Knowledge-Based Urban Development in the Middle East

Ali A. Alraouf
Qatar Urban Planning, Qatar

A volume in the Advances in Electronic Government, Digital Divide, and Regional Development (AEGDDRD) Book Series

IGI Global
DISSEMINATOR OF KNOWLEDGE

Published in the United States of America by
IGI Global
Information Science Reference (an imprint of IGI Global)
701 E. Chocolate Avenue
Hershey PA, USA 17033
Tel: 717-533-8845
Fax: 717-533-8661
E-mail: cust@igi-global.com
Web site: http://www.igi-global.com

Copyright © 2018 by IGI Global. All rights reserved. No part of this publication may be reproduced, stored or distributed in any form or by any means, electronic or mechanical, including photocopying, without written permission from the publisher. Product or company names used in this set are for identification purposes only. Inclusion of the names of the products or companies does not indicate a claim of ownership by IGI Global of the trademark or registered trademark.

Library of Congress Cataloging-in-Publication Data

Names: Alraouf, Ali A., 1964- editor.
Title: Knowledge-based urban development in the Middle East / Ali A. Alraouf, editor.
Description: Hershey, PA : Information Science Reference, [2018]
Identifiers: LCCN 2017021156| ISBN 9781522537342 (hardcover) | ISBN 9781522537359 (ebook)
Subjects: LCSH: Urbanization--Middle East. | City planning--Middle East. | Information technology--Middle East.
Classification: LCC HT384.M628 K66 2018 | DDC 307.760956--dc23 LC record available at https://lccn.loc.gov/2017021156

This book is published in the IGI Global book series Advances in Electronic Government, Digital Divide, and Regional Development (AEGDDRD) (ISSN: 2326-9103; eISSN: 2326-9111)

British Cataloguing in Publication Data
A Cataloguing in Publication record for this book is available from the British Library.

All work contributed to this book is new, previously-unpublished material. The views expressed in this book are those of the authors, but not necessarily of the publisher.

For electronic access to this publication, please contact: eresources@igi-global.com.

Advances in Electronic Government, Digital Divide, and Regional Development (AEGDDRD) Book Series

Zaigham Mahmood
University of Derby, UK & North West University, South Africa

ISSN:2326-9103
EISSN:2326-9111

Mission

The successful use of digital technologies (including social media and mobile technologies) to provide public services and foster economic development has become an objective for governments around the world. The development towards electronic government (or e-government) not only affects the efficiency and effectiveness of public services, but also has the potential to transform the nature of government interactions with its citizens. Current research and practice on the adoption of electronic/digital government and the implementation in organizations around the world aims to emphasize the extensiveness of this growing field.

The Advances in Electronic Government, Digital Divide & Regional Development (AEGDDRD) book series aims to publish authored, edited and case books encompassing the current and innovative research and practice discussing all aspects of electronic government development, implementation and adoption as well the effective use of the emerging technologies (including social media and mobile technologies) for a more effective electronic governance (or e-governance).

Coverage

- Electronic Government, Digital Democracy, Digital Government
- Knowledge Divide, Digital Divide
- E-Government in Developing Countries and Technology Adoption
- Adoption of Innovation with Respect to E-Government
- Citizens Participation and Adoption of E-Government Provision
- ICT Infrastructure and Adoption for E-Government Provision
- E-Governance and Use of Technology for Effective Government
- Case Studies and Practical Approaches to E-Government and E-Governance
- Public Information Management, Regional Planning, Rural Development
- Issues and Challenges in E-Government Adoption

IGI Global is currently accepting manuscripts for publication within this series. To submit a proposal for a volume in this series, please contact our Acquisition Editors at Acquisitions@igi-global.com or visit: http://www.igi-global.com/publish/.

The Advances in Electronic Government, Digital Divide, and Regional Development (AEGDDRD) Book Series (ISSN 2326-9103) is published by IGI Global, 701 E. Chocolate Avenue, Hershey, PA 17033-1240, USA, www.igi-global.com. This series is composed of titles available for purchase individually; each title is edited to be contextually exclusive from any other title within the series. For pricing and ordering information please visit http://www.igi-global.com/book-series/advances-electronic-government-digital-divide/37153. Postmaster: Send all address changes to above address. Copyright © 2018 IGI Global. All rights, including translation in other languages reserved by the publisher. No part of this series may be reproduced or used in any form or by any means – graphics, electronic, or mechanical, including photocopying, recording, taping, or information and retrieval systems – without written permission from the publisher, except for non commercial, educational use, including classroom teaching purposes. The views expressed in this series are those of the authors, but not necessarily of IGI Global.

Titles in this Series

For a list of additional titles in this series, please visit: www.igi-global.com/book-series

Socio-Economic and Education Factors Impacting American Political Systems Emerging Research and Opportunities
Pamela Hampton-Garland (University of the District of Columbia, USA) Lisa Sechrest-Ehrhardt (University of the District of Columbia, USA) and Benson George Cooke (University of the District of Columbia, USA)
Information Science Reference • copyright 2018 • 191pp • H/C (ISBN: 9781522538431) • US $145.00 (our price)

Media Diplomacy and Its Evolving Role in the Current Geopolitical Climate
Swati Jaywant Rao Bute (AMITY University, India)
Information Science Reference • copyright 2018 • 250pp • H/C (ISBN: 9781522538592) • US $195.00 (our price)

Handbook of Research on Women's Issues and Rights in the Developing World
Nazmunnessa Mahtab (University of Dhaka, Bangladesh) Tania Haque (University of Dhaka, Bangladesh) Ishrat Khan (University of Dhaka, Bangladesh) Md. Mynul Islam (University of Dhaka, Bangladesh) and Ishret Binte Wahid (BRAC, Bangladesh)
Information Science Reference • copyright 2018 • 452pp • H/C (ISBN: 9781522530183) • US $245.00 (our price)

Handbook of Research on Sociopolitical Factors Impacting Economic Growth in Islamic Nations
Suleyman Ozdemir (Bandırma Onyedi Eylül University, Turkey) Seyfettin Erdogan (Istanbul Medeniyet University, Turkey) and Ayfer Gedikli (İstanbul Medeniyet University, Turkey)
Information Science Reference • copyright 2018 • 472pp • H/C (ISBN: 9781522529392) • US $275.00 (our price)

Urbanization and Its Impact on Socio-Economic Growth in Developing Regions
Umar Benna (Benna Associates, Nigeria) and Indo Benna (Muhammad Al-Mana College of Health Sciences, Saudi Arabia)
Information Science Reference • copyright 2018 • 404pp • H/C (ISBN: 9781522526599) • US $195.00 (our price)

Sustainable ICT Adoption and Integration for Socio-Economic Development
Charles K. Ayo (Covenant University, Nigeria) and Victor Mbarika (Southern University, USA, and ICT University, USA)
Information Science Reference • copyright 2017 • 264pp • H/C (ISBN: 9781522525653) • US $180.00 (our price)

Digital Media Integration for Participatory Democracy
Rocci Luppicini (University of Ottawa, Canada) and Rachel Baarda (University of Ottawa, Canada)
Information Science Reference • copyright 2017 • 259pp • H/C (ISBN: 9781522524632) • US $200.00 (our price)

IGI Global
DISSEMINATOR OF KNOWLEDGE

701 East Chocolate Avenue, Hershey, PA 17033, USA
Tel: 717-533-8845 x100 • Fax: 717-533-8661
E-Mail: cust@igi-global.com • www.igi-global.com

This book is dedicated to all who firmly believe in the value of transforming the Middle East into a more prosperous place. With all its people, culture, and unique layers of knowledge and heritage, the Middle East deserves to be developed into a new productive, energetic and vibrant territory. A one which is developed based on knowledge and has the ability to invite knowledge workers and creative humans to dwell in peace within its diversified and inspiring geographies.

Table of Contents

Detailed Table of Contents

We have witnessed vast economic, social, technological, and environmental changes that have influenced patterns of urbanization. Through all these years urban planning has also experienced major reforms. During last two decades, with emergence of knowledge economy, it is claimed that the nature of urban development has changed; this new notion of development is called knowledge-based urban development. As there is not clear methodology for directing cities development process, this chapter aims to formulate a conceptual model for cities leadership towards knowledge-based urban development. This chapter considers the city of Isfahan, Iran as a case study. Finally, a model is proposed according to literature review and using ANP method for analyzing the data gathered from the context. This conceptual model has also prioritized effective factors for KBUD.

This chapter investigates the opportunities and challenges related to KBUD found in Cairo's informal settlements. Also, it explores the ability of KBUD approach in dealing with the development of such settlements instead of the adopted approaches which failed in approaching the economic aspect within these communities. The chapter provides insights on the important role KBUD could play not only in the economic growth of richer and more prestigious contexts but also in poor communities which have a lot of hidden potentials. Accordingly, the chapter investigates Cairo's informal settlements, the policies and approaches used and applied, and the related defects and shortcomings. Then, it explores the theoretical framework of KBUD. Following this, opportunities and challenges related to KBUD in Cairo's informal settlements are discussed. By the end, the chapter sheds light on some points and concludes with recommendations for readapting KBUD approach when developing Cairo's informal settlements.

As information and communication technologies (ICTs) change economic and social activities creating a new economic paradigm based on the production and processing of knowledge, all aspects of human life are being transformed, including cities people live in. All around the world, countries are trying to adopt this new paradigm referred to as a knowledge-based economy (KBE) and organize their cities to possess a more competitive position in this new context. Turkey is one of these countries wishing to build KBE. The chapter analyzes Turkish efforts in building KBE and organizing its cities in this respect. It emphasizes that Turkey once had an important advantage in building KBE due to its developed telecommunication industry that offered the material infrastructure of KBE but lost this technological capacity owing to the implementation of inappropriate strategies. Turkey also conceptualizes KBE in such a narrow sense that leads to the adoption of other wrong policies effecting the country's economy, society, and cities.

Preface

INTRODUCTION

The book covers number of interrelated and integrated topics and therefore, and for the sake of coherence, structured into three main sections. Section 1, titled "Issues, Challenges, and Theoretical Concepts," Section 2, titled "Country-Based Case Studies," and Section 3, titled "Transformations and Trends." The three sections are preceded by two introductory chapters setting the scene for the different chapters. The book contains essays contributed by scholars, professionals, and researchers from different localities and countries around the Middle East. There are a total of 13 chapters. With such structure, the hope is that book will be a resourceful reference for researchers, town planners, architects, municipality officers and decisions makers in planning and developing future knowledge cities and knowledge-bade urban development around the Middle East.

Section 1: Issues, Challenges, and Theoretical Concepts

In Section 1, three chapters focus on discussing issues, challenges, hypothetical and theoretical concepts. The first chapter is titled "The Myth of Knowledge-Based Urban Development in the Middle Eastern Cities: A Multilayered-Analysis" by Ali A. Alraouf. Alraouf investigates and validates the credibility and the authenticity of the move towards KBUD and KC in the Middle East and the Gulf. A decade ago, Middle Eastern cities and particularly Gulf cities rushed into the implementation of knowledge-Based Urban Development and knowledge cities as models for development and progress. The author suggests that unlike the Western models of knowledge and creative cities, Middle Eastern cities attempts were characterized by the mere construction of technological advanced yet isolated urban entities with the hope that they are promoting the same concepts essential for knowledge cities; integration and dissemination. By analyzing key projects selected from the Middle Eastern context, the chapter concludes that the common failure resulted from transforming these projects into a sort of gated communities fully isolated from the city and the community. The second chapter is titled "Information and Communication Technology Spine for Knowledge-Based Development of Cities" by Rabee Mohamed Reffat, Assiut University. Reffat discusses an approach for the effective employment of information and communication technology as a competitive advantage for knowledge-based development of cities. Additionally, the features of knowledge-based city compared modern and developed city are discussed. This chapter identifies the primary conditions that promote knowledge-based development of cities. The associative relationships between knowledge-base and economical development of cities are addressed. The third chapter titled "The Comparative Importance of Urban and Architectural Potentials Supporting Knowledge Cities Formation and Their Relevant Indices" is authored by Khaled Youssef Mohamed, Ayman Mohammed Mostafa and Jamal Ahmad Abdel-Hameed, Faculty of Fine Arts. Mohamed, Mostafa and Abdel-Hameed look at the physical features of knowledge cities particularly architectural and urban aspects. The chapter illustrates the methodologies adopted by several developed countries to upgrade their cities to knowledge-based economic cities. The authors demonstrate how architecture and urbanism were used to provide thorough conditions for the enhancing, creation and exchange of knowledge and innovation. While focusing on the physical aspects, the authors acknowledge that the concept of KC was found to be interdisciplinary: economic, political, social as well as being urban and architectural. So, this chapter aims to analyze the urban and architectural potentials of selected case studies. The chapter concludes with a set of indices and guidelines contributing to assessing the performance of such knowledge cities and how to envision the future impact and transformations.

Section 2: Country-Based Case Studies

Section 2 moves towards investigating cases from cities and states around the Middle East. The fourth chapter is titled "The Knowledge Urbanity in Qatar: An Alternative Dynamic" by Ali A. Alraouf. Alraouf illustrates the alternative approach to Knowledge based urban development which Qatar adopted to cope with the challenges of the post-carbon paradigm and to construct a new identity as a knowledge-based model of development within the Middle East. Using the Capital city Doha as the main case study, the chapter provides analysis of the city evolution from the discovery of oil till the contemporary stage where knowledge economy is envisioned as its future and the guiding principle for its urban and architectural projects. The analysis covers the city planning level and how future masterplan is geared towards KBUD and then some influential projects will be assessed. The chapter concludes with a holistic understanding of the case of Doha as a knowledge and creative city that succeeded to craft a new urban brand within the Gulf and Middle Eastern cities. The fifth chapter is titled "Egypt's Knowledge-Based Development: Opportunities, Challenges, and Future Possibilities" by Amal Adel Abdrabo, Alexandria University, Egypt. Abdrabo discusses both the dominant theoretical paradigms that appear within Egypt's ICT policies since early nineties and examines the practical steps of implementation. The chapter compares between the mission, vision, and goals of different ICT policies and their application in reality within four cases from the Egyptian context; the City of Scientific Research and Technological Applications in Burg Al-Arab, Bibliotheca Alexandrina (BA), Smart Village in Giza (SV), and Information Technology Institute (ITI). Abdrabo answers a crucial, complicated and multifaceted question; what are the opportunities and challenges that Egypt faces in its endeavor to transform each of the national economy into a knowledge-based economy, the Egyptian citizens into knowledge citizens, the cities into knowledge cities, and the whole Egyptian society into a knowledge society? The sixth chapter is titled "Developing a Conceptual Framework for Knowledge-Based Urban Development in Isfahan, Iran" by Marjaneh Farhangi, Municipality of Karaj. Farhangi traces how the nature of urban development has changed and focuses on the economic, social, technological and environmental changes which have influenced patterns of urbanization. The chapter aims to formulate a conceptual model for cities leadership towards knowledge based urban development. The city of Isfahan, Iran was used as a case study where a methodology for directing cities development process. The suggested model is proposed according to literature review and using ANP method for analyzing the data gathered from the context. This conceptual model has also prioritized effective factors for KBUD.

The seventh chapter is titled "KBUD as an Alternative Approach for the Development of Cairo's Informal Settlements: Opportunities and Challenges" by Ahmed Hassan Abayazeed. Abayazeed moves from the typical focus on big cities and capital and investigates the opportunities and challenges related to KBUD found in Cairo's informal settlements. Also, it explores the ability of KBUD approach in dealing with the development of such settlements instead of the adopted approaches which failed in approaching the economic aspect within these communities. The chapter provides insights on the important role KBUD could play not only in the economic growth of richer and more prestigious contexts but also in poor communities which have a lot of hidden potentials. The chapter investigates the policies and approaches used and applied and the related defects and shortcomings. Then, it explores the theoretical framework of KBUD.

The eighth chapter is titled "Opportunities for and Constraints on the Transformation Into a Knowledge-Based Economy: A Critical Analysis of Initiatives in Turkey" by Zafer Kiyan, Ankara University. Hakan Yüksel, Ankara University. Kiyan and Yüksel illustrate that information and communication technologies (ICTs) change economic and social activities creating a new economic paradigm based on the production and processing of knowledge. Accordingly, all aspects of human life are being transformed, including cities people live in. All around the world, countries are trying to adopt this new paradigm referred to as a knowledge-based economy (KBE) and organize their cities to possess a more competitive position in this new context. The authors assert that Turkey is one of these countries working on building KBE. Hence, the chapter analyzes Turkish efforts in building KBE and organizing its cities in this respect. It emphasizes that Turkey once had an important advantage in building KBE due to its developed telecommunication industry that offered the material infrastructure of KBE but lost this technological capacity owing to the implementation of inappropriate strategies. Turkey also conceptualizes KBE in such a narrow sense that leads to the adoption of other wrong policies effecting the country's economy, society and cities. The ninth chapter is titled "Creative Cities and Knowledge Capital: The Case of Dubai (UAE)" by Aly Abdel Razek Galaby, Alexandria University, Egypt. Galaby asserts that many world nations are responding to the shift from development policies that rely on intensified labor and capital into alternative policies that build on the intensification of knowledge. He discusses the innovative development paradigms of existing urban models including knowledge Cities, creative cities and the rise of knowledge society explains how they have opened up alternative prospects for development and growth. Using the Emirate of Dubai as a case study, Galaby illustrates how Dubai was among the first Middle Eastern countries that acknowledged the new development paradigms and took the initiative of transforming its economy into a knowledge economy, building development policies on the intensification of knowledge, embarked on the creation of the creative city and the formation of a knowledge capital. Hence, the chapter provides an analysis of the experience, explaining its constraints, and its impact nationally and regionally.

Section 3: Transformations and Trends

The third section of the book focuses on initiatives, emerging approaches in addition to challenges and opportunities facing KBUD in the Middle East. The tenth chapter is titled "Kuwait Urban App: The Application of Knowledge-Based Urban Development in Kuwait" by Jawaher Al-Bader, Anas Alomaim, and Robert Gurney. Jawaher, Alomaim and Gurney's attempt to articulate a methodological approach for Knowledge Based Urban Development (KBUD), select an interesting route by looking at the impact of the social media paradigm. Through an investigation of social media and contemporary smart phone applications, the authors analyze the urban landscape of Kuwait to propose a relevant reading of (KBUD) in Kuwait. Historically urban planning and design have been dominated by a formalized methodology that seeks to reinforce existing power structures. The promise of KBUD is a more balanced approach towards development, considering economic, social, environmental, and cultural factors. However, today a new structure is coalescing, one based on the interaction of individuals through social media i.e. Instagram, Snapchat and the geo-tagging technology, that supports these applications. The authors argue that the proliferation of social media applications in Kuwait covers a wide range of the population, providing insight towards the contemporary urban environment. They conclude by suggesting that these methods for social communication and social cohesions are crucial in our understanding of the current active spaces. The eleventh chapter is titled "Knowledge-Based Urban Design in the Architectural Academic Field" by Hisham G. Abusaada and Abeer Elshater. Abusaada and Elshater discuss the pedagogical aspects of introducing knowledge-based domains of investigation in the process of teaching and research. The chapter focuses on the theory of knowledge-based urban design as a tool for intellectual literacy in architecture schools. It explores the extent of the current knowledge effects in the educational process by knowing the experience gained by the students during the current learning plans, as opposed to what the urban designer should know. The authors ask a valid question; what could happen if the experts in the relevant disciplines of urban design do not accept such a paradigm shift or even recognize that there is intellectual illiteracy in a particular discipline? The chapter provides an experimental attempt to explore the relationship between illiteracy of thought and mental ability among professionals in the field of urban design to raise their intellectual and cognitive competence.

The twelfth chapter is titled "A Holistic Assessment of Education City in Doha: The Borderless Knowledge Hub" by Ali A. Alraouf. Alraouf provides a comprehensive evaluation of one of the most influential knowledge hubs in the Middle East, Education City in Qatar (EC). Qatar, while developing its vision for the future, decided to adopt the knowledge economy as the new pillar for its economy and development. The chapter focuses on examining the impact of the one of the main and iconic national mega project in the capital Doha, (EC). The chapter scrutinizes EC's contribution to a more resilient future for Qatar. The author assesses the relative roles of such an influential project in preparing or hindering Qatar's moving towards the post carbon paradigm. The project is examined using multilayered criteria which include, achieving urban diversity, relevance to Knowledge-based urban development, supporting the diversification of the local economy and accommodating multicultural society. The chapter concludes that Education city is the most crucial urban projects in Qatar geared towards sustaining the knowledge economy as it creates ripples of change, knowledge dissemination and a culture of innovation and creativity within the city. The thirteenth chapter is titled "Cities of GCC in Post-Hydrocarbon Era: Challenges and Opportunities" by Ahmed O. El-Kholei and Odeh Al-Jayyousi. El-Kholei and Al-Jayyousi call for an enabling environment for knowledge transfer, a transition towards a green economy, and institutional development by building and fostering global partnerships for knowledge, innovation, and energy. The authors acknowledge that the States of GCC countries are considered rentier states endeavored to diversify their economic base by attempting to transfer their economies from hydrocarbon-based to knowledge-based economy. Many reports and studies claim these attempts still in need to be integrated within their urban settings, not just a development at the hinterlands of existing cities. The chapter outlines key challenges and opportunities for cities of GCC to transfer their urban development into a knowledge base.

Introduction

KNOWLEDGE-BASED DEVELOPMENT OF CITIES AND URBAN INNOVATION PRECINCTS[1]

The changing and challenging conditions of the twenty-first century have been significantly impacting our economy, society and built and natural environments (Carrillo et al., 2014). Today generation of knowledge—mostly in the form of technology and innovation—is seen as a panacea for the adaptation to changes and management of challenges (Yigitcanlar, 2010a). Making space and place that concentrate on knowledge generation, thus, has become a priority for many nations and the concepts like knowledge region, city and precinct coined as places where citizenship undertakes a deliberate and systematic initiative for founding its development on the identification and sustainable balance of its shared value system and bases its ability to create wealth on its capacity to generate and leverage its knowledge capabilities (Yigitcanlar, 2008a). In recent years, the term knowledge precinct—or urban innovation precincts—in its most contemporary interpretation evolved into knowledge community precinct, which is a mixed-use post-modern urban setting—e.g., flexible, decontextualized, enclaved, fragmented—including a critical mass of knowledge enterprises and advanced networked infrastructures, developed with the aim of collecting the benefits of blurring the boundaries of living, shopping, recreation and working facilities of knowledge workers and their families—i.e., knowledge community (Pancholi et al., 2017a). Knowledge community precincts are the building blocks of knowledge cities. In the literature this type of development—a place containing economic prosperity, environmental sustainability, just socio-spatial order and good governance—is referred as a knowledge-based urban development (Yigitcanlar et al., 2016). The Foreword aims to provide an introduction to this book—Knowledge-Based Urban Development in the Middle East—by elaborating conceptual aspects of knowledge-based urban development and formation of prosperous knowledge community precincts and knowledge cities.

INTRODUCTION

Knowledge-based urban development is defined as "the new development paradigm of the knowledge economy era that aims to bring economic prosperity, environmental sustainability, a just socio-spatial order and good governance to cities, and as an end product produces a city purposefully designed to encourage the production and circulation of knowledge in an environmentally conserved, economically secure, socially just and well-governed human setting, a knowledge city" (Yigitcanlar, 2011a, p.354). Knowledge-based urban development consists of four major domains (Yigitcanlar & Dur, 2013; Yigitcanlar et al., 2017a, 2017b).

Knowledge-based economic development domain contains a perspective that places endogenous knowledge assets in the hearth of economic activities, and sees knowledge as a locally embedded strategic and vital resource rather than exogenous, imported and supplementary, and aims to build a knowledge economy within a city with economic prosperity achieved through strong macro-economic and knowledge economy foundations (Yigitcanlar, 2014b).

Knowledge-based socio-cultural development domain has a perspective that increases skills and knowledge of residents as a mean for individual and communal development and societal high-level of achievements, and aims to build a knowledge society within a city with a just socio-spatial order achieved through strong human and social capitals, and diversity and independency (Yigitcanlar, 2014b).

Knowledge-based spatio-urban (i.e., environmental and urban) development domain has a perspective that promotes conservation, development and integration of both natural and built environments, works towards building a strong spatial network relationship between urban development and knowledge clusters while driving an urban and environmental development that is ecologically friendly, high quality, unique and sustainable, and aims to build a knowledge environment within a sustainable and livable city achieved through sustainable urban development and quality of life and place (Yigitcanlar, 2014b).

Knowledge-based institutional development domain has a perspective that democratizes and humanizes knowledge, institutionalizes interdisciplinary collective learning processes and knowledge-based organizations, plays a critical role in the orchestration of the development by bringing together actors, stakeholders and sources to prepare a civic vision, plan strategically, and organize and facilitate necessary knowledge-intensive bases and activities, and aims to build a knowledge government within a well governed city achieved through strong governance and planning and leadership and support (Yigitcanlar, 2014b).

These four development domains form the main pillars of KBUD—i.e., knowledge-economy, knowledge-society, knowledge-environment, and knowledge-government. Along with these four pillars, their development processes, balance and integration with each other within the systems theory perspective, and incorporation of the knowledge-based view in the spirit of development together with organizational and sustainability capacities are among the central determinants of success the development (Yigitcanlar & Lonnqvist, 2013).

KNOWLEDGE CITIES

Many cities worldwide face the prospect of major transformation as the world moves towards a global information order. In this new era, dynamic processes of economic and spatial restructuring are radically altering urban economies. The result is the creation of knowledge cities (Metaxiotis et al., 2010; Edvardsson et al., 2016).

For the last two centuries, social production had been primarily understood and shaped by neo-classical economic thought that recognized only three factors of production: land, labor and capital. Knowledge, education, and intellectual capacity were secondary, if not incidental, factors. Human capital was assumed to be either embedded in labor or just one of numerous categories of capital. In the last decades, it has become apparent that knowledge is sufficiently important to deserve recognition as a fourth factor of production. Knowledge and the social and technological settings for their production and communication are now seen as keys to development and economic prosperity (Baum et al., 2009).

The rise of knowledge-based opportunity has, in many cases, been accompanied by a concomitant decline in traditional industrial activity. The replacement of physical commodity production by more abstract forms of production (e.g., information, ideas, and knowledge) has, however paradoxically, reinforced the importance of central places and led to the formation of knowledge cities (Lonnqvist et al., 2014).

Knowledge is produced, marketed and exchanged mainly in cities. Therefore, knowledge cities aim to assist decision-makers in making their cities compatible with the knowledge economy and thus able to compete with other cities. Knowledge cities enable their citizens to foster knowledge creation, knowledge exchange and innovation. They also encourage the continuous creation, sharing, evaluation, renewal and update of knowledge (Yigitcanlar & Sarimin, 2011).

To compete nationally and internationally, cities need knowledge infrastructures (e.g., universities, research and development institutes); a concentration of well-educated people; technological, mainly electronic, infrastructure; and connections to the global economy (e.g., international companies and finance institutions for trade and investment). Moreover, they must possess the people and things necessary for the production of knowledge and, as importantly, function as breeding grounds for talent and innovation (Yigitcanlar, 2008b).

The economy of a knowledge city creates high value-added products using research, technology, and brainpower. Private and the public sectors value knowledge, spend money on its discovery and dissemination and, ultimately, harness it to create goods and services. Although many cities call themselves knowledge cities, currently, only a few cities around the world (e.g., Austin, Barcelona, Boston, Delft, Helsinki, Melbourne, Montreal, San Francisco, Singapore and Stockholm) have earned that label. Many other cities aspire to the status of knowledge city through urban development programs that target knowledge-based urban development. Examples include Brisbane, Copenhagen, Dubai, Dublin, Istanbul, Manchester, and Shanghai (Yigitcanlar et al., 2008c).

KNOWLEDGE-BASED URBAN DEVELOPMENT

To date, the development of most knowledge cities has proceeded organically as a dependent and derivative effect of global market forces. Urban and regional planning has responded slowly, and sometimes not at all, to the challenges and the opportunities of the knowledge city. That is changing, however. Knowledge-based urban development potentially brings both economic prosperity and a sustainable socio-spatial order. Its goal is to produce and circulate abstract work (Yigitcanlar, 2010c; 2014a).

The globalization of the world in the last decades of the twentieth century was a dialectical process. On one hand, as the tyranny of distance was eroded, economic networks of production and consumption were constituted at a global scale. At the same time, spatial proximity remained as important as ever, if not more so, for knowledge-based urban development. Mediated by information and communication technology, personal contact, and the medium of tacit knowledge, organizational and institutional interactions are still closely associated with spatial proximity. The clustering of knowledge production is essential for fostering innovation and wealth creation (Yigitcanlar, 2011c; Yigitcanlar et al., 2014).

The social benefits of knowledge-based urban development extend beyond aggregate economic growth. On the one hand, the possibility of a particularly resilient form of urban development secured in a network of connections is anchored at local, national, and global coordinates. On the other, quality of place and life—defined by the level of public service (e.g., health and education) and by the conservation and development of the cultural, aesthetic and ecological values give cities their character and attract or repel the creative class of knowledge workers—is a prerequisite for successful knowledge-based urban development. The goal is a secure economy in a human setting: in short, smart growth or sustainable urban development (Yigitcanlar, 2010b).

CREATIVE CLASS OF KNOWLEDGE WORKERS

One of the greatest challenges of the knowledge city is its social and environmental setting. In the production of places of knowledge, image is as important as reality. The presence of knowledge professionals and creative talent attracts innovative, knowledge and technology-based industries. Home to a creative class of knowledge workers, social interactions drive value creation and further concentrate creative knowledge workers—e.g., computer and mathematical occupations; architecture and engineering; life, physical and social science occupations; education, training and library occupations; and arts, design, entertainment, sports and media occupations (Yigitcanlar et al., 2007).

A key determinant in attracting and retaining these people is the quality of life of a place. Knowledge workers do not simply select their residence to maximize their salary. They are also concerned with consumption opportunities. Typically, knowledge workers value a whole series of place-based characteristics, not the least being cultural activities and amenities. Consequently, quality of place and life is a factor of growing importance for knowledge-based cities. Besides that, the city's heritage, the meanings attached to the past and present from the foundations of social, political, and cultural knowledge, can attract additional talented workers (Esmaeilpoorarabi et al., 2016a, 2016b).

One of the goals of knowledge-based urban development is a virtuous circle of attraction that retains skilled and creative people who, in turn, attract smart industries and businesses that need their labor, and investors looking to invest in high value production. With a strong sense of community and a pool of skilled and talented people, a knowledge city will enjoy robust growth at way above average rates (Yigitcanlar, 2011b).

KNOWLEDGE COMMUNITY PRECINCTS AS ESSENTIAL INNOVATION CLUSTERS

The on-going transformation of advanced economies from manufacturing to services and knowledge-based activities has important implications for the formation of knowledge cities. Firms increasingly use technology as their prime source of competitive advantage, while the economic wealth of nations is increasingly tied to their technological competence (Yigitcanlar et al., 2016).

The increasing interconnectedness of the world economy as part of the ongoing process of globalization depends on technologies such as information and communication technology. These are the keys to corporate success and national growth. Such technologies impose an almost irresistible drive to be part of international growth. Similarly, since the end of the 1980s, the development of the knowledge-based economy, globalization, and international competitive pressure has increased the importance of innovation. Simultaneously, globalization increases local differences arising from local capabilities and environments (Yigitcanlar et al., 2012; Pancholi et al., 2014).

New developments in globalization and communications technology have prompted countries and cities to focus their competitive strategies on improving innovation. This shift has increased the value of knowledge-based activity. Knowledge-based production, however, generally clusters in areas with a rich base of scientific knowledge tied to specific industries. This spatial imperative has polarized high growth activity in a limited number of areas of the world (Yigitcanlar, 2009).

Proximity generates and transfers knowledge. Thus, new knowledge-based activities cluster in specific geographic localities. Proximity is essential to stimulate company learning, create compatible knowledge spillover effects, and establish positive feedback among various local agents. Such clusters are built around advanced technological infrastructure and mature networks of innovation (Yigitcanlar & Dur, 2013).

Knowledge clusters are not all equal but have differing dynamics. Amongst the forms already identified are knowledge park, knowledge precinct or knowledge community precinct, knowledge village, knowledge corridor, knowledge hub, knowledge district, and beyond knowledge city knowledge region. Tacit knowledge embedded in a city is also critical. The most successful cities are those able to combine the structural or spillover, effects of a rich local knowledge with international best practice (Yigitcanlar et al., 2015).

For example, the successful development of Silicon Valley in the USA was based on a knowledge network that encompassed both regional learning institutions (i.e., the universities of Northern California) and for-profit industry research teams. Innovations produced in the knowledge network were adopted and developed economically by proximate industries operating in an environment of flexible development. Silicon Valley has inspired knowledge-based urban development around the world. Since the 1970s the establishment of technology parks and precincts in both developed and developing countries has become widespread. (Sarimin & Yigitcanlar, 2011)

Knowledge precincts—also science and technology parks, research parks, business parks, industrial parks, and innovation parks or innovation precincts/districts have been used interchangeably—are high growth knowledge industry clusters. The term knowledge precinct distinguishes the functional activity in an area and refers to an area where agglomeration of knowledge and technological activities has positive externalities for individual firms located there (Pancholi et al., 2015).

Knowledge precincts are generally established with two primary objectives in mind. The first objective is to be a seedbed and an enclave for knowledge and technology and to play an incubator role nurturing the development and growth of new, small, high-technology firms, facilitating the transfer of university know-how to tenant companies, encouraging faculty-based spin-offs and stimulating innovative products and processes. The second objective is to act as a catalyst for regional economic development that promotes economic growth and contributes to the development of a knowledge city (Yigitcanlar & Bulu, 2015).

While there are many different models of knowledge precincts, a knowledge precinct generally provides both support and an environment of technology transfer that nurtures the start-up, incubation, and development of innovation-led, high-growth, knowledge-based businesses. Although these precincts strive to focus research and development (R&D) and innovation in its area, the types of R&D and the sectors they focus can vary widely. Overall, attracting new firms, technology parks can create substantial agglomerative effects for the regional economy Yigitcanlar & Sarimin, 2015).

Knowledge community precincts are the most contemporary knowledge precincts initiatives that have the following characteristics. They: have knowledge and technology-based enterprises, knowledge workers, research and development and educational institutions; provide living facilities that promote creativity, cater for emerging lifestyle choices, and celebrate the experience of place; and are guided and managed by partnerships between governments, real estate developers, educational or research institutions, and information and new media companies. Examples of knowledge community precincts include one-north in Singapore, Brainport in Eindhoven, Kelvin Grove Urban Village in Brisbane, Hermia in Tampere, Monash Employment Cluster in Melbourne, Macqaries Innovation District in Sydney, and Crossroads in Copenhagen (Sarimin & Yigitcanlar, 2012; Pancholi et al., 2017b).

STRATEGIES FOR BUILDING SUCCESSFUL KNOWLEDGE CITIES AND COMMUNITY PRECINCTS

Attempts to building new knowledge community precincts and transform cities into knowledge cities will likely fail if they are not guided by sound strategic visions. These strategic visions should incorporate policies for attracting and retaining knowledge workers and industries and also empowering citizens as knowledge creators and innovators. The top-tier knowledge cities specialize in a few sectors only and set ambitious goals for each, and develop their knowledge-based policies carefully (Velibeyoglu & Yigitcanlar, 2010).

The common strategies include: political and societal will; strategic vision and development plans; financial support and strong investments; agencies to promote knowledge-based urban development; enhancing international, multi-cultural character of the city; robust online public information networks; value creation for citizens; creation of urban innovative engines; assurance of knowledge society rights; low-cost access to advanced communication networks; research excellence; and high standards of quality of life and place (Yigitcanlar & Velibeyoglu, 2008).

Implementation of these strategies and policies requires a broad intellectual team with expertise in urban development, urban studies and planning, socio-economic development, models of intellectual capital and knowledge management. It also requires understanding of the diverse spatial forms of the knowledge city where a large number of knowledge clusters are particularly important in promoting the spillover effects vital for long-term economic prosperity (Yigitcanlar et al., 2008d).

FINAL THOUGHTS

Planning for prosperous knowledge cities and knowledge community precincts through knowledge-based urban development requires understanding the diverse socio-economic and socio-spatial forms of creative urban regions and their valuable knowledge assets. Beyond this the knowledge-based urban development conception is still evolving in order to produce more sustainable outcomes for urban planning and development. Global financial crises and rapid urbanization (i.e., driving urban growth with high consumption patterns without fully considering the environmental and social needs and occupants' behavior and aspirations) along with the changing climate in many countries worldwide has become a major concern because of its detrimental effects on the environment and societies. Especially, in a century that urbanization rate is globally over 50% and moving rapidly to reach up to 70 percent by 2050, knowledge-based development of our cities is seen as probably the last resort for achieving a sustainable urban development—a development seeking to respond to: integration of conservation and development; satisfaction of basic human needs; achievement of equity and social justice; provision of social self-determination and cultural diversity, providing welfare and prosperity, and; maintenance of ecological integrity. The debate in the literature signifies that the process of implementing knowledge-based urban development approaches and strategies is neither simple nor quick and some argue that the issues should be viewed from the multidisciplinary angles. However, for the time being knowledge-based urban development seems to be the only systematic way out from the rising economic, societal and environmental crises and disasters.

Tan Yigitcanlar
Queensland University of Technology, Australia

REFERENCES

Baum, S., O'Connor, K., & Yigitcanlar, T. (2009). The implications of creative industries for regional outcomes. *International Journal of Foresight and Innovation Policy, 5*(1/2/3), 44-64.

Carrillo, J., Yigitcanlar, T., Garcia, B., & Lonnqvist, A. (2014). *Knowledge and the city: concepts, applications and trends of knowledge-based urban development.* New York, NY: Routledge.

Edvardsson, I., Yigitcanlar, T., & Pancholi, S. (2016). Knowledge cities research and practice under the microscope: A review of the literature. *Knowledge Management Research and Practice*, *14*(4), 537–564. doi:10.1057/s41275-016-0003-0

Esmaeilpoorarabi, N., Yigitcanlar, T., & Guaralda, M. (2016a). Towards an urban quality framework: Determining critical measures for different geographical scales to attract and retain talent in cities. *International Journal of Knowledge-Based Development*, *7*(3), 290–312. doi:10.1504/IJKBD.2016.078556

Esmaeilpoorarabi, N., Yigitcanlar, T., & Guaralda, M. (2016b). Place quality and urban competitiveness symbiosis? A position paper. *International Journal of Knowledge-Based Development*, *7*(1), 4–21. doi:10.1504/IJKBD.2016.075444

Lonnqvist, A., Kapyla, J., Salonius, H., & Yigitcanlar, T. (2014). Knowledge that matters: Identifying regional knowledge assets of Tampere Region. *European Planning Studies*, *22*(10), 2011–2029. doi:10.1080/09654313.2013.814621

Metaxiotis, K., Carrillo, J., & Yigitcanlar, T. (Eds.). (2010). *Knowledge-based development for cities and societies: an integrated multi-level approach.* Hersey, PA: Information Science Reference. doi:10.4018/978-1-61520-721-3

Pancholi, S., Yigitcanlar, T., & Guaralda, M. (2014). Urban knowledge and innovation spaces: Concepts, conditions and contexts. *Asia Pacific Journal of Innovation and Entrepreneurship*, *8*(1), 15–38.

Pancholi, S., Yigitcanlar, T., & Guaralda, M. (2015). Place making facilitators of knowledge and innovation spaces: Insights from the European best practices. *International Journal of Knowledge-Based Development*, *6*(3), 215–240. doi:10.1504/IJKBD.2015.072823

Pancholi, S., Yigitcanlar, T., & Guaralda, M. (2017a). Place making in knowledge and innovation spaces: The Australia experience. *Technological Forecasting and Social Change.* doi:10.1016/j.techfore.2017.09.014

Pancholi, S., Yigitcanlar, T., & Guaralda, M. (2017b). Governance that matters: Identifying place-making challenges of Melbourne's Monash Employment Cluster. *Journal of Place Management and Development, 10*(1), 73–87. doi:10.1108/JPMD-08-2016-0053

Sarimin, M., & Yigitcanlar, T. (2011). Knowledge-based urban development of Multimedia Super Corridor, Malaysia: An overview. *International Journal of Knowledge Based Development*, *2*(1), 34–48. doi:10.1504/IJKBD.2011.040623

Sarimin, M., & Yigitcanlar, T. (2012). Towards a comprehensive and integrated knowledge-based urban development model: Status quo and directions. *International Journal of Knowledge Based Development*, *3*(2), 175–192. doi:10.1504/IJKBD.2012.047035

Velibeyoglu, K., & Yigitcanlar, T. (2010). An evaluation methodology for tangible and intangible assets of city-regions: The 6K1C framework. *International Journal of Services Technology and Management*, *14*(4), 343–359. doi:10.1504/IJSTM.2010.035783

Yigitcanlar, T. (2009). Planning for knowledge-based development: Global perspectives. *Journal of Knowledge Management*, *13*(5), 228–242. doi:10.1108/13673270910988079

Yigitcanlar, T. (Ed.). (2010a). *Sustainable urban and regional infrastructure development: technologies, applications and management*. Hersey, PA: Information Science Reference. doi:10.4018/978-1-61520-775-6

Yigitcanlar, T. (Ed.). (2010b). *Rethinking sustainable development: urban management, engineering and design*. Hersey, PA: Engineering Science Reference. doi:10.4018/978-1-61692-022-7

Yigitcanlar, T. (2010c). Making space and place for the knowledge economy: Knowledge-based development of Australian cities. *European Planning Studies*, *18*(11), 1769–1786. doi:10.1080/09654313.2010.512163

Yigitcanlar, T. (2011a). Position paper: Redefining knowledge-based urban development. *International Journal of Knowledge Based Development*, *2*(4), 340–356. doi:10.1504/IJKBD.2011.044343

Yigitcanlar, T. (2011b). Moving towards a knowledge city? Brisbane's experience in knowledge-based urban development. *International Journal of Knowledge-Based Organizations*, *1*(3), 22–38. doi:10.4018/ijkbo.2011070102

Yigitcanlar, T. (2011c). Knowledge-based development processes of an emerging knowledge city: Brisbane, Australia. *A|Z Journal,* 8(1), 53-67.

Yigitcanlar, T. (2014a). Innovating urban policymaking and planning mechanisms to deliver knowledge-based agendas: A methodological approach. *International Journal of Knowledge-Based Development*, *5*(3), 253–270. doi:10.1504/IJKBD.2014.065300

Yigitcanlar, T. (2014b). Position paper: Benchmarking the performance of global and emerging knowledge cities. *Expert Systems with Applications*, *41*(12), 5549–5559. doi:10.1016/j.eswa.2014.03.032

Yigitcanlar, T., Baum, S., & Horton, S. (2007). Attracting and retaining knowledge workers in knowledge cities. *Journal of Knowledge Management*, *11*(5), 6–17. doi:10.1108/13673270710819762

Yigitcanlar, T., & Bulu, M. (2015). Dubaization of Istanbul: Insights from the knowledge-based urban development journey of an emerging local economy. *Environment & Planning A, 47*(1), 89–107. doi:10.1068/a130209p

Yigitcanlar, T., & Dur, F. (2013). Making space and place for knowledge communities: Lessons for Australian practice. *Australasian Journal of Regional Studies, 19*(1), 5–32.

Yigitcanlar, T., Edvardsson, I., Johannesson, H., Kamruzzaman, M., Ioppolo, G., & Pancholi, S. (2017a). Knowledge-based development dynamics in less favoured regions: Insights from Australian and Icelandic university towns. *European Planning Studies, 25*(12), 2272–2292. doi:10.1080/09654313.2017.1358699

Yigitcanlar, T., Guaralda, M., Taboada, M., & Pancholi, S. (2016). Place making for knowledge generation and innovation: Planning and branding Brisbane's knowledge community precincts. *Journal of Urban Technology, 23*(1), 115–146. doi:10.1080/10630732.2015.1090198

Yigitcanlar, T., Inkinen, T., & Makkonen, T., (2015). Does size matter? Knowledge-based development of second-order city-regions in Finland. *disP-The Planning Review, 51*(3), 62-77.

Yigitcanlar, T., & Lonnqvist, A. (2013). Benchmarking knowledge-based urban development performance: Results from the international comparison of Helsinki. *Cities (London, England), 31*(1), 357–369. doi:10.1016/j.cities.2012.11.005

Yigitcanlar, T., Lonnqvist, A., & Salonius, H. (2014). Analysis of a city-region from the knowledge perspective: Tampere, Finland. *VINE: The Journal of Information and Knowledge Management Systems, 44*(3), 445–466. doi:10.1108/VINE-09-2013-0056

Yigitcanlar, T., Metaxiotis, K., & Carrillo, J. (Eds.). (2012). *Building prosperous knowledge cities: policies, plans and metrics*. London: Edward Elgar Publishing. doi:10.4337/9780857936042

Yigitcanlar, T., O'Connor, K., & Westerman, C. (2008c). The making of knowledge cities: Melbourne's knowledge-based urban development experience. *Cities (London, England), 25*(2), 63–72. doi:10.1016/j.cities.2008.01.001

Yigitcanlar, T., Sabatini-Marques, J., Da Costa, E., Kamruzzaman, M., & Ioppolo, G. (2017b). Stimulating technological innovation through incentives: Perceptions of Australian and Brazilian firms. *Technological Forecasting and Social Change*. doi:10.1016/j.techfore.2017.05.039

Yigitcanlar, T., & Sarimin, M. (2011). The role of universities in building prosperous knowledge cities: The Malaysian experience. *Built Environment, 37*(3), 260–280. doi:10.2148/benv.37.3.260

Yigitcanlar, T., & Sarimin, M. (2015). Multimedia Super Corridor, Malaysia: Knowledge-based urban development lessons from an emerging economy. *VINE: The Journal of Information and Knowledge Management, 45*(1), 126–147. doi:10.1108/VINE-06-2014-0041

Yigitcanlar, T., & Velibeyoglu, K. (2008). Knowledge-based urban development: Local economic development path of Brisbane, Australia. *Local Economy, 23*(3), 197–209. doi:10.1080/02690940802197358

Yigitcanlar, T., Velibeyoglu, K., & Baum, S. (Eds.). (2008a). *Knowledge-based urban development: planning and applications in the information era*. Hersey, PA: Information Science Reference. doi:10.4018/978-1-59904-720-1

Yigitcanlar, T., Velibeyoglu, K., & Baum, S. (Eds.). (2008b). *Creative urban regions: harnessing urban technologies to support knowledge city initiatives*. Hersey, PA: Information Science Reference. doi:10.4018/978-1-59904-838-3

Yigitcanlar, T., Velibeyoglu, K., & Martinez-Fernandez, C. (2008d). Rising knowledge cities: The role of knowledge precincts. *Journal of Knowledge Management*, *12*(5), 8–20. doi:10.1108/13673270810902902

ENDNOTE

1 This is a revised version of "Yigitcanlar, T., (2015). *Knowledge based urban development.* In Encyclopedia of information science and technology. 3rd Edition. Khosrow-Pour, M., (Eds.). Hersey, PA: IGI Global, pp. 7475-7485".

Introduction

THE INEVITABILITY OF KBUD IN THE MIDDLE EAST

Globally, Knowledge Based Urban Development (KBUD) has rapidly developed as an independent domain of studies articulating the relation between the knowledge and the city. Yet, the Middle East was unfortunate to foster research, knowledge transfer and cases examination in this swiftly emerging domain. There is an ample of opportunity through the publishing of this book, to achieve a critical platform of interest, research and practice on KBUD within the Middle Eastern context. Due to the multidisciplinary nature of KBUD, the book invites researchers and contributors from diverse fields, such as architecture, urban studies, planning, geography, social studies and knowledge and creative economy investigators, to share their insights. The quality and quantity of transformations which are taking place in the Middle East are unprecedented particularly in the last decade. Middle Eastern States and cities are changing rapidly to cope with the challenges and aspirations of their people. The pace by which Middle Eastern cities and particularly Gulf Cities are approaching the post Carbon paradigm is extraordinary. With the sever drop in oil prices and lack of political and social stability, Middle Eastern cities are obliged to investigate its future. Transforming Middle East and Gulf cities into knowledge and creative ones is a newly evolving strategy to deal with the challenges created by the new economic realities, the population growth and rapid urbanization. But more significantly to better prepare Gulf cities to the post carbon paradigm.

Extending the boundaries of the Middle East to incorporate the Turkish and Iranian experiences would shed light on a paradigm shift in this ever turmoiled part of the world. The Middle East has a long-established reputation for radicalism, extremism, human rights abuses and failing economies. To divert the blame, most of the region's leaders tend to point the finger of responsibility for these failings at foreign actors and forces. Such attitude paved the way for the conspiracy theory to be always used to justify mistakes and bad decisions. A shift to a 'knowledge economy' could transform the Middle East, on the condition; it respects the holistic nature of such a needed shift. A knowledge economy paradigm refers to the post-agricultural, post-industrial global economic dynamic which can be traced in developed States around the world. This paradigm signifies an economy in which an individual's professional value is not evaluated by what he/she can manufacture or draw from the ground, but by what that individual knows and his/her creative contribution. Middle East countries struggle to adapt to this new reality emerged from such a paradigm shift transforming from resources and industrial economy to knowledge and creative economy. Many of their economies are still based on agriculture and industry and not moving yet to knowledge economy.

The events of the Arab Spring in 2011, constructed a clear manifestation that the new generations in this region, are aspiring for a different quality of life. Therefore, the idea of the book stems from the necessity to provide a new vintage point on the future of Middle Eastern cities in a challenging world. In the last decade and with the impact of the post-globalization condition and the establishment of knowledge economy as an alternative to future development in the Middle East, knowledge-based urban development (KBUD) of cities is becoming a timely topic for research and investigation. KBUD has been lately perceived as a catalyst for cities around the world to successfully compete, survive and prosper. As suggested in recent research, many cities and regions that have not chosen a knowledge-based development pathway are facing the imminent risk of being left behind, diminishing and perishing (Yigitcanlar, 2011; Carrillo et al., 2014). A decade ago, reports were suggesting the need for a move towards knowledge economy with the needed shift in investment priorities (Aubert and Reiffers, 2004). The global knowledge revolution presents Middle East States with challenges and opportunities. They need to take advantage of this new source of growth and employment. To date, related investments in education, information infrastructure, research and development (R&D), and innovation have been insufficient or inappropriate in most Middle East countries. Moreover, inadequate economic and institutional frameworks prevent these investments from yielding desired results.

A PARADIGM SHIFT IN THE MIDDLE EAST

Evidently, the world is experiencing a different era and witnessing a different history as from now to 2050, it will spend the amount of financial resources which were invested since the dawn of humanity. By 2050, the world's population will be nearly 10 Billion and the challenge is how to better plan cities to accommodate the greatest demographic upheaval using the unprecedented financial resources? A mere economic growth rate as an independent indicator of prosperity can be misleading. It suggests prosperity but fails to inform about the credibility of the just distribution of growth to all citizens rather than to the privileged few. Major events in the Middle East, particularly the consequences of the Arab Spring revolutions and uprisings and the sever drop in oil prices, forced major financial institution including World Bank and International Monetary Fund (IMF) to revisit the criteria used in evaluating the economic performance of Middle East countries. The context of Gulf Cities is rather controversial with such accelerating economic and political changes. While some argue that this paradigm is a fundamental crisis for the Gulf, an alternative argument suggests that it is totally the opposite (Alraouf, 2017).

The inconvenient truth of oil depletion and decreased prices is a blessing to the Gulf States if the historical opportunity is used to revisit their expenditure, society lifestyle, modes of production, culture of consumption and social integration. Therefore, a trend emerges in which a number of Gulf and Middle East cities turn towards the knowledge-based rather than the resource-driven fields of industries. Major consequences are expected on cities' planning, urbanism and architecture. To address obvious discrepancy in research, scientific development and knowledge production, certain Middle East leaders have turned to knowledge hubs and innovation clusters intended to concentrate local and international entrepreneurs and offer the resources to incubate their ideas (Engelke, 2015). Some Middle Eastern leaders primarily Gulf leaders orientate to building knowledge economies as a solution for the region's long-lasting problems. Recognizing that their countries' fossil-fuel-driven wealth will come to an end in the future, leaders of the six Gulf Cooperation Council (GCC) countries (Bahrain, Kuwait, Oman, Qatar, Saudi Arabia, and the United Arab Emirates) are investing heavily in the infrastructure necessary to create economies driven more by innovation than by energy exports. They have created ambitious national strategies to build research-and-development capacity, enable venture capital, attract highly skilled foreign workers, and create innovation clusters. As (Engelke, 2015) argues when it comes to building the knowledge economy, the Gulf is one of the most ambitious regions in the world.

The book, KBUD in the Middle East, collectively scrutinize mega knowledge-based projects like Abu Dhabi's Masdar City, Dubai's Techno Park, Doha's Science and Technology Park, Smart Village and Scientific Research City in Egypt, and the King Abdullah University of Science and Technology in Saudi Arabia among others as they represent prominent examples of KBUD in Middle East and Gulf States. Due to contextual peculiarities, I would also argue that the shift is required in the conception of future development in the Middle East and the Gulf to be founded on four main categories of solutions; Nature - based solutions, Heritage - based solutions, Knowledge - based solutions and more significantly Democratic - based solutions. The notion of democracy is crucial in establishing KBUD. The role of the community and the significance of listening to its diverse voices is a must condition for such development to take place. Democracy is a huge challenge in most of the Middle East countries. Most of the countries are governed by royal families, monarchies, coup leaders, or falsely elected presidents. Hence, engaging people should transcend the cosmetics practice represented in selecting some community representatives to look at the very final results to another level by allowing people to be present from the very early stage. With such practice, people will define challenges which need to be confronted as they experience in daily struggles.

The contemporary history of the Middle East is continuous waves of turmoil and conflicts. Even the glimpse of hope which emerge during the Arab Spring, had been swiftly dissolved into chaos and bloodshed (Danahar, 2015). Evidently, the Arab Spring changed the Middle East forever. The events known today as the Arab Spring began in Tunisia in 2011 and spread to several other Arab States in North Africa and the Middle East; Egypt, Libya, Iraq and also Syria. Among many consequences, the role of the youth is becoming crucial and considered. The young generations in the Middle East are dreaming about a new paradigm which transcends the endless energy drain in conflicts and artificial disputes (Bayat, 2009). Therefore, significant aspect about the future of the Middle East is related to the presence of youth as they represent the majority of populations in most of the countries. These new generations are also educated as e result of increased public accessibility to education during the 90s, especially at the level of primary education, which experienced the greatest degree of expansion in the region. Relatedly, adult literacy rates increased tremendously from 1990 to 2010. Hence, the current generation of Middle East and North Africa (MENA) youth, which accounts for 21.5 percent of the region's total population, is more educated than their predecessors (The World Bank, 2008). At the same time, the rise of independent media and internet usage across the regime gave intellectuals, along with human rights and women's activists, valuable tools to advocate for human rights and democracy. So, a growing number of youth are becoming more educated, exposed and aware of regional and global issues. Bayat (2009) acknowledges the vitality of these newly emerging classes in the Middle East and their desire for change and illustrates that such classes were responsible for the accumulated energy resulted in the Arab Spring.

Additionally, the book KBUD in the Middle East provides a platform to a better understanding of the different patterns of growth of knowledge-based urban development (KBUD) within the Middle East. This platform is constructed to illustrate that the concepts of KBUD and related Knowledge Cities (KC) are not about establishing ICT clusters in Middle East cities. A more dynamic and holistic development of the knowledge cities in this part of the developing world is an alternative approach which transcends the regional limited view of KBUD in the Middle East. This book aims to be an essential reference source for universities, researchers, institutions and decision makers concerned about contemporary Middle

Eastern Cities. The book builds on previous literature in the field of contemporary theory of architecture and urbanism in the advent of knowledge and creative economy. It provides the resources necessary for education in contemporary architecture and urban politics, local development and research practice. The book develops a political and critical perspective on contemporary practices of planning, urban design and architecture, their implementation, political effects and social results. The significance of the book stems from the fact that the topic and the related issues where never examined and collected in a scientific and holistic manner. While there is substantial literature on the topics of Knowledge and creative cities, Knowledge based urban development and knowledge economy but none of which confronted the challenges of contemporary Middle Eastern cities.

Within the different chapters of the book, a number of key conceptual and empirical issues of urban development and planning in cities around the Middle East are interrogated. Primarily, the discussion of the role of knowledge and its spatial form in urban development is included. In addition, identifying the preconditions for innovative use of urban resources for cities is discussed. Topics like review of the existing urban information and communication (ICT) policy and the implications of ICT use for conventional land use regulation were confronted. The impacts of ICTs upon localized, physical space to provide new perspectives for planners and managers were discussed in the cases. The book also as echoed in number of chapters interrogate the concept of smart cities. In at least two chapters, the concept is challenged as it is promoted as a qualitative approaches to interact the digital systems controlling and monitoring aspects of the city like infra structure, transportation and energy consumption. The extended understanding of the concept should deal with urban growth as smart, sustainable and inclusive growth.

The book aims at pin point new methods to evaluate the potential of urban planning to delivery knowledge-based development. Eventually, the book determines and share KBUD experiences of the successful knowledge cities. The chapters of this book will further explore a number of broad and specific research questions. Essentially, this interrogation includes what is the role of the city in the knowledge economy? What are the main characteristics of KBUD? What are the forces and factors of successful KBUD? What is the capacity of urban planning in the transformation of cities into knowledge cities? Specifically, the book can be seen as an integrated tool to explore and examine the issues of KBUD In the Middle Eastern context as it sheds light on a number of themes interactively structure the argument of the book. The first theme of the book is the notion of knowledge economy and The Middle East's interpretation of Knowledge and creative Economy. Second theme is articulated around exploring Middle Eastern Cities in post-hydrocarbon paradigm. Within this theme, an assessment of knowledge cities initiatives within the Middle Eastern context is conducted. Knowledge-based urban development of cities and regions in the Middle East and the contemporary competition in the Gulf and the Middle East in constructing the knowledge city image. The third theme focuses on knowledge city in practice suggesting best practices, frameworks for the development of knowledge cities and case studies from the Middle East. Urban services and infrastructure for knowledge cities, Key success factors and planning approaches for knowledge-based urban development are deliberated. Additionally, a clarification to distinguish the differences and overlaps between concepts like Knowledge, creative, smart, or intelligent cities, regions and societies is provided. Chapters also discussed the future of knowledge/creative workers and Intellectual, Social and human capital of Middle East cities. Therefore, creativity, innovation technology and learning communities, knowledge, globalization, and dynamics of cities, the role of cultural and educational buildings (museums, universities, etc.) in constructing models of KBUD in the Middle East.

The main obstacle towards building viable knowledge economies in the region is creating soft infrastructure and this needs to be fully acknowledged (Engelke, 2015). Such soft infrastructure is concerned with values and principles needed for KBUD more than buildings and physically constructed facilities. The building blocks of the knowledge economy are creativity, freedom of expression, social inclusion, and interaction with global cultures. Therefore, one of the most important lessons that need to be learned in the Middle East is no positive results would come from investing in the knowledge economy while maintaining the authoritarian and patriarchal status quo. Most of Middle East leaders fear taking the holistic steps to build knowledge economies as they fully acknowledge that every investment into a knowledge economy brings societies a step closer to understand the value of the struggle and the social and political transformations needed to from an authoritarian political culture to a more democratic one. Sadly, the Arab Spring crystalized the dilemma that while it's the one thing long-suffering peoples need most, corrupted leaders and their regimes will do everything to hinder liberating their people and equip them with the conditions for a knowledge economy and society.

The recent Gulf crisis between Qatar and Saudi Arabia, United Arab of Emirates and Bahrain, resulted from the blockade on Qatar activated on the 5th June 2017, proved that aspiring leaders for implementing knowledge economy in Middle East and particularly in the Gulf won't reach their goals without deeper political and social reforms (MacDonald and Fattah, 2017; Tharoor, 2017). As discussed, knowledge economy and knowledge-based urban development are more inclined to be perceived as social and political engines of change. Without such perception, it will be only limited in erecting buildings and infrastructure without substantial and qualitative changes and transformations. Obviously, the dilemma is while Residents of the Middle East, like most people in the world, want what comes with the knowledge economy. Their leaders, however, rarely wish to see the drastic social transformations that accompany it. What leaders and decision makers need to understand that knowledge economies give rise to debates about good governance, accountability, multiculturalism, gender equality, and worker's rights among other topics. Without creating platforms for such debates, it is impossible to seek a knowledge economy. They also need to fully comprehend that knowledge economy is about attracting and retaining knowledge workers who will never reside in an environments fails to provide the quality of life that draw creative classes to innovation and knowledge hubs (Foray, 2004). So the needed infrastructure for knowledge economy and knowledge-based urban development is not only about cement-based achievements but about value-based infrastructure. Dubai was a very promising case and invested heavily in the cement and steel based infrastructure but failed totally when tested during the Arab Spring, the 2017 Gulf crisis and in any situation related to pluralism, rule of law, and rights and freedoms.

With such unprecedented compilation of regional researchers and academics' interpretations of the impact of Knowledge on the Middle East urbanity, Knowledge-Based Urban Development in the Middle East will interest a wide range of academic disciplines from Gulf and Middle East studies to architecture, from urban planning to sociology and more significantly the emerging generation of researchers in the post carbon paradigm within the boundaries of the Middle East. It will also appeal to economic development planners, public service agencies and policy-makers in public sector, urban and regional development/planning bodies. By bringing together research, action research, best practice and case studies in an integrated form, the book will have a wide-ranging audience across the main components of KBUD throughout the world.

Ali A. Alraouf
Qatar Urban Planning, Qatar

REFERENCES

Aubert, J., & Reiffers, J. (2004). *Knowledge Economies in the Middle East and North Africa: Toward New Development Strategies. WBI Learning Resources.* Washington, DC: World Bank. doi:10.1596/0-8213-5701-8

Al-Nakib, F. (2016). *Kuwait Transformed: A History of Oil and Urban Life*. Stanford University Press.

Alraouf, A. A. (2017). Interrogating Qatar's Urbanity as a Catalyst for Building Knowledge-Based Societies and Economies. In Strategies of Knowledge Transfer for Economic Diversification in the Arab States of the Gulf. London: Gerlach Press.

Alraouf, A. A. (2008). Emerging Middle Eastern Knowledge Cities: the Unfolding Story. In T. Yigitcanlar & V. Koray (Eds.), *Knowledge Based Urban Development: Planning and Application in the Information Era* (pp. 240–259). IGI Global. doi:10.4018/978-1-59904-720-1.ch014

World Bank. (2008). *The Road Not Traveled: Education Reform in the Middle East and North Africa.* Washington, DC: World Bank.

Bayat, A. (2009). *Life as Politics: How Ordinary People Change the Middle East.* Cairo: AUC Press.

Carrillo, F. J., Yigitcanlar, T., García, B., & Lönnqvist, A. (2014). *Knowledge and the City: Concepts, Applications and Trends of Knowledge-Based Urban Development.* London: Routledge.

Danahar, P. (2015). *The New Middle East: The World After the Arab Spring*. London: Bloomsbury.

Engelke, P. (2015). Brainstorming the Gulf: Innovation and the Knowledge Economy in the GCC. Washington, DC: The Atlantic Council's Brent Scowcroft Center on International Security.

Foray, D. (2004). *The Economics of Knowledge*. Cambridge, MA: MIT Press.

MacDonald, F., & Fattah, Z. (2017). 100 Days of the Big Gulf Feud. *Bloomberg Business Week.*

Tharoor, I. (2017). The Persian Gulf crisis over Qatar, explained. *The Washington Post.* Retrieved from https://www.washingtonpost.com/news/worldviews/wp/2017/06/06/the-persian-gulf-crisis-over-qatar-explained/?utm_term=.507e62718366

UNESCO. (2005). *Towards knowledge societies.* Paris: UNESCO Publishing.

United Nations Development Program (UNDP). (2003). *Arab human development report 2003: Building a knowledge society*. New York: United Nations Publications.

Yigitcanlar, T. (2011). Redefining knowledge-based urban development. *International Journal of Knowledge Based Development*, *2*(4), 340–356. doi:10.1504/IJKBD.2011.044343

Section 1

Issues, Challenges, and Theoretical Concepts

Chapter 1
The Myth of Knowledge-Based Urban Development in the Middle Eastern Cities:
A Multilayered Analysis

Ali Alraouf
Qatar Urban Planning, Qatar

ABSTRACT

A decade ago, Middle Eastern cities and particularly Gulf cities rushed into the implementation of knowledge-based urban development and knowledge cities as models for development and progress. Unlike the Western models of knowledge and creative cities, Middle Eastern cities attempts were characterized by the mere construction of technologically advanced yet isolated urban entities with the hope that they are promoting the same concepts essential for knowledge cities: integration and dissemination. By analyzing key projects selected from the Middle Eastern context, the chapter concludes that the common failure resulted from transforming these projects into gated communities fully isolated from the city and the community.

INTRODUCTION

Advances in information and communication technologies (ICTs) are inevitably making societies and cities increasingly knowledge-based. In the 21st century, more than ever before, cities around the world bank on on the knowledge of citizens, institutions and enterprises. It creates local spaces and professional environments, which offer the quality of life to the citizens who are seeking to cope with the challenges of modern life in a competitive world. The nature of city development changes accordingly as activities in the knowledge sector are becoming more important and they require conditions and environments which are different from commodity-based manufacturing activities (Knight, 1995). Castells (1996 and 1998) has argued that a new type of society is rising in our contemporary cities due to the consequences of the information revolution. Evidently, scholars, planners and decision-makers have started to debate

DOI: 10.4018/978-1-5225-3734-2.ch001

Copyright © 2018, IGI Global. Copying or distributing in print or electronic forms without written permission of IGI Global is prohibited.

the need for a new urban planning approach in order to achieve a development that is sustainable and knowledge-based (Castells, 1994; Hall, 2004). The value and the relevance of knowledge-based urban development (KBUD) stems from the dire need for an alternative ways of planning cities to better face the unprecedented challenges of contemporary time.

Within the Middle Eastern and Gulf cities, the objective of developing a knowledge-based economy is clear and well declared as stated in their strategic visions. The plans of the Gulf Cooperation Council (GCC) States bank on the diversified and knowledge-intensive economies. Principally, the emerging Gulf cities Kuwait City (Kuwait), Manama (Bahrain), Doha (Qatar), Abu Dhabi, Dubai, Sharjah (UAE), and Muscat (Oman) exhibited a commitment towards adopting the knowledge economy principles. The same was echoed in the rest of the Middle Eastern cities with different levels of focus including Cairo (Egypt), Khartoum (Sudan), Riyadh (Saudi Arabia) and Morocco. It is also extended to include evidences of KBUD in Iran and Turkey. Yet, such effort needs to be examined to answer the important question, are those development plans realistic? Most of Middle Eastern cities have a lot in common; primarily; language, religion. Yet, contextual differences are so radical. Hence the chapter is also geared towards understanding how political, cultural, social, and economical factors will facilitate or rather hinder transforming a Middle Eastern city into a knowledge one. The common understanding of planning and cities evolution suggests that cities develop organically over hundreds of years. Particularly in the case of Gulf cities, they were able to provide a solid example opposing this conceptual interpretation of gradual urban development. In the last few decades, contemporary Gulf cities expanded rapidly in terms of size, buildings, infrastructure, and population. Another crucial research investigation is related to the demographic structure. While most of the Middle Eastern cities experience normal increase in population, during the last decade, Gulf cities became poles of attraction for people coming from almost every part of the world to generate more income and secure their futures. Workforces from different levels, backgrounds and ideologies are pouring into these cities. The percentage of foreigners in Kuwait city and Muscat is around 60- 65 percent. In all of the other cities, the percentage is about or higher than 80 percent. The situation is more serious in Doha as the expatriates form around 85 percent while in Dubai, more than 90 percent of the population are expatriates. Research questions like how newly emerged Gulf knowledge cities will engage their inhabitants (locals and expatiates) positively and creatively? is of an essential significance. Knowledge cities main principles like equity, transparency, equal rights, and minority groups' consideration should be reinterpreted in the light of the existing yet controversial Gulf cities demographic structure.

The economical, political, social and cultural changes which took place in the context of the last decade suggest that radical changes are needed to cope with the aspiration of communities particularly young generations around the Middle East. Middle Eastern cities are struggling to be part of a movement of change and development. For instance, discussing the economical factors dynamics in the last decades might reveal interesting conclusions. The protests of the youth (Also documented as the Arab Spring) which started in Tunisia in the end of 2010 and traveled through the Middle East, all the way to Bahrain, emerged from the lack of decent life, absence of social justice and lack of dignified sense of citizenship. People in most of the Middle Eastern cities realized that they were manipulated and betrayed. In the same time, the rich Middle Eastern countries, basically located around the Arabian Gulf are becoming fully aware of the necessity for diversifying their economical bases. They have been trying to move from an oil-based economy towards a more multi-dimensional one that will help them surviving the inevitable dry up of their oil resources (Alraouf, 2008). Other cities that are located in the rest of the Middle East have also realized that a new paradigm is approaching where the typical production of physical commodities

Figure 1. Gulf cities are witnessing the dawn of a new urban paradigm centered on KBUD, the case of NYU in Abu Dhabi overlooking the city's global urban skyline (Source:Author)

is replaced by the knowledge production which is based primarily on the power of human brains and the unlimited creativity. While acknowledging that coping with this new paradigm is inevitable, obviously a major confrontation with the contextual realities of these cities is a fundamental challenge.

THE KNOWLEDGE CITY: A NEEDED FORM OF URBANISM

Any city is a spatial platform where hundreds of human interactions and exchanges occur. These interactions are holistically human because of the inclusion of cultural, ideological, intellectual, symbolic, political, informational, and of course commercial and economical. Missing this holistic nature particularly while planning for knowledge-based urban development would result on yet again value-free developments. This holistic perspective is clearly stressed in substantial literature articulating the approaches to knowledge cities and KBUD (Carrillo, 2006; Divr, 2005; Komninos, 2002). Knowledge Cities are cities that possess an economy driven by high value-added exports created through research, technology, and brainpower. In other words, these are cities in which both the private and the public sectors value knowledge, nurture knowledge, spend money on supporting knowledge dissemination and discovery (i.e. learning and innovation) and harness knowledge to create products and services that add value and create wealth. Knowledge cities (KCs) play fundamental roles in knowledge creation, economic growth and development. Edvinsson (2003) sees KC as a city that was purposefully designed to encourage the nurturing of knowledge. The notion of KC is interchangeable to a certain degree with similar evolving concepts such as 'knowledge-based clusters' (Arbonies & Moso, 2002), 'ideopolis' (Garcia, 2004) or 'technopolis' (Smilor et al., 1988a; Smilor et al., 1988b; Dvir & Pasher, 2004).

KC is also seen as an umbrella metaphor for geographical entities, which focus on knowledge creation and covers other knowledge zones such as 'knowledge corridors', 'knowledge harbors', 'knowledge villages' and 'knowledge regions' (Dvir, 2003). Ergazakis et al. (2004) refer to KC as a city that aims at a knowledge-based development, by encouraging the continuous creation, sharing, evaluation, renewal and update of knowledge. This can be achieved through the continuous interaction between its citizens and also between them and other cities' citizens. The citizens' knowledge-sharing culture as well as the city's appropriate design, ICT networks and infrastructures support these interactions. Obviously, the previous definitions are suggesting a multi-layered concept which involves developing a path towards a more viable, vibrant, and sustainable development. KCs have embarked on a strategic mission to firmly encourage the nurturing of innovation, science and creativity, within the context of an expanding knowledge-based economy and society. KCs are seen as fundamental to the economic growth and development of the 21st century cities. KC is a new perspective of development which is based on knowledge, innovation and creativity. Leif Edvinsson (Dvir, 2004) defines KC as "a city that purposefully designed to encourage the nurturing of knowledge". KC is not just a regular city. It is a growing space of exchange and optimism in which each and every one can devote himself to personal and collective projects and aspirations in a climate of dynamism, harmony, and creativity. What is unique about this definition is the focus on KC as a holistic environment for comprehensive development. Hence, it calls for different process of articulating the city structure and subsequently raises issues and concepts like transparency, democracy and sustainability. It is also suggesting new paradigm in city planning. Based on knowledge-based development, Carrillo (2005) shows how knowledge can be and is placed at the center of city planning and economic development to enable knowledge flows and innovation to provide a sustainable environment for high value-added products and services.

INTEROGATING THE CONCEPT OF CREATIVE AND KNOWLEDGE CITIES

For Carrillo, Yigitcanlar, García and Lönnqvist (2014, p. xvii), "cities are taking a leading role as both knowledge-consumption and knowledge-production hubs." One basic aspect of knowledge cities conveys "the conglomeration of intense scientific, technological, academic, cultural and innovation activities in urban spaces operating as engines of economic productivity" (Carrillo et al., 2014, p. 3). To illuminate the connection between creativity, knowledge and city planning, Richard Florida's "Creative City" (2008, 2006, 2005, and 2002) theory is an essential tool for understanding how cities have become central to the achievement of competitive advantage. Therefore, the real economic competition today plays out among cities, not nation states as Florida rightly argues. An essential part of Florida's theory is the notion of creative class; the body of talented people that would be attracted to a specific city. Florida's theory emphasizes three main factors; Technology, Talent, and Tolerance, as responsible for attracting the "Creative Class", contributing to the national economy and establishing the requisite framework for sustaining competitive advantage. The creativity of cities is attributed to various factors, including openness to diversity, level of tolerance and the peaceful coexistence of differences in a society. Levels of technological innovation and a population comprised of talented and innovative people are also believed to have a direct impact on the creativity and hence, development of a city. Florida (2008) asserts that people can now choose the cities in which they want to live in, and this choice is shaped by the characteristics of the cities.

A misconception about creative and knowledge cities as Hall (2004) argues lies in the mere focus on the atmosphere and the image of the city. So, as he argues, it is not about import a community of artists, sprouting galleries and coffee shops and the sensational new airports designed by one of star architects. More profoundly, the new urban economy is based on creative activities and creative people; openness and tolerance are crucial elements. While big cities like London, Paris or New York will keep on attracting creative people and knowledge workers, the focus should be extended to the second tier of cities, small ambitious developing cities. Some Middle Eastern cities particularly Gulf cities fall into this category. Those in the next rank, aiming to raise into the 'global city' league by a combination of policies to attract knowledge workers and physical development – plus, in many cases, programs to encourage cultural life, like the Barcelona Forum. Barcelona is an excellent case as the city dells on the concept of "*Festivalization*" as Hall argues and promoting the city through periodic international events.

THE INEVITABLE PARADIGM: KBUD

Knowledge-based urban development (KBUD) is a new development Paradigm. The (KBUD) concept has first emerge in the urban planning and development discourse during the last decade of the 20th century as a promising paradigm to support the transformation process of cities into knowledge cities and their societies into knowledge societies (Ergazakis et al., 2006). The concept aims to increase the region's competitive edge, the attraction of highly skilled human resources and investments, and support the people of the region in reaching high standard of living and welfare. KBUD is based on the premises of Knowledge Economy (KE) which play a crucial role in the improvement of competitiveness of cities and urban regions (Yigitcanlar and Lönnqvist, 2013). Knight (2008) argues that knowledge-based urban development is a social learning process in which the knowledge capital is utilized in the development of a sustainable urban region. Kunzmann (2008) characterize the knowledge-based urban development concept as a collaborative development framework that provides guideline to the public, private and academic sectors in the make-up of future development strategies that attract and retain talent and investment, as well as to the creation of knowledge-intensive urban and regional policies. Yigitcanlar (2011) looks upon KBUD in the era of the global knowledge-based economy as a novel development paradigm, which is aimed to create economic prosperity, social order, sustainable environment and appropriate municipal governance.

The conceptual structure of KBUD is based on integrated set of pillars (Carrillo et. al., 2014; Yigitcanlar, 2011; Alraouf, 2008). The economic development pillar of KBUD is aimed to set the knowledge capital in the center of economic activities, because according to this concept knowledge is not a supplementary factor of development, but a key resource. The socio-cultural pillar aims to improve people's knowledge to develop a knowledge-based society, with main characteristics of strong human capital, acceptance of diversity and social equality. The third pillar of KBUD is the environmental and urban (enviro-urban) development which aims at finding the harmony between preservation and improvement of the built and natural environments. Positive spatial sustainable development in KBUD emphasize the Quality of life and place as it would guarantee the spatial quality needed to attract knowledge workers and to establish knowledge milieu. The environmental and urban pillar reflects the dimension of sustainable urban development and the creation of quality of life. The fourth, final pillar is the institutional development which aims to form a group of local actors who - in cooperation with stakeholders - determine the common vision of future and plan the strategy needed for the implementation of it. Thus, the fourth pillar is about to develop a knowledge-based governance, that can provide the effective institutional background that is essential for design and implementation of the development ((Yigitcanlar, 2011). As a result of coordinated development of the four dimensions an appropriate social, environmental, institutional and economic climate will develop, that will create economic prosperity, social equity, and environmental sustainability.

THE CHALLENGE OF ATTACTING KNOWLEDGE WORKERS

For a direct understanding of the knowledge-based society, cities need to recognize that Knowledge will be its key resource and knowledge workers (KW) will be the dominant group in its Workforce. A knowledge-based society is defined as "one where knowledge diffusion, production and application become the organizing principle in all aspects of human activity: culture, society, the economy, politics, and private life" (UNDP, 2003, p. 2). Therefore, the economic success of such a society is related to the ability of a place to attract the creative class, and that 'quality of place' is a key determinant. Members of the 'creative class' are thought to prefer lively and mixed environments, excellent urban infrastructures and cultural facilities (Florida, 2002). Knowledge workers (KW), as important individual agents who embody, exchange, create and exploit knowledge, contribute to regional competitiveness and growth (Thierstein et al., 2017). Urban and regional planning has displayed a recent interest in designing policies to attract international investment and encourage economic growth in KCs. These policies also focused on creating social amenities and communities to attract knowledge workers (Martin, 2001; Chen & Choi, 2004). The key factors in attracting knowledge workers to KCs are mainly social relationships and quality of life provided (Mathur, 1999; Leamer & Storper, 2001; Robinson, 2002; Santagata, 2002). One of the most crucial challenges in constructing a model of knowledge-based urban development in any city is related to the ways by which they can be attracted and retained. Hence, it is necessary to have a better understanding of their fundamental spatial needs particularly in housing choices, workplace environments, and commute choices. The spatial choices of Knowledge Workers as Thierstein et al. (2017) argue, are related to diversified residence alternatives, stimulating working environments and reliable public transportation as they tend to use it to allow for more social interactions and reflections on ideas and concepts. The choices of knowledge workers clearly display distinct choices of residential location and commute mode may provide insights for urban planners and policy-makers regarding the attraction and retention of knowledge workers.

Because of their role as individual agents of knowledge creation in knowledge-intensive economies, knowledge workers tend to manifest a distinguished case when it comes to the way they decide about where to live or work and also about how to move around in the city. Knowledge creation has become unrestricted and is no longer bounded to the physical workplace (Thierstein et al., 2017). (KW) also regard their residence together with their commute path as offering opportunities to find the inspiration that their job requires. When knowledge workers choose a residence, the function of maintaining social contacts is as important as, or even more important than the dwelling function. They select locations that match their "social pattern of contact" (Kaplan et al., 2016). When knowledge workers had the choice, they preferred public modes of transportation form the sake of more social interaction and external environmental exposure. Such experiences wouldn't be possible if cars are used as the prim mode of commuting. Accordingly, when (KW) select their commute mode, they also consider the degree of exposure to potential influences along the commute path, aside from travel efficiency (Thierstein et al., 2017). The notion of (KW) acquires a distinct importance in the context of Gulf cities as the demographic structure shows clearly the majority of expatriates moving to work and life in cities around the Gulf. Hence, a crucial question is what happens if the knowledge is not transferred to nationals? The creation of a knowledge economy of which entrepreneurship is a key component, is hugely important to the economic growth of the Middle East. But it is vital that knowledge is transferred to and shared by locals rather than residing only with expatriates who are likely to take the knowledge outside the country once they travel back. There are also issues related to social structure and cultural values. For

Figure 2. The process of knowledge and economic flow in cities (source: Author)

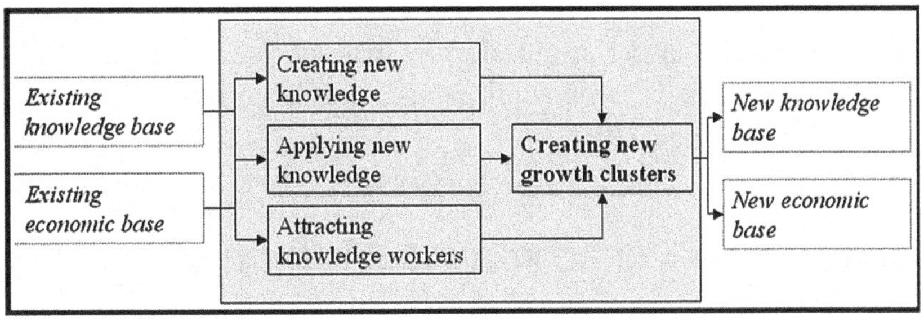

the knowledge economy to flourish, especially small-to-medium sized enterprises and micro enterprises, a middle class is needed. The importance of this class for flourishing local economy is not always appreciated and encouraged in the Middle East context. Creating opportunities for local-level business to interact with international corporations is hugely needed. If innovation is to flourish, and the knowledge economy thrives, people and organizations must also be prepared to take more risk. Risk taking is not encouraged in the Middle East and this needs to be addressed. Transparency, risk taking encouragement, access to financing, good governance, and educated workforce are all critical to the development of the Arab world's knowledge economy.

GLOBAL OR KNOWLEDGE CITIES: THE NEW DYNAMICS IN CITY FORMATION AND TRANSFORMATION

The discussion on the transformation from global to knowledge cities is of a great importance to the context of the Middle East. While the discussion is relevant to cities in the developed world, only limited number of Middle Eastern cities aspires for a global position. Therefore, a distinction between global and knowledge cities is crucial for evaluating the contemporary status of Middle Eastern cities. A major misunderstanding of the evolution of global cities, characterized the attempts of some Middle Eastern cities mainly in the Gulf to claim being globalized. As numerous researchers suggest, Gulf cities, in their trail to gain a place on the global stage, focused on the imagery nature of globalization (Al-Nakib, 2016; Alraouf, 2017; 2010; Wippel, 2014; Fromherz, 2012; Wiedmann, 2010). Hence, the construction of skyscrapers similar to the ones in New York and Chicago was more important than investing in the real components that would construct a knowledge city. While cities like New York, Chicago and Hong Kong are full of skyscrapers but this is not the reason for putting them on the top of global cities. Planners and decision makers in the Gulf were not able to see the other layers needed to label a city as a global one.

The illuminating work in explaining this point is the contribution of Saskia Sassen (1991; 2000). Sassen (1991), identifies four major interrelated functions that cities should perform in their attempt at becoming global. Cities should become "highly concentrated command points in the organization of the world economy; second, as key locations for finance and for specialized service firms, which have replaced manufacturing as the leading economic sectors; third, as sites of production including production of innovations, in these leading industries; and fourth, as markets for the products and innovations produced" (pp. 3-4). Hence, Sassen (2000) elaborates that cities in the information age should be re-perceived as nodes of an immense network of cultural, commercial and political transactions. Sassen

(2002) investigates emerging global cities in the developing world; Sao Paulo, Shanghai, Hong Kong, Mexico City, and Buenos Aires. She concludes that these cities show how globalizing zones are not only replicating many features of the top tier of global cities, but are also generating new socio-economic patterns as well. In other words, cities need to utilize the value of their local assets in the transformation process to be acknowledged as global cities.

THE POST CARBON ERA: A NEED FOR AN ALTERNATIVE URBANISM

All Gulf States came to the conclusion that a focus on development strategies for a post carbon paradigm is essential. The decline in oil prices during the last five years, from 100 $US per barrel to a less than 40 $US, suggests a swift change in the way Gulf States envisioned their future. The oil reserves are limited and will be exhausted in the near future. To secure wealth and further economic prosperity, the Gulf cities bank, among other prospects, on knowledge-driven industries and on well-educated knowledge workers. Therefore, the principles of knowledge economy was declared as the backbone in all Gulf States' future visions including Bahrain 2030, Dubai 2030, Abu Dhabi 2032, Qatar 2030, Kuwait 2035 and Riyadh 2025. Recently, notions as important as the knowledge economy, the related Knowledge Based Urban Development (KBUD), the impact of the Creative Class are seen as strategically important for the future development of Middle Eastern and Gulf cities. Cities' planners and strategists in the Middle East are talking about attracting the knowledge workers and the creative class, establishing knowledge-based economical activities and plan cities as knowledge and creative ones. For the "Qatar National Development Strategy" the main goal is to build on knowledge: "As Qatar's economy diversifies more from its reliance on gas and oil, success will increasingly depend on the ability to compete in a global knowledge economy. Educating and training Qataris to their full potential will be critical to continuing progress" (GSDP, 2011, p. 122). In the "Dubai Strategic Plan 2015" two knowledge-based aims are described: (1) "Preparing Dubai's workforce for the high-value, knowledge-driven economy, which requires attracting and retaining highly skilled employees, improving Nationals' qualifications and increasing their motivation" and (2) "Turning Dubai into a vibrant science and technology hub in targeted sectors, by supporting the development of existing sectors, and establishing the right environment for nurturing the post 2015 economy" (Dubai Strategic Plan, 2007, p. 22). Emerging knowledge cities in the Gulf, mainly Doha, Manama, Dubai, Abu Dhabi and more recently Riyadh are trying, in different capacities, to transform from their previous status as oil producing economies to cities celebrating education, research, innovation and attracting knowledge workers. For this process to thrive, a different kind of urbanism is required. The needs of knowledge workers moving to Gulf cities will change the spatial contents, boundaries and qualities of these cities. Knowledge-based urban development (KBUD) can be an appropriate vehicle towards a new planning paradigm for Gulf cities. More specifically, establishing a creative or knowledge city implies its ability to affect the spatial properties. New patterns of urban spaces should be articulated. The ultimate goal is to increase the innovation and creative capacity of cities based on a new set of knowledge patterns.

The main dilemma of some Middle Eastern cities' struggling to establish a knowledge and creativity identity is related to the notion of time. This is a long process and can't cope with the desire to build fast and instant cities like Dubai. As the pioneer work of Castells and Hall (1994) and Hall (1998) concluded that building innovative or creative cities was a long and slow, sometimes excruciatingly slow, process, and that the outcome could by no means be guaranteed in advance. There are favorable preconditions,

Figure 3. New York University in Abu Dhabi, one of the evidences of new urbanity in Gulf cities aiming towards establishing knowledge and creative cities (Source: Author)

to be sure, but they are difficult to achieve and their presence will not automatically generate the desired outcome. Further, creating these preconditions is itself a long process. Such conclusion is crucial as it is a requirement if the aim is to build a truly creative city full of cultural interactions, inspiration and continuous knowledge dissemination. In this sense, we need to differentiate between cities built for cultural consumption versus the ones built for culture production and the latter is the aspired for as a genuine creative city. If the creative city is more related to the production of culture, then the point is that cities have to start with something. They have to discover their best points and build on them. Further, they have to engage the local community and not only focus on cultural tourism. Social and cultural base is essential for cities to incubate creativity to ensure economic growth, urban development, and socio-cultural and psychological wellbeing of their residents. Cultural resources are embodied in people's creativity, and Landry (2000) highlights that knowledge cities aim to create the conditions for people think, plan, and act creatively.

MIDDLE EASTERN CITIES: NEW CENTRES AND ALTERNATIVE MODELS

Cairo, Baghdad, and Damascus used to be the intellectual, cultural, social, and political centers of the Arab and Islamic world. These cities have structured the models of development to be followed in the Middle East for centuries (Al Hathloul, 2004). Even after the Gulf's oil boom back in the early seventies, they have been able to maintain their leading capabilities (Alraouf, 2008). Historically, Cairo exercised strong influence on the whole region of the Arab world. This influence can be traced culturally, politically, socially and architecturally (Mitchell, 2002; Sakr, 1996). However, the city is losing its regional leading role. Cairo' status is a reflection of Egypt struggles to cope with problems caused by massive population growth, urban sprawl, economic failures, political instability and growing poverty rates. Due to long conflicts and the complexity of their recent political and economical situations, both Baghdad, and Damascus lost their capability of sustaining their sense of leadership. Hence Cairo is left alone as the only old center struggling to maintain and develop its previous status. Yet, after the 25th January revolution and then the military coup in 2013, Egypt has completely derailed from regaining its unique status as the leader of Middle East. Evidently, the traditional centers of Middle East culture and knowledge have been immersed in political and social conflicts and the same goes with the North African States including Morocco, Tunis and Algeria. Sudan suffered from a long civil war ended up with splitting the country into two states. Alternatively, in the last two decades new centers in the Middle Eastern region are emerging (Al Qassemi, 2013). New cities are flourishing within the context of the Gulf. Cities, like Dubai· Doha and Abu Dhabi are creating new models of development which are so new, swift and dynamic. These Gulf cities have made big strides in such a short time in terms of business and cultural development as well as their ambition to become more than just financial hubs but rather expand their influence across the region.

In the face of the growing competition between countries, cities, organizations, and individuals a new way of thinking is required if all are to achieve economic success. To date, only some of the Middle East countries have been fortunate. They are oil-rich states, although reserves are dwindling and have been able to use oil revenues to develop projects to diversify their economies. The grand plan for most of these economies is to become knowledge-based which means that the service sector will become more important. Consequently, the need for governments to educate and nurture local talent will become paramount and they will need to encourage people to think differently. In other words, shifting towards knowledge-based economy is becoming a necessity rather than a development optional direction. Gulf countries are constructing a very clear case in the relevance of knowledge based development in the post oil paradigm using the outstanding oil sales revenues which have accumulated in the Gulf countries due to unprecedented increase in oil prices. When the price of the oil barrel reached $70 in 2005, the way was paved for an economic revolution that started with the real estate boom. In addition, a lot of gulf financial capitals saved in American and European banks were withdrawn and redirected locally as a consequence of 9/11's culture of fear. Fear of embargo, assets freezing or sever punishments on Arab and Muslims has urged considerable number of Gulf most rich people to invest locally. Real estate was an ideal answer for the exceptional presence of liquidity in Gulf/Arab modern history (Alraouf, 2008). These projects are the most recent packaged residential environments in the Gulf, Their different themes and design concepts, as well as the different amenities and services allow inhabitants to engage in an exclusive lifestyle. The supremacy of image, projected in the media and promoted internationally through technological advances in mass communication, has resulted in the construction of global architectural fantasies and the pursuit of planning whims that offer no local identity or sense of contextual authenticity.

Within this perspective, Dubai constructs an interesting experience. In the last ten years, and at a remarkable pace, it has developed into a global crossroads, and is now thriving on a new type of post-global condition. New Dubai cityscape is emerged through the implication of a set of developmental models that emphasizing the global objectives and aspirations of the city. A creation of icons in Dubai or Iconic Development seems to be the governing strategy for all its current and upcoming projects. Hence, projects and buildings are becoming urban brands waited to be exported and then consumed by other Arab and Gulf cities in their strive to join the global paradigm. Most of Arab world cities are competing to imitate Dubai in its unprecedented effort to build the tallest, the biggest and the largest ever built architectural and urban statements (Wipple, 2014; Wiedmann, 2010). Dubai is this sense is becoming an urban brand which was successfully marketed within its regional boundaries (Alraouf, 2005; 2008). One problem of the explosion of growth in cities like Dubai and its followers is the creation of "Gated Regions". The result has been the creation of what demographer William Frey calls "Gated Regions"-places like New York, London, Tokyo-in which both the city and many of the surrounding suburbs have become unaffordable for all but the very wealthy. Such development tendency contradicts the main principles and promises of Knowledge Cities as the spread of such gated regions and communities is antithesis to its commitment to creating KCs.

TIME TO LEARN FROM HISTORY: LESSONS FROM THE PAST

The common understanding which relates KC to advanced information and communication technologies encourage decision makers to overcome the significance of people, heritage and culture. Knowledge in itself is a process accumulated overtime. The concept of 'Knowledge Cities' is deeply rooted in the urban, cultural and even architectural structure of traditional Middle Eastern cities. Some traditional cities in Egypt, Iraq and Syria were designed as an arena for knowledge exchange. Therefore, an attempt to foster this concept in today's Middle Eastern cities would not be possible by building isolated technological statement scattered around the city (Alraouf, 2008). Alternatively, the rise of the network society, global networks, linked cities and existence of smart communities should construct the basis for shaping Middle Eastern Knowledge Cities. A close examination of the urban and architectural structure of a typical Islamic/Arab city reveals that many of the city's experiences were based on exposing community members to knowledge either consciously or subconsciously. Three main building types can be used in the context of this discussion to illustrate how the physical built environment was positively supporting a distinguished relation between city and knowledge. These buildings are: the Mosque (*Al-Jameaa*), the School (*Al-Madrassa*), and the Market (*Al-Souq*).

Integrated Mosques, schools and universities like Sultan Hassan in Cairo or Al-Mustansiriyah in Baghdad are excellent examples in showing how knowledge and spirituality were interconnected. The Mosque was perceived intellectually and spiritually as the most public space in a traditional Islamic city. Complexes like Sultan Hassan and Al-Mustansiriyah are the cases where the mosque and the school were physically integrated to form an accessible, hence democratic knowledge center. Additionally, those centers showed the highest degree of tolerance by including the different Islamic school of thoughts and doctrines within the same knowledge entity of the Madrassa. The case of sultan Hassan is very interesting where the architectural spatial composition were divided into four sections to accommodate the main four doctrines of Islam. The Souq has always played an important role in the economy and social life of the traditional Middle Eastern city (Alraouf, 2012; Al Hathloul, 2004). In the broadest sense of the term, the Souq is an organized system grouped into guilds. In most of Souqs which were located in Islamic cities, the shops are usually grouped by profession; thus one alleyway may be occupied by carpet sellers, another by goldsmiths and yet another by coppersmiths. It acts as an interface between the town and the country, and has close links with the clergy. Strolling the Souq for shopping purposes was an indirect knowledge transfer experience especially for the young generation.

SCRUTINIZING THE REGIONAL MODELS OF KBUD

In a post-global and a post-oil paradigm, most of the Middle Eastern cities are thriving into diversified economic industries. Knowledge economy is perceived by both leaders and intellectuals as a valid vehicle for bridging into the new paradigm. Gulf cities countries within the middle East are working seriously in this direction as they fully acknowledge the negative impacts of oil depletion and devaluation.

Enormous investments which used in the last decade to finance iconic real estate developments are now shifted towards planning and financing knowledge based economic centers. Additionally, unprecedented concerns regarding the production and dissemination of information and knowledge are rising within all of those cities. The by-products of knowledge development, that go through the stages of knowledge creation, dissemination and utilization, form the core of "Knowledge Economy". A knowledge city as clearly explained earlier, becomes a geographical area with an expanding knowledge society, and with knowledge as a strong pillar of its economy. The concept of Knowledge City though being a familiar term in Western countries is merely interpreted in the Middle Eastern context as a geographical concentration of Special Economic Zones (SEZ's) and I.T. Companies. This has led to the development of various "Knowledge City" areas, which merely consist of several knowledge based and knowledge intensive industries. However, one needs to realize that the SEZ's, I.T. companies and the other industries, are an integral part of the city of knowledge, and by themselves do not constitute a Knowledge City. Alraouf (2008) provides critical analysis of the first attempts to create knowledge based urban developments within the Middle East.

In this section, a more elaborated analysis is conducted on selected cases from the Gulf Statas, North Africa and particular influential cases from the Middle Eastern context. To begin with, Emirate of Dubai initiated a number of projects in the direction of KBUD. As was explained earlier, opposite to the international applications of KC's principles, Dubai model was more centralized and divorced from the real community. Both the Media city (DMC) and The knowledge Village (KV) projects in Dubai fail to construct a knowledge pole (Alraouf, 2005). The first one is becoming the headquarters of foreign media agencies and the second one is transformed into rental places for modest universities branches, collages or training centers. Part of the substantial criticism directed to projects like Knowledge village, Dubai internet city, or Media city is based on the role of such projects in being merely business parks and are not innovation clusters. Dubai Internet city is an excellent manifestation of such interpretation. It was established in the Dubai Technology and Media Free Zone, a tax-free commercial site set up to support the development of knowledge-based industries. Apart from Dubai Internet City, this Free Zone today

Figure 4. Knowledge Village (KV) in Dubai is an example of how KBUD can be implemented in a distorted way (Source: Author)

includes separate clusters for the media and education industries that were mentioned earlier; KV and DMC. Over the past decade, Dubai Internet City has been developed to provide a complete business and community infrastructure for ICT companies. There are now 16 office buildings in Dubai Internet City. The buildings are set amidst an exquisitely designed landscape of lakes and gardens. Dubai Internet City is home for about 1,200 companies and accounts for more than 10,000 knowledge workers.

Another promising case is Emirate of Abu Dhabi, the capital city of UAE. It is also seeking prominence on the global stage with the $28 billion Saadiyat Island project, a cultural island that accommodates New York University campus, franchises of the Louvre and Guggenheim museums, and other leading cultural institutions in an attempt to capitalize on the 'Bilbao effect', garner international credibility, and attract further foreign investment (Ponzini & Nastasi, 2011). Other interesting knowledge-based educational institutions in Abu Dhabi include Khalifa University for Science, Technology and Research (KUSTAR), and Masdar Institute of Science and Technology (MIST). KUSTAR is a science-focused university, and was established in 2008 as an "independent, non-profit coeducational institution, dedicated to the advancement of learning through teaching and research and to the discovery and application of knowledge" (KUSTAR, 2008). KUSTAR is known for its Khalifa University Robotics Institute (KURI) which is dedicated to establishing an internationally recognized center of excellence in Robotics research and ICT Innovation Center. Meanwhile, Masdar Institute of Science and Technology (MIST) was established in 2009 in Abu Dhabi "To be a world-class graduate-level institution, seamlessly integrating research and education to produce future world leaders and critical thinkers in advanced energy and sustainability" (MIST, 2010).

Manama, Bahrain, was fully aware of the depletion of its oil resources, tried to gear towards KBUD. As early as 2006, the State announced the launch of a $1 billion Science and Technology Park plan in Bahrain (Alraouf, 2007; 2008). The world-class park will host small, medium, and large technology companies to grow niche markets, and will attract global science and technology companies to the Kingdom. This initiative will boost and encourage innovation in technology and scientific research, while providing a solid infrastructure for the development of the technology sector in Bahrain. The $1 billion project will be executed in three term phases. The first phase will focus on the infrastructure of the project, with the second and third phases on development of science laboratories, educational partnerships and lifestyle aspects. When interviewed, Sh. Mohammed bin Essa Al-Khalifa, Chief Executive of the Economic Development Board in Bahrain stated that "This park reflects the importance Bahrain places on science and technology. A world-class park will attract prestigious international technology-based companies into Bahrain, from where they can serve the region and build up a local knowledge base. This project will also provide jobs for Bahraini graduates, and help establish Bahrain as the science and technology hub of the region. Sh. Mohammed called upon the private sector to take the initiative to establish specialised science and technology clusters in the Kingdom to reinforce Bahrain's expertise in the sector. According to the financing agency (KFH), the Bahraini economy will be supported and step rightly in the process of diversification with such a project. This initiative will attract two types of projects; technological, and scientific research and development. The target sectors for the new park include new technologies, such as clean technology, renewable energy, environment, information and communications. Unfortunately, and after more than a decade, the project still in an ambiguous status as it was delayed because of the financial crisis in 2008 and then due to the instable political situation resulted from 14 February - March 2011 uprising erupted to confront claims of discrimination against Shias, unemployment, slow pace of democratization and Inspiration from the Arab Spring and concurrent regional protests (Murphy, 2011; Alraouf, 2013; Shehabi and Jones, 2015).

Muscat, Oman, while essentially focus on tourism to replace the dependence on oil economy, the city resorts to KBUD declaring the establishment of a science park named Knowledge Oasis Muscat (KOM). The park was opened in 2003 and built to encourage technology-oriented and thus knowledge-intensive businesses. As the project site suggests, KOM symbolizes successful public-private partnership in nurturing knowledge-based businesses. KOM is committed to creating an environment in which budding entrepreneurs, small and medium-sized enterprises and established multi-nationals can coexist, innovate and flourish within a Middle East setting (www.kom.om). The science park consists of over sixty companies, and even two IT-Colleges are located in the Knowledge Oasis Muscat (Al Shmeli, 2009). Controversially, KOM is an excellent evidence of how KBUD was seen within the Middle East as a fashionable development trend without the required understating of the nature of such projects and commitment to achieve it. While the project title is talking about science park and research oasis, in reality, it is just a building with very limited activities in research and knowledge-based activities and geared more to real-estate investment where companies rent spaces. Another interesting case form the Middle Eastern context is the initiative adopted by the city of Khartoum, Sudan. The Sudanese State with all its political and economical challenges embarked on the same limited interpretation of establishing KBUD and KC as isolated entities within the city. As Hassanein and Mohamed (2007) illustrate the experience of establishing the Sudan Electronic City (SEC). The project was declared by the Ministry of Science and Technology (MOST) to promote the culture of innovations and the competiveness between knowledge-based institutions. The first evidence of the limited interpretation of KBUD is in selecting an ICT consultant from India to envision the project. Limiting the understanding of KBUD projects to the mere establishing of ICT center is a fundamental problem represents the narrow perception of KBUD. Even the objective of the project intensifies the lack of understanding. The declared objective is that SEC is being developed to promote the Sudanese IT and computer industry. More controversially, an area of around 680 acres at Soba city of Khartoum is designated for the project to facilitate accommodating education and research center, convention and expo center, landmark tower and related facilities (Hassanein and Mohamed, 2007. P.173). This case yet again proved that thinking of KBUD as a mere ICT project confined in a limited and gated territory is a distorted understanding. Logically, plenty of obstacles faced the project and resulted in repetitive delays and then almost a total freeze of the whole development

In Egypt, an isolated city for scientific research called Mubarak Scientific City was inaugurated in August, 2000. Its location is almost 200 km from Cairo and was built to promote a new knowledge era for Egypt. Three month after the outset of Mubarak in 11th February 2011, the title of the project was changed to City of Scientific Research and Technological Applications (SRTA-City). In the capital, Cairo's experience in building the Smart Village project as a model for KBUD constructs an investigation case. The project was allocated almost 40 km away from the Cairo city center and was designed to communicate a high-tech identity about the future of Egypt. The reality of Smart Village shows that the concept of a community knowledge center was totally abounded. In addition the public access and allocation of open spaces were denied. Therefore, the village is totally isolated from both the city and the community. Even architecturally, a naive reproduction of Pharaonic (Ancient Egyptian) architecture was created. Although international giants like Microsoft and other major ICT companies move their local headquarters to the project yet their presence stressed more the isolated nature of the project (Alraouf, 2005; 2007). Security issues are becoming a top priority limiting the accessibility of the project especially

Figure 5. City of scientific research and technological applications (SRTA-City) (Source: Author)

when two years ago the Egyptian ministry of Information and Communications moved to the village's central zone. Currently, the reality of Smart Village is far from the concept of KBUD and more close to a gated business park disguised in a Pharaonic architectural costume.

Morocco also took steps towards seizing the value of moving towards KBUD. Inspired by Masdar city in Abu Dhabi, the State declared the start of the first Green City in the country and Africa as the official statements claim. The city, named King Mohamed VI Green City, is located between Casablanca and Marrakesh, adjacent to Benguerir, an existing city of 80,000 people. The city intended population is 120,000 with an area of 10 square Kilometers with an anticipated economic drivers mainly higher education and research. The aim is to be a development engine, incubator and research hub centered on universities, and research and development activities. It is the first city of its kind in the African continent that promotes its inhabitants' well-being, diversity and social and cultural blossoming. The Mohammed VI Polytechnic University, within the city, is designed to attract high quality candidates from around the world to produce a thriving new sociocultural "engine" for the city. It is a hub for research, training and innovation, and a real bridgehead between Morocco, Africa and the world. This world-class university is the core of the Mohammed VI green city, Partnerships with leading engineering and science institutions in France and the United States, namely Ecole des Mines de Paris and Massachusetts Institute of Technology (MIT) lend further legitimacy to the university. King Mohammed VI, on January 12, 2017 inaugurated the first phase of the project, mainly the new university. Safouane (2015) argues that King Mohamed VI Green City represents a transformational change in a non-crisis mode that will provide an all-encompassing make-over of not only Benguerir, but the region as a whole. The Green City project has the aspirations of shifting the role of the city, namely from one focused on phosphate development and mining, to one that will promote education and a knowledge-oriented ecosystem.

Another controversial context for establishing KBUD within the Middle East is Saudi Arabia. The State hosted the first international Symposium on Knowledge Cities ever held in the Middle East in Al-Madinah Al-Munawarah in 2005. The cities leaders and planners were able to get a closer look at the holistic understanding of establishing KCs and KBUD (AUDI, Saudi Arabia, 2005). The first major attempt to transform a Saudi city into a knowledge city was documented in (Abu-Anzeh and Ledraa, 2007). The narrative of the Riyadh city, the Saudi capital, proved that establishing a knowledge city is not only about the physical entities including ICT centers, universities and research institutions. Riyadh city promotes itself as a city of profound Middle Eastern importance. Riyadh, with all its financial assets, infrastructure and unprecedented recent development, asserts itself as a world class city capable of competing on a regional/world stage. As Abu-Anzeh and Ledraa (2007) argue Riyadh enjoys many of world class city characteristics which make the city well integrated in a networked global economy. They claim that the city is striving towards greater openness, creating a vibrant milieu that attracts talented people and providing workers with the incentives both to explore and to exploit technological possibilities (p.131).While an excellent urban milieu is a must for any knowledge city that cares to attract and retain knowledge workers, scrutinizing the meaning of openness and intellectual freedom is a must in a severely conservative context like Saudi Arabia. If Riyadh is to assert itself as a knowledge city, it must embark on making every effort to develop transparent, democratic, diversified and tolerant environment which would credibly attract knowledge workers from all over the world. The city is making significant steps in the direction of establishing the physical aspects of KC. One can finds an accelerated rate of building universities, research and development centers and science parks in different parts of the city.

The second revealing case in Saudi Arabia is King Abdulla Economic City (KAEC) and University of Science and Technology which were established to declare the move towards a post-oil era in the future development of Saudi Arabia. In an attempt to learn from the limitations faced the trial to transform Riyadh into a knowledge city, KASTC is based on the concept of providing unprecedented compromises within the conservative Saudi context. KAEC has looked to Singapore as a model, seeking to emulate the city state's strong international economy, its port as a major source of revenue, and its use of public–private investment strategies in order to nurture a knowledge economy, develop advanced manufacturing, and attract global talent (Moser, 2014a). KAEC features six distinct zones: a university, an industrial zone, a business district, a resort area, a sea port, and residential areas. The Saudi government bills King Abdullah Economic City and the economic cities as a solution to diversify the economy away from oil and provide a comparatively relaxed and liberal way of life. Given the unique context of a private, socially liberal gated city located in a combination of an absolute monarchy and Islamic theocracy, many questions emerge about how the city will operate on a day-to-day basis upon completion Moser et al. (2015). But Will Saudi authorities allow a formal two-system policy with a different legal system in KAEC? How much will shareholders of KAEC influence the political and economic development of the lived city? What voice will residents of KAEC have in governance issues? Regulations around tourism and foreign residents are another example of a governance issue that will challenge the city's future economy. While KAEC officials reassure foreigners that they may purchase real estate in KAEC, there is currently no tourist visa to enter Saudi Arabia. Entering Saudi Arabia is limited to strict alternatives mainly religious pilgrims, business activates and government official visits. These restrictions severely limit the flow of people, talent and ideas into KAEC and make it challenging to expand tourism beyond the domestic market as Moser et al. argue (2015, p.78).

KAEC's relationship to the rest of the Saudi kingdom is likely to create social and political tension. KAEC is already publicized as a unique context for more relaxed and westernized social norms. For instance, women were permitted to drive, men and women are allowed to associate in public, women are not required to wear the legally mandatory black traditional *"Abaya"* or the head scarf *"Hijab"* in public. As construction in KAEC proceeds rapidly, questions about its future continue to increase. There is a high level of ambiguity regarding how KAEC and will become socially integrated or separated from the rest of the country. Applying radically different sets of social values within the same country or city would emphasize the isolation and fragmentation of the KBUD. KAEC could represent a new

Figure 6. KAEC is publicized as a new paradigm in Saudi Arabia urbanity and development (Source: Author)

era of social change and liberalization in Saudi Arabia as Moser et al. (2015) argues. Yet, this should be perceived in inviting the whole of Saudi Arabia and not only a walled project, into a different social and cultural paradigm transforming the conservative kingdom into a cosmopolitan, global context that prioritizes innovation, youth and creativity over unchanging parochialism. Hence, Moser et al. (2015) warns that without such transformation, KAEC could easily become yet another example of neoliberal development that places corporate interests above all else and strengthens the ruling elite's hold on society.

The previously discussed cases from the context of the Middle East, illustrate the validity of KBUD for the reinventing of cities aspiring for an alternative development scenario. Clearly some main pillars of KBUD still need more consideration like democratic approach to development and transparency in decision making process. Participatory mechanisms and collaborative methodologies to incorporate diversified pool of stakeholders need more elaboration and consideration in the development process. Additionally, discussing strategies to activate the role of knowledge workers and allowing the creative class contributes to urban development reveals two distinct scenarios. The first is a top down approach based on a political decision taken from top leaders supported by the appropriate financial resources. Such approach was practiced in Middle Eastern cities by activating political power in some cases or exploiting financial resources in other cases particularly Gulf cities. In Morocco, Tunisia, Sudan and Egypt, political leaders imposed projects to gain credibility. Also, as it was observed in most of the Gulf States, this approach is highly adopted. Evidently, State's national vison is in all the cases based on the vison of the leader and use his name as a reference. It is evident for cities adopting the this strategy to attract global brands and invest unconditionally in architectural glamour. The model of Dubai would appear as a prime case in this category. In the Middle Eastern and Gulf context, Dubai used architecture extensively to construct a city brand by building controversial global landmarks like the highest tower on earth, Burj Khalifa or the Palm real-estate and recreational projects.

The second strategy requires a more liberal and democratically structured society which would allow a more grass roots and bottom up approach to engaging knowledge workers and creative class. The second alternative is based on shaping an appropriate tangible context where knowledge economy will perform. In this approach, architecture, design and technology are used to attract strategic brands, highly educated individuals, and high added value services. Another documented scenario is based on the Fabrication of a city brand with one major art or architecture initiative. The case Bilbao and the Guggenheim museum designed by Frank Gehry and its impact on the prosperity of the city is a classic example. In the case of Bilbao, It is the city that activated a substantial mobilization by the city council to engage in a transformational process. This process, which took about two decades, helped transform the city from post-industrial decay to a thriving culture and knowledge based economy. The post Arab Spring and the post oil Middle East requires Strategies driven from the ground. A more organic process which would allow the community members to participate in decision making and planning decisions. Such approach moves from focusing on isolated projects to initiate an urban development process of district, neighborhoods and city improvement and rejuvenation.

CONCLUSION

The narrative recited in this chapter suggests that the question still relevant and gaining more importance and momentum, how to profoundly transform contemporary Middle Eastern cities into knowledge cities? Any attempt towards establishing a contemporary Middle Eastern Knowledge City should acknowledge its holistic nature. KC is a comprehensive organization; it is a place where knowledge is produced and spread all over its parts. As seen in most of the claimed KBUD or KCs projects in the Middle East, the challenge is to shift Middle Eastern /Gulf cities' strategies towards creating a holistic knowledge cities rather than scattered, fragmented and isolated projects is fundamentally required. Contemporary Middle Eastern cities have great potentials to be transformed into KCs. Hence, for the establishment of contemporary Knowledge Cities in the Middle East, two integrated conditions are required. The process of creating Middle Eastern knowledge cities should be shifted from focusing on creating isolated and separated knowledge centers based on the presence of ICT centers or higher education facilities to a process by which a knowledge network is established and shared by different sectors of the community. Additionally, a comprehensive examination of the history of Middle Eastern Cities is urgently needed to provide contemporary planners, urban designers and architects with tools and patterns which were used successfully to disseminate knowledge in the Middle Eastern traditional built environments. Research is also a prerequisite of a KC. It requires infrastructure of research, an issue which has not been developed in the Middle East. Hence, an inclusive initiative to prepare the grounds for a major transformation must be translated into strategy.

This chapter analyzed the context of KBUD within the paradigm of the post oil economy and the Middle Eastern cities formation and transformation. The knowledge-based development of Middle Eastern cities is not a theoretical doctrine, but it is an excellent approach to plan and develop knowledge and creative cities. The major challenge in the Middle East is to fully comprehend that knowledge and creative cities are complex entities, and attempts to transform cities into knowledge cities would likely result in failure unless they are guided by holistic strategic visions. These strategic visions should incorporate KBUD policies for attracting and retaining knowledge workers and industries and also empowering citizens as knowledge creators and innovators. Planning for KBUD of cities requires a holistic approach to development which would include socio-economic development, urban development, and governance, political stability, democratic environment, freedom, investing in intellectual capital and urban diversity. Planning for KBUD also requires understanding that there is no ideal blue print for a knowledge city but different formal and spatial configurations based on the local context and embedded potentials. KBUD needs a move from a focusing on a single project within the city to a large number of connected zones, clusters and environs all of which are physical and intellectual manifestation of KBUD principles and policies primarily political and societal will.

In a post Arab Spring and post-carbon paradigm, KBUD should be perceived as the opportunity for new sustainable growth and prosperity in the global knowledge-based economy. Therefore, the emerging knowledge cities in the Middle East should be seen within a regional and global knowledge network. The ultimate goal is to increase the innovation and creative capacity of cities based on a new set of knowledge patterns. However, in order for promising and emerging Middle Eastern cities like Dubai, Abu Dhabi, or Doha to become inspirations of Middle Eastern culture and be truly considered as centers of the Middle East, they must engage in culture creation and production rather than adoption and appropriation. These cities must involve in the creation of art, the production of knowledge, the publishing of scientific research, and the exchange of social and political discourse, if they are considering being KBUD models and centers of the Middle East.

For a holistic KBUD to be attained, a number of integrates and inseparable conditions need to be planned and implemented. Principally, strategic vision and dynamic log-term development plan coupled with political and societal will and good governance and supported by strong financial investments from public and private sectors. Secondly, on the level of place making, KBUD requires multi-cultural character of the city, international diversity, and excellent quality of place, life and affordable housing and urban services, just environment and democratic atmosphere. It promotes urban connectivity and accessibility to all community facilities specifically knowledge-based and technologically advanced. KBUD is about creating affordable and attractive way of life and not exclusive lifestyle geared only for the wealthy sector of the community and therefore it calls for tolerating human diversity and being socially just and equitable. Thirdly, KBUD is about the creation of urban innovativeness engines, unique research culture manifested in research-based universities, research and development institutions and continuous and sustainable development, social upgrading and capacity building for all citizens. Finally, establishing the needed legal infrastructure to protect intellectual property. Without well-defined rules and regulations, people will be discouraged from innovation and creative contributions. KBUD is a form of development which is based on the ultimate respect for nature and therefore, it is an eco-friendly form of development. It promotes sustainability in all its aspects particularly the concern for the future generations. In sum, KBUD is human and nature oriented holistic strategy for growth evidently applicable to the context of the Middle East if holistically comprehended.

REFERENCES

Abu-Anzeh, N., & Ledraa, T. (2007). Planning the Knowledge City: Can it be an option for Riyadh? In *Knowledge Cities, Future of Cities in The Knowledge Economy* (pp. 116–141). Scholar Press.

Al Hathloul, S. (2004). Planning in the Middle East, moving Toward the Future. *Habitat International, 18*(5), 641–643. doi:10.1016/j.habitatint.2004.04.004

Al-Nakib, F. (2016). *Kuwait Transformed: A History of Oil and Urban Life*. Stanford University Press.

Al Qassemi, S. S. (2013). Thriving Gulf Cities Emerge as New Centers of Arab World. *Al-Monitor: The Pulse of the Middle East*. Retrieved from http://www.al-monitor.com/pulse/originals/2013/10/abu-dhabi-dubai-doha-arab-centers.html#ixzz4sLNSlI3A

Alraouf, A. (2005). Knowledge Cities: Examining the Discourse: Smart Villages, Internet Cities or Creativity engines. *Proceedings of the International Symposium on Knowledge Cities*. The World Bank and Arab Urban Development Institute.

Alraouf, A. (2006). *Dubaization vs. Glocalization: Territorial Outlook of Arab/Gulf Cities Transformed.* The 9th Sharjah Urban Planning Symposium (SUPS), Sharjah, UAE.

Alraouf, A. (2016a). "Dohaization": An Emerging Interface between Knowledge, Creativity, and Gulf Urbanity. In *Gulf Cities as Interfaces* (pp. 47–68). Cambridge, UK: Gulf Research Centre Cambridge.

Alraouf, A. (2016b). *One Nation, One Myth and Two Museums Heritage, Architecture and Culture as Tools for Assembling Identity in Qatar.* In P. Erskine-Loftus (Ed.), *Representing the Nation: Heritage, Museums, National Narratives, and Identity in the Arab Gulf States* (pp. 79–94). Routledge.

Alraouf, A. (2017). Interrogating Qatar's Urbanity as a Catalyst for Building Knowledge-Based Societies and Economies. In R. G. Bertelsen, N. Noori, & J.-M. Rickli (Eds.), *Strategies of Knowledge Transfer for Economic Diversification in the Arab States of the Gulf* (pp. 53–66). London: Gerlach Press.

Alraouf, A. A. (2008). Emerging Middle Eastern Knowledge Cities: the Unfolding Story. In T. Yigitcaular & V. Koray (Eds.), *Knowledge Based Urban Development: Planning and Application in the Information Era* (pp. 240–259). IGI Global. doi:10.4018/978-1-59904-720-1.ch014

Alraouf, A. A. (2013). Manama, Bahrain. In M. Fraser & N. Golzari (Eds.), *Architecture and Globalization in The Persian Gulf Region*. London: Ashgate.

Barcelona City Government. (2003). *Culture, The Motor of the Knowledge City: Strategic Plan of the Cultural Sector of Barcelona*. Barcelona: Steering Council of the Strategic Plan of the Cultural sector of Barcelona.

Bounfour, A., & Edvinsson, L. (2005). *Intellectual Capital for Communities: Nations, Regions, and Cities*. London: Routledge.

Carrillo, F. (2006). The century of knowledge cities. In Knowledge cities: Approaches, experiences, and perspectives. New York: Butterworth–Heinemann.

Carrillo, F. J. (Ed.). (2005). *Knowledge Cities: Approaches, Experiences, and Perspectives*. London: Routledge.

Carrillo, F. J., Yigitcanlar, T., García, B., & Lönnqvist, A. (2014). *Knowledge and the City: Concepts, Applications and Trends of Knowledge-Based Urban Development*. London: Routledge.

Castells, M. (1989). *The Informational City: Informational Technology, Economic Restructuring and the Urban-Regional Process*. Oxford, UK: Basil Blackwell.

Castells, M. (1997). *The Information City: Economy, Culture and Society*. Oxford, UK: Blackwell.

Castells, M. (1997). The Rise of the Network Society (Vols. 1-3). Blackwell.

Castells, M., & Hall, P. (1994). *Technopoles of the World: The Making of 21st-Century Industrial Complexes*. London: Routledge.

Cooke, P. (2006). *Regional Development in the Knowledge Economy (Regions and Cities)*. London: Routledge.

Dovey, K. (2005). *Fluid City: Transforming Melbourne's Urban Waterfront*. London: Routledge.

Dubai Strategic Plan. (2007). Emirate of Dubai. UAE: Academic Press.

Dvir, R. (2003). *Innovation Engines for Knowledge Cities*. In ENTOVATION 100 roundtable and the Latin American Knowledge Development forum, Monterrey, Mexico.

Dvir, R., & Pasher, E. (2004). Innovative Engines for Knowledge Cities: An Innovation Ecology Perspective. *Journal of Knowledge Management*, *8*(5), 16–27. doi:10.1108/13673270410558756

Edvinsson, L. (2003). *Introduction to issues in Knowledge Management*. Henley Knowledge Management Forum.

Ergazakis, K., Metaxiotis, K., & Psarras, J. (2004). Towards Knowledge Cities: Conceptual Analysis and Success Stories. *Journal of Knowledge Management*, *8*(5), 5–15. doi:10.1108/13673270410558747

Ergazakis, K., Metaxiotis, K., & Psarras, J. (2006). Knowledge cities: The answer to the needs of knowledge-based development. *Journal of Information and Knowledge Management Systems*, *36*(1), 67–81.

Florida, R. (2002). *The rise of the creative class and how it is transforming work, leisure, community and every-day life*. New York: Basic Books.

Foray, D. (2004). *The Economics of Knowledge*. Cambridge, MA: MIT Press.

Fraser, M., & Golzari, N. (Eds.). (2013). *Architecture and Globalization in The Persian Gulf Region*. London: Ashgate.

Fromherz, A. (2012). *Qatar: a Modern History*. Washington, DC: Georgetown University Press.

GSDP. (2011). *(General Secretariat of Development Planning) National Development Strategy 2011–2016*. Doha, Qatar: Gulf Publishing and Printing Company.

Hall, P. (1998). *Cities in Civilization*. London: Weidenfeld and Nicolson.

Hall, P. (2000). Creative cities and economic development. *Urban Studies (Edinburgh, Scotland)*, *37*(4), 639–649. doi:10.1080/00420980050003946

Hall, P. (2002). *Cities of Tomorrow: An Intellectual History of Urban Planning and Design in the Twentieth Century*. Blackwell Publishing.

Hall, P. (2004). Knowledge Creativity, Culture, and the City. *Built Environment*, *30*(3), 256–258. doi:10.2148/benv.30.3.256.54306

Hassanein, N., & Mohamed, M. (2007). Sudan Electronic City, an Integrated Technology Park. In *Knowledge Cities, Future of Cities in The Knowledge Economy* (pp. 160–183). Scholar Press.

Jayne, M. (2006). *Cities and consumption*. London: Routledge. doi:10.4324/9780203358733

Kaplan, S., Grünwald, L., & Hirte, G. (2016). The effect of social networks and norms on the inter-regional migration intentions of knowledge-workers: The case of Saxony, Germany. *Cities (London, England)*, *55*, 61–69. doi:10.1016/j.cities.2016.03.017

Khalifa University of Science, Technology and Research (KUSTAR). (2008). *Our mission*. Retrieved from http://www.kustar.ac.ae/main/index.php?page=themission

King, A. D. (2004). *Spaces of Global Cultures, Architecture, Urbanism, Identity*. London: Routledge.

Knight, R. (1995). Knowledge-based development: Policy and planning implications for cities. *Urban Studies (Edinburgh, Scotland)*, *32*(2), 225–260. doi:10.1080/00420989550013068

Knight, R. (2008). Knowledge based development. In Knowledge-based urban development. IGI Global.

Komninos, N. (2002). *Intelligent Cities: Innovation, Knowledge Systems and Digital Spaces*. London: Routledge.

Kunzmann, K. (2008). Spatial dimensions of knowledge production. In Knowledge-based urban development. IGI Global.

Laguerre, M. S. (2006). *The Digital City: The American Metropolis and Information Technology*. Palgrave Macmillan.

Landry, C. (2000). *The creative city: a tool kit for urban innovators*. London: Earhscan.

Masdar Institute of Science and Technology (MIST). (2010). *Vision & mission*. Retrieved from http://www.masdar.ac.ae/aboutus/VisionMission.php

Miles, M., & Hall, T. (Eds.). (2003). *Urban Futures*. London: Routledge.

Mitchell, T. (2002). *Rule of Experts, Egypt, Techno-Politics, Modernity*. Berkeley, CA: University of California press.

Morse, S. (2004). *Smart Communities*. Jossey-Bass.

Moser, S., Swain, M., & Alkhabbaz, M. H. (2015). King Abdullah Economic City: Engineering Saudi Arabia's post-oil future. Cities, 45, 71–80.

Murphy, B. (2011, February 15). *Bahrain Square Becomes New Center for Arab Anger*. Associated Press.

Pol, P., Winden, W., Woets, P., & Berg, L. (Eds.). (2005). European Cities in the Knowledge Economy: The Cases of Amsterdam, Dortmund, Eindhoven, Helsinki, Manchester, Munich, Munster, Rotterdam and Zaragoza (EURICUR. Institute for Comparative Urban Research). Ashgate Publishing.

Ponzini, D., & Nastasi, M. (2011). *Starchitecture: Scenes, actors and spectacles in contemporary cities*. Turin: Allemandi.

Safouane, Y. (2015). Inventing New Cities: Case Studies from Morocco. In *(Re)inventing Cities: Successful Cases seminar*. Retrieved from http://www.ocppc.ma/events/seminars-series/reinventing-cities-successful-cases#.WbjEoFEjFnI

Sakr, T. (1993). *Early Twentieth-Century Islamic Architecture in Cairo*. Cairo: American University in Cairo Press.

Sassen, S. (1991). *The Global City*. Princeton University Press.

Sassen, S. (2002). *Global Networks, Linked Cities: Urban connections In a Globalizing World*. New York: Routledge.

Shehabi, A., & Jones, M. O. (Eds.). (2015). *Bahrain's Uprising*. London: Zed Books.

Taylor, P., Derudder, B., Saey, P., & Witlox, F. (2006). *Cities in Globalization: Practices, policies and theories*. London: Routledge.

Thierstein, A. (2017). Residence, workplace and commute: Interrelated spatial choices of knowledge workers in the metropolitan region of Munich. *Journal of Transport Geography, 62*, 197-212.

Thierstein, A., & Schein, E. (2008). Emerging Cities on the Arabian Peninsula: Urban Space in the Knowledge Economy Context. *Archnet-IJAR: International Journal of Architectural Research, 2*(2), 178–195.

UNESCO. (2005). *Towards knowledge societies*. Paris: UNESCO Publishing.

United Nations Development Program (UNDP). (2003). *Arab human development report 2003: Building a knowledge society*. New York: United Nations Publications.

Wagner, C. (2001). Megacities of the future. *The Futurist, 35*(6), 8–9.

Wiedmann, F. (2010). *Post-oil Urbanism in the Gulf*. Stuttgart, Germany: University of Stuttgart.

Wippel, S. (Ed.). (2014). *Under Construction: Logics of Urbanism in the Gulf Region*. London: Ashgate.

Yigitcanlar, T. (2005). The Making of Knowledge Cities: Lessons Learned from Melbourne. In *Proceedings of the International Symposium on Knowledge Cities*. The World Bank and Arab Urban Development Institute.

Yigitcanlar, T. (2011). Redefining knowledge-based urban development. *International Journal of Knowledge Based Development, 2*(4), 340–356. doi:10.1504/IJKBD.2011.044343

Chapter 2
Information and Communication Technology Spine for Knowledge-Based Development of Cities

Rabee M. Reffat
Assiut University, Egypt

ABSTRACT

The chapter presents the approach of effective utilization of information and communication technology as a competitive advantage for knowledge-based development of cities. Knowledge investment, creation, and diffusion are the essential nodes of the information and communication technology spine for developing knowledge-based cites. The features of knowledge-based city compared to the modern and developed city are introduced. This chapter identifies the primary conditions that promote knowledge-based development of cities. The associative relationships between knowledge-base and economical development of cities are addressed.

1. INTRODUCTION

Cities are considered the principal manifestations of civilizations and are conceptualized in terms of population size and physical attributes such as geographic location, land area, morphology, equipment, etc. Development of cities is viewed from the perspective of city planning with a focus on physical form and the built environment including infrastructure, land use, zoning, buildings, recreation and parks, safety codes, health, aesthetics, etc. Urbanization and globalization have rapidly change the development rate and nature of cities. However, the knowledge resources of cities and the role of cities in knowledge production are essential pillars for cities in order to be transformed to knowledge-based cities. Due to the evolving nature of knowledge there is always a challenge for cities to enhance and build on the strengths of knowledge resources.

DOI: 10.4018/978-1-5225-3734-2.ch002

Copyright © 2018, IGI Global. Copying or distributing in print or electronic forms without written permission of IGI Global is prohibited.

Cities have been witnessing during the recent decades immense pressure to cope with the rapid growth of production and unprecedented levels of development in information communication and technologies (ICT). Cities had to adapt with these ever changing developments but in parallel a various problems environmentally and socially have emerged along with urban sprawling and increase of metropolitan cities. With the rise of ICT-based development and decline of industrial-based development, it becomes a necessity and challenge to create opportunities for cities to continue developing technologically, economically, socially, environmentally and culturally in a sustainable manner. In order pave the roads for sustainable development of cities, knowledge resources should be transformed within the local context but a universal perspective. Accordingly, realizing the potential of knowledge resources in cities requires increasing the recognition and comprehension of both nature of knowledge cultures and knowledge development within these cities. Reinforcing and supporting the culture base of a city with a distinctive quality of life will certainly strengthen the knowledge-base of this city (Knight, 1995, Kothin et al, 2001). The quality of life in cities is determined by various factors including safety, security and provision of basic services. However, the appropriate utilization of technologies allows achieving optimization of urban infrastructure through compiling and analyzing huge amount of real-time data. Accordingly, the ability of city inhabitants to effectively and efficiently navigate city resources will be improved (Monreal, 2016). Therefore, there is an apparent need for developing approaches to effectively prosper and manage cities' knowledge.

The evolution of knowledge management supported by ICT is manifested in advanced business applications, online and virtual education, e-government, etc. and implemented in international organizations. For example, knowledge frameworks are adopted in the strategic directions for global development at the European Commission (2000) and the United Nations Organization (2001). Accordingly, a new link is created between knowledge management and knowledge-based development (Carrillo, 2002; Metaxiotis et al., 2004) which has also been articulated by Ergazakis et al (2004). Consequently, the concept of knowledge-based city is emerged.

This Chapter introduces the approach of information and communication technologies (ICT) as the driver and motivator for the knowledge-based cities. The characteristics of information including its conditions, tradability and appropriation are affected by ICT wherein the role of business services is favored and considered as forces of interaction for the new technology generation especially between knowledge components. The results obtained from empirical analysis (Lever, 2002) assert that the communication services and usage of business are correlated with high output elasticity.

2. TECHNOLOGICAL ADVANCES ARE PRECURSORS FOR CITY DEVELOPMENT

Technological advances are continuing to shape and reform the economic and physical development of cities. With the emerge of industrial revolution in the 19th century, factories and manufacturing plants have arisen, seaport cities have grown and expanded due to the steam engine, while cities and towns were linked by a system of railroads. The advancement of transportation technology in the 20th century has led to major urban growth dispersing people to suburban areas. These technological trends have been reinforced by the development of highways construction of airports. Furthermore, the transformation and growth from seasonal communities to year-round populations are contributions from the extensive use of air-conditions. Recently, the emergence and rapid development of ICT are reformulating the pattern and nature of physical development of cities along with their economic role. Accordingly, activities that are some information-intensive (such as development and research laboratories, customer service centers, and back offices), are attracted in some cities, while others cities that were for long time known as manufacturing centers and corporate headquarters have lost their roles. Furthermore, a major challenge is posed by the rapid advancement in ICT to city-based finance, healthcare, educational institutions and cities' roles as centers for culture and commerce (Moss, 1998).

ICT is changing the breadth, depth, accessibility, retrieval, communication and processing for the information with its different kinds and types. The wide use of ICT makes it possible to increase transportation, separation, trade, and division of information. The diffusion of new information technology makes it possible for information networks to increase its connectedness and receptiveness so as to enhance the innovative capability of economic systems and lead to the introduction of an array of process and product innovations. The diffusion of new ICT is likely to act as a powerful factor of structural change of the capability for innovation and competitive economy of cities (Antonelli, 1997).

3. IMPACT OF INFORMATION AND COMMUNICATION TECHNOLOGY ON CITY DEVELOPMENT

There are two types of impacts of information and communication technology on city development. First, from a social perspective, it is viewed that ICT will exponentially increase the online communications which will replace most of face-to-face communications and will cause a decline of cities due to the reduction of live activities between people in public and urban places within cities. For instance, Gilder (1995) claimed that because of the advancement of distributed organization and continuous growth of using personal computer, the result will be heading for the death of cities. According to such claim, various cultural and educational activities will take place virtually and real places in cities will not be required to conduct these activities, while reading a book from libraries, viewing a concert, or attending business meeting can be conducted remotely from home or elsewhere. The wide spread of using portable computing, smart phones, online streaming, satellite channels allow people to enjoy many activities of urban life while avoiding the chronic problems of cities including problem of commuting, security, crowd, pollution. This was anticipated in Castells's Informational City (1989) that the technological change of facilitating information flow through computer networks will suppress various places in cities. Consequently, the place-based societies and cultures will be disarticulated and that the emergence of the places for information flow will be dominated in societies without control. Furthermore, Negroponte (1995) expected that the limitations of geography will be virtually dissolved in the digital revolution age. While, Moss (998) argued that the need of presence at specific time and place in cities will decrease and people will be much less dependent on physical presence in the digital age while places in cities will be transformed.

Second, from the perspective of economics, as Gottmann (1977) long ago forecasted the impact of technology on economic activities either through concentrating and dispersing such activities. The rapid advancement of ICT allowed linking the branches and subsidiary offices distributed in various cities to be easily linked together and decentralization has become the norm compared to centralization that was dominant during the industrial revolution. Accordingly, some cities have been transformed from centers of good production in specific places to distributed centers of information production around the world. The ICT has led centers for information-intensive activities to extend the global reach of such cities, and caused as set of globally linked cities to emerge. Therefore, gaining a rapid access to the Internet and obtaining a high capacity bandwidth along with providing Internet access almost everywhere in the city have been crucial in recent years and are considered as necessary steps towards developing the knowledge-based city and its economy.

The competitive advantage of cities can be highly obtained by appropriate investment in ICT in terms governance and strategies in cooperation with hard and soft information technologies. McAfee and Brynjolfsson (2007) suggested for six elements for the processes of successful utilization of ICT: wide span, production of immediate results, preciseness, consistency, easy monitoring, and embedded enforceability. They also argued that the investment of ICT should focus on rethinking the processes of ICT as an enabler than as an operational.Turner (2010) asserts a strong governance is required for ICT to be become an enabler. However, Weill and Ross (2009) suggests that standardization and integration are essential incorporation of ICT, whereas the former deals data and the latter with incorporation of ICT.

4. FEATURES OF KNOWLEDGE-BASED CITIES

The development of urban areas in cities should consider improving quality of life by supporting environmental sustainability, social cohesion and economic competitiveness. The smart and knowledge city concept emerged due to the unprecedented development and innovations of ICT which should be utilized achieve efficient and sustainable urban development in cities (Monzon, 2015). A smart and knowledge city is viewed as one with a "comprehensive commitment to innovation in technology, management and policy" (Nam and Pardo, 2011). Encouraging and nurturing knowledge should be the primary purposes for developing a knowledge city. Therefore, a city that has an economy driven by "value added exports created through research, technology and brainpower" can be viewed a knowledge city (SGS Economics, 2002). Accordingly, a significant investment in education, training and research is essential for the successful development of knowledge-based cities. The main pillars of obtaining knowledge-based development in cities include "encouraging the continuous creation, sharing, evaluation, renewal and update of knowledge". Facilitating and supporting continuous interaction between the city residents and other cities' residents is essential for achieving knowledge-based development. The effectiveness of such interaction requires establishing and nurturing the culture of knowledge-sharing of city residents along with the provision of appropriate ICT infrastructures in well designed urban places. Ergazakis et al (2004) have attempted to differentiate knowledge-based cities from modern and well-developed cities as represented in Table 1.

It is argued that the functionality and applicability of the traditional model of cities development are diminishing compared to the advantages of adopting the knowledge-based development (Laszlo et al, 2002; Malone et al, 2002). The primary benefits of knowledge cities towards knowledge-based development are articulated by Ergazakis et al (2004) which can be categorized into two main issues:

- Enhancing city's economical prospects
  - Revitalization of traditional industries
  - Improving community's income and wealth with a faster rate of growth
  - Increasing community's capacity for sustainable economy based on attracting off-shore investment and adoptions of technological innovations

Table 1. A comparison between the features of a modern, well-developed city and a knowledge-based city (after Ergazakis et al, 2004)

Features of a Modern and Well-Developed City	Features of a Knowledge-Based City
• Provision of **high quality life** • Provision of efficient, dependable and **access to infrastructure** for transport of people, goods and information that is cost competitive • **Critical mass economy** to support world competitive specialization • **Central educational** strategy including all cultural facilities and services • Incorporation of **new technologies** in urban design and architecture • **Networks of commercial influence**, in order to attract funds • **Market access** and awareness • Competitive and collaborative **business culture** • Creative and **responsive public services** • Merit based culture and **tolerant society**	• Provision of **access** for all citizens to new **information and communication technologies** • **New knowledge-based goods** and services emerging from research excellence • Provision of **accessible knowledge** to citizens in a systematic, efficient, and effective way • Provision of **high quality services and packages** to generate, attract and retain highly skilled knowledge experts • Provision of **distinctive civic centers** to foster diversity and face-to-face relations

    - Boost to tourism
    - Creation and increase of employment with well-payment
- Improving life quality of city's residents
    - Sharing wealth by providing investment opportunities in public facilities such as cultural facilities, public transport, parks and gardens,
    - Provision of funding and mechanisms of effective social safety nets
    - Reinvestment of local capital for boosting city's pride and confidence and improving local economy
    - Provision of right knowledge at the right time to communities
    - Provision of high quality educational services

5. THE INFORMATION AND COMMUNICATION TECHNOLOGY SPINE FOR KNOWLEDGE-BASED DEVELOPMENT OF CITIES

For a society to be transformed into knowledge-based, there is a need to change the nature of city development especially by fostering the knowledge sector with high priorities in terms of processes, funding, creation new urban environments that attracts knowledge workers and experts. Advances in information and communication technology help in facilitating and differentiating activities in the production sector from those in the knowledge sector. However, in the knowledge sector, activities are culturally based and require extensive efforts to be uprooted. The development of knowledge-based activities is primarily concerned with promoting human and organizational capacities and developing environments that supports and nurtures change, learning, creativity and innovation. Accordingly, the types of environments that are required to be developed for knowledge-based activities should be based on different development strategies that vary significantly from strategies of developing commodity-based activities. There are two primary factors affecting development of a knowledge-based city: (a) integrity of knowledge resources, and (b) the livability of city where the knowledge resources are based. Hence, if a city is to realize the potentials of its knowledge resources, it must develop environments that offers facilities and conditions that support knowledge-based activities and ensures that knowledge resources are valued, and highly secured and anchored. It must be noted that integrity of knowledge resources is a necessary but not a sufficient condition for knowledge-based development either within organizations or within cities. In order to advance knowledge, organizations in the city must be able to "attract, develop and retain talent", and "offer challenging career opportunities and work environments which are intellectually stimulating and healthy, with high-quality living environments for their families" (Knight, 1995). These are essential requirement in order to respond to the sophisticated and high quality expectations of knowledge workers and their families require. Monetary income cannot necessarily compensate for the insufficiency of distinctive living environments. Talented knowledge workers anticipate appreciation in working environments and leisure and safety in living and public environments. Misuse, exploitation and endanger in working and living environments will be resulted in brain drain and great loss of knowledge workers and experts.

Knowledge-based development relies on (a) establishing conditions to support creative and innovative use of resources, and (b) realizing synergies between various levels and types of knowledge. Formulating strategies for knowledge-based development requires innovation in knowledge fields, types and levels. Cities should not be overwhelmed or intimidated by "big science". However, cities' citizens should begin by scrutinizing their own knowledge resources, capitalizing and reinforcing their own strengths, while learning, diffusing and valorizing their distinctive varieties of knowledge. Activities which establish the knowledge-based development include knowledge investments, creation, and diffusion and distribution. These three activities comprise the information and communication technology spine for developing a knowledge-based city as illustrated in Figure 1.

There are main pillars that must be furnished to support developing knowledge-based cities. These conditions are introduced and sorted based on their importance and impact on the development of knowledge-based cities and are illustrated in Figure 2.

There is a need for policies for cities in transition (such as most of the cities in the Middle East), in order to furnish the main pillars to support the development of knowledge-based cities outlined above.

Figure 1. Activities that comprise the information and communication technology spine for developing a knowledge-based city

Figure 2. Main pillars to support the development of Knowledge-Based Cities (KBC)

Such policies should aim for achieving a shift in both ground-breaking initiatives and paradigms towards developing the knowledge-based cities. For instance, one of the essential elements of restructuring initiatives is privatization but it will achieve the restructuring by itself. On the contrary, if privatization is pursued as an aim and not as means, it will inhibit restructuring especially if associated with rapid and mass sell-offs, (e.g. the experience of the Czech Republic and Russia). It should also be noted in order to ensure that the capital will be directed towards exports and industry, privatization of banks is not sufficient and could result in investing the capital in real estate, securities and imports (Gower, 1997). Furthermore, another necessary rather than sufficient condition for restructuring is the liberalization of prices and foreign trade. In fact, the radical opening-up of an economy may result in freezing or hindering the structural change. Therefore, for cities in transition, a better integration of structural and transition policies is essentially required in order to appropriately initiating structural change, and promoting economic growth for developing knowledge-based cities (Dyker, 2000).

6. ASSOCIATION OF KNOWLEDGE-BASED CITY SUPPORTED BY INFORMATION AND COMMUNICATION TECHNOLOGY AND ITS ECONOMICAL DEVELOPMENT

The diffusion of information and communication technology is likely to engender a significant shift in the condition of accessing, storing, processing and communicating information. The effects of the use of information and communication technology are quite relevant on information trade, diffusion, and transportation. The use of new information and communication technology will possibly cause a direct increase in both the "connectivity and the receptivity of information networks" underlying business relations of the city (Antonelli, 1997). The relationship between utilizing research and development with innovation and economic growth, and creating new knowledge is not evident with empirical results at the local level of cities. In related empirical studies, simple means of measuring the city knowledge-base are used in terms of numbers of research and development establishments. This assumption is based on the potentials of new generated knowledge in reaching the public domain and enhancing overall local competitiveness favoring research establishments (e.g. universities, public laboratories) over privately 'in-house' generated knowledge which may not be made widely available. On the other hand, Lever (2002) adopted a more multidimensional measure of the knowledge-base which seeks to incorporate composite measures of knowledge including: "tacit knowledge, codified knowledge and knowledge infrastructure". A correlation analysis is conducted between these composite measures of knowledge and the economic performance of 19 European cities. The analysis showed that one of the most effective discriminate measures is the "shift-share residual value" which takes into account both the economic structure of the individual cities and the overall European growth. This indicated some correlation between the growth rates above predicted levels and knowledge-base, wherein positive growth residuals correlates with good access to the knowledge-base.

Furthermore, with respect to the Italian economy due to adoption of ICT, the empirical results assert that there are: (a) strong correlations between the use of information technology in business services and levels and rates of growth, and (b) enhancement of productivity due to the co-evolution of use of business and communication services. Also, there is confirmed correlation between the diffusion of communication and business services and the rates of productivity growth. A significant portion of the increase of total productivity "is the outcome of the interactions between diffusion of new information and communication technologies and their effects on the tradability, divisibility and transportability of information". This is addition to the "growing role of business service industries in the introduction of new technologies" (Antonelli, 1997). Accordingly, advocating policy-makers should consider the indirect effects of non research and development intangibles into consideration when framing innovation and ICT digital policies, whereas the "intangible capital is the knowledge capital resulting from investments in research and development, design, brand equity, firm-specific training and organizational change" (Corrado et al,2017).

6. CONCLUSION

The information and communication technology is categorically reshaping the landscape of world cities in terms of redefining space and time and is accelerating the speed with which information is processed and disseminated. With the rapid advancement of ICT, today's cities are continuously facing new opportunities and challenges. The opportunities are manifested in the recognition of digital economy acceleration. The impacts of knowledge, experience, innovation, skills and talents of city residents are far greater in value than capital equipment or even capital itself. The high mobility of talented individuals can reward the cities that will be able to attract and retain them to advance its knowledge-based activities and knowledge outcomes.

Similarly, the loss of talented individuals in cities will be sever for these cities and cannot be compensated by any alternative natural resources or goods production. Simply, this is due to the fact that the competitive advantage in the knowledge-based economy can never be obtained without the talented human capital. Therefore, cities that focus on the knowledge assets will benefit from the talented human capital and will do whatever it takes to attract and retain them to reinvigorate the knowledge-based economic growth. Furthermore, cities have to continually provide high quality education to their residents, otherwise being left behind in the new economy will be inevitable.

The knowledge-based economy provides urban areas in cities an opportunity to interchanges its geography and identify distinctive potentials that are city dependent for sustainable development. Cities exploring and exploiting these opportunities will attract and appeal to creative talents and will certainly reap the benefits of knowledge-based economy. Cities in transition including most of the Middle East are best suited to take advantage of these opportunities by appropriately investing in the ICT as a driver to boost the digital economy. This paper has introduced an approach of the information technology spine for developing knowledge-based cities in transition. The main pillars that are essential for supporting knowledge-based development of cities are identified and graphically represented based on importance within a hierarchal approach. The correlations of information technology to a knowledge-based city and its economical development were addressed based on empirical results. However, there will be various challenges for the successful implementation of the proposed approach for developing ICT knowledge-based cities. Such challenges will vary from city to another based on each city's potentials and constraints that should be carefully considered while pursuing this adventure with a well articulated strategic plan for developing a knowledge-based city as the first pillar of the proposed approach.

REFERENCES

Antonelli, C. (1997). New Information Technology and the Knowledge-Based Economy. The Italian Evidence. *Review of Industrial Organization, 12*(4), 593–607. doi:10.1023/A:1007798532691

Carrillo, F. (2002). Capital systems: Implications for a global knowledge agenda. *Journal of Knowledge Management, 6*(4), 379–399. doi:10.1108/13673270210440884

Corrado, C., Haskel, J., & Jona-Lasinio, C. (2017). Knowledge Spillovers, ICT and Productivity Growth. *Oxford Bulletin of Economics and Statistics, 79*(4), 592–618. doi:10.1111/obes.12171

Dyker, D., & Radosevic, S. (2000). Building the Knowledge-Based Economy in Countries in Transition – from Concepts to Policies. *Journal of Interdisciplinary Economics, 12*(1), 41–70. doi:10.1177/02601079X00001200103

Economics, S. G. S. (2002). *Towards a knowledge city strategy, Technical Report*. Melbourne, Australia: Melbourne City Council.

Ergazakis, K., Metaxiotis, K., & Psarras, J. (2004). Towards knowledge cities: Conceptual analysis and success stories. *Journal of Knowledge Management, 8*(5), 5–15. doi:10.1108/13673270410558747

European Commission. (2000). *Innovation Policy in a Knowledge-Based Economy*. Brussels: Office for Official Publications of the European Communities.

Gilder, G. (1995, February 27). *Forbes ASAP*.

Gottmann, J. (1977). Megapolis and Antipolis: The Telephone and the Structure of the City. In P. de Sola (Ed.), *The Social Impact of the Telephone*. Cambridge, MA: MIT Press.

Gower, P. (1997). *Banking Development in the Czech Republic: an Analysis of Credit Allocation* (Ph.D. Thesis). University of Sussex.

Knight, R. (1995). Knowledge-based Development: Policy and Planning Implications for Cities. *Urban Studies (Edinburgh, Scotland)*, *32*(2), 225–260. doi:10.1080/00420989550013068

Kothin, J., & Devol, R. (2001). *Knowledge-Value Cities in the Digital Age*. Santa Monica, CA: Milken Institute.

Laszlo, K., & Laszlo, A. (2002). Evolving knowledge for development: The role of knowledge management in a changing world. *Journal of Knowledge Management*, *6*(4), 400–412. doi:10.1108/13673270210440893

Lever, W. (2002). Correlating the Knowledge-base of Cities with Economic Growth. *Urban Studies (Edinburgh, Scotland)*, *39*(5–6), 859–870. doi:10.1080/00420980220128345

Malone, T., & Yohe, G. (2002). Knowledge partnerships for a sustainable, equitable and stable society. *Journal of Knowledge Management*, *6*(4), 368–378. doi:10.1108/13673270210440875

Manuel, C. (1989). *The Informational City*. Williston, VT: Blackwell.

McAfee & Brynjolfsson. (2007). Investing in the IT That Makes a Competitive Difference. *Harvard Business Review*.

Metaxiotis, K., & Psarras, J. (2004). Applying knowledge management in higher education: The creation of a learning organization. *Journal of Information and Knowledge Management*, *6*(4), 1–7.

Mitchell, W. (1995). *City of Bits: Space, Place, and the Infobahn*. Cambridge, MA: MIT Press.

Monreal, C. O. (2016). Intelligent Technologies for Mobility in Smart Cities. *Hradstechnika*, *71*, 29–36.

Monzon, A. (2015). Smart Cities Concept and Challenges: Bases for the Assessment of Smart City Projects. *Proceedings of the Smartgreens 2015, Smart cities, Green technologies, and Intelligent Transport Systems*, 17–31.

Moss, W. (1998). Technology and Cities. *Cityscape: A Journal of Policy Development and Research*, *3*(3), 107-127.

Nam, T., & Pardo, T. (2011). Smart City as Urban Innovation: Focusing on Management, Policy, and Context. *Proceedings of the 5th International Conference on Theory and Practice of Electronic Governance*, 185–194. doi:10.1145/2072069.2072100

Negroponte, N. (1995). *Being Digital*. New York: Alfred A. Knopf.

Turner, P. (2010). *On IT strategies*. Enterprise Architecture Summer Camp.

United Nations Organization. (2001). *Making new technologies work for human development, The Human Development Report 2001*. New York, NY: UNO.

Weill, P., & Ross, J. (2009). *IT Savvy: What Top Executives Must Know to Go from Pain to Gain*. Harvard Business School Press.

Chapter 3
The Comparative Importance of Urban and Architectural Potentials Supporting Knowledge Cities Formation and Their Relevant Indices

Khaled Youssef Mohamed
Minia University, Egypt

Ayman Mohammed Mostafa
Minia University, Egypt

Jamal Ahmad Abd el-Hameed
Minia University, Egypt

ABSTRACT

In 1996, the OECD coined the term knowledge city. This caused several developed countries to seek developing and adapting the features of their cities to be upgraded to knowledge-based economic cities. Hence, various experts worked on demonstrating and identifying the features of this concept. An objective of these cities was drawn: providing sound conditions for the enhancing, creation, and exchange of knowledge and innovation. The concept was found to be interdisciplinary: economic, political, social, as well as being urban and architectural. So, this chapter aims to observe the urban and architectural potentials of these cities, as well as their comparative importance. The comparative importance of these potentials is deduced through the study and analysis of some recognized KC models. Finally, a number of indices contributing to assessing the performance of such potentials are deduced.

DOI: 10.4018/978-1-5225-3734-2.ch003

Copyright © 2018, IGI Global. Copying or distributing in print or electronic forms without written permission of IGI Global is prohibited.

1. INTRODUCTION

In the 21st century, the emergence of some economic and environmental problems in cities led to rethinking of the methods and strategies adopted by cities for overcoming these piled up problems (Tan Yigitcanlar, 2006). As a result, the OECD coined the term Knowledge Economy in 1996. The emergence of this term stimulated various researchers from different disciplines, including planners, to establish several elements supporting this concept. This, in turn, led to the emergence of the so-called *Knowledge-based Urban Development (KBUD).* Knowledge cities became the first urban formation specifically developed for meeting the needs of Knowledge Economy. The rapid advance of ICT, in the last two decades, led to establishing the infrastructure that would enable those responsible for KBUD to extend the domain of their work (Tan Yigitcanlar, 2007).

Establishing these cities aims at achieving sustainability and quality of life by providing the required services. It also aims at enriching the variation of cultural and knowledge life within the city, as well as increasing the skills and knowledge of citizens and workers in the city as being the means of human intellectual development (Tan Yigitcanlar, Muna Sarimin, 2010). These cities also depend on state-of-the-art technologies for achieving development and providing infrastructure (Tan Yigitcanlar, Koray Velibeyoglu, Cristina Martinez-Fernandez, 2008). Another aim is maintaining the domestic image of the city, as well as enabling the city to become a vivid center that can face problems and challenges (Kostas Ergazakis, Kostas Metaxiotis, John Psarras, Dimitris Askounis, 2006).

Hence, the chapter addresses the urban and architectural potentials which contribute to the creation of a KC. To this end, the chapter is divided into four parts. The first part addresses the main concepts of KBUD and KCs, and reviews the common features of KCs and their analysis framework. The second part addresses deducing the architectural and urban potentials. The third part will be an analysis of the urban and architectural potentials in some knowledge cities. The fourth, final, part aims at deducing the comparative importance of these potentials, and reviewing some indices for measuring the performance of such potentials.

2. KNOWLEDGE BASED URBAN DEVELOPMENT

In the Knowledge economy era, cities started to increase their investments in the physical, social, and knowledge infrastructure for enhancing, attracting, and retaining talents. Knowledge-based development is a system that supports Knowledge economy and a new method of planning and development that turns cities into globally competitive ones (Tan Yigitcanlar, Muna Sarimin, 2010). *Knight* was the first to coin the concept of KBUD. He indicated the KBUD is a process where citizens take part in developing their cities through enhancing cultures and knowledge production in the city. Yigitcanlar described KBUD as the knowledge development model in the knowledge economy era. It aims at achieving economic welfare and environmental sustainability, and establishes the optimal social/spatial regime of a city. Also, he stated that KBUD is a methodology for knowledge production; one that aims at enhancing knowledge production and spreading while maintaining the environment and achieving social and economic security (Tan Yigitcanlar, Antti Lonnqvist, Jonna Kapyla, Henna Salonius, 2012). 2000, the OECD defined KBUD as decisive set of strategies that seek to achieve quality of life. In the mid-2000s, Tan Yigitcanlar reformulated the concept of KBUD as a strategic tool for developing and enhancing the competitive power of cities in the context of KBUD (Tan Yigitcanlar, 2011). KBUD aims at achieving the following (Tan Yigitcanlar, Koray Velibeyoglu, Cristina Martinez-Fernandez, 2008) (Tan Yigitcanlar, Shinyi Lee, 2009) (Tan Yigitcanlar, 2007):

- Sustainable urban development.
- Achieving a sustainable, safe knowledge economy.
- Making cities vivid with cultural life.
- Designing a knowledge city that encourages, produces, and expands knowledge work.
- Increasing skills and knowledge of residents as a means for social development.
- Boosting the quality of life through providing services needed for achieving social development.

There are many models for KBUD assessment. The Makci model was adopted in selecting case studies; being the only model which was transformed into an annual prize awarded to the best KC. The Makci award was established to set general criteria and frameworks which would contribute to transformation of cities into KCs. The award measures eight elements (The World Capital Institute & Teleos, 2010):

- Identity capital.
- Intelligence capital.
- Financial capital.
- Relational capital.
- Human individual capital.
- Human collective capital.
- Instrumental-material capital.
- Instrumental knowledge capital.
- Cities nominated for this award fall into two categories:
- **Knowledge City**: These cities were classified as largest to medium urban conglomerate, often national capitals, and gather over 3.5 million inhabitants.
- **Knowledge City-Region**: These are small cities, often acting as cultural and economic centers, with a 0.5-3.5 million inhabitants.
- Analysis of the eight factors reveals connection of some to urban and architectural components. Also, it is shown that knowledge cities are complex entities as they are linked to many interrelated factors. It can be seen that attempting to transform a city into a KC is doomed to failure unless guided by sound visions and strategies.

3. KNOWLEDGE CITIES

Under the KBUD concept, the concept of Knowledge cities (KCs) emerged. Economy of such cities depends on knowledge-based economy. Such cities seek to achieve economic and environmental sustainability, and improve the social and cultural situation in the city. Therefore, researchers and planners view KCs as the geographic entities of knowledge based urban development. To understand and formulate a clear mental image of knowledge cities, the following have to be addressed:

- Knowledge cities definition.
- The general analytic framework of a knowledge city.

3.1. Knowledge Cities Definition

The concept of knowledge city is a universal one which can take in, create, and develop all aspects of the social, economic, and cultural life in a city (Khaled Ali, Amer Taiba). It can also be a concept of the future sustainable city. *Delijen* argues that it is the ability of the knowledge city to understand, control, and generate growth via the effective usage of all city features (Xuefeng Wang, 2009). *Michard* defines a knowledge city as being excellent in knowledge creation in the first place. It is also a city which can transform knowledge capital into products of high value. According to Michard, a knowledge city is characterized by intensity of knowledge generated by three main components (Pascale Michaud, Alexandra Tcheremenska, 2003):

- Degree of knowledge production.
- Speed of understanding and using novice types of knowledge.
- Circulation of knowledge.

The Work Foundation defined a knowledge city as a city which embraces knowledge and culture. A city creates various practices for knowledge production within its borders (Xuefeng Wang, 2009). *Edvission* views a knowledge city as a geographic entity embracing knowledge and culture in order to create a knowledge-based economy (Tan Yigitcanlar, 2005). *Ergazakis* defines a knowledge city as a city which seeks to achieve knowledge-based urban development through continuous encouragement for knowledge creation, assessment, renovation, and updating. This can be done via continuous interaction between its residents and residents in other cities. Such interactions are supported by the proper design of the city, the infrastructure, and ICT networks (Kostas Ergazakis, Kostas Metaxiotis, John Psarras, 2004). Figure 1 shows *Ergazakis'* definition of a knowledge cities simplified.

3.2. The General Analytical Framework of Knowledge Cities

A knowledge city aims at providing conditions for citizens to support knowledge economy. Knowledge and cultural and social bases are the key of transformation into a KC. Understanding the general analytical framework helps increase realization of the knowledge city concept. Thus, decision makers, planners, and policy makers can have a clearer understanding of the general framework. The general framework of a knowledge city is more like a building as shown in Figure 2 (Willem van Winden, Leo van den Berg, 2004).

- **Knowledge City Base:** The base of knowledge city is the start point for the whole city in knowledge economy. The base of the KC includes the economic base of the city, the knowledge base, the urban system, variation of urban areas, accessibility to city and its services, and the quality of life (Xuefeng Wang, 2009).
- **The Knowledge Base:** The economic base seeks to achieve strong knowledge on the long run, leading to enhancing city potential for achieving economic prosperity. It includes implicit knowl-

Figure 1. Ergazakis' definition of a knowledge city (Kostas Ergazakis, Kostas Metaxiotis, John Psarras, 2004)

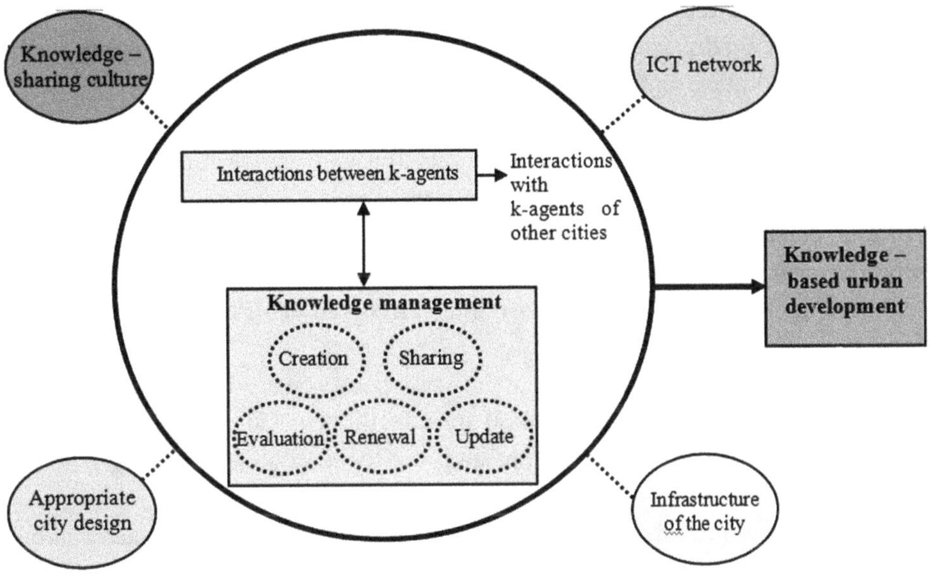

Figure 2.The general analytical framework of a KC (www.slideshare.netGemeenteDelftmasterplan-technologische-innovatiecampus-delft)

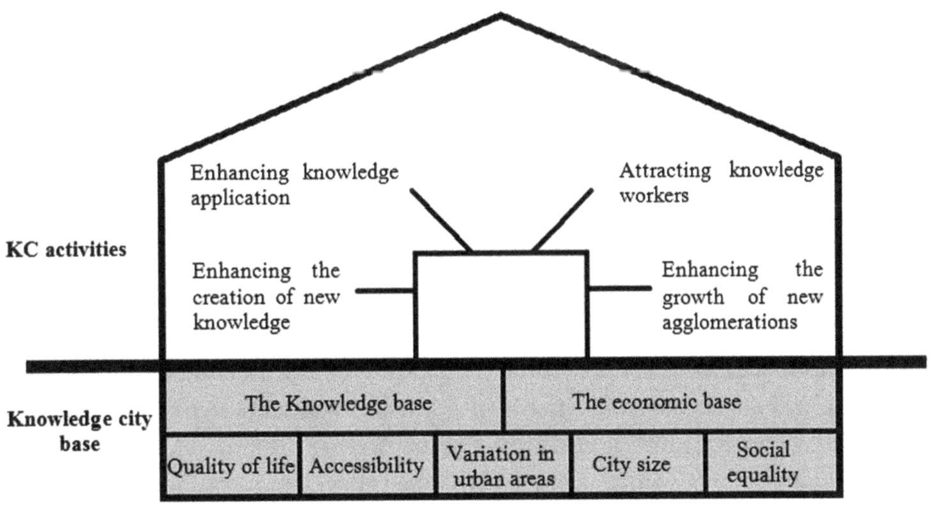

edge, technical knowledge, variation university institutions and their numbers. The level of the knowledge base specifies the position of the city at the onset of transformation to knowledge economy (Willem van Winden, Leo van den Berg, 2004).

- **The Economic Base:** A KC seeks to add value to products. So, the economic base specifies the economic abilities and obstacles encountered by the city. Services are a starting point for knowledge-based economy. Cities with various economic activities are incubators of novice developments and economic innovation (Xuefeng Wang, 2009).

- **Quality of Life:** The quality of life is the main factor in attracting and retaining knowledge workers in the city. The built environment, urban facilities, the natural environment, and different cultural institutions act as attractions. Also, providing and improving other systems; such as transportation, which facilitate accessing city facilities; and environmental systems – which seek to reduce pollution and noise; enhances the quality of life.
- **Accessibility:** Knowledge economy is a network economy which relies on high quality ICT infrastructure, providing rapid and easy communication with the surroundings of the city. It also provides fast and easy access to the city - via a network of international airports, TGV, and regional links to other urban knowledge centers, particularly by the rail roads and regional roads – to facilitate transferring knowledge and knowledge production. So, the basic infrastructure network must be active and effective (Willem van Winden, Leo van den Berg, Luis Carvalho, Erwin van Tuijl, 2011).
- **Variation in Urban Areas:** Variation in urban areas boosts creativity and innovation. Such variation is a measure of city development. These areas facilitate social inclusion which, in turn, leads to increasing interaction among inhabitant and, consequently, knowledge generation (Xuefeng Wang, 2009).
- **City Size:** Knowledge-intensive activities are particularly run in medium sized and big cities. Big cities have many merits, which provide for attracting and retaining knowledge workers, such as including a variety of knowledge activities. Such cities have the opportunity to establish and create various centers for marketing knowledge products; include various amenities, international transportation infrastructure, and embrace cultural that makes it culturally vivid (Willem van Winden, Leo van den Berg, 2004).
- **Social Equality:** Sustainable urban growth aims at achieving economic sustainability, improving income, and reducing social gaps in order to attain social coherence which directly impacts the safety and security of city inhabitants and workers. Urban safety has become essential for achieving sustainable economic growth in urban areas (Xuefeng Wang, 2009).
- **KC Activities:** Knowledge cities have four types of knowledge activities, which enhance the knowledge-based economy. The first type is encouraging the creation of new knowledge through universities that produce science or other types of knowledge such as culture. The second type is boosting knowledge application. This is about the possibility of knowledge transfer and transformation into knowledge products; indicating the inevitability of cooperation between the knowledge infrastructure and the business sector. The third type is attracting and retaining knowledge workers. A KC is regarded as one capable of attracting and retaining creative industry workers in general. Cities depending on transforming industries are viewed as capable of attracting and retaining a certain group of workers. The fourth type is developing the growth of new agglomerations, which increases the city's capacity for attracting and developing new economic activities to enlarge the economic base and boost the size of the knowledge base (Willem van Winden, Leo van den Berg, 2004).

From the above it can be seen the KC basic components support existing activities in a KC, as shown in Table 1. The knowledge base supports creating new knowledge. Also, a knowledge base, economic base, and city size contribute to enhancing knowledge application. The economic base of the city, quality of life, and social equality support the attraction and retention of knowledge workers. All components of the KC base contribute to enhancing the growth of new agglomerations (Xuefeng Wang, 2009).

Table 1. Contribution of KC basic components to supporting KCs activities (Researchers)

General analytical framework of a KC		KC Activities			
		Enhancing the creation of new knowledge	Enhancing knowledge application	Attracting knowledge workers	Enhancing the growth of new agglomerations
KC Basis	Knowledge base	●	●		●
	Economic base		●	●	●
	Quality of Life			●	●
	Variation of urban areas				●
	accessibility				●
	City size		●		●
	Social equality			●	●

Last, but not the least, the organizational capabilities in urban areas formulate and execute policies the respond to the main developments for creating conditions for sustainable economic growth through setting strategies, executing policies, and observing results. Hence, the objective of the KC basis is supporting knowledge activities within the city.

4. COMMON FEATURES OF KCS

A number of scholars; Emmanouil Ergazakis, Kostas Ergazakis, Kostas Metaxiotis and Yannis Charalabidis; have analyzed the case studies to draw the common features of KCs. It was shown that all such cities provide good conditions for knowledge creation, enhancing, and exchange; being crucial in future business activities. The study concluded that that common features fall into two categories: development and operation. Development-related features are important for knowledge cities construction. Operation-related features are important for knowledge city development and upgrading.

4.1. Development

Features under development are described as essential for constructing knowledge cities. They include social and political will, strategic vision, development plan, financial support and big investments, agencies for enhancing knowledge-based regions, racial variety, a website of the city, creating value for citizens, establishing urban innovation engines, and maintaining the rights of knowledge society citizens (Khaled Ali, Amer Taiba, 2011).

- **Political and Social Will is Indispensable:** This is the most important factor being the main initiative for embracing KBUD; a general feeling arises about the need for change for improving city position in the knowledge era as a response to many emerging problems, deterioration of traditional industries in the city, or lack of domestic resources. Such social desire for change can be the motive for transformation, and is translated into a political will. A city may not be transformed into a KC without obvious support from domestic and governmental leaders (Khaled Ali, Amer Taiba, 2011).

- **Having a Strategic Vision and a Development Plan:** Any attempt to transform a city into a knowledge city must be guided by a clear strategic vision. This strategic vision should incorporate and take into account the entirety of in-depth knowledge concerning the city status. Therefore, it is compiled by community leaders and actors being responsible for the city's future and results to a set of specific objectives and a series of measures and actions.

The plan usually seeks to make balance among the resources available in the city. These cities target developing a quality system of higher education, and to establish a mechanism for increasing the quality of life of city inhabitants, with a vision to improve social services (Kostas Ergazakis, Kostas Metaxiotis, John Psarras, 2004).

- **Financial Support:** Before the implementation of any actions or measures related to the strategic plan, the appropriate funding of the initiatives and plans should have been ensured; crucial to the success of the strategic plan objectives. Through marketing actions, the city can attract outside investments.
- **Setting-up of Agencies to Promote the Development of Knowledge-Based Regions**: The setting-up of agencies that promote the development of knowledge-based regions is essential for a knowledge city to succeed. These agencies can take various forms: technology foundations, research centers and institutions, technology parks, universities, as well as other institutions having almost the same features. They take part in different kinds of activities such as designing and implementing relevant projects, conducting research and strengthening scientific co-operation and knowledge sharing, attracting and retaining knowledge workers, sustaining economic development, and marketing the knowledge city concept.
- **Multi-Ethnic Character**: For a knowledge city to succeed, it must also be built on diversity. Knowledge workers prefer to live in cities with populations characterized by diversity, tolerance, and openness, because such an atmosphere stimulates cross-fertilization of ideas and practices and promotes faster flow of knowledge.
- **Having a Metropolitan Website**: Effective metropolitan website development improves responding in an integrated way to citizens' needs and expectations in their search for information and their desire to be assimilated into different communities. Quality of the website services is proof of the city's appeal and creativity.
- **Value Creation to Citizens**: This feature is quite crucial for a KC to succeed. Examples of such practices include creating and establishing places for permanent community dialog, and building high quality websites and networks. KCs are characterized by the speed of assimilation and dissemination of new types of knowledge.
- **Establishing Urban Innovation Engines**: An urban innovation engine is a system that supports, generates, fosters and catalyzes innovation in a city. It is crucial for change and economic growth which attract and retain knowledge workers (Khaled Ali, Amer Taiba, 2001). It is a complex system that depends on many components such as people, relationships, values, tools, and technological infrastructure.
- **Assurance of Knowledge Society Rights of Citizens:** A KC assures the rights of knowledge society citizens. These rights are: access to information right, a city must ensure connecting to broadband networks for all citizens; information rights, which ensure citizens ease of use and

requires information efficiency and diversity, continuous updating, and transparency of available information; the education and training right, which ensures citizens of a KC education and training to effectively benefit from the available knowledge and services through the ICT. The last one is the participation right: enhancing citizens' participation in management; thus strengthening and enhancing the civil society.

4.2. Operation

Categories under operation are essential for updating and upgrading a KC. This category includes: low costs of connecting to advanced networks, research excellence, public libraries network.

- **Low-Cost Access to Advanced Communication Networks:** Knowledge cities must ensure low-cost and integrated access to advanced communication networks and broadband services. Well-developed communication networks maintain steady knowledge supply. IT and connectivity are essential features of a knowledge city.
- **Research Excellence:** Research excellence is concerned with producing researches which have the capacity to create new knowledge in the areas of science and technology. Research excellence provides the basic infrastructure for new knowledge-based goods and services. A successful knowledge city is primarily characterized by the wealth of its produced knowledge, which essentially revolves around its research centers and learning institutions. Knowledge production proceeds largely from what are known as a city's engines of economic development such as its research centers and educational institutions. Knowledge production remains intensive thanks to the so-called economic development engines such as research centers and universities.
- **Existence of Public Libraries Network:** A basic attribute of a knowledge city is the existence of a public libraries network. Libraries serve as a place of innovation and knowledge dissemination. They can be active, lively places, where knowledge may be created and exchanged, ideas may be generated through conversations, and innovation can occur (Francisco Javier Carrillo, 2006).

5. THE URBAN AND ARCHITECTURAL POTENTIALS OF KCS

Studies reveal that knowledge-based city development requires urban and architectural potentials different from those of cities depending on manufacturing. Knowledge industries depend on culture and knowledge and technology-intensive industries; attracting knowledge workers and investments. From the above review of the theoretical framework of KBUD and KCs, the urban and architectural potentials supporting knowledge cities formation may be drawn. The analytical framework was mentioned as accessibility is essential in a KC. Accessibility is achieved by having a highly efficient roads and transportation network; a main component in the basic infrastructure. It also addressed the variation of urban areas; urban facilities, and cultural and creative infrastructure. According to the definition introduced by Ergazakis, a KC must have an ICT network that supports interaction among citizens. This may be translated via the basic infrastructure of a city. Research excellence is another common feature; as well as having a knowledge base as an essential component of KCs. Hence the urban and architectural potentials supporting knowledge cities formation are (Researchers):

- Basic infrastructure.
- Urban facilities.
- The cultural and creative infrastructure.
- The ICT infrastructure.
- Knowledge institutions.

5.1. The Basic Infrastructure

The basic infrastructure includes: potable water and sanitary networks, energy networks, as well as road and transportation networks. Transportation network is essential for city success. It connects the whole city and, thus, workers are easily transported to knowledge industry zones. It also facilitates access to different city facilities. It includes high-quality public transportation means, active transport network, rail roads, highway network, and international transportation and shipping means (The World Capital Institute & Teleos, 2010), (Jones Alexandra, Williams Laura, Lee Neil, Coats David, Cowling Marc, 2006) The basic infrastructure plays a crucial role in boosting economic growth and welfare. City development depends largely on the main infrastructure that improves urban regions and enables residents to live there (H.S. KUMARA, 2008).

5.2. Urban Facilities

Urban facilities include open green areas, public parks, sports centers, and social services areas. Providing urban facilities reflects in the Quality of life and a level of luxury. A city trying to be a KC without having urban facilities would suffer in attracting knowledge workers and knowledge investments (Khaled Youssef, Jamal Ahmed, Ayman Mohammed, 2006).

5.3. Cultural and Creative Infrastructure

The cultural and creative infrastructure can be divided into two sets. The first includes cultural heritage of a city: historic sites, archaic records, and museums. The second includes cinemas, theatres, conference halls, expositions, music concert places, and public libraries (The World Capital Institute & Teleos, 2010). The cultural and creative infrastructure helps create a high level of community development. It also helps in attracting and retaining knowledge workers and talents, and making the city culturally vivid. This is the core of KC success. Attraction and retention leads to knowledge base building, generation, and enhancing (Yigitcanlar Tan, O'Connor Kevin and Westerman Cara, 2008).

5.4. ICT Infrastructure

Such infrastructure contains a telecommunications network and internet network that keep the city connected to the outside world, in addition to some smart cities supporting and contributing to the establishment of the information and communication technology (The World Capital Institute & Teleos, 2010). Information and communication technology infrastructure facilitates the dissemination of knowledge in the community and improves knowledge exchange opportunities. It also contributes to the existence of knowledge-intensive regions areas that produce knowledge-intensive technologies. ICT is regarded as an essential element for ensuring the success of knowledge cities that defiantly ensure public access to information and services (Yigitcanlar Tan, O'Connor Kevin and Westerman Cara, 2008).

5.5. Educational Institutions

These include universities, research centers, and science parks. Universities and higher education institutions are particularly important to knowledge intensive cities. Educational institutions enhance knowledge publishing and exchanging ideas (Khaled Youssef, Jamal Ahmed, Ayman Mohammed, 2006). They also aim at providing a high level of education to city residents (Tan Yigitcanlar, Muna Sarimin, 2010). All KCs have universities closely connected to companies according to university majors; consequently contributing to knowledge society founding and creation (Jones Alexandra, Williams Laura, Lee Neil, Coats David, Cowling Marc, 2006). Hence, educational institutions may be regarded as a catalyst that aids in citizen interaction within the society and accepting racial variety which is essential in knowledge societies (Yigitcanlar Tan, O'Connor Kevin and Westerman Cara, 2008).

6. ANALYSIS OF SOME KCS

Having observed the urban and architectural potentials of KCs, the comparative importance of such potentials can be drawn via analyzing some KCs. Singapore, Manchester, and Valencia were selected for the following reasons:

- **Winning the Makci Award**: Singapore came first in 2012, Manchester second in 2009, and Valencia first in the very same 2009.
- The difference in economic growth for the three cities.
- **Different Sizes**: Manchester and Valencia are small KCs, whereas Singapore is a large one.

With such variation in nature and size, the urban and architectural potentials are quantitatively observed in the three cities. Cities are followed for studying potentials that were influential on city transformation, in order to deduce the comparative importance of such potentials.

6.1. Manchester

Manchester is located in England as presented in Figure 3. The Manchester City Region (MCR) is the second largest conurbation in the UK with a population of over two and a half million people. The climate is moderate all year round. The city is surrounded by hills and mountains, with several rivers through. The city centre lies on the east bank of the River Irwell, near its confluences with the Rivers Medlock and Irk.

The River Mersey flows through the south of Manchester. Although the city is not a coastal one, it is directly connected to the sea by the Manchester Canal. In 2008, Manchester was in the best 14 European cities. In 2010, Manchester won the MAKCI award as a Knowledge City Region. That's why the urban and architectural potentials of that city (The World Capital Institute & Teleos, 2010).

Figure 3. Location of Manchester

6.1.1. Basic Infrastructure

The Manchester City Region has an extensive, modern transport network which provides connectivity across the conurbation and the rest of the UK and the world. Manchester is located north of the highway, which provides good connectivity with other highways. Officials of the public transportation network aim at promoting the use of public transportation.

Manchester has a rail network of 142 miles and 98 stations. A number of stations in Manchester have benefited from extensive refurbishment in recent years. As the North's only major international gateway, Manchester provides vital transport links to the rest of the globe via Manchester Airport which was awarded the best UK airport 2008 (The World Capital Institute & Teleos, 2010).

6.1.2. Knowledge Institutions

Manchester has significant physical infrastructure assets to support its knowledge-based development. These assets make the city one of Europe's most-intensive student cities. The city has several educational institutions: Four reputable universities, providing various majors; Manchester Science Parks, providing laboratory and office space for many key knowledge-based companies; Manchester Bioscience Incubator; and Bolton Innovation Zone – a 67 hectare project set to include leisure space, hotels and student accommodation (The World Capital Institute & Teleos, 2010).

6.1.3. ICT Infrastructure

Information and Communications Technology and digital connectivity are vital to the development of a knowledge city. The Manchester Digital Development Agency was created in 2003 to attract and sustain further investment in ICT and e-commerce across all sectors of the economy. The agency includes: Media City: A new creative hub, the first of a kind in the UK, over 200 acres of space, a new region for creativity; A broadband super-speed Internet service, with a developed wireless network for the internet;

An E-government for providing public services to all; The East Serve Project: the largest ICT project, located east of Manchester. It is the Manchester gateway to the internet for providing interactive public services. This project played an important role in filling the digital gap (The World Capital Institute & Teleos, 2010).

6.1.4. The Culture and Creativity Infrastructure

Manchester has a very strong cultural offering and heritage. The city center, a creativity center for the city, is among the World Heritage Sites.

It consists of a network of canals and mills, which were constructed in the 19th century. On the other hand the city center was renovated and transformed into high-quality projects in order to enhance the existing urban texture. These projects include the Betham Tower, the highest residential building in Western Europe. The city center has the Lowry Theater, an art & glass gallery, and the Imperial War Museum. Manchester's creative and cultural institutions include: Royal Northern College of Music, other venues for introducing music, an opera house and 5 theaters, an exhibition center, and Museums such as: The Manchester Museum, the Museum of Science and Industry, Imperial War Museum North and the People's History Museum (The World Capital Institute & Teleos, 2010).

6.1.5. Urban Facilities

The city includes a number of urban facilities that directly contribute to enriching life in the city. The city includes: an open space, one of largest in Europe, with an approximate area of 3 km^2; winner of the Heaton Park Award. Manchester has a total of 135 parks, gardens and open spaces within the city. A commercial district in the city center: a mixed use project with vast office spaces, restaurants, and shopping centers.

The Manchester City Region faces many challenges in the area of public health with poor health statistics and inequalities in healthcare provision. The city has implemented a number of initiatives to address these challenges including. The Manchester Academic Health Science Centre (MAHSC) is a UK first; a federal partnership of six major teaching hospitals in Greater Manchester and the University of Manchester covering the full spectrum of healthcare. Manchester officials hope that by 2015, Manchester citizens will be the wealthier and healthier (The World Capital Institute & Teleos, 2010).

6.2. Valencia

Valencia is located in Spain as presented in Figure 4. It is the third main economic city in Spain, after Madrid and Barcelona. The climate is good all year round. There are 807000 inhabitants in Valencia. The strategic plan of Valencia aims to turn Valencia into Europe's Green City of integrated social and cultural activities. The plan aims also to turn the city for knowledge economy by concentrating advanced services and using ICT facilities. Those services resulted in economic growth; as well as increasing cultural and artistic activities, recreational activities, and R&D activities – characteristic of knowledge economy- by 41% between 2001 and 2005. Hence, such activities became the most important to economic structure. Scientific progress in healthcare and biotechnologies such as biomedicine and Genetics contributed to supporting the city's economy.

Figure 4. Location of Valencia

In 2009, Valencia won the first place in the MAKCI award as a KC region. So, the urban and architectural potentials of the city will be analyzed (Khaled Youssef, Jamal Ahmed, Ayman Mohammed, 2006).

6.2.1. Basic Infrastructure

Transportation in Valencia uses the underground, the tram, local trains, and buses. The transportation infrastructure in continually extended; road network is adapted to the challenges of regional and metropolitan communication. The city has a very efficient network of roads and railroads. There is also a super-speed railroad network that connects Valencia to Spanish cities, such as Barcelona, and many European countries such as France.

The international airport of the city attained the highest domestic and international growth percentage in the last few years. The airport was extended to 36000 m^2 in 2008; a corresponding 33% increase in capacity to 6500000 passengers annually. Another extension in 2008-1011 will increase to capacity to 15000000 passengers.

The city has three sea ports; with Valencia port on top as being the pioneering force for driving growth across the Mediterranean – by building a service activity zone in the port complying with the environmental standards. This resulted in Valencia being the Euro-Mediterranean Commodities city. This Valencia became the most important marine gate on the Mediterranean basin (The World Capital Institute & Teleos, 2009).

6.2.2. Urban Facilities

Valencia is located on the Mediterranean Sea, with 24 kilometers of beaches. It has various green areas, with lots of urban facilities that aim to achieve the quality of life. Urban facilities of the city include: a recreational sports centre, on the Mediterranean beach, for winter games; 4,384,075 m^2 of green areas, Urban greenness per inhabitant is at 5.5m^2 and the total per inhabitant is 84,2 m^2; a great number of spaces for enjoyment: 11 urban parks (1,772,031 m^2), 14 stretches of the River Turia Gardens (9km), and more than 716 neighbourhood green spaces (25 parks and 691 gardens, 500 of them with playgrounds); 240 areas exclusively for children's playgrounds; and 95 sports facilities, 147 sports hall, and 39 swimming.

As for housing there is a new project for establishing a new model for residential neighbourhood. The project aims to propose new inhabitable environments that reflect the social conditions. The project promotes for establishing houses that respond to the needs of young people, the elderly and one-parent families in a high quality environment urban environment with landscaped areas, social amenities, and special architectural works for creating urban excellence.

Valencia cares for the health of its citizens. The city possesses hospitals with multiple specialties: 6 hospital centers, 4 specialist clinics, and 26 local clinics (The World Capital Institute & Teleos, 2009).

6.2.3. Knowledge Institutions

Valencia is an education intensive region, in number and diversity (primary schools to higher education to advanced research). Valencia has an integrated network of available educational infrastructure; 7 universities (5 public and 2 private). The 26 technology institutes contributed to additions of the knowledge economy (Sara Izquierdo García, 2009).

6.2.4. The ICT Infrastructure

Valencia has one of the largest wired & wireless communications infrastructures; cable cover 98% of the city. It also provides a wired internet service. Internet users are 77.8% of inhabitants. 55% has computers; 41% of those have broadband internet. An ICT institute was established for connecting Valencia to the internet to be close to major European cities (The World Capital Institute & Teleos, 2009).

6.2.5. The Culture and Creativity Infrastructure

Setting the Valencia Strategic Plan, the culture and creativity environment was extended, constructions and events, for the purpose of renovating and refreshing Valencia's historic heritage. The culture and creativity infrastructure includes various constructions: 34 museums and more than 66 art galleries, 29 conference halls, more than 50 libraries and book archives, 19 theatres and 21 cinemas, and 9 km on the Turia river bank were transformed into a cultural and recreational pathway.

The Resource Centre for young creative people is designed as a space equipped with the necessary technical resources to enable young people to carry out their creations. The center is an intermediate space between schools and industry to promote the development of the creative processes that affect especially in disciplines related to new technologies, as well as video, video art, design or multimedia, etc (The World Capital Institute & Teleos, 2009).

6.3. Singapore

The unique location of Singapore resulted in easy connection with global markets such as Japan, China, and Australia as shown in Figure 5. As a consequence Singapore was the best place for conference hosting in the world in 2009. Also, Singapore comes first in shopping all over the world. Hot humid climate prevails in Singapore. Singapore is relatively safe from seismic activities in the region. The approximate area of Singapore is 710 km^2, with about 5.2 people living there.

In 2009, the government established an economic strategy committee for investigating the challenges facing Singapore. The committee recommended a critical transformation for enhancing growth through

Figure 5. Location of Singapore

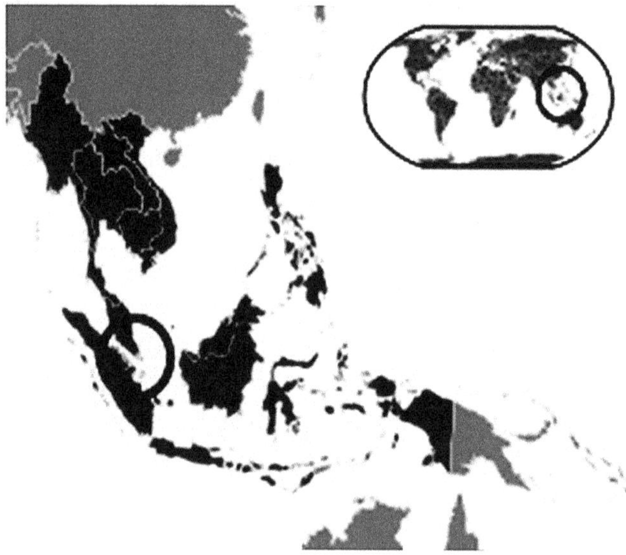

skills and innovation. The committee also recommended that Singapore should become a vivid, open, diverse city.

In 2012, Singapore came first in the MAKCI award as a knowledge city. So, the urban and architectural potentials of the city will be analyzed (The World Capital Institute & Teleos, 2012).

6.3.1. Basic Infrastructure

Singapore also has world-class infrastructure (ranked 4th), leading the world in the quality of its roads, ports, and air transport facilities (The World Capital Institute & Teleos, 2012). The road network extends for 3356 km, with 161 km of highways. Roads occupy 12% of the total area of Singapore. The underground network is taken for a public transportation network that extends over 130 km, and includes 85 stations (George Sun, LTA Academy, 2010).

The railroad network will be extended, leading to an increase in the total length of the network from 148 km to 278 km in 2020. The residential and commercial densities around railroad stations will be increased for achieving more development (Khaled Youssef, Jamal Ahmed, Ayman Mohammed, 2006).

The World Economic Forum (WEF) ranked Singapore the 1st country holding the best quality of air transport and sea port infrastructures and making its best services available. In terms of quality of trade and transport related infrastructure (e.g. Ports, railroads, roads, and information technology), Singapore scored the 3rd position, in World Bank's International Logistics Index Ranking 2009 (The World Capital Institute & Teleos, 2012).

6.3.2. Urban Facilities

Singapore reviews and formulates the concept plan every 10 years to ensure providing lands for meeting future economic needs that directly contribute to enriching life within the city and achieving a higher standard of clean environment. Hence, Singapore has various urban facilities (The World Capital Institute & Teleos, 2012):

- A recreational spa on 49 acres, with six hotels.
- An arts park.
- The Water Front Promenade.
- Various bay overlooking gardens.
- Green areas, with about 50% of the total area of Singapore.

Housing occupies 15% of the area, with housing options for all income levels – in high quality. Singapore was ranked globally the 4th in the Legatum Prosperity Index 2009 for having attained a high level of health service satisfaction. On the other hand the World Health Organization (WHO) acknowledged that Singapore has the best quality of health care (The World Capital Institute & Teleos, 2012).

6.3.3. Knowledge Institutions

The Singapore education system aims to help students discover their talents, realize their potential, and develop a passion for learning that lasts them through their lives. Singapore has various knowledge institutions having strong ties to ICT companies (http://www.universitiesinsingapore.sg/List-of-Universities-InSingapore.html):

- 5 public universities, 10 private universities and institutes.
- 852 research organization.
- More than 350 schools; primary and secondary.

Singapore is constantly working to enrich and transform the learning environments of its students and to equip them with the critical competencies to succeed in a knowledge-based economy. A key thrust is the purposeful integration of ICT into all types of lessons to enhance the students' learning experience.

Additional funding and resources enable schools to seed innovative teaching methods. A group of "future schools" are partnering industry players to use state-of-the-art technology to pilot new teaching and learning experiences (Ministry of education, in Singapore, 2012).

6.3.4. ICT infrastructure

Starting in the early 1980s, the government played a crucial role in promoting and enhancing the use of Internet & ICT. The aim was to boost advanced technological activities that would rank Singapore high in that field; by using IT for boosting the economy. Hence, Singapore came in advanced positions in various conferences and economic forums (The World Capital Institute & Teleos, 2012):

- Singapore was ranked the 1st in the international e-government ranking.
- Singapore was ranked the 11th in UN e-Government Development Index 2012.
- In the Enabling Trade Index, the World Economic Forum (WEF) ranked Singapore the 1st country holding the best quality of air transport and sea port infrastructures and making its best services available.

- Singapore was ranked the 4th in the WEF's The Networked Readiness Index 2008–2009.

Singapore also has other ICT means (Khaled Youssef, Jamal Ahmed, Ayman Mohammed, 2006):

- Domestic & International radio and TV channels.
- Broadband Internet network.
- The first Universal Studios; the only in Southeast Asia.

6.3.5. Culture and Creativity Infrastructure

In 1992, the Government initiated the Advisory Council for Culture and the Arts (ACCA). The belief then was that arts and culture were integral in developing a culturally vibrant society, giving Singapore a unique national identity and providing the social bond that holds our people together. Cultural facilities in Singapore include (Ministry of Information, Communications and the Arts, 2012):

- 56 museums (5 arts, 10 culture, 10 military & social, 5 health, 13 historical, 3 lifestyle, and 10 for science and innovation).
- 24 public libraries, as well as the National Library and 100 reading clubs.
- Theaters, galleries, and concert halls.

7. THE COMPARATIVE IMPORTANCE OF URBAN AND ARCHITECTURAL POTENTIALS AND THEIR MEASURING INDICES

From the theoretical framework of KBUD and KCs, as well as analysis of the case studies, the urban and architectural potentials supporting knowledge cities formation may be drawn, and some indicators measuring their performance may be inferred.

7.1. The Comparative Importance of Urban and Architectural Potentials

Having reviewed the common features of KCs, emphasizing the importance of having an urban innovation engine for the city to attract and retain knowledge workers, and by reviewing the analytical framework of a KC, which stresses ease of access, diversity of urban areas and quality of life in a city to support KC formation; and by studying the role of each potential and following the case studies (Singapore, Manchester, and Valencia) it was found the basic infrastructure and urban facilities provide access to the city and services, as well as achieving the quality of life; thus enabling citizens to live in the city. The other three potentials support and promote the city brand, being an urban innovation engine at the same time; leading to attraction of knowledge workers and enhancing the creation of new knowledge: knowledge city activities according to the analytical framework. The basic infrastructure in Singapore led to providing many knowledge-based industries. Educational institutions, particularly universities, supported the transformation of Manchester as for Valencia, the cultural and creative infrastructure, particularly its cultural heritage, played a major role in supporting transformation. So, the last three potentials attract knowledge workers. The urban and architectural potentials can be summarized in a

Table 2. The influence of urban and architectural potentials on transforming case study cities (Researchers)

Potentials case studies	Basic infrastructure	Educational institutions	ICT Infrastructure	Culture and creativity infrastructure	Urban facilities
Manchester	●	◒	○	○	●
Valencia	●	○	○	◒	●
Singapore	●	○	◒	○	●
●	Potential exists, Essential for transformation.				
○	Potential exists, subordinate for transformation.				
◒	Potential exists, acts as urban innovation engine in transformation.				

table for comparison as in Table 2 to show their impact on the process of transforming a city into a KC; eventually identifying the comparative importance of such potentials (Researchers).

Having reviewed the urban and architectural potentials supporting KCs transformation, their role and aim, and by analysis of the case study cities; the urban and architectural potentials comparative importance may be inferred as shown in Figure 6.

Figure 6. Role played by the urban and architectural potentials in transforming a city into a KC (Researchers)

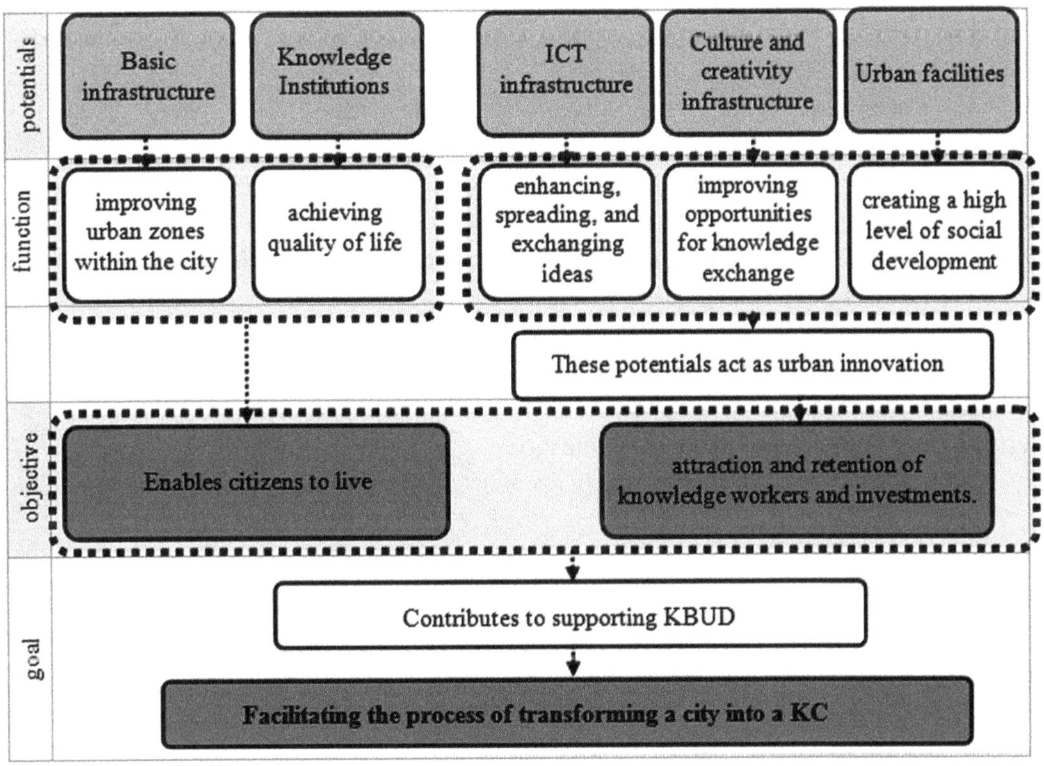

Hence, a city that aspires for transformation must upgrade the basic infrastructure and urban facilities, followed by identifying the KC value and brand and upgrading one of the three other potentials to act as urban innovation engine. This should be followed by upgrading the remaining two potentials to support the urban and architectural environment to assimilate the KBUD concept and transform into knowledge-based cities.

7.2. Indicators for Measuring the Urban and Architectural Potentials Supporting Knowledge Cities Creation

Various performance measuring indicators can be inferred. Such indicators contribute directly to evaluating the efficacy of a potential before or after transformation.

Indicators for measuring the efficacy of public transportation, active transport, and road network are (Brisbane City Council, 2012) (Department of Transport and Main Roads, 2011) (Queensland Government, 2011):

- Percentage of using public to private transportation daily.
- Percentage of available information of public transportation means at stations.
- Percentage of accidents due to road defects/
- Annual deceleration of accidents causing mortalities.
- Annual deceleration of accidents causing casualties.
- Percentage of satisfaction with public transportation cost per individual.
- Percentage of accessibility to public transportation services.
- Percentage of residents' satisfaction with diversity of public transportation options.
- Trip time in public and active transportation means to reach active city areas and business areas compared to time taken by private vehicles.
- Percentage of increase in public transportation during peak times.
- Percentage of citizens' satisfaction with transportation means efficiency and comfort.
- Percentage of safety and security, and availability of shaded areas in public transportation stations.
- Degree of integration of public transportation systems.
- Degree of heavy transport penetration into active city centers and residential areas.
- Percentage of complete strategic heavy transport highway network.
- Percentage of active and public transport users to private vehicles users.
- Percentage of pollution caused by private and public vehicles compared to other sources of pollution.
- Percentage of active transport routes in the city.
- Percentage of available information and maps of active transport routes and means to the citizens.

Urban facilities efficiency indicators (Brisbane City Council, 2012) (Manchester City Council, 2012) (the Commission for Architecture and the Built Environment and the Greater London Authority, 2009):

- Individual's share of green and open areas.
- Increase in urban facilities variety in the city.
- Percentage increase of major global events Attraction to the city.
- Percentage of annual increase in green and open areas in commercial and industrial areas.

- Percentage of environmental pollution in the city.
- Percentage of accessibility and walking distances to urban facilities.
- Percentage of accessibility to great green and open areas in the city via active or public transport.
- Percentage of citizens' satisfaction with the size and quality of urban facilities in the city.
- Percentage of satisfaction with information availability on urban facilities features.
- Percentage of covering basic infrastructure in urban facilities.

Cultural and creativity infrastructure efficiency indicators (Department of Science, Information Technology, Innovation and the Arts, 2014) (Minister for the Arts, 2009):

- Percentage of increase in cultural industries contribution to the city's economy and annual GDP.
- Percentage of contribution of cultural products to the GDP compared to existing industries in the city.
- Percentage of using heritage places as spaces of creativity.
- Percentage annual individual's share of cultural infrastructure in the city.
- Percentage increase of digitizing cultural, artistic, and knowledge production.
- Percentage of information availability on cultural life in the city.
- Percentage of citizens' satisfaction with the cultural life.
- Percentage increase of hosting events and festivals in the city.
- Percentage of increase in citizens participating in such cultural events and festivals.
- Percentage of access to the cultural infrastructure via active or public transportation means.
- Percentage of city visitors for cultural events compared to the annual total number of visitors.

ICT efficiency indicators (Brisbane City Council, 2012):

- Annual increase in the digital sector companies.
- Annual increase in employment in the digital sector.
- Percentage of citizens supported by a digital work zone.
- Annual increase in services provided via the internet.
- Percentage of citizens having access to broadband network.
- Percentage of existing urban areas having access to broadband network.
- Percentage of existing urban areas supported by fiber-optics network.
- Percentage of ICT users in different governmental services.

Educational institutions efficiency indicators (Federation University Australia, 2015) (University of Salford, 2011):

- Percentage of educational institutions contribution to the domestic product.
- Percentage increase in global ranking of educational institutions.
- Access to educational institutions via ICT.
- Annual scientific production.
- Percentage of international students to the total number of students in educational.

8. CONCLUSION

Various parameters contribute together in transforming cities into KCs. The urban and architectural potentials comprise the physical environment of a city; participating directly in the transformation process. One conclusion of the study is that there are five urban and architectural potentials in knowledge cities:

- The basic infrastructure.
- The educational institutions.
- The ICT infrastructure.
- The culture and creativity infrastructure.
- The urban facilities.

Each one of these potentials plays a significant role in transformation. Basic infrastructure enables citizens to live in the city. ICT infrastructure improves the opportunities for knowledge exchange, and aid the creation of high-intensity knowledge regions that contribute to establishing knowledge-based technology industries. The culture and creativity infrastructure leads to a high level of social development and creates a vivid life. Finally, urban facilities achieve the quality of life.

The urban and architectural potentials may be classified under three categories. The first is an essential; the basic infrastructure and urban facilities, as they provide the appropriate living environment within the city. The second is a subordinate one. It includes: knowledge institutions, ICT infrastructure, and the culture and creativity infrastructure. The third originates from the second; potentials that act as urban innovation engines. Hence, the process of transforming a city into a KC requires the existence of basic infrastructure and urban facilities. Then, a study has to be conducted to identify the city value and methods of upgrading through a strong urban innovation engine that aids in the process of attracting and retaining knowledge workers. The last step is complementing the urban and architectural potentials for improving the physical conditions of the city and contributing to the process of knowledge and ideas generation, enhancing, and exchange; leading in the end to preparing the city for transformation.

The cities that aspire to transformation knowledge cities can measure the efficiency of the performance of the urban and architectural potentials through some indicators before and after the process of upgrading, and compare them either at the standard global rates or models of other cities of knowledge.

REFERENCES

Alexandra, J., Laura, W., Neil, L., David, C., & Marc, C. (2006). *Ideopolis: Knowledge City-Regions*. London: The Work Foundation.

Brisbane City Council. (2012). *Brisbane Long Term Infrastructure Plan 2012 – 2031*. Brisbane City Council.

Carrillo, F. J. (2006). *Knowledge Cities Approaches, Experiences, and Perspectives*. Elsevier's Science & Technology Rights.

Department of Science. (2014). *Information Technology, Innovation and the Arts: " Queensland Cultural Precinct*. Queensland Government.

Department of Transport and Main Roads. (2011). *Connecting SEQ 2031 – An Integrated Regional Transport Plan for South East Queensland*. The State of Queensland.

Ergazakis, Metaxiotis, & Psarras. (2004). Towards knowledge cities: conceptual analysis and success. *Journal of Knowledge Management, 8*(5).

Ergazakis, K., Metaxiotis, K., Psarras, J., & Askounis, D. (2006). A unified methodological approach for the development of knowledge cities. *Journal of Knowledge Management, 10*(5), 65–78. doi:10.1108/13673270610691189

García, S. I. (2009). *Valencia, awarded as one of the Most Admired Knowledge Cities 2009*. Retrieved from http://www.globalcitiesdialogue.com/index.php/home/88-news-from-our-members/122-valencia-awarded-as-one-of-the-most-admired-knowledge-cities-2009.html

George Sun, L. T. A. Academy. (2010). *Land Transport in Singapore*. Retrieved from http://www.gist.edu.sg/cmsresource/Travel%20conference/Land%20Transport%20in%20Singapore.pdf

Kumara. (2008). Speed implementation for provision of urban infrastructure: A case of Mysore city. *ITPI Journal, 5*(4).

Manchester City Council. (2015). *2015 – UK-GBC City Conference Summary Report*. Manchester, UK: Green Building Council.

Michaud, P., & Tcheremenska, A. (2003). *Montreal, Knowledge city*. Retrieved from http://ville.montreal.qc.ca/pls/portal/docs/page/contenus_partages_en/vie_montreal/media/documents/mtl-knowledge.pdf

Ministry of Education. (2012). *Education in Singapore*. Retrieved from www.moe.gov.sg

Ministry of Information, Communications and the Arts. (2012). *Singapore culture statistics 2012*. Retrieved from www.mica.gov.sg

Queensland Government. (2011). *Western Brisbane Transport Network strategy*. Minister for Transport.

Tan, Y. (2011). Knowledge-based urban development redefined: from theory to practice knowledge-based development of cities. *Proceedings of the 4th Knowledge Cities World Summit*.

Tan, Y. (2007). The Making of Urban Spaces for the Knowledge Economy: Global Practices. *Proceedings The 2nd International Symposium on knowledge cities: future of cities in the Knowledge Economy*.

Tan, Y., & Muna, S. (2010). Orchestrating knowledge-based urban development: lessons from multimedia super corridor, Malaysia. In Knowledge-Based Development for Cities and Societies – Integrated Multi-Level Approaches. IGI Global.

The Commission for Architecture and the Built Environment and the Greater London Authority. (2009). *Open space strategies Best practice guidance*. Blackmore Ltd.

The World Capital Institute & Teleos. (2009). *The Most Admired Knowledge Cities (MAKCi) Report*. Retrieved from http://www.worldcapitalinstitute.org/

The World Capital Institute & Teleos. (2012). *The Most Admired Knowledge Cities (MAKCi) Report*. Retrieved from http://www.worldcapitalinstitutc.org/

University of Salford. (2011). *The campus plan: Urban initiatives*. Author.

van Winden, W., & van den Berg, L. (2004). *Cities in the knowledge economy: new governance challenges*. European Institute for Comparative Urban Research.

van Winden, W., van den Berg, L., Carvalho, L., & van Tuijl, E. (2011). *Manufacturing in the New Urban Economy*. Routledge.

Wang. (2009). *Knowledge-based urban development in China* (PhD dissertation). The Newcastle University.

World Capital Institute & Teleos. (n.d.). *The Most Admired Knowledge Cities (MAKCi) Report*. Retrieved from http://www.worldcapitalinstitute.org/

Yigitcanlar & Sarimin. (n.d.). Orchestrating knowledge-based urban development: lessons from multimedia super corridor, Malaysia. *International Journal of Knowledge-Based Development, 2*(1).

Yigitcanlar, T. (2011). redefining knowledge-based urban development. *International Journal of Knowledge-Based Development*, *2*(4), 340. doi:10.1504/IJKBD.2011.044343

Yigitcanlar, T. (2007). The Making of Urban Spaces for the Knowledge Economy: Global Practices. *Proceedings The 2nd International Symposium on Knowledge Cities: Future of Cities in the Knowledge Economy*.

Yigitcanlar, T. (2005). *The Making of Knowledge Cities: Lessons Learned from Melbourne*. International Symposium on Knowledge Cities, Medina, Saudi Arabia.

Yigitcanlar, T., & Lee, S. (2009). *Moving towards a knowledge city: Brisbane's experience in knowledge-based urban development*. The State of Australian Cities National Conference, University of Western Australia, Perth, Western Australia.

Yigitcanlar, T., Lonnqvist, A., Kapyla, J., & Salonius, H. (2012). Tampere region under the microscope: a critical analysis from the knowledge perspective. In *7th International Forum on Knowledge Asset Dynamics (IFKAD)*. University of Basilicata.

Yigitcanlar, T., O'Connor, K., & Westerman, C. (2008). The making of knowledge cities: Melbourne's knowledge-based urban development experience. *Cities (London, England)*, *25*(2), 63–72. doi:10.1016/j.cities.2008.01.001

Yigitcanlar, T., Velibeyoglu, K., & Martinez-Fernandez, C. (2008). Rising knowledge cities: The role of urban knowledge precincts. *Journal of Knowledge Management*, *12*(5), 8–20. doi:10.1108/13673270810902902

Youssef, K., Ahmed, J., & Mohammed, A. (2013). The comparative importance of the architectural and urban potentials of knowledge cities (KCs). The 6th knowledge cities world summit, Istanbul, Turkey.

Youssef, K. A., & Taiba, A. (2011). *Knowledge Cities Approaches, Experiences, and Perspectives*. Dar El Marafa.

Section 2

Country-Based Case Studies

Chapter 4
The Knowledge Urbanity in Qatar:
An Alternative Dynamic

Ali A. Alraouf
Qatar Urban Planning, Qatar

ABSTRACT

This chapter illustrates the alternative approach to knowledge-based urban development that Qatar adopted to cope with the challenges of the post-carbon paradigm and to construct a new identity as a knowledge-based model of development within the Middle East. Using the capital city, Doha, as the main case study, the chapter provides analysis of the city evolution from the discovery of oil until the contemporary stage where knowledge economy is envisioned as its future and the guiding principle for its urban and architectural projects. The analysis covers the city planning level and how future masterplan is geared towards KBUD and then some influential projects will be assessed. The chapter concludes with a holistic understanding of the case of Doha as a knowledge and creative city that succeeded to craft a new urban brand within the Gulf and Middle Eastern cities.

INTRODUCTION

In the last 20 years of the 20th century, Gulf urbanity was mainly characterized by a commitment to use oil revenues to allow primitive, small and simple Gulf cities to rapidly transform into modern status. A process of massive transformation of the endless deserts into real estate mega projects coupled with qualitative upgrade of cities' infrastructure to get ready for a new modern condition. Observing skylines of cities in the Gulf or tracing their geographical boundaries during the last two decades would prove what diverse researchers have considered unprecedented momentum of development (Kamrava, 2013; Gray, 2011; Davidson, 2008; Alraouf, 2008). Yet, during the last five years, major Gulf cities have emerged as rapid growing knowledge economy localities as they realize the inevitability to go beyond the oil-based economy (Ulrichsen, 2011). The chapter narrates critically the case of Doha, the Capital city of Qatar and illustrates its distinction from neighboring Gulf cities particularly the city of Dubai, United

DOI: 10.4018/978-1-5225-3734-2.ch004

Copyright © 2018, IGI Global. Copying or distributing in print or electronic forms without written permission of IGI Global is prohibited.

Arab of Emirates. Dubai was a dominant development model for a number of Gulf and Middle Eastern cities in the recent decade (Davidson, 2008; Al-Thani, 2011; Alraouf, 2016). Qatar is now capturing the world's imagination with a remarkable balance between global aspirations and local necessities. Doha is planned as a future hub in different areas such as education, research, culture, sports and knowledge-based economy initiatives. The chapter illustrates how the urban development is guided by this vison. For instance, the city is becoming the host for an unprecedented assembly of international branch campuses. Additionally, one of the clear directions for Doha's development is based on transforming the city into a sports hub. This was manifested in the city's ability to host a considerable number of world class events including the Asian Games of 2006 to the successful bid for World Cup 2022. Consequently, Doha is gradually becoming a knowledge based urban development territory as manifested in the intensive activities of building universities, museums and cultural centers, research institutes, science and innovations incubators and sports and recreational facilities. Clearly, Doha is constructing a new brand based on the authenticity and the credibility of its adherence to the vison towards knowledge as the main governor and generator of its future development. Such vison transcends the typical image of Gulf cities development initiated by Dubai as will be explored. The critical narrative of constructing such a brand is the focus of this chapter. The chapter examines the vision and strategy of Qatar to use its oil and gas revenues to pave the way for a new identity for the city as a holistic manifestation of the knowledge-based urban development paradigm.

CONTEXT AND TERRITORIAL BACKGROUND

The State of Qatar is a small peninsula, with a total area of 11,500 km2 of flat, featureless terrain, with various sand dunes in the south and rocky desert in the north. The Country is connected to the Arabian Peninsula from the south where its borders with Saudi Arabia are located. It has population of more than 2.5 million, at least 85% of them are expatriates (Qatar Statistics Authority (QSA), 2012). Just a few

Figure 1. Doha's contemporary urbanity, a paradigmatic shift (Author)

years ago, Doha was referred to as a "sleepy town" (The New Frontier, 2008). The city was perceived as one of the dullest cities in the world. In 2008, the Lonely Planet guidebooks rated the city as the most boring city on earth (Lonely Planet, 2008). Development in Qatar has occurred at an unprecedented pace. In the matter of a few years, the country has gone from being one of the poorest countries to being the richest country on earth. Measured in purchasing power parity terms, its per capita GDP is now the highest in the world. Qatar surpassed Luxembourg as the world's richest nation in 2010 and is set to pull away with wealth that's almost twice that of the US, latest estimates from the International Monetary Fund show. The IMF's Chart of the Day shows Qatar's gross domestic product per capita at $88,221 in 2010, according to IMF data. The figure may reach $111,963 by 2016, surpassing Luxembourg's $94,621 and Singapore's $70,992, the IMF said. US GDP per capita is forecast at $55,622 in five years, from $46,860 in 2010.With enormous and increased revenues from its exports of gas and oil, Qatar has invested heavily in economic and social infrastructure, as well as, in the well-being of its people.

Until few decades ago, Qatar was dominated by nomadic people whose livelihood depended on fishing and pearling. However, the discovery of oil and gas has encouraged not only socio-economic changes, but environmental changes as well. Today, the capital, Doha is home to more than 90% of the country's 2.5 million people, the majority of whom are professionals from all around the globe (QSA, 2015). Up to the mid-1960s, the majority of Doha's built environment was composed of traditional houses that represent local responses to the surrounding physical and socio-cultural conditions. During the 1970s and 1980s Doha was transformed into a modernized city (Othman, 1984; El Mallakh, 1979; Zahlan, 1979). Over the past decade, Qatar has become one of the major producers and exporters of Liquefied Natural Gas (LNG) in the world (Gray, 2013; Fromherz, 2012). The wealth produced by Qatar's oil and gas exports has generated a construction development boom in the capital, Doha, and the surrounding vicinity. This resulted in significant growth at all levels from urban development and infrastructure provision to cultural and educational facilities. The tremendous economic boom seen in Qatar has been supported largely by an influx of expatriate workers. The country is becoming the main attraction for external workforce in the last five years. A fact which dramatically transcends the estimations of World Bank and UN. World Bank (2005) estimates of population growth for Qatar were to reach approximately 600,000 by 2006. In actuality, the population increased to nearly 800,000. Predictions by the UN for Qatar for the year 2025 placed a high estimate at 850,000, while the planning Council figures for 2015 was 1.4 million. Yet, both predictions were gross underestimates because by the end of 2007, the population had reached 1.5 million (Gulf Times, 2008). More significantly, the current population already reached the limit of 1.7 million by the end of the first half of 2012 (QSA, 2012). Demographic structure of Doha while considered, by some regional researchers, as a threat to national identity can also be seen as a great potential in constructing Doha's new identity. Landry (2006) argues that we need to blend our differences together even if we don't understand each other. In this sense, culture diversity is actually a positive feature in the conditions for constricting knowledge and creative city as Doha is aspiring for.

THE EVOLUTION OF THE CITY (PRE-OIL ERA - 2000'S)

The city of Doha's pre-oil settlement history could be traced back to the 18th century when tribal settlements occupied the northern and eastern part of the peninsula. The *Al Bidda* settlement (Doha's original name) was founded in 1847 on the east coast and it consequently grew into eight distinct settlements with a total area of 1.23sq km (Hassan, 1994). In early 1800's, *Al Bidda*, the original site of Doha and other cities in Qatar were developed at a distant from the tribal conflicts that took place at Al Zubara territory in the north of the peninsula. Moreover, it was considered as partially secured from the conflicts among Abu Dhabi Emirate and Bahrain (Rahman, 2005). At the turn of the 20th century, *Al Bidda* and its southern satellite Al Wakrah, accounted for 74% of Qatar's urbanized population (Lorimer, 1970). *Al Bidda* had subsumed several towns' populations to arrive at an estimated 12,000 inhabitants by mid-20th century, while the country-wide population reached 30,000 (Nagy, 2000). Between Doha's foundation and until the mid-20th century, Doha continued to grow as a small port settlement. It remained as fishing and pearling center even after the arrival of oil until the 1950's. Although, oil was discovered in 1939, its exploitation was halted between 1942 and 1947 because of World War II and the Bahrain embargo (El Mallakh, 1979; Zahlan, 1979; 1998). Accordingly, the oil wealth acted as a catalyst for the urban development and the true sense of development in the country began at 1955 where the need to accommodate expatriates joining the oil industry, emerged. The early expansion of the 1950's and 1960's was determined by the provision of roads infrastructure and required workers housing developments (Alraouf, 2017; Wiedmann, 2012; Al Buainain, 1999).

Following the withdrawal of the British, the State of Qatar declared its independence on September 3, 1971. During early seventies, Qatar has witnessed an extreme increase in the construction of its institutional buildings, offices, ministries and governmental authorities resulted in a major change in the city's urbanity. The notion of public administration came into effective control manifested in several ministries that dealt with Qatar's urbanization, the most important of which was the Ministry of Municipal Affairs and Agriculture (MMAA) with its town planning section established in 1974 (Al Buainain, 1999, 207). With the shift in power in Qatar, a new young ambitious Amir took the responsibility of leading the State into a new phase of development. Sh. Hamad bin Khalifa Al-Thani clearly acknowledged the

Figure 2. An aerial photo showing the Doha as a portal settlement in 1947(Source: Courtesy of MME, Qatar)

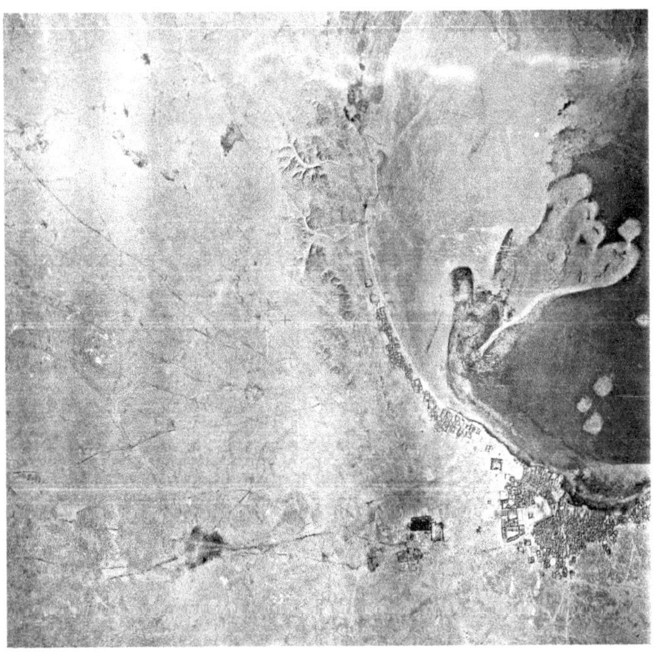

Figure 3. An aerial photo captured in mid-forties showing Doha's waterfront, AL Jessra Area, the cemetery and Al Khot Fort (Source: Courtesy of MME, Qatar)

potential of his small yet very promising State. For many Gulf cities, going beyond modernization and basic development, was a major objective. Qatar was inspired to open up to development and reproduce Dubai's rapid boom. Also, with all the similarities between Dubai and Doha and the pace at which Doha is developing, questions concerning Doha's development are raised. As Al- Thani (2011, p: 38) rightly asked will Doha be the next Dubai or will the country maintain control over its pace of development and social repercussions. The impact of Dubai on Doha's development was evident particularly in the first years of this decade. Doha's development plans seem on the same path as Dubai. Compelling aspirations towards a place on the global stage reflected in a new kind of urbanism based again on iconic and vertical development (Alraouf, 2016). Yet, Doha was so swift, even before the financial crisis of 2008 and its sever impact on Dubai, to realize that imitation is antithesis to uniqueness and distinctiveness.

AN INTERROGATION OF A KNOWLEDGE CITY: A DECADE OF CHANGE

In the last decade, Qatar has transformed itself into a major hub for numerous economic and cultural activities. Hosting a number of top-level sporting tournaments, culminating in the successful FIFA World Cup 2022 bid, is contributing in establishing Doha as an emerging urban and development brand within the Gulf and Middle Eastern contexts. Whether to counter regional economic competitors or to further tie Qatar to the economies of the world's leading countries, this brand is designed innovatively to counter a range of security concerns; in short, Qatar is diversifying its dependencies (Roberts 2015; Alraouf, 2016). Furthermore, Qatar has become attractive as a place for foreign knowledge workers and the creative class. This is the class of people who are moving around the world and attracted to the quality of urban environments which maintain their creative and intellectual outputs (Florida, 2002; 2005). Qatar's national vision for the year 2030 consists of basic foundations focused on the necessity of continuous social development in order to achieve a fair and safe society based on upholding human

Figure 4. The 1980s modernization of Doha as clearly changing the urban fabric of the city and introducing different architectural language particularly in governmental and institutional buildings (Source: Courtesy of MME, Qatar)

values and social welfare and aims to maintain and improve its economic standards in order to further strengthen its national economy and remain competitive, while continuing to secure and satisfy the needs of its citizens (QNV 2030). Maintaining the current growth of its urban population and fostering quality of life is seen as critical to the future development of the country, as indicated in the national development strategy 2011–2016 (QSDP, 2011). Such vision is supporting the way by which the new generation of knowledge workers decide on where to live as Florida argues (Florida, 2008). Qatar's economy has experienced three transformations.

It has been 39 years since the British left Qatar and much has changed during the last four decades. Hydrocarbons have replaced pearls as Qatar's main source of revenue, bringing previously unimagined wealth to the former British protectorate as White (2010) rightly argued. With a per capita income of $83,000, second in the world, the leaders of Qatar are building a new future for their country. In 2005, Qatar Investment Authority (QIA) was established with a vision to reinvesting oil and gas revenues and building a diversified international asset portfolio. According to financial analysis done by RGE Monitor New York, Qatar has around $75bn worth of investments outside the country. Strategically, Qatar has been on a multibillion spending spree to acquire assets across the globe. Yet, the country's leaders fully acknowledge the importance of development from within. So, while Qatar is spending a fortune on foreign shores, it is not forgetting to invest at homeland. As part of this development the face of Doha will change immeasurably over the coming years. So far, Doha is a more successful example in incorporating knowledge within the city. As clearly reflected in its future vision, Qatar's rulers acknowledged the shift towards a post oil paradigm (QNV 2030). More significantly, realized the global competition between cities around the world. Hence, acknowledge that in the context of international competition, new strategies for development have to emerge. Undoubtedly, architecture and urbanism are excellent tools that help cities create its niche in the global competition. Doha, while investing in positioning itself on the map of world emerging economies, was alert to use architecture and urbanism as a manifestation of a new era of planning and urban development (Jodido, 2014; Alraouf, 2013; 2016).

A PARADIGM SHIFT FORM RESOURCE TO KNOWLEDGE ECONOMY

As the Qatar economy diversifies more from its reliance on gas and oil, success will increasingly depend on the ability to compete in a global knowledge economy. Educating and training Qataris to their full potential will be critical to continuing progress (GSDP, 2011, p. 13).

Starting from 2008, Qatar adopted a new vision towards achieving a holistic development which was crystallized in the doctrinal document Qatar Vision 2030. It is structured around huge investments in education, science, and research. In other words, the knowledge economy was explicitly declared as the selected economic platform for the country's future. While Doha's position is radically different from cities like Manama and Dubai when it comes to oil and Gas reserves, Qatar leaders were convinced that the post-oil paradigm is becoming a reality. Hence, moving from a resources economy to a knowledge-based economy is a global and inevitable transformation that requires understanding and better engagement. To pave the way for this process to be implemented, main steps were made. Roberts (2015) argues that rarely has a state changed its character so completely in so short a period of time. In 1995, Sh. Hamad Al Thani authorized the establishment of Qatar Foundation (QF). Qatar Foundation is a comprehensive and dynamic knowledge structure which includes all level of educational services from basic to university education. More importantly, QF accommodates creativity and innovation forums, a leadership academy, a sports academy, research centers, intellectual debates and state of the art conference facilities. For the sake of this chapter, a focus on some specific projects from within Qatar foundation is provided. Such projects are used to evaluate Qatar's effort to construct its identity as a knowledge and creative city within the Gulf's emerging urbanism. The analysis will suggest that Qatar is using this new paradigm to create an identity for its capital city; "Dohaization". This brand is based on number of factors including national vision, quality of urbanism and adopted strategies. Roberts (2015) argues that rarely has a state changed its character so completely in so short a period of time. Yet, the paradigm shift form resource to knowledge economy requires courageous decisions and radical transformations. In this following part, a discussion of the three main strategies adopted by the country's leaders to create a new identity for Qatar amid the Gulf States is provided.

THE VISION, THE MISSION AND THE ADOPTED STRATEGIES

Extended Global Investment Arm

Oil and gas reserves have made Qatar one of the most rapidly growing economies in the world. Qatar became the world's top liquefied natural gas (LNG) exporter in 2007. Qatar's copious supplies of (LNG) allowed its small population to enjoy being one of the world wealthiest countries and have the globe's highest per capita income. Fascinatingly, Qatar is trying hard to diversify its economy and its future vision named Qatar 2030 is forecasting an economy based on knowledge and creativity rather than soon to be depleted natural carbon resources. Qatar changed the classical slogan of different Gulf States known as earn locally, spend globally into earn locally, invest globally. The traditional method of international investment was based on moving oil revenues to foreign banks and stocks. Qatar is paving a new route by focusing on substantial global investment. Qatar pays close attention to the diversification of its economy. Although the oil and gas related sectors still constitute the majority of state revenues,

Figure 5. The Aspire zone and its related facilities moving Doha to be one of the most sports friendly ready cities in the Middle East (Source: Courtesy of MME, Qatar)

varying yearly from about 50 to 70 percent, diversification is high on the agenda. As a good example of this sensitivity, the country's Sovereign Wealth Fund (SWF), the Qatar Investment Authority (QIA), valued at approximately US $115 billion at the end of 2012, "does not invest in the Qatari energy sector" (Gray, 2013, p. 105). In light of this, Gray claims that QIA "was created either primarily or partly as a deliberate strategy of the Emir toward balancing out the fluctuations in energy rents and diversifying the economy" (Gray, 2013, p. 107).

Political Credibility: A New Global Mediator

Qatar is, as Kamrava (2013), explains a "tiny giant": although severely lacking in most measures of state power, it is highly influential in diplomatic, cultural, and economic spheres. In the process of reinventing itself as a potential Arab super power, Qatar focuses on gaining global credibility. The Gulf State tries to build a niche as conflict mediator within the Middle East and Africa. Using a combination of its financial power and its increasing diplomatic credibility, Doha is winning global respect as an able negotiator. Financed by gas exports, Qatar diversified its foreign relations to include Iran and Israel, and carved a leading role in international mediation (Roberts, 2015). Currently, Qatar is successfully building a reputation as the mediator of choice in regional and international conflicts. Qatar gained political credibility among Arab and foreign states alike. It has endeavored to cut a unique profile as a diplomatic mediator and peace negotiator in recent years, intermingling in conflicts from Lebanon to Yemen and Darfur and most recently, the Arab spring countries. Qatar's prominent role in the Arab Spring follows a similar pattern, yet the gamble it is taking in supporting elected presidents and people's choices proved to be of a high cost. Qatar used the Arab Uprisings as an opportunity to seize rather than a challenge to be contained (Ulrichsen, 2014).The state's strategy was to achieve regional and global prominence. Qatar has a palpable desire to be a trendsetter at the forefront in all domains, whether it is education, media or diplomacy (Farha, 2010, The Gulf). Therefore, the Amir is expected to continue to give priority to mediation efforts, boosting Qatar's stranding diplomatic circles. Qatar's effective use of its subtle power, Kamrava (2013) argues, challenges how we understand the role of small states in the global system. Qatar's diplomatic triumph is a result of clear vision that Doha is the ideal environment for regional conflict resolutions and constructive negotiations. Kamrava (2013), points to the changing nature of power in international arena in general and its utilization by Qatar in particular, labeling the new form of power that Qatar has carved out "subtle power".

Branding Qatar via Doha's Emerging Knowledge-Based Urbanism

Architecture, urbanism and planning are used, as will be explained in the coming sections, to prepare the country for the post-carbon era and establish a model which transcends the Dubai's dominance as a reference for development in the gulf. Dohaization is consciously perceived as a process to brand Doha in a balanced manner focused on the image and the content (Alraouf, 2016). Such preparation includes creating the environment which would attract knowledge workers and creative people from around the world to settle in Qatar and contribute in its new economical and development paradigm. On a planning level, the new blueprint for the urban development of Qatar titled "Qatar National Development Framework (QNDF)" is the outcome of Qatar's urban planning department and its focus group envisioning Qatar National Master Plan (QNMP). The main pillars of the framework suggest a new form of urbanism for Qatar articulated around planning for sustainable growth, compacted settlements, transit oriented urban development, walkability, mixed use urban centers and positive public realm. Such new planning principles aim at transforming Qatari cities and municipalities into people-friendly places and spaces and create the attractive environment which speaks to knowledge and creative workers considering Doha and other Qatari cities as their new homes. For instance, enhancing walkability within the West Bay development is considered as a catalyst to transform the city business district from a composition of isolated towers and skyscrapers into a network of activities which would enhance social integration, walkability, public real and urban connectivity.

More significantly, according to QNDF and all municipal spatial development plans, Qatari cities are planned to accommodate a number of mixed use urban centers. The centers go all the way form the level of the neighborhood to the level of the whole city. All centers provide the needed community services and facilities including open and green spaces (QNDF, 2016). To enhance the sense of walkability, the centers are designed around either a metro station or a public bus node to emphasize the transit oriented development strategy adopted in all of Qatar. Additionally, the National Spatial Strategy (2032) and Metropolitan Doha Plan (2032) are providing a future vision for the Qatari Capital. The vision is founded on a multi-centered approach to urban development. Metropolitan Doha contains three capital city centers include Downtown Doha, Airport City and West Bay. The three centers are characterized by mixed use development which can guarantee vibrant, attractive and sophisticated public realm. Also, numbers of sustainable patterns of development are introduced including bicycles and water buses and taxies. All of these policies and strategies substantiate QNDF's main aim to provide an excellent spatial strategy which provides sustainable urban living for locals and expatriates. Another crucial point related to the qualitative understanding of Qatar's future population. QNV 2030 asserts the value of attracting knowledge workers to reside in Doha. To better cope with the conditions of establishing knowledge economy, the vision suggests revisiting the country's demographic structure. While the current population is approaching 2.5 million, the vision is estimating around the same number for 2030. The rational as explained in the vision, stems from the fact that Qatar's population will experience qualitative and not quantitative change. At least 800,000 construction and infrastructure workers will leave the country by 2019/2020 when most of the mega projects are finalized. This 35% of the total population will be replaced by knowledge workers and creative class members to occupy position in education, research, innovation, arts, banking, services and all other aspects of knowledge-based development (QNV, 2008; QNDF, 2016).

Qatar has lost its bid for the 2016 Olympics, but has vowed to try again. On the second of December, 2010, Qatar was selected as the host country for the FIFA Cup 2022. The tiny Gulf state was awarded the honor of organizing and hosting the most important sports event in the world. The remarkable decision was yet another crucial boost for the city's efforts in carving a unique place on the global stage. More significantly, it is creating a great momentum in the process of constructing the new brand of urbanity that Doha is envisioning. The quantity and the quality of architectural and urban projects which will be added to the city's urbanity to facilitate hosting the World FIFA Cup would definitely make Doha a very unique world destination. Significantly, Doha has gained global significance through the growth of knowledge economy related projects. The city's new urban development and its spatial qualities contribute to the global attractiveness of Doha for knowledge economy investments, firms and people. Such urbanism fulfills the requirements of knowledge workers coming to the city from literally every spot of the globe anticipating an attractive smooth quality of life which would foster their creativity and innovation.

KBUD IN CONTEMPORARY DOHA

On the levels of architecture and urbanism, two main categories of can be observed within the boundaries of Doha, as the main channels for articulating the new urban brand. Knowledge-based Urban Development (KBUD) is the first category. The balanced combination between local and global urbanism is the second. Qatar underwent a radical transformation to go beyond the typical image of a Gulf city relying on presumably endless assets of oil and gas. Significant investment has been made in knowledge-based urban development in the country during the last decade. Architectural and urban evidences of the new trend towards knowledge based urbanism can be observed around Doha including iconic projects like Education City, Qatar Science and Technology Park, National Library, Qatar National Museum (QNM),

Figure 6. Doha waterfront as a manifestation of an unprecedented development in the last decade (Author)

and Museum of Islamic Art (MIA). Architecture and urbanism, as various researchers have suggested, used to be the physical representation of Muslim communities' creativity, and positive contributions in mankind development (Hawker, 2008; Al-Hahtlul, 1981; Hakim, 1986). Specifically art and architecture were seen in some historical eras as a manifestation of science, cosmology and geometry (Brend, 1992; Hillenbrand, 1998; Grabar, 1983, Nasr, 1987). In the Middle East, museums were geared towards the elite and well-educated minority in addition to foreigners and tourists (Alraouf, 2016). However, museums are now using a different approach to blend in the cities where they are located and expand their target audience by engaging all segments of the local community (Hein, 2000; Anderson, 2004; Black, 2005). Within the Gulf context, the last five years have witnessed extensive and rapid growth in museum activity, with the regeneration of existing museums, the founding of major new ones, and the creation of international satellite museums ((Bharadwaj, 2012; Erskine-Loftus,2013; Exell and Rico, 2014; Wakefield, 2015). MIA in Doha is an interesting example in showing how museums are moving from independent and isolated buildings to a vibrant urban entity where exhibition spaces, public places, educational facilities and entertainment venues are blended harmoniously. To learn more about these projects, I would start with the two iconic museums MIA and QNM as they are both helping in envisioning Doha as a new arts capital in the Middle East. MIA opened its door to visitors in December 2008. Pei took inspiration from the thrilling geometry of Ahmad Ibn Tulun Mosque in the heart of Islamic Cairo (Bharadwaj, 2012). The museum is a contemporary representation of generative architecture produced from applying three dimensional geometrical complexities (Jodidio, 2009). Despite the building's size and purpose, the architecture seems positively modest. Humbleness and modesty are underlying values of Islamic architecture and urbanism (Hillenbrand, 1998). MIA situated Qatar on a global stage, connected it to regional and local architectural trends, and enabled it to display its adherence to the creation of KBUD (Alraouf, 2008; 2012).

Without places for active and passive socialization, with no opportunity for casual and formal interactions, our cities and towns would be no more than agglomerations of privatized spaces and buildings, devoid of the space for the individual to be a complete citizen: a landscape that affords a limited ability to explore, create, express and share; to encounter difference and learn; and to confront, tolerate and resolve. Mehta, V. (2015).

Qatar Museums (QM) which constructs the umbrella underneath MIA and other museums are covered, has its own cultural development strategy for Qatar. Subsequently, constructing museums would substantiate Qatar's vision for Doha as an emerging knowledge city amid other Gulf Cities. Marking the next stage of its program to develop Qatar into a hub of culture and communications for the Gulf region and the world, the Qatar Museums (QM) revealed its plans for the new National Museum of Qatar, as expressed in a striking and evocative design by Pritzker Prize-winning architect Jean Nouvel. The project is also seen as manifestation of knowledge based urban development trend in Doha and other Qatari cities. Unlike the MIA that was situated on a man-made island in the bay, the QNM is at the south end of Doha's Corniche, QNM will be located on a 1.5 million-square-foot site where the old museum is in the city's heart. Unlike Pei with the MIA who looked to architecture of Muslim communities for inspiration, Nouvel looked locally to the actual site, environment and adjacent Gulf coast. The organic design allowed the new museum to literally embrace the old museum and intensify its value, emphasizing the appreciation of the old heritage. The masses of the new museum articulated around the old one give a message of integration and appreciation rather than separation and discontinuity between old and new. Precisely, the form of the desert rose, a unique feature of the Gulf coast, made a huge impact on the architect's quest for a local natural element to be reinterpreted geometrically to provide the formal composition of the museum. A move towards being a regional center for education, knowledge and culture is the new aspired sense of identity for Qatar. The two museums, MIA and QNM, are designed and planned to engage the community in various activates some of which transcend the typical role of the museum as a mere container of art works. The rational here is related to the necessity of confronting the fact of limited museum goers in the Gulf. The urban scenarios suggested by the design of the two museums allow people to be attracted via unique amentias like the open park at MIA with its regular concerts, bazaars and recreational activities for families of locals and expatriates alike. The MIA Park proved to be the primary destination for visitors as it was concluded from my numerous interviews with park visitors.

Figure 7. I. M. Pei was inspired by the architecture and geometrical poetics of Ibn Tulun Mosque in the heart of Cairo, Egypt. Such geometrical structure acts as an icon and a landmark in the visual fabric of Doha (Author)

Figure 8. The construction of the unique architectural and urban composition of Qatar National Museum (Courtesy of QM)

Figure 9. The vibrancy of MIA Park and its promenade overlooking Doha's skyline (Author)

Another keystone in the vision of Qatar as a platform for KBUD is manifested in projects related to the culture of education, research and knowledge dissemination. Education City (EC) is creating a culture of research and knowledge which is located in a unique campus on the outskirts of Doha (See Alraouf's holistic analysis of EC in this volume). EC hosts branch campuses of some of the world's leading universities, as well as numerous other educational and research institutions. EC is envisioned as a hub for the generation of new knowledge: a place that provides researchers with world-class facilities, a pool of well-trained graduates, the chance to collaborate with like-minded people, and the opportunity to transfer ideas into real-world applications. To be confident that EC is playing its social role within Doha, a deliberate effort is geared towards the internal and external integration of EC with greater Doha. To achieve this goal some strategies were suggested including the borderless campus, inviting local community to use the city's facilities, providing new amenities which speak to the needs of the surrounding community and the residents of Qatar as a whole. On the same path, Qatar's Science and Technology Park (QSTP) aims at turning Doha into a vibrant science and technology hub and attracting and retaining highly skilled employees are outlined in the Qatar Strategic Plan 2030. QSTP was established to provide the ideal environment to develop and market hi-tech intensive innovations and products and for providing services and locations with international standards for global companies to incubate new technological projects. The fact that QSTP is located close to EC's top universities adds a positive element particularly when it comes to research collaboration, innovation, and creativity.

EMBRACING LOCAL HERITAGE AND GLOBAL URBANISM

Due to the urban impact of oil revenues in the late 70s and 80s, most Gulf countries have neglected and demolished their heritage in their accelerated effort to modernize their cities (Al-Buainain, 1999; Davidson, 2009; Formherz, 2012; Rabbat, 2014). As illustrated earlier, a well balanced mixture of local and global approaches in developing Doha's architecture and urbanism highlights the emerging urbanity of the city. While the Waterfront's development is characterized with icons and signatures from the top architects of the world, a good number of projects which preserve, conserve and promote local culture

Figure 10. Qatar's Science and Technology Park, QSTP. (Author)

and architectural heritage can be observed. To substantiate my point of view regarding the importance of local architecture and urbanism, I will provide a short analysis of some projects which substantiate this trend of development. One interesting project which brings people together to enjoy leisure time and also confront cultural and knowledge experiences is The Cultural Village (Katara). Katara, Qatar's cultural village is situated on Doha's eastern coast at West Bay, near the Qatar International Exhibition Center. Katara's concept is to create an environment suitable for nurturing and activating the cultural and innovative activities in the country; to be a cultural hub and meeting place for the educated and creative; to raise public cultural awareness through festivals, exhibitions, forums and other cultural events; to conduct researches and studies relevant to the objectives and activities of Katara; and to invest in the buildings and facilities.

Another unique example is Souq Waqif was originally a weekly market for local Bedouins. The souq acquired its name "Waqif," which means "standing" in English because merchants stood up to peddle their goods. Coinciding with the emerging of modern Qatar, the souk developed to expand in space and activities. The Souq recent renovation is considered one of the most successful projects which took place within Doha in the last decade. It has become one of Doha's most popular sites. After renovation, Souq Waqif becomes a showcase of traditional architecture, handicrafts and folk art. The Souq evokes the feeling of traditional Qatar heritage. The successful renovation highlights the nobility and wisdom behind the region's traditional architecture in the face of modern construction devoid of any cultural identity. This traditional experience made Souk Waqif imperative and the prime place to visit for locals, expatriates and tourists alike. Souq Waqif was nominated for prestigious Aga Khan Award for Architecture in the 2010 cycle. It has been described as a revitalization project, a unique architectural revival of one of the most important heritage sites in Doha aimed to reverse the dilapidation of the historic structures and remove inappropriate alterations and additions.

After renovation, Souq Waqif becomes a showcase of traditional architecture, handicrafts and folk art. The Souq evokes the feeling of traditional Arabic heritage. Beginning in 2004, it was renovated according to traditional Qatari architectural principles and by using authentic materials (Tichar, 2010;

Atar and Abdullah, 2006). The renovation has returned it to a typical 19th century souq; an intricate maze of streets offers a natural shelter from the country's harsh climate (Kaaki, 2008). The successful renovation highlights the nobility and wisdom behind the region's traditional architecture in the face of modern construction devoid of any cultural identity. According to Mohamed Ali Abdulla (2006, p: 13), the architectural designer of the souq, the renovation and restoration plan was based on number of evidences and principles. A comprehensive study of Qatar traditional architecture, analysis of Ariel photos captured the souq's urban fabric in the 40[s] and 50s of last century, archival records, building records and finally local elderly people narrative of place memories structured the renovation plan This traditional experience made Souk Waqif imperative and the prime place to visit for locals, expatriates and tourists alike. The spatial experience currently provided is so unique. Strolling in open air along the winding souk streets and the twisting narrow alleyways is itself an interesting journey; evoking a sense of connecting to the past and reliving Qatar's ancestors lives before development (Abdullah, 2006; Nafi, 2015, Alraouf, 2012).

CONCLUDING REMARKS

As people and capital move more freely around the world, people will have the option to choose which area to live. This creates competition among global cities. Qatar is using the design and planning of the built environment to disseminate a positive message and to create a global and regional brand promoting the quality of life expected in its cities. Contemporary Qatari cities are being designed to attract knowledgeable and entrepreneurial people from around the globe to their locals so that the state may benefit socially and economically from the ideas, goods and services provided by such people. Doha has gained global significance through the growth of knowledge economy related projects. The city's new urban development and its spatial qualities contribute to the global attractiveness of Doha for knowledge

Figure 11. The daily and weekly events adding to the vibrancy of the Souq and sustaining its status as a prim destination in Qatar (Source: Author)

economy investments, firms and people. Such urbanism fulfills the requirements of Knowledge workers coming to the city from literally every spot of the globe anticipating an attractive smooth quality of life which would foster their creativity and innovation. While Dubai's model was based on glittering facades, high-end hotels, artificial islands, huge shopping malls, and the tallest constructions of the world, Doha strategically decided to move to another development model. A model that would better prepare the city to go beyond oil and attracts people from all over the world to settle in Doha as a new center for education, research and culture (Alraouf, 2012; 2016). Therefore, Doha's regional and global importance has amplified significantly over the last decade. The city of Doha is experiencing continual rapid growth. Maintaining the current growth of its urban population and fostering quality of life is seen as critical to the future development of the country, as indicated in the national development strategy 2011–2016 (QSDP, 2011). From an urban planning perspective, the last decade in Doha's urbanity is characterized by a paradigmatic shift towards Knowledge-based urban Development as a base for city planning and development. The rational was the commitment to go beyond the oil economy and move towards the post carbon era. Also, this direction was related to the realization that Dubai can't be the model for every single city in the Gulf or the Middle East.

Qatar, considering the paramount importance of its culture and identity, is not aiming at copying the model of Dubai, rather maintaining an economic boom without compromising its own culture. Qatar acknowledged culture as a main catalyst for a new era of development. Knowledge based society as Qatar national vision suggests, considers culture as a crucial asset that should be preserved. The holistic understanding of culture implies not only preserving the value of the past but moving aggressively towards the knowledge and education paradigm. Knowledge economy and the commitment towards transforming Doha into a creative and knowledge city govern every step the Qatar government is taking to shape the future of its Capital city, Doha. Hence, the government emphasizes the importance to embrace Qatari culture and identity, ensuring that development will not have a negative impact on culture and social norms. Looking at the major measures taken by the government, Qatar's path looks optimistic in terms of ensuring that economic development will not compromise its culture. With an unprecedented financial resources and political commitment, Qatar is constructing a new brand "Dohaization" which would be disseminated within the Gulf and the Middle East. Dohaization is a brand but also a continuous dynamic process. A large part of the motivation behind the projects is clearly the desire to establish Qatar as both a tourist destination and as an ideal place where knowledge workers might be prepared to relocate. Making global and knowledge workers happy by innovating and creating might be the new definition of 21st century urban knowledge and creative city. Qatar acknowledged culture as a main catalyst for a new era of development. Knowledge-based society as Qatar national vision suggests, considers culture as a crucial asset that should be preserved. Knowledge economy and the commitment towards transforming Doha into a creative and knowledge city govern every step the Qatar government is taking to shape the future of its Capital city, Doha. Hence, the government emphasizes the importance to embrace Qatari culture and identity, ensuring that development will not have a negative impact on culture and social norms. Looking at the major measures taken by the government, Qatar's path looks optimistic in terms of ensuring that economic development will not compromise its culture. In sum, Qatar and its capital city Doha seem to provide a motivating case on how radical, daring, and courageous decisions and transformations are needed in the age of sever urban competitions regionally and globally.

REFERENCES

Abdullah, M., & Atar, M. (2006). *Souq Waqif.* Doha: Al Diwan Al Amiri.

AKDN. (2013). *AKDN – Aga Khan Development Network.* Retrieved from http://www.akdn.org/architecture/project.asp?id=3564 〉

Al Buainain, F. (1999). *Urbanisation in Qatar: A Study of the Residential and Commercial Land Development in Doha City, 1970 -1997* (Ph.D. Thesis). University of Salford, Salford, UK.

Al-Kholaifi, M. J. (2003). *The Traditional Architecture in Qatar.* Doha: National Council for Culture, Arts and Heritage. (In Arabic)

Al-Thani, A. (2011). *The Paradox of Development: A Comparison between.* Dubai, UAE: Intellectual Magazine of SFS-Q.

Alraouf, A. (2017). Interrogating Qatar's Urbanity as a Catalyst for Building Knowledge-Based Societies and Economies. In R. G. Bertelsen, N. Noori, & J.-M. Rickli (Eds.), *Strategies Of Knowledge Transfer For Economic Diversification In The Arab States Of The Gulf* (pp. 53–66). London: Gerlach Press.

Alraouf, A. A. (2008). Emerging Middle Eastern Knowledge Cities: the Unfolding Story. In T. Yigitcaular & V. Koray (Eds.), *Knowledge Based Urban Development: Planning and Application in the Information Era* (pp. 240–259). IGI Global. doi:10.4018/978-1-59904-720-1.ch014

Alraouf, A. A. (2010). *From Knowledge to Creativity Economy, Qatar Urbanity Transformed. In Third Knowledge Cities Summit (KCS) 2010* (pp. r16–r19). Melbourne, Australia: Academic Press.

Alraouf, A. A. 2011. Assembling Identity for an Emerging Urbanity. Doha, Qatar, as a Creative City. *The City: 2nd International Conference The City: Culture, Society, and Technology.*

Alraouf, A. A. 2012. An Emerging Urbanity in Knowledge Economy Paradigm: The Case of Doha, *Qatar. International Conference on Realigning Power Geometries in the Arab World.* Leipzig University.

Anderson, G. (2004). *Reinventing the Museum, Historical and Contemporary Perspectives on the Paradigm Shift.* AltaMira Press.

Anholt, S. (2009). *Places: Identity, Image and Reputation.* Palgrave Macmillan. doi:10.1057/9780230251281

Bharadwaj, V. (2012). *Museums, Cultural Jewels in the Gulf.* NYTimes.com

Black, G. (2005). *The Engaging Museum: Developing Museums For Visitor Involvement.* London: Routledge.

Carrillo, F. J. (2005). *Knowledge Cities: Approaches, Experiences, and Perspectives.* Butterworth-Heinemann.

Davidson, C. M. (2008). *Dubai: The Vulnerability of Success.* Colombia University Press.

Dinnie, K. (2011). *City Branding: Theory and Cases.* Palgrave Macmillan. doi:10.1057/9780230294790

El Mallakh, R. (1979). *Qatar, Development of an Oil Economy.* London: Croom Helm.

Erskine-Loftus, P. (2013). *Reimagining Museums: Practice in the Arabian Peninsula*. Cambridge, MA: MuseumsEtc.

Evans, G. (2009). Creative Cities, Creative Spaces and Urban Policy. *Urban Studies (Edinburgh, Scotland)*, *46*(5-6), 1003–1040. doi:10.1177/0042098009103853

Florida, R. (2002). *The Rise of the Creative Class*. New York: Basic Books.

Florida, R. (2005). *Cities and the Creative Class*. New York: Routledge.

Florida, R. (2008). *Who's your city?* New York: Basic Books.

Fromherz, A. (2012). *Qatar: a Modern History*. Washington, DC: Georgetown University Press.

Gehi, J. (2010). *Cities for People*. Island Press.

Gray, M. (2011). *A Theory of 'Late Rentierism' in the Arab States of the Gulf.* Occasional Paper No. 7, Center for International and Regional Studies, Georgetown University School of Foreign Service in Qatar.

Gray, M. (2013). *Qatar: Politics and the Challenges of Development*. Boulder, CO: Lynne Rienner Publishers.

Harvey, D. (2009). *Social Justice and the City (Geographies of Justice and Social Transformation)* (Revised edition). University of Georgia Press.

Hassan, A. (1994). *City planning in the state of Qatar. Doha*. Doha: Qatar University Publications. (In Arabic)

Hillenbrand, R. (1998). *Islamic Art and Architecture*. London: Thames & Hudson.

Jaidah, I., & Bourennane, M. (2010). *The History of Qatari Architecture 1800-1950*. Skira.

Jodidio, P. (2009). *Museum of Islamic Art, Doha, Qatar*. New York: Prestel.

Jodido, P. (2014). *The New Architecture of Qatar* (1st ed.). New York: Skira Rizzoli Publications.

Kaaki, L. (2008). *The stunning renovation of Souq Waqif.* Arab News. Retrieved from http://archive.arabnews.com

Kamrava, M. (2013). *Qatar: Small State, Big Politics*. New York: Cornell University Press.

King, A. D. (2004). *Spaces of Global Cultures, Architecture, Urbanism, Identity*. London: Routledge.

Kotler, P. (1993). *Marketing Places*. Free Press.

Landry, C. (2006). *The Art of City Making*. London: Earthscan Publications Ltd.

Landry, C., & Wood, P. (Eds.). 2007. The Intercultural City: Planning for Diversity Advantage. London: Earthscan Publications Ltd.

Lorimer, J. (1970). *Gazetteer of the Persian Gulf.* Dohah.

Mehta, V. (2015). *Public Space*. London: Routledge.

Nafi, S. I., Alattar, D. A., & Furlan, R. (2015). Built Form of the Souq Waqifin Doha and User's Social Engagement. *American Journal of Sociological Research*, *5*(3), 73–88.

Nagy, S. (2000). Dressing Up Downtown: Urban development and government public image in Qatar. *City & Society*, *12*(1), 125–147. doi:10.1525/city.2000.12.1.125

Othman, N. (1984). *With Their Bare Hands: The Story of the Oil Industry in Qatar*. London: Longman.

Qatar General Secretariat of Development Planning (QSDP). (2009). *Qatar National Vision 2030. Advancing Sustainable Development, Qatar's Second Human Development Report*. Gulf Publishing and Printing Company.

Qatar General Secretariat of Development Planning (QSDP). (2011). *National Development Strategy 2011- 2016*. Doha: Gulf Publishing and Printing Company.

Qatar National Development Framework (QNDF). (2016). *The Ministry of Municipality and Environment*. Author.

Qatar Statistics Authority. (2015). *QSA Population*. Retrieved February 22, 2015, from http://www.qsa.gov.qa/eng/populationstructure.htm

QSDP. (2011). *Qatar General Secretariat of Development Planning National Development Strategy 2011–2016*. Doha, Qatar: Gulf Publishing and Printing Company.

Rahman, H. (2005). *The emergence of Qatar: the turbulent years, 1627-1916*. London: Kegan Paul.

Richer, R. (2009). *Conservation in Qatar: Impacts of Increasing Industrialization. Center for International and Regional Studies (CIRS)*. Qatar: Georgetown University.

Rico, T., & Exell, K. (Eds.). (2014). *Cultural Heritage in the Arabian Peninsula - Debates, Discourses and Practices*. London: Ashgate.

Roberts, D. B. (2015). *Qatar: Securing the Global Ambitions of a City-state*. London: C Hurst & Co Publishers Ltd.

Sassen, S. (2001). The Global City: New York, London, Tokyo (2nd ed.). Academic Press. doi:10.1515/9781400847488

Thierstein, A., & Schein, E. (2008). Emerging Cities on the Arabian Peninsula: Urban Space in the Knowledge Economy Context. *Archnet-IJAR: International Journal of Architectural Research*, *2*(2), 178–195.

Ulrichsen, K. C. (2011). *Insecure Gulf: The End of Certainty and the Transition to the Post-oil Era*. London: C Hurst & Co.

Wakefield, S. (2015). Museum Development in the Gulf: Narrative and Architecture. In K. Mitchell & G. Katodrytis (Eds.), *UAE and the Gulf: Architecture and Urbanism Now. Architectural Design* (pp. 20–27). London: Wiley. doi:10.1002/ad.1851

Weil, S. (2007). *Making Museums Matter*. Smithsonian Institution Press.

White, A. (2010). How Doha's Dollars are changing the World. Arabian Business, 11(28), 26-34.

Wiedmann, F. (2010). *Post-oil Urbanism in the Gulf*. Stuttgart, Germany: University of Stuttgart.

Wiedmann, F. (2012). Post-oil Urbanism in the Gulf: New Evolutions in Governance and the Impact on Urban Morphologies. Academic Press.

Wippel, S. (Ed.). (2014). *Under Construction: Logics of Urbanism in the Gulf Region*. London: Ashgate.

Wood, P., & Landry, C. (2008). *The Intercultural City: Planning for Diversity Advantage*. London: Earthscan.

Woodman, E. (2008). *I.M. Pei's MIA opens in Doha*. Retrieved from http://www.bdonline.co.uk/story.asp?storycode=3129204

Zahlan, R. S. (1979). *The Creation of Qatar*. London: Harper and Row Publishers Inc.

Zahlan, R. S. (1998). *The Making of the Modern Gulf States: Kuwait, Bahrain, Qatar, the United Arab Emirates, and Oman*. Reading, UK: Ithaca Press.

Chapter 5
Egypt's Knowledge-Based Development:
Opportunities, Challenges, and Future Possibilities

Amal Adel Abdrabo
Alexandria University, Egypt

ABSTRACT

This chapter discusses both the dominant theoretical paradigms that appear within Egypt's ICT policies since the early nineteenth century along with the practical steps of implementation of those policies in reality that may/may not depict such theoretical paradigms. Following a qualitative approach (using SWOT analysis, FGDs, and in-depth interviews), this chapter compares between the mission, vision, and goals of different ICT policies and their application in reality within four cases of the Egyptian KPs, which are the City of Scientific Research and Technological Applications in Burg Al-Arab, Bibliotheca Alexandrina "BA", Smart Village in Giza "SV", and finally Information Technology Institute "ITI". The main question is: What are the opportunities and challenges that Egypt faces in its endeavor to transform each of the national economy into a knowledge-based economy, the Egyptian citizens into knowledge citizens, the cities into knowledge cities, and the whole Egyptian society into a knowledge society?

BACKGROUND

Global Milestone Forums and Local Knowledge-Based Initiatives

Globally, the World Summit on the Information Society (WSIS) was held in four phases. The first phase took place in Geneva, hosted by the Government of Switzerland from 10 to 12 December 2003, the second phase took place in Tunis, hosted by the Government of Tunisia from 16 to 18 November 2005, the third phase was in New York City in the United States 15-16 December 2015, and finally the WSIS fourth phase returned to Geneva early this year (12-16 June 2017). Since its first phase, WSIS has been held annually with several interim preparatory meetings each year. The main idea behind WSIS started

DOI: 10.4018/978-1-5225-3734-2.ch005

Copyright © 2018, IGI Global. Copying or distributing in print or electronic forms without written permission of IGI Global is prohibited.

from The Millennium Development Goals (MDGs- 2000) to establish the foundations for an Information Society for all people, reflecting the myriad different interests at stake; in order to "develop" our human communities. However, in order to develop within the Information Societies, economies should go beyond the traditional definition of development using the tangible assets and the natural limited resources, and instead begin generating intangible assets in terms of knowledge creation and investment in human capital. Considering the case of Egypt, the question here is: Does the Egyptian government follow this global trend regarding achieving "Knowledge-Based Development" within Egyptian society? To answer this question, two steps must be followed; first, examination of different knowledge-based public policies and strategies. Second, examination of whether, and how, these policies have been implemented in reality.

Locally, since the early Nineteenth Egypt showed a commitment to the global development discourse where new Knowledge-Based Urban Development policies (KBUD) were issued and new projects of Knowledge Precincts (KPs) were initiated. Since the beginning of the 1990s, Egypt has launched a series of Knowledge-Based Development strategies. The milestone steps of the Egyptian KBUD policies started with Egypt's National Vision for Information Society (2000- 2005); then Egypt's ICT National Strategy 2007- 2010[1]; followed by Egypt's ICT National Strategy 2012- 2017 (The Egyptian Digital Society in Knowledge Economy). Recently, during the last Economic Development Conference (EEDC) "Egypt The Future", Sharm El-Sheikh, 13-15th March 2015, the economic development strategy for the country was announced with a general aim of transforming Egypt into a knowledge-based society while fostering a knowledge-based economy through the launch of seven new KPs[2], one of which was declared to be the first Egyptian knowledge city known as The Capital Cairo (Egypt's 2030 Vision for Sustainable Development, 2016). However, many studies have shown that the process of creating a knowledge society cannot be considered as easy or fast, because it requires genuine support from all social agents including local government, citizens, civil society, and universities (Parry and Deog-Song 2007; Alraouf 2008; UNECA 2009; UNESCO 2016). Within this frame, KPs have been endorsed as the engines of KBD policies for cities that choose knowledge production as a key goal in their development strategy (Yigitcanlar 2008).

Figure 1. Knowledge-based global milestones initiatives (source: the researcher)

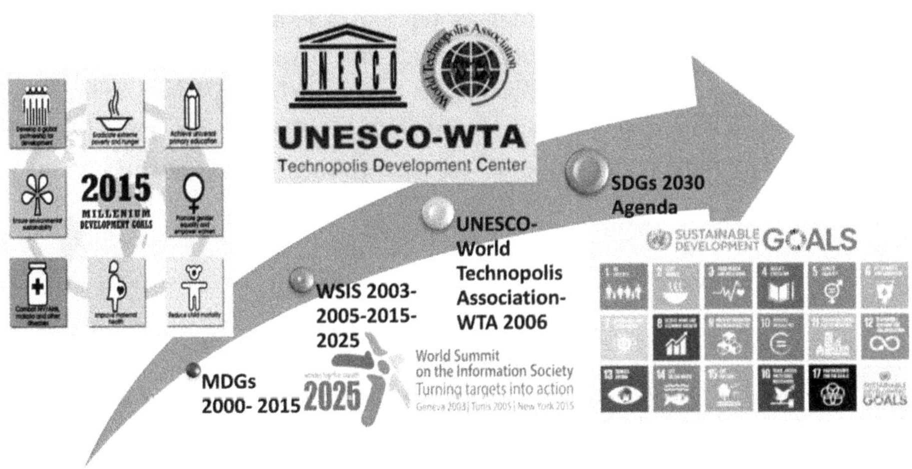

Figure 2. The Capital Cairo Project- Egypt's first Smart City (photo extracted from the Capital Cairo-Egypt's First Smart City website)[3]

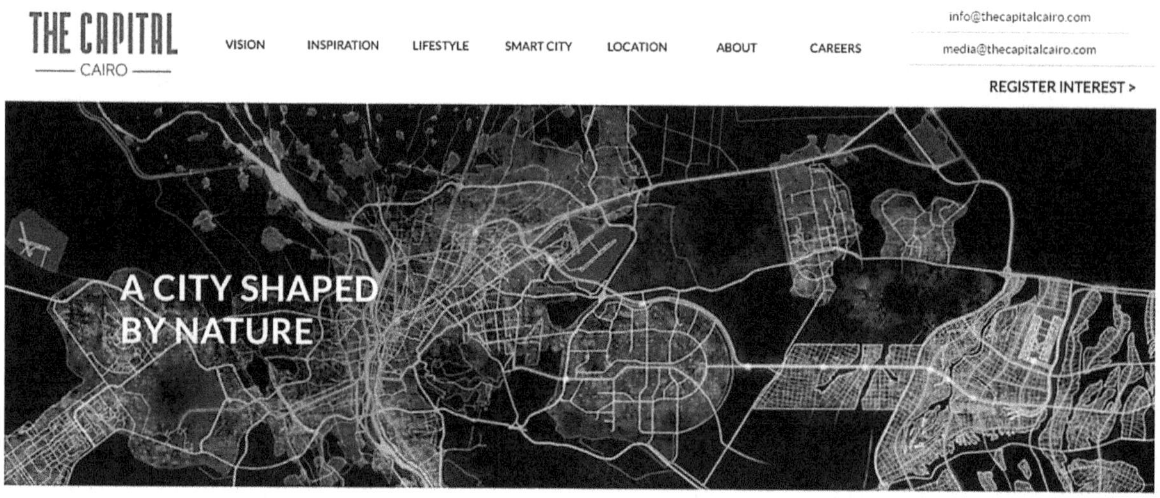

DEFINITIONS OF THE MAIN CONCEPTS WITHIN THE EGYPTIAN CONTEXT

Knowledge Precincts Concept

Within the frame of Knowledge-Based Urban Development "KBUD," knowledge precincts (KPs) have been endorsed as the engines of KBUD policies for cities that choose knowledge production as a key goal in their development strategy. A Knowledge Precincts "KPs" is also seen as an urban phenomenon and a distinct part of a city with a recognizable identity to which knowledge gives its unique character (Yigitcanlar 2008). Regarding the terminology "knowledge precincts (KPs)", the research relies on the definition of (Yigitcanlar 2008), who stated that precinct formation is actually an urban phenomenon. In other words, a knowledge precinct can be defined as "place-centered and highly refers to a distinct part of a city with recognizable identity to which knowledge gives its unique character" (Yigitcanlar, et al. 2008). The same study highlighted three major types of potential KPs zones; the first type called Knowledge-intensive service clusters, which operate in tandem with clusters of high-order financial service. The second type is scientific innovation clusters, which are largely based on high-tech, ICT, and biotechnology production within regional learning institutions. The last type called Creative industry clusters, which are largely based on cultural knowledge generating, social networking, business oppor-

Figure 3. Three major types of Knowledge Precincts (source: the researcher)

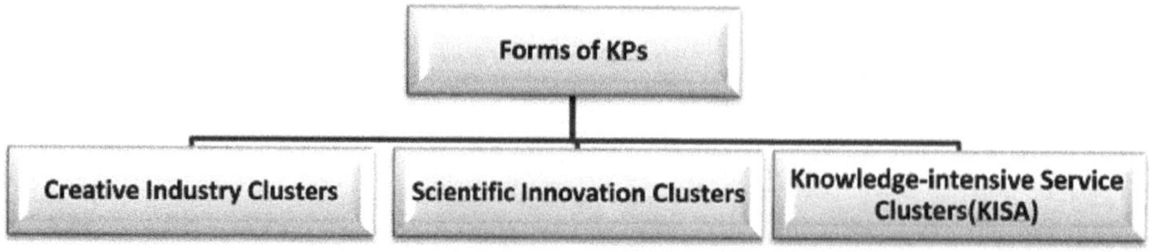

tunities, and face-to-face communications. Within this frame, KPs have been endorsed as the engines of KBD approach for cities that choose knowledge production as a key goal in their development strategy (Yigitcanlar et.al 2008).

The available literature around KPs shows three main types emerging: (Creative Industry Precincts, Scientific Innovation Precincts, and Knowledge-intensive Services Precincts). All types rely on the technological (IT) component as the main foundation of its services (Yigitcanlar et. al 2008). The Knowledge-intensive Services Precincts can be seen as knowledge hubs that are located in the heart of the global cities that provide the population with knowledge-intensive services. Within the Egyptian context we can find Smart Village (SV), Information and Technology Institute (ITI), and Bibliotheca Alexandrina (BA) as three examples of knowledge precincts. The first example, SV, is known for its highly intensive logistics services that are provided to the investment sector. The ITI case is known for its building capacities and human knowledge based development services. Finally Bibliotheca Alexandrina can be classified as a knowledge precinct designed for the purpose of creating and disseminating knowledge, which emphasizes the importance of the dimension of knowledge capital itself amongst other dimensions of KBUD.

Within the theoretical frame of Knowledge Society, Knowledge Precincts (KPs) can be considered as the key of Knowledge-based Development approach as it combines three main components by which a comprehensive development can be achieved. As seen within successful KPs worldwide, a typical successful KPs combines the efforts of three main motifs. The first one is science and technology activities that initiate the knowledge production process. The second main component is investment and industrial entities that facilitate the application of knowledge produced through research and technology entities. The last component is the governmental entities that support the entire process of knowledge production, dissemination, and transfer. This last component achieves its goals through providing the suitable and necessary technological infrastructure, encourage a secure and productive investment climate, facilitate land tenure, build roads to reach KPs and link them to their nearest urban areas and airports.

Additionally, Egypt has initiated new projects of knowledge precincts (KPs), such as[4]: ITI, SV, SRTA, BA. Thus, there exists the official discourse conveying not just KBD strategies, but also practical steps of implementing these strategies realistically through various mega projects of different KPs. The problem, as mentioned in previous studies (Alraouf 2008; Nasar 2008) is these former KPs presented isolated ivory towers. Therefore, the existence of these inactivated KPs may deplete the financial resources of

Figure 4. Knowledge precincts' triangle (source: the researcher)

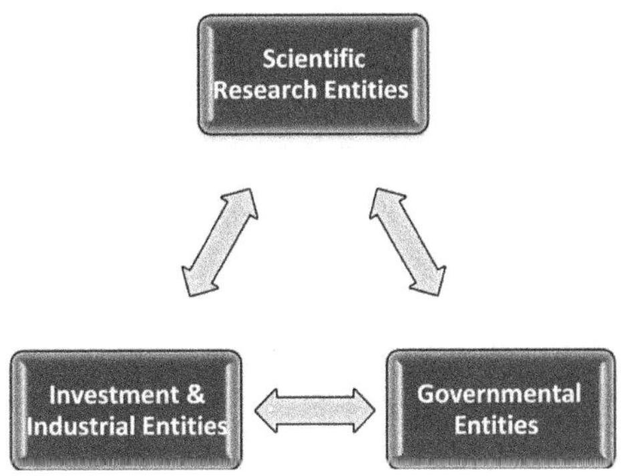

the state in vain without a visible impact on establishing and developing a Knowledge Society in Egypt. Unfortunately, very few of the above-mentioned specialized studies addressed the topic of knowledge society and KPs in Egypt within the field of Sociology. From an architecture perspective, (Alraouf, 2008) argues that examination of the contemporary status of global knowledge cities reveals tangible achievements and collective efforts for declaring and building such cities around the globe. On the contrary, Middle Eastern cities are building technologically isolated entities with the hope that they are promoting the knowledge city concept. This study derived its results from the analysis of some Arabian Knowledge projects, including Egypt's Smart Village, Dubai's Internet City and Knowledge Village, finally Qatar's Educational City and Science and Technology Oasis, and argues that studying such projects is insightful in the evaluation of emerging Middle Eastern Knowledge Cities. The study, drawing upon (Alraouf 2008), divided the former knowledge projects into 2 categories: The Arabian Gulf cities which achieved significant steps toward fostering a knowledge-based economy in their societies; and the other cities located in the remainder of the Middle East which still have considerable challenges to improve human resources quality and invest in human capital and unlimited creativity. Within another study, Alraouf argues that most of the KPs within the Arab region have failed to achieve their goals. He argues that some of the Egyptian KPs did not achieve their primary goals and turned out to be like Knowledge Ivory Towers, presenting isolated technological spots scattered around the city (Alraouf 2012).

Knowledge Society Concept

Theoretically, many studies have shown that the process of creating a knowledge society cannot be considered as an easy or fast process, because it needs a real support from all social agents including, but not limited to, local government, citizens, civil society organizations, and universities. Therefore, "Knowledge Society" cannot be defined as a society based only on knowledge sharing, because it includes capabilities to identify process, transform, disseminate and use information to build and apply knowledge for human development. It requires the empowering of a social vision that encompasses plurality, inclusion, solidarity and participation. Finally, in knowledge society everyone must be able to move easily through the flow of information submerging them, and to develop cognitive and critical thinking skills to distinguish between "useful" and "useless" information (UNESCO 2005). Thus, it is not merely about consuming different technological productions imported from the developed countries, as much as it is about the ability to create a unique version of knowledge.

In reality, since the 25th of January Revolution, Egyptian society has been going through crucial events and changes on a daily basis. Regarding the state's development policies, one can witness changes within these policies addressing a new creative development approach. Recently, Egypt's ICT strategy (2012-2017) pointed out that in order to achieve development in Egypt it is necessary to adopt the democratic revolution witnessed in Egyptian society by all its targets, investing in Egyptian potential with new perspectives regarding effective societal participation, and finding effective ways of achieving digital citizenship through innovative technology applications[5]. This last ICT strategy adopted four main goals: support democratic transformation; foster digital citizenship; support sustainable social development; and finally foster knowledge-based national economy. For the last goal to be achieved, the strategy set several steps: work to increase rates of knowledge workers to reach 75 thousand in PBO industry, 30 thousand in ICT domain, and 10 thousand in creativity fields; also work to increase number of knowledge hubs to reach 20 areas covering Egyptian society. All should work alongside toward increasing growth rates within ICT sector to reach 7-10% during the next five years. In addition, work must be done to increase the contribution of the telecommunications sector in the national income up to 5% of the return sovereign state, and the outsourcing exports to reach $2.5 billion, and expand the overall size of investment to $55 billion, with percentage up to 20%[6].

Comparing what is there within academia with what is there within the reality of society; two different forces can be noticed within the process of crafting different development policies. The first force is driven by the global economic and political transformations and can be known as an up-down influence from different international actors such as WB, IMF, UN. The second force is a down-up influence which highlights several political, economic, and social demands that have been raised by many inactive groups who engaged in the socio-political movement across the country during the last couple of years. With specific concentration on the development of national policies in Egypt in the post-January era, can it be said that they truly reflect people's needs now? Or do they just continue to mimic the successful global development experiments without regard to the special national characteristics, potentials and needs? What are the main goals of the three KPs which the study focuses on? Have these KPs managed to achieve their goals? Could these Egyptian KPs achieve a sustainable development according to the main criteria and indicators guiding KBUD approach? The study also will try to answer some subsidiary questions surrounding whether these KPs adopt new goals derived from new development approaches like KBD and KBUD?

The researcher works to utilize the existence of a genuine desire to rebuild Egyptian society on solid foundations considering the radical changes that have taken place at all levels for almost a decade. Thus, the main questions addressed within the following section are:

- Could these Egyptian KPs achieve comprehensive development according to the main criteria and indicators guiding KBD approach?
- Can these KPs adopt new goals derived from new development approaches like KBD?
- What are the main social dimensions of KBUD as shown within different Knowledge based development strategies in Egypt?

Knowledge-Based Urban Development Dimensions

Many scholars have argued that the concept of knowledge-based development has emerged as a new scientific movement, as a result of the growing role of knowledge in contemporary human societies and of the many transformations that globalization has engendered. They use KBD approach to represent both a theoretical and an applied strategic concept which in practice comprises three levels: cognitive capital, human capital, and social capital (Carrillo 2002).

Theoretically, this concept has strengthened its position within the evolutionary development themes and trends as an independent concept that conveys both a theoretical paradigm and a developmental strategy that is highly credible in those countries where the highest levels of sustainability and development have already been achieved (Center for Knowledge Systems, 2003). However, as a result of the misuse of that concept and the drawback that it does not cover all developmental dimensions, another complementary concept has emerged known as "knowledge-based urban development- KBUD", which is based upon the adoption of three additional comprehensive developmental goals that involve economic development, additions to human and social development, and finally increasing spatial relations and networking among knowledge precincts (Yigitcanlar et al 2008). Such conceptual evolution can be highlighted through the following illustration:

Figure 5. Illustrates the evolve of developmental goals to be achieved though different Knowledge-Based approaches (source: the researcher)

Based on the above mentioned, the study combines the objectives of the knowledge-based development approach and the knowledge-based urban development approach to arrive at a procedural definition of the social dimensions of knowledge-based development, which will guide the field study within the peculiar context of Egyptian society. Also helpful is the study of different KPs established within the urban context of Egyptian society in Alexandria, Cairo, and Giza, bearing in mind that the study addresses the previous theoretical approaches under one name, "Knowledge-Based Urban Development." The study examines the social dimensions of knowledge-based urban development driven by the dimensions extracted from theoretical heritage, literature review, and best practices and case studies globally. Four dimensions of knowledge-based urban development as defined by previous studies and the theoretical heritage are economic, social, environmental, and administrative dimensions, explained as follows:

Economic Development: generally increases the financial assets of the community by supporting all industrial and production activities that attract investments, create new employment opportunities, generate and produce knowledge. Eventually, this will improve the quality of life within society. Economic development, through the prism of knowledge-based development, also aims at achieving economic growth and prosperity through endogenous self-reliance on knowledge or local origin rather than depending on the permanent import of the latest global innovations and knowledge from abroad. Economic development reaches its main goal by transforming the economic system into a Knowledge Economy to achieve prosperity and create a general climate attractive to investment and business (Lever 2002).

Social Development: according to the Knowledge-Based Urban development perspective, seeks to develop the skills and knowledge of the population, as an essential means to achieve high levels of individual and collective development, along with high levels of societal achievements in general; ultimately to build and establish a knowledge society within urban areas based on social equity. This will lead to the development of Human Capital, promotion of diversity and independence, and hence the creation of a supportive climate for community dialogue and human development by supporting transformations, promotion of a culture of innovation and creativity, building societies in the upward direction from bottom to top based on human beings, changing cultural concepts supporting quality of life, productivity, work mastery and other concepts seen within knowledge-based societies as a basis for their development. It works also to change community culture and individuals mind-set in the direction of supporting the culture of innovation and creativity (Ovalle et. al 2004).

Environmental Development/Spatial development/ development of the place: promotes integrated and balanced development through the integration of human-produced environments from different urban buildings and enterprises with the surrounding natural environments, with a view to working towards creating spaces for living, working and recreational and leisure purposes, as well as providing spaces for community services within cities, taking into account the generation of minimal negative effects on the environment and the depletion of natural resources. In other words, knowledge-based development is an environmentally friendly development that promotes the sustainability and conservation of natural resources for future generations by conserving and developing natural resources by integrating them with the buildings of the projects of Knowledge Precincts. This relies on building a strong spatial network between the knowledge precincts, which play the role of spatial linkages within the framework of KBUD approaches and strategies. Finally achieves high-quality environmental sustainability, real developmental returns and the building of the so-called green environment (Knight 1995).

Institutional/Administrative development: KBUD approach considers governance as an integral part of management, planning and urban development processes, as Institutional development involves the development of policies, processes, roles and responsibilities that improve city management and the development of its performance. It controls how institutions and societies can achieve and guide their development goals. The institutional dimension of development aims to operationalize knowledge from a human and democratic perspective to serve the objectives of "knowledge humanization" and to make it a more human-oriented perspective, and strengthen collective learning processes in order to create balance between all dimensions of the developmental process within institutions that depend on the use of knowledge to achieve balance and synchronization of development efforts in all its dimensions. This synchronization and networking is the backbone of the achievement of knowledge-based development, which works to collect efforts of all involved beneficiaries and stakeholders (Yigitcanlar 2014).

From the foregoing, it is clear that knowledge-based development is both: a theoretical and applied approach, a development policy and a planning strategy, based on the achievement of development through four main dimensions: economic development, socio-cultural development, environmental development and administrative development. This is achieved by working to create a space for the production of knowledge within the community depending on the potential and resources that the communication and information technology ICT that facilitates the production of knowledge and its sustainable employment in development processes through different specialized projects of Knowledge Precincts.

Figure 6. Dimensions of Knowledge-Based Urban Development- KBUD (source: the researcher)

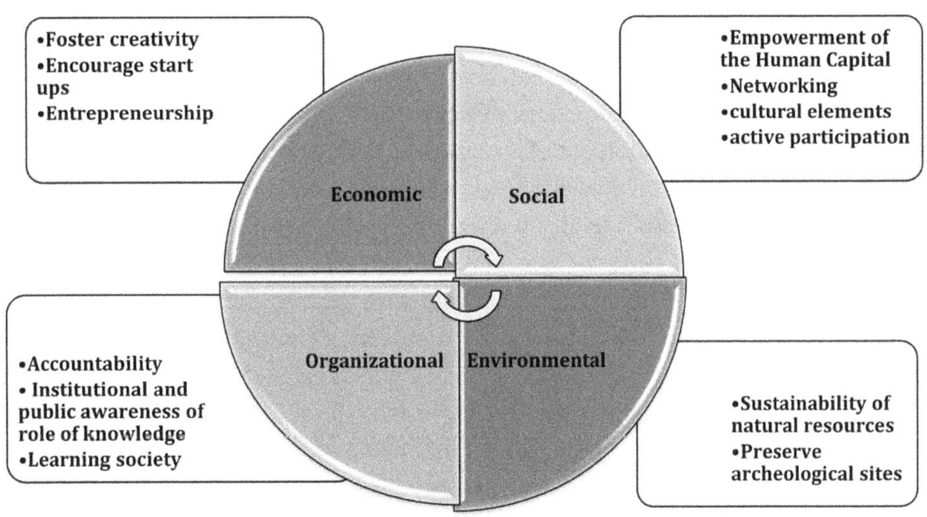

The analysis of different KBUD policies within the Egyptian context also reveals the importance of adopting a knowledge-based development perspective in its various dimensions is demonstrated by raising popular awareness for prosperity, economic progress, social justice and environmental sustainability, as well as the development of government institutions in accordance with the principles of strategic planning within state institutions, decision makers, and public policy makers. Thus, it may be preferable to ensure the success of future development plans of Egyptian society that the state institutions begin to look at the needs of the citizen and the nature of the radical changes that have struck the Egyptian public sphere as a result of the political transformations that have taken place during the last years starting 2011 till now, relying on development from the bottom and not from the top, which is consistent with seeing Amartya Sen of the fundamental freedoms of individuals is not only an end in itself, but also an important one, as it entails contributing to the expansion Freedoms for other aspects of the life of every human being, which ultimately is in the interest of development processes in general, and which it has divided into: (political freedoms, free use of economic installations and facilities, social opportunities, then ensuring transparency, and finally ensuring security protection or preventive security).

EGYPTIAN KNOWLEDGE PRECINCTS

Challenges and Opportunities

Given that there is very little literature on Knowledge Precincts in Egypt from a sociological point of view, the current research depended on qualitative methods in order to bridge the gap that exists in literature. During the fieldwork, the researcher conducted several in-depth interviews and focus group discussions with former ICT ministers, academic experts, and policy makers within the circles of KBD and KPs. Comparing what exists within academia with what exists within the reality of society, two different forces can be perceived within the process of crafting different development policies. The first force is driven by the global economic and political transformations and can be called as an up-down influence from different international actors such as WB, IMF, and UN agencies. The second force is a down-up influence which highlights a myriad of political, economic, and social demands that been raised by many inactive groups of people who engaged actively in the socio-political movement across the country during the last few years. The researcher also interviewed experts working in four Egyptian Knowledge Precincts: Smart Village (SV), City of Scientific Research and Technological Applications in Burg Al-Arab (SRTA-City), Bibliotheca Alexandrina (BA), and Information Technology Institute (ITI), using the theoretical lenses of Knowledge-based Development approach to evaluate to what extent different ICT policies[7] are mirrored in reality within the Egyptian context through an evaluation study of these four knowledge precincts.

The researcher applied the SWOT analysis in dealing with these in-depth interviews in order to identify four elements – internal strengths and weaknesses, plus their external opportunities and threats – of the working cases of Knowledge Precincts). The primary questions that emerged at this stage are if and how the Egyptian Knowledge Precincts contribute to establish an Egyptian knowledge society. Does Egypt have all required potentials to be transformed into a knowledge-based society within the coming fourteen years through establishing significant knowledge-based areas and knowledge precincts? What was the role played by these knowledge precincts in achieving the different dimensions of Knowledge-based Development? What are their internal elements of strength/ weakness? What are the external opportunities/ threats?

The distinctive characteristics of the four knowledge Precincts studied are diverse and varied: Institute of Information Technology-1992, City of scientific research and technological applications, Burj Al Arab city--1993, Smart Village project in Giza-year 2000, the Bibliotheca Alexandrina Project, 2002. Each formed a self-standing unit with different characteristics and conditions surrounding it from one Precinct to the other, this is illustrated by the reality of field study and the qualitative data of the in-depth interviews and focus group discussions, and from the statistics and ready-made data (vision/mission/ construction decisions) of each Precinct.

Information and Technology Institute (ITI)

As mentioned via the ITI website: The Information Technology Institute (ITI) was first established in 1993 under the affiliation of the Egyptian Cabinet's Information and Decision Support Center, with a mission to develop IT caliber to cater to the government's decision support functions, as well as the development of the ICT industry in Egypt. Camping on its success throughout the years, in 2005 the affiliation of the ITI moved to the Ministry of Communications and Information Technology as one of its main arms for ICT capacity building and industry development in Egypt. Within the MCIT's strategy led by His Excellence the Minister of Communications and Information Technology Eng. Yasser ElKady, to develop the ICT infrastructure and industry, transforming Egypt into a global digital hub. Information Technology Institute works to empower Egypt's youth with the tools and skills needed to develop and live in a knowledge-based society, while using the ICT tools to boost the country's competiveness, productivity and the national, regional & international development[8].

Figure 7. Information and Technology Institute, established in 1993, headquarter located in Smart Village, Giza Governorate with several branches spread over the country in: Ismailia, Alexandria, Mansoura governorates, Egypt (source: the researcher's fieldwork, May 2016)

Table 1. Information Technology Institute (ITI): opportunities and challenges

Internal Strengths/ Opportunities	Internal Vulnerabilities/ Challenges
1. Enlightened and responsible leadership that is committed to success and adopts personal initiatives to improve the human capital level of the Institute through pursuing a strict follow-up policy of level of achievement of the human product graduated from the ITI within the labour market. 2. Adoption of personal initiatives for the development of the institute and modification of its training programmes. 3. The existence of a follow-up policy on employment ratios among graduates. 4. Working to support organizational behaviours during the organizational structure of the Institute's staff (knowledge workers). 5. Promote a culture of teamwork and creativity. 6. Community responsibility of the Institute towards its local surroundings and society in partnering with the Ministry of Social Solidarity to support and train Productive Families to market their products and supporting the Port Authority with its technological needs in customs and others. 7. Flexibility in dealing with students applying to the institute in accepting papers, for example: modification of the deadline for admission of the Institute's enrolment papers according to the student exams schedule. 8. Investing in human capital. 9. Government support and legislative background are available as a basis for the work of the Institute and the achievement of its objectives. 10. Provide programs to support researchers working at public university institutes such as Digital Market Programs.	1. The Institute's policy does not include a corrective action in the case of a weakened human capital graduated from the institute. The Institute's policy requires that the operating ratios be followed up only without any corrective actions. 2. Lower operating ratios for the graduates of the Information Technology Institute in recent years. 3. Lack of numbers of the qualified staff of Knowledge Workers working in the Institute, which is limited by the qualitative weakness of the graduates of Egyptian universities along with the absence of new employment opportunities at the Institute. 4. The working staff at the institute is used to leave their posts for other overseas jobs and better jobs abroad. 5. Increased administrative and managerial burdens on the current staff of the Institute. 6. The lack of continuous coordination between the University institutions and faculties and the ITI to communicate with students and urge them to submit to the various training programmes offered by the Institute; Although that ITI's programmes are financially subsidized by the Government and provide financial stipend for students every month. 7. Limited time available for training programmes in general. 8. Non-participation of staff of the Knowledge Workers of the Information and Technology Institute in the drawing and development of the Institute's policies, strategies, vision, mission. Following a top-down approach when developing the institute's strategy. In case being asked for their opinion of the institute's policy, it is done informally and uncorroborated; it is merely an oral expression of views. 9. Higher proportions of female trainees compared to male applicants, at the same time parents are not encouraged to allow their daughters accept any job opportunity available abroad that would require travelling and taking evening shifts, which affects the employment ratios of graduates of the Institute in general.
External Opportunities	**External Challenges/ Risks**
1. There are future opportunities for networking with Alexandria University, particularly with the TAFL Center- Faculty of Arts (Teaching Arabic as Foreign Language) to rely on the TAFL's foreign students to train the institute's students in the English conversation[9]. 2. Contribute to the establishment of a sustainable learning society in Egypt. 3. Investing in people to achieve Comprehensive Development within the Egyptian society in general, through providing transformative training programmes to change the course of graduates of the university and qualify them for real jobs opportunities in a competitive labour market. 4. The opportunity to hold future bilateral partnerships with research, scientific and university institutions specializing in Egyptian society such as the Japanese University, the German University, The American University, the Canadian University, the Arab Academy for Science and Technology and the City of scientific research and technological applications in Burj al-Arab. 5. Potential for networking and future partnerships with companies working in the Arab countries in the outsourcing industry (BPO). 6. Emphasize the normative and moral dimension and strive for comprehensive community development by inculcating a culture of hard work, diligence and teamwork. 7. To affirm the idea of community role models and to inculcate the positive values of a culture of innovation, creativity and the importance of scientific research. 8. Promote a culture of success based on the importance of imagination, knowledge, culture and innovation. 9. It is possible to use information technology to change the behavioural and cultural values of Egyptian society and to develop certain needed behaviours by disseminating success stories to information technology professionals.	1. Deterioration of the outsourcing industry (Business Process Outsourcing- BPO) in general and decreasing employment opportunities at customer service centres (Call Centers) within the Egyptian society. 2. The failure of others to play their respective roles in the field of outsourcing, attracting and encouraging investments in the Egyptian market to provide employment opportunities for graduates of the Institute, in particular the Information Technology Industry Development Authority (ITIDA). 3. The lack of a business market for the BPO industry within Egyptian society to absorb the graduating human capital graduated from the institute. 4. The level of the Egyptian educational institution has deteriorated, which has had a negative impact on the level of university graduates applying for training programmes who apply for the Institute's various transformative training programmes. 5. Low quality of the graduated product from the public Universities. 6. The supremacy of the cultures of chaos and fraud and the lack of encouragement of innovation in Egyptian society in general. 7. The lack of clarity of strategic vision of ITI and the lack of clarity of practical steps to implement them. 8. Increase of the competitiveness within the global markets for outsourcing industry. The high cost of technical training in information technology domains in light of the accelerating technological changes and globalization processes. 9. Some training programmes and projects have been discontinued or suspended for their association with certain people and are being supported by the former political systems (for example, the Institute was supported by the former Prime minister Ahmed Nazeef).

The City of Scientific Research and Technology Applications (SRTA-City)

As mentioned through its main online page, The City of Scientific Research and Technological Applications (SRTA-City) is:

one of the leading research institutes in Egypt that was directed to the development and renovation of industry. A decision to develop a science park in the Alexandria region was reached in 1993 in order to acquire and improve scientific technologies in different areas of human life. The SRTA-City occupies 250 acres in the industrial area located at New Borg El Arab City, west of Alexandria. This region also inhabits about 40% of the Egyptian industry. The science park comprises 12 research centers to be developed at different intervals. The first stage of SRTA-City was inaugurated on the 13th of August, 2000 and included Genetic Engineering and Biotechnology Research Institute (GEBRI), Informatics Research Institute (IRI), Advanced Technology and New Materials Research Institute (ATNMRI) and Arid Lands Cultivation Research Institute (ALCRI). In addition, a Scientific & Technological Capabilities Development Center (STCDC) is fully functioning in the Dekhlia Branch and Investment zone. SRTA-City works to achieve various objectives[10].

According to the above mentioned, it seems that the Egyptian policy maker has initiated SRTA-City project to fulfill the objectives of a science park to generate the economic development in Egypt. A science park has to have many other facilities to reach that goal, among which centers of Scientific Excellence, startups, innovation and business incubators, training facilities, consultancy agencies; all to serve both economic and social developments of the Egyptian Society in general.

Figure 8. The City of Scientific Research & Technology Applications (SRTA-City), opened on the 13th of August 2000. New Borg Al Arab City, Alexandria Governorate, Egypt (source: the researcher's fieldwork, July 2013).

Table 2. The City of Scientific Research and Technology Applications (SRTA-City): opportunities and challenges

Internal Strengths/ Opportunities	Internal Vulnerabilities/ Challenges
1. Guided by the national visions and public policies of the state to define the city's operational policy. 2. Inter-governmental cooperation at the level of various ministries and bodies in the administration of the city (networking among different government actors that facilitate the work of SRTA-City). 3. The intensity of the scientific production of the city in the form of scientific research published globally and in form of local patents. 4. Knowledge Workers and researchers working in the city are seen as a strategic treasure and ambassadors to Egypt abroad at various universities and international research institutes.	1. The administrative pyramid of the city is an inverted pyramid (A broad administrative base and a few researchers at the top of the pyramid even though the city is specialized in the scientific research as a research and technology hub. 2. Dispersion of the decision between multiple governmental bodies requires their approval before real steps are taken for the development of SRTA-city. For example, Approval of projects within the city area requiring approval by several government agencies which has delayed the lunching of the investment area of SRTA-City for more than a decade now, since 1990's till the final approval was taken (The cornerstone of the investment zone was developed in early 2016). 3. Weak and conflicting legislative structure governing the production of scientific knowledge and research.
External Opportunities	**External Challenges/ Risks**
1. The visibility of the vision is that knowledge is the basis of the progress of contemporary societies. 2. Finalization of a new science and technology Law which will open new horizons and provide more opportunities for scientific research in the SRTA city, especially, and within the entire Egyptian society. 3. The beginning of the adoption of the concept/ term "Science and Technology Valleys" in the New Science Act. 4. Modify the legislative background in line with the requirements of contemporary global transformations. 5. Expansion of the vision of a possible transition to a knowledge economy in the areas of technological applications, the tourism industry and cinema. 6. The possibility of expanding the establishment of specialized technological zones at a horizontal level. 7. The possibility of increasing investment opportunities through the establishment of the investment zone, which offers opportunities for networking between the Research foundation, the Industrial Foundation, infrastructure institutions and basic services. 8. Opportunities for the creation of business incubators and support for small and medium-sized young entrepreneurs and entrepreneurs. 9. Increased opportunities to send researchers and experts in the field of scientific research abroad to obtain training. 10. Increased opportunities for self-reliance in the production and manufacture of technology.	1. The separation of the specialized scientific concepts from the experts' way of thinking from which the general strategies of such Precincts are developed and drawn. 2. The act on tenders and auctions hinders the importation of raw materials needed for scientific research. 3. The multiplicity and divergence of names, used to define these KPs, between the existing construction decisions and the operational policies and the names used by the experts working in those KPs (the conceptual confusion of the names used to refer to the knowledge precincts). 4. Poor funding opportunities for project creation and operation. 5. Deterioration of the level of the educational institution and the low level of graduates. 6. Lack of trained human capital to work in the field of scientific research. 7. Weak cooperation between industry institutions and scientific research institutions. 8. Lack of strong national industries already in place. 9. A community culture that hinders creativity and not conducive to innovation. 10. Weak research and development sectors located in factories. 11. Corruption of the system of promotions, and the recruitment of research institutions. 12. Government orientation to support major projects with far-reaching returns.

Smart Village

Smart Village was initiated as a "Business Park" as their home page describes:

SMART VILLAGES DEVELOPMENT AND MANAGEMENT COMPANY (SVC) was founded in November 2001 as a Public-Private-Partnership (PPP) investment with a mandate to establish and manage a branded chain of Technology cluster and Business parks-especially in three governorates of Cairo, Alexandria and Damietta- as well as variety of other products and services available here. We special-

Figure 9. Smart Villages Development and Management Company (SVC) 2000. Located in the 6th of October City, Giza Governorate, Egypt (source: the researcher's fieldwork, May 2016).

ize in the establishment and management of communities through innovative thought and practical work. Our multipurpose ecosystems are built on quality, collaboration and trust to the satisfaction of all stakeholders[11].

Bibliotheca Alexandrina

The Library of Alexandria was reborn in October 2002 to reclaim the mantle of its ancient namesake. It is not just an extraordinarily beautiful building; it is also a vast complex where the arts, history, philosophy, and science come together. Moreover, the myriad activities it offers have made it a place for open discussion, dialogue, and understanding. The Bibliotheca Alexandrina website conveys its rebirth, and later its mission, vision, and objectives[12]:

The New Library of Alexandria, the New Bibliotheca Alexandrina is dedicated to recapture the spirit of openness and scholarship of the original Bibliotheca Alexandrina. It is much more than a library. . . The Bibliotheca Alexandrina aims to be: A center of excellence in the production and dissemination of knowledge and to be a place of dialogue, learning and understanding between cultures and peoples. . .The unique role of the Library of Alexandria, as that of a great Egyptian Library with international dimensions, will focus on four main aspects, that seek to recapture the spirit of the original ancient Library of Alexandria. It aspires to be:

- *The world's window on Egypt.*
- *Egypt's window on the world.*
- *A leading institution of the digital age.*
- *A center for learning, tolerance, dialogue and understanding*[13].

Table 3. Smart Village: opportunities and challenges

Internal Strengths/ Opportunities	Internal Vulnerabilities/ Challenges
1. A genuine partnership between the public and private sectors while giving the opportunity to the private sector to work freely and the lack of control by the government sector overall project assets. 2. Provide a geographical space for the pooling and agglomeration of investment companies in a single place with all required infrastructure. 3. Starting from a clear working plan and strategy and periodic follow-up of the evolution and progress achieved since 2001 to the present time 2016 (SV Master Plan). 4. Creating an environment conducive to business and investment. 5. Standardization of exterior design and architectural character. 6. Strengthen the culture of beauty, following order and cleanliness. 7. Confirming the place factor and upgrading the human characteristics of its employees. 8. Strict adoption of the law without favouritism (the law applies to everyone). 9. Offering employment opportunities to train Egyptians by foreign experts through foreign companies operating in Egypt. 10. Providing services to the local community such as promoting a culture of belonging and preserving the cultural heritage.	1. Weak sources of funding and declining profits with the increasing financial burden of repayment of outstanding loan shares (financial difficulties). 2. Lack of publicity and marketing globally and even locally. 3. Difficulties associated with the changing political environment in Egyptian society The village was linked to the names of political figures such as former prime Minister Ahmed Nazeef.
External Opportunities	**External Challenges/ Risks**
1. Considering the Smart village as a center of civilized radiation with the possibility of transferring the SV's culture, style, and way of operating as a smart Technopole to the Egyptian society as a whole. 2. Provide opportunities to support initiatives to empower women and young people and promote entrepreneurship thinking and culture. 3. Strengthen the thought and culture of technological poles "technopole". 4. Support the creation of Centers of Excellence, Business Incubators and Science and Technology Valleys. 5. Provide real investment opportunities in people by supporting small and medium-sized industries and by supporting companies, emerging projects, and startups. 6. Support new trend and thinking of decentralization and to the importance of initiating real administrative reform within different governmental bodies. 7. Provide support for the new trend of legislative reforms and reform the system of laws and legislation stimulating investment and competitiveness.	1. The deterioration and weakness of the technological infrastructure of the Egyptian society in general. 2. Industrial separation from scientific research in Egyptian society. 3. Disruption of the political environment and the interruption of some projects and support provided to the village because these projects are linked to the name of former prime Minister Ahmed Nazeef. 4. The weakness of the product graduating from the educational institution (The Egyptian students graduated from the public universities). 5. Blurred vision (no clear strategic vision of the State is shared and implemented transparently with different categories of citizens). 6. The supremacy of community cultures that are impeding progress is not encouraging for innovation. 7. Domination of the culture of ugliness through the entire society with the failure of the Government to solve vital problems such as garbage collection and prevention of illegal residential buildings. 8. The supremacy of the culture of Administrative and governmental corruption. 9. Excessive interference by the government in future projects, especially with regard to the management of smart village projects all around the Egyptian society. 10. Lack of local capacity building to work with Smart Village projects (unqualified human capital while having large numbers of graduates in Egyptian universities Qualitative weakness of human capital versus quantitative increase in the number of specialists per year.

From the previous presentation, it is clear that there are many obstacles, or what can be termed as (threats) using SWOT analysis, that faces knowledge presents as a mechanism for implementing knowledge-based development policies, as followed:

Figure 10. Bibliotheca Alexandrina- BA, opened on the 16th of October 2002, Alexandria governorate-Egypt (source: the internet)

Table 4. Bibliotheca Alexandrina: opportunities and challenges

Internal Strengths/ Opportunities	Internal Vulnerabilities/ Challenges
1. Follow the policy of providing knowledge free of charge or at a simple cost. 2. Support for globally published Arabic content (Export local knowledge abroad/global dissemination of Egyptian knowledge). 3. Support for the Egyptian cultural and historical heritage in many ways. 4. Observance and compliance with intellectual property rights. 5. Take into account the scientific quality of the publication. 6. To decentralize the administrative, legislative and financial independence of the library and its direct subordination to the President of the Republic. 7. Adopt non-traditional advertising methods for the library, such as creating a private channel on YouTube site. 8. Inter-departmental administrative cooperation between the departments and units of the internal library.	1. Poor outreach to the public at street level to raise awareness of the role of the library, its achievements and the many services it provides. 2. Limit communication to specific cultural circles, which has reduced the visibility of the library on Egyptian street.
External Opportunities	**External Challenges/ Risks**
1. Partnering with the Egyptian public universities to train students and qualify them for the labour market, especially within domains associated with the work of libraries and the proofreading, maintaining, and preserving of historical manuscripts and others. 2. Dissemination of knowledge outside the spatial space of the Library to reach all over the Egyptian society (as known as The BA Embassies of Knowledge project[14]). 3. Support international networking after the library window Egypt to the World and window to the world on Egypt 4. International partnerships with global publishing houses and major international universities. 5. Support for networking at the African Level (known as BA Africa Networks project[15]).	1. The narrowed perception of some audiences (citizens) about the library as a limited geographical space that provides a set of books only; neglecting its cultural role in the production and dissemination of knowledge. 2. Give a bad impression of the library as a result of the security complications in the library perimeter.

1. The lack of clarity of the operational steps to achieve public policies and strategic visions.
2. The following a single top-down approach in the design of public policies for knowledge precincts.
3. Blurred names and the use of loose and variable concepts to refer to knowledge precincts.
4. The separation between industry institutions, scientific research institutions, and universities.
5. The relative separation of knowledge precincts from their societal surroundings as "fenced communities" and weakness of its mass communication.

FUTURE OPPORTUNITIES AND PROPOSED SOLUTIONS

From the foregoing, it is clear that networking between different types of knowledge precincts, whether at the local, regional or global levels. The study also emphasized the identification of the social dimensions of knowledge-based development within the global theoretical heritage, consisting of four main dimensions: after economic development and after social development and after environmental development and finally after institutional development. These dimensions focus on the development of cognitive capital by knowledge workers, citizens of knowledge or a creative class in general, as well as the activation of relationships networking between different knowledge circles, and the extent to which the social justice policies of those circles are being achieved and are meant to work towards horizontal development at the level of society as a whole, not just the focus on specific geographical areas through which vertical development is achieved, in addition to the social empowerment of all segments of the Egyptian society and its sectors, without any distinction as a result of geographical, cultural or ethnic considerations. This is a hope for the development of an inclusive truth in Egyptian society in which knowledge production is the basic building block.

The study is based on the premise that more attention is being given to establish technological hubs and magnificent architectural institutions for the purpose of knowledge production, Knowledge Precincts-KPs, which through their policies emphasize the importance of knowledge capital, and human and social capital. In reality, in order to maximize the returns of knowledge-based development policies, that are specific to the framework of these knowledge precincts and works through them, there is a need to network between different knowledge precincts to operationalize the foundations and knowledge-based principles of development within the entire society. In other words, the more interest that exists in the development of cognitive, structural, administrative, economic, human, and social capitals the better to strengthen sustainable learning, networking and social empowerment processes and increase the quality of life within society in general. Different dimensions of development have to be enclosed within the policies of the knowledge precincts.

The state strategy also must pay closer attention to the enclosing of various types of capital in general and human capital, particularly within the developmental goals and strategies of the country. In addition, there is a need to raise awareness of the importance of development in general and of "knowledge" in development in particular. That also could be achieved through learning about successful experiences in this domain globally and locally within the Arab world while taking into account the cultural and social specificities of the Egyptian society. That is, the more knowledge, institutional and social strength of the society, the greater the awareness of the importance of the entry points of knowledge-based development in shaping state development policies, which are linked to the needs and aspirations of society. This will maximize the outcomes of the knowledge-based policies and knowledge precincts in achieving genuine and comprehensive development of society.

CONCLUSION

Departed from the field of Area Studies, this chapter discussed both the written strategies and the implemented steps taken by different governmental bodies that seek knowledge-based development within the Egyptian context. Thus, to make research relevant to the current developmental challenges

Figure 11. The researcher's vision of networking different types of KPs for the purpose of knowledge production and dissemination within the Egyptian society (source: the researcher)

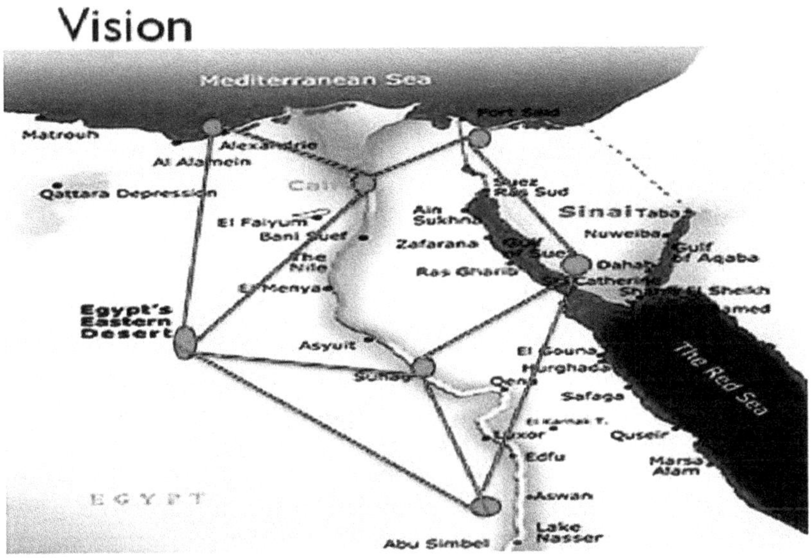

that face different African countries, researchers need to go to the field armed with different theoretical and conceptual perspectives while keeping in mind the reflexivity of the social sciences research based on what the reality reveals. Within the African context, Africa is a very rich continent not just by its natural resources, but more importantly by its human capital of genuine Africans who work in different domains to make the best of their continent. Within academia, it is the role of scholars to criticize the dominant development paradigms that are adopted by different international actors; not to refuse, but to examine them within the African reality in order to achieve the maximum utilization and perhaps reach different African-knowledge-based societies for the coming generations. For the Egyptian case, one can perceive the separation of knowledge-based development policies from their implemented steps on the ground, different knowledge precincts whose policies are not in line with the state's strategic plans to achieve a knowledge-based development. Within the particular four cases of the Egyptian KPs under study, each faces different obstacles and has its unique characteristics. This chapter attempted to investigate the possibilities for establishing and developing knowledge cities, within the Egyptian context, through knowledge precincts which are the key engines for achieving a knowledge-based development. The researcher faced many obstacles during the fieldwork phase that have to be highlighted. The first was using the term "social dimensions" of KBUD policies. Most of the interviewees did not agree on the usage of the term "social dimensions" as it meant for them as an opposite of what is "economic" in regard to the development goals. The second problem was related to gathering the high administrative officials and experts within the field of research in one room at the same time due to their strict schedules or to political considerations. This dilemma affected the research methodology and changed it from depending only on focus groups discussions to depend on in-depth interviews. Also, the methodology tended to shorten the sample of interviewees to include experts, policy makers, and knowledge workers only as it did not include beneficiaries.

REFERENCES

Alexandria University, Faculty of Arts. (n.d.). *TAFL Center (Teaching Arabic as Foreign Language)*. Retrieved from http://arts.alexu.edu.eg/tafl/

Alexandrina, B. (n.d.a). *BA African Networks*. Retrieved from http://afn.bibalex.org/GeneralPortal.aspx

Alexandrina, B. (n.d.b). *Overview, Mission, Objectives*. Retrieved from https://www.bibalex.org/en/page/about

Alexandrina, B. (n.d.c). *The BA Embassies of Knowledge*. Retrieved from https://www.bibalex.org/en/project/details?documentid=1300&keywords=

Alraouf, A. A. (2008). Emerging Middle Eastern knowledge cities: the unfolding story. In *Knowledge-Based Urban Development: Planning and Applications in the Information Era*. Retrieved from http://www.igi-global.com/chapter/emerging-middle-eastern-knowledge- cities/25495

Alraouf, A. A. (2012). *Knowledge Cities: Examining the Discourse Smart Villages, Internet Cities or Creativity Engines*. Retrieved from http://qu.academia.edu/AliAlraouf/Papers/126203/Knowledge_Cities_Examining_The_Discourse_Smart_Villages

Arab Republic of Egypt. (2012). *Egypt's ICT strategy 2012-2017: The Egyptian Digital Society in Knowledge Economy*. Ministry of Communications and Information Technology. Retrieved from http://www.mcit.gov.eg/Upcont/Documents/ICT%20Strategy%202012-2017.pdf

Arab Republic of Egypt, Ministry of Communications and Information Technology (MCIT). (n.d.a). *Building Digital Bridges: Egypt's Vision of the Information Society 2003*. Retrieved from http://www.mcit.gov.eg/Upcont/Documents/BuildingBridges_all.pdf

Arab Republic of Egypt, Ministry of Communications and Information Technology (MCIT). (n.d.b). *Egypt's Information Society 2005*. Retrieved from http://www.mcit.gov.eg/Upcont/Documents/Egy-Info_Society.pdf

Bibliotheca, A. H. P. (n.d.). *About the BA*. Retrieved from https://www.bibalex.org/en/default

Bibliotheca Alexandrina. (n.d.). Retrieved from http://www.bibalex.org/ar/Page/About

Carrillo, F. J. (2002). Capital Systems: Implications for a Global Knowledge Agenda. *Journal of Knowledge Management*, *6*(4), 379–399. doi:10.1108/13673270210440884

Center for Knowledge Systems. (2003). *Forum on Knowledge-based Development, 2003*. Retrieved from http://www.knowledgesystems.org/

ITI. (n.d.). *Vision and Mission*. Retrieved from http://www.iti.gov.eg/overview.aspx?page=1

Knight, V. R. (1995). Knowledge-based development: Policy and planning implications for cities. Urban Studies, 32(2), 225-260.

Laszlo, K. C., & Laszlo, A. (2007). Fostering a Sustainable Learning Society Through Knowledge-based Development. *Journal of Systems Research and Behavioral Science, 24*(5). Retrieved from http://onlinelibrary.wiley.com/doi/10.1002/sres.850/pdf

Lever, W. (2002). Correlating the knowledge-base of cities with economic growth. Urban Studies, 39(5-6), 859–870.

Mieg. (2012). Sustainability and innovation in urban development: concept and case. *Journal of Sustainable Development, 20*(4), 251-263.

Ministry of Communications and Information Technology. (2007). *Egypt's National Vision for Information Society (2000- 2005); Egypt's ICT National Strategy 2007- 2010.* Author.

Nguyen, T. (2010). Knowledge Economy and Sustainable Economic Development. De Gruyter Saur, Munich. *International Journal of Knowledge-Based Development*, *5*(3), 2014.

Ovalle, M., Marquez, J., & Salomon, S. (2004). A compilation of resources on knowledge cities and knowledge-based development. *Journal of Knowledge Management, 8*(5), 107–127.

Scott, J. C. (1999). *Seeing like a State: How Certain Schemes to Improve the Human Condition Have Failed.* Yale University Press.

Sen, A. (1999). *Development as Freedom.* Oxford University Press.

Smart Village Egypt. (n.d.). *About Us.* Retrieved from https://www.smart-villages.com/en/page/page/147

SRTA-City. (n.d.). *Vision & Mission.* Retrieved from http://mucsat.org/index.php?option=com_content&view=article&id=46&Itemid=63

UNESCO. (2005). *Towards Knowledge Societies.* Paris: UNESCO Publications.

Village, S. (n.d.). *Vision & Mission.* Retrieved from http://www.smart-villages.com/en/page/page/147

Yigitcanlar, T. (2011). Position paper: Redefining knowledge-based urban development. *International Journal of Knowledge-Based Development*, *2*(4), 340–356. doi:10.1504/IJKBD.2011.044343

Yigitcanlar, T. (2014). Innovating urban policymaking and planning mechanisms to deliver knowledge-based agendas: A methodological approach. *International Journal of Knowledge-Based Development*, *5*(3), 257. doi:10.1504/IJKBD.2014.065300

Yigitcanlar, T., Velibeyoglu, K., & Martinez-Fernandez, C. (2008). Rising knowledge cities: The role of urban knowledge precincts. *Journal of Knowledge Management*, *12*(5), 8–10. doi:10.1108/13673270810902902

ENDNOTES

1 Ministry of Communications and Information Technology. Egypt's National Vision for Information Society (2000- 2005); Egypt's ICT National Strategy 2007- 2010. (May 2007). -Egypt.

2 Egypt Economic Development Conference (EEDC) "Egypt The Future", Sharm El-Sheikh, 13-15th March 2015. http://www.egyptthefuture.com/
Egypt's Vision 2030 website: http://sdsegypt2030.com/
Borg Al Arab Tech and Science Park: http://www.mcit.gov.eg/Investment_Opportunities/Technology_Parks/BorgAlArab_TechPark

New Assuit Tech Park- Silicon Waha: http://www.siliconwaha.com/about-assiut.html
Maadi Technology Park: http://www.itida.gov.eg/EN/OURPROGRAMS/INDUSTRYINFRASTRUCTURE/MAADIPARK/Pages/default.aspx
10th of Ramadan City Tech and Science Park: http://www.mcit.gov.eg/Investment_Opportunities/Technology_Parks/10thofRamadan_TecPark
New Suez Canal Technology Valley: http://newcanal.suezcanal.gov.eg/
Sinai Technology Valley (STV): https://www.unescwa.org/sinai-technology-valley
Northern Coast Technology Valley: This proposed technopole is still at the study stage. The project is being considered by Alexandria Governorate, the Ministry of Higher Education, and the Ministry of State for Scientific Research and the Social Fund for Development. https://www.unescwa.org/ar/northern-coast-technology-valley

3 The Capital Cairo- Egypt's Firat Smart City: http://thecapitalcairo.com/.

4 Smart Village. "Vision & Mission". Accessed: 17th August 2016. http://www.smart-villages.com/en/page/page/147, ITI. Vision and Mission. Accessed: 17th August 2016. http://www.iti.gov.eg/overview.aspx?page=1, SRTA-City. Vision & Mission. Accessed" 17th August 2016. http://mucsat.org/index.php?option=com_content&view=article&id=46&Itemid=63. 13 February 2013. Bibliotheca Alexandrina main website page: http://www.bibalex.org/ar/Page/About. Accessed: 17th August 2016.

5 Arab Republic of Egypt (2012). *Egypt's ICT strategy 2012-2017: The Egyptian Digital Society in Knowledge Economy*. Egypt. Ministry of Communications and Information Technology. http://www.mcit.gov.eg/Upcont/Documents/ICT%20Strategy%202012-2017.pdf.

6 Ibid. P.p. 6-7.

7 Egypt's Vision of the Information Society 2003
Egypt's Information Society 2005
Egypt's ICT strategy 2007-2010. Ministry of Communications and Information Technology- Egypt. (May 2007).
Egypt's ICT strategy 2012-2017: The Egyptian Digital Society in Knowledge Economy. Egypt. Ministry of Communications and Information Technology.
Egypt's Vision 2030

8 Information and Technology Institute Website. "About". http://www.iti.gov.eg/Site/AboutUs

9 Alexandria University, Faculty of Arts. TAFL Center (Teaching Arabic as Foreign Language). http://arts.alexu.edu.eg/tafl/.

10 SRTA-City Website. "About". http://www.mucsat.org/
SRTA-City Objectives: "Developing new technologies and provide new scientific methods in different fields of industry to link research programs to national development plans. Providing training, consultancy and technology transfer to different production and services agencies in Egypt. Conducting applied projects to ensure better performance in different areas that can benefit Alexandria region and the national economy. Cooperating with different national and international institutes in the various areas of technology."

11 Smart Village- Egypt. "About Us". Accessed 13th July 2017. https://www.smart-villages.com/en/page/page/147.

12 Bibliotheca Alexandrina Home Page. "About the BA". Accessed 13th July 2017. https://www.bibalex.org/en/default

13 Bibliotheca Alexandrina. "Overview, Mission, Objectives". Accessed 13th July 2017. https://www.bibalex.org/en/page/about

14 Bibliotheca Alexandrina. "The BA Embassies of Knowledge." Accessed 13th July 2017. https://www.bibalex.org/en/project/details?documentid=1300&keywords=

15 Bibliotheca Alexandrina. "BA African Networks." Accessed 13th July 2017. http://afn.bibalex.org/GeneralPortal.aspx

Chapter 6
Developing a Conceptual Framework for Knowledge-Based Urban Development in Isfahan, Iran

Marjaneh Farhangi
Municipality of Karaj, Iran

ABSTRACT

We have witnessed vast economic, social, technological, and environmental changes that have influenced patterns of urbanization. Through all these years urban planning has also experienced major reforms. During last two decades, with emergence of knowledge economy, it is claimed that the nature of urban development has changed; this new notion of development is called knowledge-based urban development. As there is not clear methodology for directing cities development process, this chapter aims to formulate a conceptual model for cities leadership towards knowledge-based urban development. This chapter considers the city of Isfahan, Iran as a case study. Finally, a model is proposed according to literature review and using ANP method for analyzing the data gathered from the context. This conceptual model has also prioritized effective factors for KBUD.

1. INTRODUCTION

During the last two decades, a global knowledge-based economy has emerged so called "knowledge economy" which is named variously: "knowledge-based economy", "new knowledge" and "creative economy". In 21st century, the need for the power of knowledge has reduced the importance of tangible factors and has led to new era in which knowledge dominates (Yigitcanlar, 2011). Moreover, in this new economy, knowledge-based activities, especially creativity as a tacit form of knowledge, has been signified in order to employment and wealth creation and maintaining economic growth and place-making (Friedmann, 2010). Meanwhile, it is claimed that cities have a pivotal role in knowledge economy and the

DOI: 10.4018/978-1-5225-3734-2.ch006

Copyright © 2018, IGI Global. Copying or distributing in print or electronic forms without written permission of IGI Global is prohibited.

nature of urban development in relation with knowledge sectors needs conditions and environments which differ from commodity-based production (Carrillo, 2004, 2006, 2009; Knight, 1995, 2008; Yigitcanlar, 2007, 2010a,b). This has resulted in an evolving literature that seeks the concept of knowledge-based development in cities as a development approach which goals are creating a place includes economic prosperity, environmental sustainability, a social-spatial order and good governance. This notion has been widely mentioned and accepted especially for competitive cities in knowledge economy (Knight, 1995; Lever, 2001; Yigitcanlar, 2011).

Therefore, it seems that entering knowledge economy to urban arena would have significant consequences for urban planning both practically and theoretically. Although there is consensus among theoreticians and researchers in the field of knowledge-based urban development that the knowledge economy changes the nature of urban development, but there is no precise and clear methodology that clarifies a theoretical framework to lead the development process. It seems that this notion is in the pre-paradigm level and no definite paradigm has been formed. So, still some questions have remained in this field:

- Does this way of development require characteristics and prerequisites in cities or can be adopted in any urban area?
- Which benefits and qualities separate it from the former urban development paradigms?
- What would be the consequences of this notion on the theory and practice of urban planning?

As the notion of KBUD has not been considered much in the field of urban planning in an Iranian context, this paper is going to examine the opportunities and perquisites of Esfahan to act as a knowledge city and also to develop a conceptual model for leading the city towards knowledge-based urban development.

2. KNOWLEDGE ECONOMY AND CITIES

The first delineation of the Knowledge Economy was introduced by the OECD in their 1996 report:" The Knowledge-Based Economy". According to this report, a Knowledge Economy creates, distributes, and uses knowledge to generate value and gives rise to "a network society, where the opportunity and capability to access and join knowledge and learning intensive relations determines the socio-economic position of individuals and firms". Moreover, knowledge and creativity are perceived as the engines of economic growth. In 21th century, the need for knowledge power has reduced the significance of tangible factors and conduced to new era in which knowledge is dominated (Yigitcanalar, 2011). In this new economy, knowledge-based activities, especially creativity has been emphasized as a tacit form of knowledge in order to create employment and wealth, maintaining economic growth and place-making (Friedman, 2010).

In the global knowledge economy, knowledge and information and the social and technological contexts for their creation and communication are now regarded as a solution for economic growth and prosperity (Lever, 2002).The replacement of physical products with intangible forms of production (e.g. information, ideas and knowledge) has significantly increased the role of cities and has led to the formation of knowledge cities (Yigitcanlar, 2010). The reason for this is the city nature that provides a context for knowledge production, supplication and exchange. According to this notion, knowledge cities should be capable to provide a context to promote knowledge production, exchange and innovation (Ergazakis et al., 2004). Therefore, the first linkage between knowledge economy and city is its prominence and position to produce, share, evaluate, renew and update knowledge. Knowledge has always played an important role in economic value creation and has always been in the center of urban development. Nevertheless, only recently knowledge has been recognized as the main factor in leading urban development (Knight, 2008).

3. KNOWLEDGE-BASED DEVELOPMENT

Historically, knowledge has always been the source of development. Nevertheless, what has been changed is the role of knowledge which has been evolved significantly. Last two decades increasingly witness the importance of knowledge in the development challenges and turnovers. So, the term of "knowledge" has become a prefix in development-related concepts, for example "knowledge economy", "knowledge society", "knowledge citizens", "knowledge-based development", "knowledge city" and so on. Meanwhile, "development" definition (which was economic based), has been expanded to consider social, environmental, political and cultural subjects (Pike et al., in Wang, 2009).

Although there is consensus that the city's knowledge base constitutes the foundation of its future development, but knowledge-based development has been founded on a set of completely different characteristics, which are not only vary by type of culture producing knowledge, but also by place (Knight, 2008).

Carrillo (2002) believes that there are two different perspectives on knowledge-based development; the first is mostly about the increase in the monetary accumulation and productivity based on technology and education. On the other hand, knowledge-based development is known as a dynamic equilibrium between all common value elements in a society namely social-cultural, physical and fiscal ones (Carrillo, 2009). In the current literature on the knowledge-based development the victory is by economic perspectives. Mostly, they see knowledge-based development a powerful strategy for economic growth and post-industrial development of cities and countries to participate in knowledge economy.

4. THE EVOLVING PROCESS OF KNOWLEDGE-BASED DEVELOPMENT

The concept of knowledge based development has not emerged as its current form, but it has been recognized during time and with the evolvement in the concept of "knowledge" and "development". Carrillo (2004) has studied the relation between and found out that knowledge based development had evolved in three consecutive stages. In the first stage, when knowledge was only an instrument for development, KBD was a method to promote economic growth. In the second stage, when knowledge was recognized as production factor to replace common material capital, KBD improved towards human capital development. Finally, when knowledge deployed for development and included all kinds of knowledge and intellectual capital, KBD transformed to an oriented strategy to social, economic and environmental sustainability in global scale where knowledge society is achievable.

5. KNOWLEDGE-BASED URBAN DEVELOPMENT AND KNOWLEDGE CITIES

Knowledge based urban development (KBUD) is a term which encompasses a wide range of perspectives on the relation between knowledge, space and place in the context of emerging global debates around knowledge economy and the respective importance of production factors. In its widest level, KBUD indicates this notion that realization of knowledge economy has urban aspects based on place. This will cause significant changes: knowledge based development which has urban aspect; urban development that could be knowledge based or strategies in which knowledge is seen as a symbol, product or process which collecting, harnessing or remembering would have potential advantages in urban scale.

Development changes are widely seen in the changes of development thoughts, theories and approaches. The knowledge based era starts with the success of silicon valley and Cambridge science park in 1970s which has resulted in the aim of urban development with focus on the development of techno poles or industrial parks in order to optimum use of technological resources in 1980s (Castells and Hall, 1994). 1990s witness rapid growth of science and technology parks to promote entrepreneurship and the emergence of "digital cities" as a way to optimize the use of information technology.

With the raise of the idea of knowledge cities emergence in 21st century by Carrillo(2004), many cities all over the world face the promise of predominant changes along with the world progress towards a global information order. In this regard, KBUD was indicated as a mechanism for directing urban development towards knowledge cities.

There is a wide range of definitions that attempt to define knowledge based urban development: KBUD can be considered as an instrument or approach to help to reform and renovate cities towards knowledge cities and their economies to knowledge economy(Yigitcanlar, 2005).Social advantages of KBUD exceed economic growth. On one hand, it is a flexible and special form of urban development realized in a chain of linkages harnessed at local, national and global scales; On the other hand, it is the quality of place and life not only defined by the level of public services(e.g. health and education), but also by maintaining and developing cultural, aesthetics and ecological values that gives cities identity and attract or repel knowledge workers. The promise of KBUD is a secure economy in a human context that briefly means smart growth or urban and economic sustainable development (Yigitcanlar and Velibeyoughlu, 2008).

The numerous interpretation of KBUD may be due to insignificant separation between different activity context and increasing porosity of borders between science, knowledge, culture, society, geography and economy (Perry and May, 2010). This has resulted in wide range of inter- and multi- disciplinary manuscripts with different perspectives. From agglomeration, industrial zones, locational theories to increasing concentration on innovative environments, learning regions and economic advantages which has induced to changes from concentration on national innovation systems to regional systems. New ways of knowledge creation have strong local and regional dimensions. Others focus on the relations between science, knowledge and cultural dynamics of city/regions through considering social, cultural and organizational growth needed for economic development at local and regional levels.

6. KNOWLEDGE CITIES

According to this wide spread of perspectives, various and different definitions have been presented for knowledge cities. The Prominent view on KC believes in evolvement in notions such as "technopolis" and "idea-polis" toward a more practical, spirituous and sustainable style of urban development. In this perspective the main characteristic of knowledge city is application of local innovation, science and creativity within the urban economic and social texture. In some perspectives, knowledge city is considered an integrated city that has incorporated the functions of a science and technology park with urban and residential functions (Yigitcanlar, 2007).

Edvinsson (2003) describe KC as a city that purposefully has been designated to promote knowledge education and training. Accordingly, it is asserted that in societies that are increasingly get knowledge-based, the nature of urban development changes because the activities in knowledge sector would be more significant and require conditions and environments that differ from those required by commodity production activities (knight, 1995; Yigitcanlar et al., 2007).

Various studies have been performed on current knowledge cities to seek their common qualities. Although they are different in concentration and consideration, but this study has tried to search for similarities and has categorized current notions on KC according to their main characteristics.

6.1. Technology and Networking

So many researchers and scholars that information and communication technologies is a separating factor between developed and under developed countries. Therefore, IT infrastructures provide essential and defining situation for an innovative knowledge cities (Dvir and Pasher, 2004; Ergazakis et al., 2004). Also Maynard (2008), Larsen (1999), Van Winden et al. (2007).

6.2. Culture and Creativity

Some researchers conceptualize knowledge cities by understanding non-material flows and assets (Kunzmann, 2008; Ritter, 2008; Musterd and Gritsai, 2012). Culture and Creativity are dominant factors in creating identity and image of a city and undoubtedly, nowadays it is more probable for urban areas to create new ideas. Knight (1995) also indicates that " knowledge-based development requires strengthening all aspects of cultural foundation of a city". The main reason for emphasizing on culture and society is that places with cultural wealth and consolidation provide external activities and facilities parallel with high-tech industries.

6.3. Human and Social Capital

Educational institutions are effective on creating skills and talents within cities. Universities are considered as innovation engines not only generate skills, but also promote communications and connections among citizens in knowledge precincts (Dvir and Pasher, 2004; Garret Jones, 2007; Perry, 2008; Crossa et al., 2010). Van Winden et al. (2007) demonstrated that evaluation of qualifications, capabilities and academic documents of a knowledge precinct and understanding the immigration movement of knowledge workers will provide criteria for knowledge cities growth and development. It is believed that creative knowledge workers improve the efficiency of local and national economy through providing solutions for problems, all life learning and innovative skills. Human capital is an important element in Florida's(2002) perspective which constitutes the linkage between science, creativity, skills and economic development. Florida's notion of "creative class" asserts that creative people choose their place considering "soft" factors other than just classic "hard" factors.

6.4. Structural and Relational Capital

Knowledge clusters with structural capability for directing innovations and creating new industries, are central places in a knowledge oriented perspective. In other words, there are in a more extensive structure than knowledge production and distribution. Such organizations in knowledge clusters are Universities and colleges, research institutes, state research offices and knowledge-intensive firms (Ever et al., 2010).

Clusters propagation reveals significant insights on the competitive micro economy and role of place in competitive advantage. Although, the aggregation reasons have diminished by globalization, but clusters new influences on the economic competence would be significant (porter, 2002). In some studies, knowledge activities aggregations with the title of "knowledge precincts" are considered as spatial correlations mostly encompass knowledge activities that have linkages with mixed use environments include residential, business, education and entertainment within a semi urban context (Yigitcanlar et al., 2008a; Yigitcanlar and Lonqvist, 2013).

6.5. Innovative Networks and Spatial Communications

Spatial communications provide essential opportunities to communicate and share knowledge in order to create new ideas. More than simple aggregation of economic activities, Gospondiana (2005) considers the role of cultural aggregations in a knowledge city that make them lively and renovate them to cultural hubs.

Consequently, the notion of knowledge city is vague to some extents and several terms have been used to describe to which we can refer as science parks, research parks, techno-polis, innovation centers and science cities. Currently, the concept is developing and evolving to a more practical, lively and sustainable of urban development. According to both Charles and Wray (2008) and Ergazakis et al. (2006) who has investigated the evolving process of knowledge cities although at the beginning these cities were planned and constructed by national Governments to follow fundamental researches. Unlike the first generation, currently KCs are based on coordination and direction through sub-national institutes and organizations participation. These governance networks in sub-national level tend to provide a strategic vision and knowledge city outbreak.

7. KNOWLEDGE-BASED URBAN DEVELOPMENT LITERATURE REVIEW

According to above mentioned issues, it is revealed that the notion of urban development or reform to "knowledge cities" is widely accepted by scholars and researchers in this field, policy makers and urban practitioners and developers (Carrillo, 2006; Van winden et al., 2007; Knight, 2008; Yigitcanlar et al., 2008b; Ergazakis et al., 2009). Nevertheless, current urban planning and development approaches do not represent a vivid image of planning knowledge-based method. Metaxiotis and Ergazakis (2008) believe that in knowledge economy, urban functions and shape are mostly formed by global market forces rather than urban planning.

In recent years, researchers have begun to concentrate their activities in order to develop frameworks, methodologies, tools, systems and measurements for evolving and developing in the context of knowledge based urban development. Investigating the process of KBUD notion formation has revealed an evolutional trend that has been categorized in three generations. Although we can't draw exact border lines between these categories, but it will help to have a better understanding of the concept evolution process in recent decades.

7.1. KBUD First Generation: Separated and Distinct Contexts

Since the beginning of third millennium, we witness an intense focus of scholars and researchers on the context of KCs and KBUD, that their variation in a short period of time is interesting. During first half of 2000s, several scholars have discussed the concept from different point of view. These studies mostly have a special perspective to the concept and have less attention to its multi-dimensional nature and do not represent a vivid image of how the new development strategies should be formulated to specify the effective use of urban planning mechanism:

Carrillo (2004) represents a theoretical and methodological framework to design, evaluate and measure KCs on the basis of knowledge social capital. Ergazakis et al., (2004) have declared some characteristics and advantages of knowledge cities, principle success factors and also some examples of real life experiences. Gonzalaz Ovalle et al., (2004) provided integrated and organized information related to knowledge cities, region and country innovation. Baqir and Kathawala (2004) have introduced a KC model via creating knowledge homes using futuristic technology building blocks that can help in implementing the concept of virtual Ba to share, manage, and create knowledge. Chen and Choi (2004) asserted three inter-related process that generate and distribute tacit knowledge to create successful knowledge cities. Garcia (2004) reviews the theoretical background of KCs and KBUD. She asserts that one of the most severe experiences in modeling KC and KBUD is utilization of theoretical variables to measurable equivalent or quantitative criteria. Chatzkel (2004) represents a strategic perspective for better identification of essential elements to create a successful knowledge capital. Dvir and Pasher (2004) investigate the concept of innovation engines (big events, library, museum, university, digital infrastructure, etc.) and their significance for developing knowledge cities. Cheng et al. (2004) provide insights for policy makers in designing or developing global cities through debates about the linkage between knowledge management and knowledge cities growth.

7.2. KBUD Second Generation: Addressing Multi-Dimensional Nature of KBUD

After various prospects were put in KBUD first generation, the related literature witnessed considerable evolvement in the next generation. In this stage of theoretical development, the multi-dimensional nature of Knowledge based urban development has been considered. In this stage of studies, theoreticians mostly have represented their ideas through conceptual models:

Ergazakis et al. (2006) have proposed *KnowCis Model* on the analysis and evaluation of the common characteristics of successful knowledge cities. Its findings are formulated as a framework to design, develop and implementing knowledge cities. Corey and Wilson (2006) have presented *ALERT Model* that is a prescriptive approach and supporting system for local and regional planning practice in global economy and network society.

The *Knowledge-based Urban Development Characteristic Model* by Van winden et al. (2007) introduces seven structural characteristics that make the city adjust with knowledge era essentials. These seven principals include: knowledge base, quality of life, accessibility, urban diversity, urban scale and social equity. Although this model does not provide an instruction for designing knowledge city but represent a framework for analysis.

7.3. KBUD Third Generation: Integrated Models

In this way, KBUD studies are experiencing a kind of convergence which has led to emergence of KBUD third generation. In this phase, that Carrillo (2009) refer to as pre-paradigm stage, there is consensus among theoreticians about four pillars of knowledge based urban development: economic development, social-cultural development, urban development and management.

Knowledge-based urban development analysis model by Yigitcanlar (2008) categorize the requirement of cities have the vision of knowledge based development into four main groups which are society, environment, management and economy. *Knowledge based urban development integrated model* which was represented by Sarimin et al., (2010) added the weight factor to previous model which was neglected before and tried to offer a more integrated and effective model for KBUD.

Comparative analysis of knowledge-based urban development by Yigitcanlar (2010c) has been formulated based on this notion that KBD evaluation in knowledge cities in order to determine the performance of KBD and city ranks and determination of their accessibility criteria to KBD is necessary. This is also essential for making awareness for decision making as it refers to strategic guidelines that help to identify a development that is more sustainable and knowledge-based. Again in this model four pillars of KBUD are: economic, socio-cultural, environmental-urban development. This model also represents 8 criteria and 32 indicators for these four pillars which are chosen based on different factors including measurement ability, analytical appropriateness, comparativeness, location coverage, accessibility to data and inter-relatedness. *Sustainable development Conceptual frame work* by Fernandez-Maldonado and Romein (2010) has special attention to sustainability and mention economic, social and organizational quality development as main benchmark for knowledge based urban development.

8. THEORETICAL FRAMEWORK OF THE RESEARCH

Investigating theoretical literature on knowledge based urban development and knowledge city reveals that knowledge based urban development is a development approach which aim is making a place that encompass economic prosperity, environmental sustainability, a social-spatial order and urban good governance. It is accepted that this notion is widely appropriate for competitive cities in knowledge economy (Knight, 1995, 2008; Lever, 2002; Yigitcanlar, 2011, 2013a). This development notion embraces the following prominent qualities:

- Knowledge-based urban development has purposefully been formulated for reasonable economic, social, cultural and environmental development in a sustainable way based on the use of knowledge economy capabilities.
- Clustering thought in knowledge-based development in contrast with industrial policies, not only considers the significance of innovation and competitive advantage at local and regional levels, but also demonstrates this reality that more sections of government have effects on competitiveness.
- In this development notion, there is much attention to human values and social and cultural dimensions. Human capital constitutes an important factor; Moreover, equity and social inclusion are significant qualities in this way of development. Therefore, equal opportunities (public accessibility to knowledge) both for individual development and social development.

- Networking has a considerable position in this notion that provides suitable condition for exchanging knowledge and new knowledge production. These communication networks are not confined to government, scientific, occupational and formal networks, but also include all social and informal networks. Knowledge which is discussed in KBUD is not just technical knowledge and encompasses all kinds of knowledge. Accordingly, continuous and mutual communication among different economic, social, scientific and government departments and consequently, related infrastructure are necessary.
- Knowledge based urban development is a complicated project that needs numerous resources, skills and organizational models. This will require organizational routines and models which are practically flexible enough to adjust with existing terms. Therefore, KBUD creates pervasive influences within organizational structure of local governments. Planning for KBUD is a long and sophisticated process that is not a straight line from beginning to end. Over time, economic, social and political conditions change that would have wide spread consequences for planning process. Therefore, the role of guidance and leadership in development is vital and determinant.
- KBUD realization undoubtedly requires a planning approach which is strategic and based on urban privileges and assets for endogenous development. So the role of planners is to study and identify urban resources and potential qualities in all pillars of KBUD, meanwhile cooperating with other organizations.
- A transition is needed from hierarchical government-based methods with the logic of dominance to governance methods based on networks with the logic of negotiation. As in the age of knowledge economy, the role of local institution in development has been signified, mutual governance both up-down and down-up is essential. Therefore, government structure renewal is required to for coordination and effective knowledge synergy for urban development.
- Although, some specifications like the existence of universities and research centers and scientific, cultural and historical image of the city may be important factors that improve the position of cities in KBUD process, it seems that factors such as quality of life and quality of place which was emphasized by Florida as a pre-condition for development and an effective element in attracting creative class (human capital) are mostly the consequences of development rather that a precondition.
- Therefore, in order to follow knowledge based urban development it is essential to make a connection between knowledge-based economy system and local planning system. Joint proceeding between these two systems in order to benefit from the capabilities of both systems is necessary.

According to these findings Figure 1 shows the proposed model for leading knowledge based urban development.

9. CASE STUDY: ISFAHAN

9.1. Historical, Scientific and Artistic Background of Isfahan

Geographic position of Isfahan near the river of *Zayandehrood* caused the city become a center of human civilization. The city of Isfahan always has been a major city of Iran through history and in three historical

Figure 1. The proposed model for leading KBUD

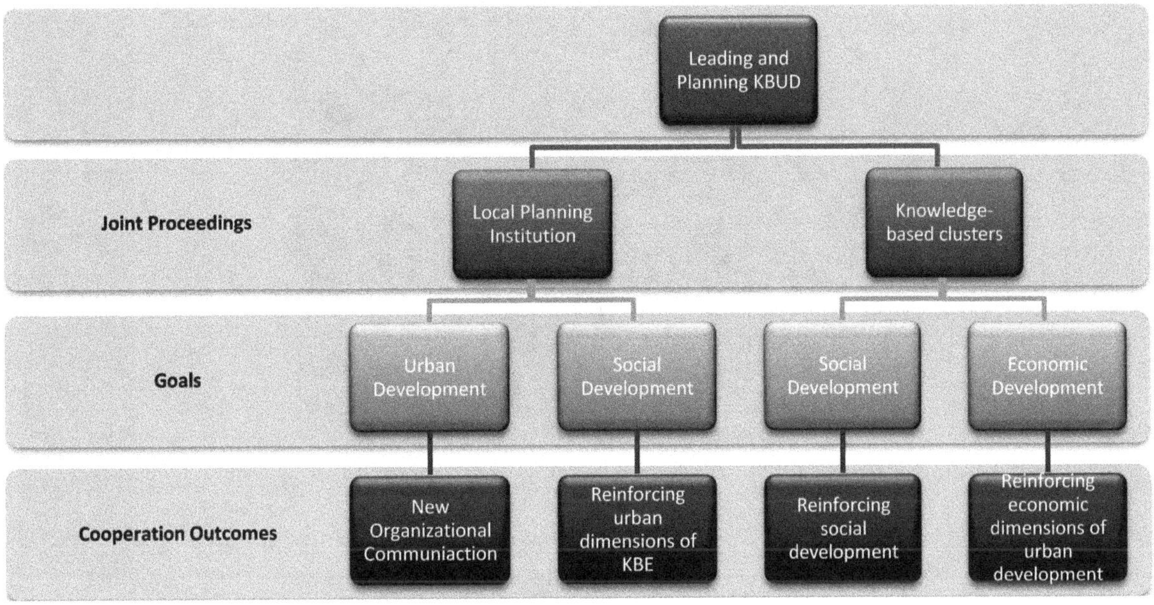

eras it was the political, cultural and civilization center of Iran and in 17th century it became a city with global communications and currently, it is also the interest focus of thousands of international tourists.

One of the honors of Isfahan is its civilization and artistic prosperity. This city has had several architectural artworks before Islam and in Islamic era. This city also has been origin of scientists and intellectuals that have had inevitable impression in different scientific areas, culture and human knowledge. Isfahan is registered as one of the seven historical cities in the world by Unesco.

9.2. Knowledge-Based Urban Development Pillars in Isfahan

According to the findings from theoretical studies and the formulated theoretical framework for leadership towards knowledge-based development, at first it is essential to investigate urban planning system

Figure 2. 40 Sotoon, Isfahan

Figure 3. 33 pole, Isfahan

Figure 4. Aalighapoo- Isfahan

Figure 5. Imam Mosque

and knowledge based economic system in Isfahan. According to Iranian planning system, municipalities, as local institutes, are responsible for urban planning. So at first we engage in reviewing Isfahan municipality approach in urban planning and strategic thinking and then Isfahan science and technology town (ISTT) will be introduced as a complex which mission is knowledge-based economic development through supporting innovative firms, promoting entrepreneurship culture, creating science and technology parks and incubators and facilitating knowledge flow among universities, scientific centers, knowledge-based firms and the market.

9.3. Planning System in Isfahan Municipality, the Opportunities and Constraints

Isfahan municipality is one of few Iranian metropolises which has been able to prepare and execute four physical, cultural and social strategic programs, " Isfahan22+, Isfahan85, Isfahan90 and Isfahan95) rather than conventional master plans. In a concentrated planning system, as Iran is, the most important policies and programs, whether national or local, are determined in country political center. In this condition, local organizations like municipalities have few impressions in governing local affairs and are mostly the implementers of major policies adopted at national level. In such a situation, Isfahan urban managers have intended to make changes in urban planning and management method that demonstrates a positive evolution in urban management thought. On the other hand, inconsistency among different organizations involved in urban management and interference in their responsibilities are serious barriers in urban development.

9.4. Isfahan Science and Technology Town

Science and technology parks in Iran are one of effective social institutes in technology development and consequently knowledge-based economic development. Science and technology parks are appropriate environments for SMEs, industries research and development units and research institutes establishment that are interacting together and with universities. Isfahan science and technology town and incubators founded in 1993 in order to coordinate the scientific and technical capabilities of research, academic and industrial centers in Isfahan.

In 2010, Islamic Development Bank prize went to ISTT. This selection was due to the town's activities in economic development, creating more than 300 knowledge-based firms, registering more than 179 patents, innovations and their commercialization, and continuous and productive relations with industries.

Isfahan has several advantages for broadcasting knowledge economy: the existence of science and technology parks, three premier universities of country, 26 non-profit universities and benefitting 11% of country's researchers.

10. CONCEPTUAL MODEL FOR ISFAHAN KBUD

After data acquisition through documentary studies and observations, this research has performed several in-depth interviews with identified informed individuals in both Isfahan municipality and ISTT. From analyzing data achieved through this process and by using the technique of *pattern matching*, which compares the pattern achieved based on experience and the model resulted from theoretical surveys (Yin, 2003), the conceptual model for Isfahan KBUD has been formulated.

According to findings from theoretical framework, effective factors in KBUD are categorized in 4 main pillars of economic development, urban planning and development, social-cultural development, guidance and leadership. In this step, we have attempted to categorize the data achieved through interviews in these four groups and the model has been proposed as shown in Figure 6.

The pattern is the result of integrating findings from theoretical studies and case studies. Accordingly, the findings from the analysis are as follows:

- In KBUD, none of the development principals are independent and the main point is the balance between all dimensions of development. The inter-relations of development factors are inevitable.
- In social, human and cultural development, factors such as social equity are effective in just distribution of all facilities especially knowledge accessibility. Therefore, social infrastructures, universities and research centers will have an important role. Also citizen's image of the city as a soft dimension is considered. Entrepreneurship culture and creativity is also considered. Networking for knowledge and idea transaction is also of importance.
- In urban planning and development, it is believed that in current situation of increasing complexity, policy system and local planning lack resources (information, skills, capital and legitimacy) to organize the process of KBD. So, participation and aggregation are significant elements in successful knowledge economy. This differ with conventional planning methods, therefore there is a need to make change in urban planners and managers thoughts.
- In economic development, Knowledge workers, Knowledge-based clusters and addressing urban competitive advantages are effective factors of development. Moreover, considering all kind of knowledge, not just technical ones is essential.

Figure 6. Conceptual model of affective factors on Isfahan knowledge-based urban development

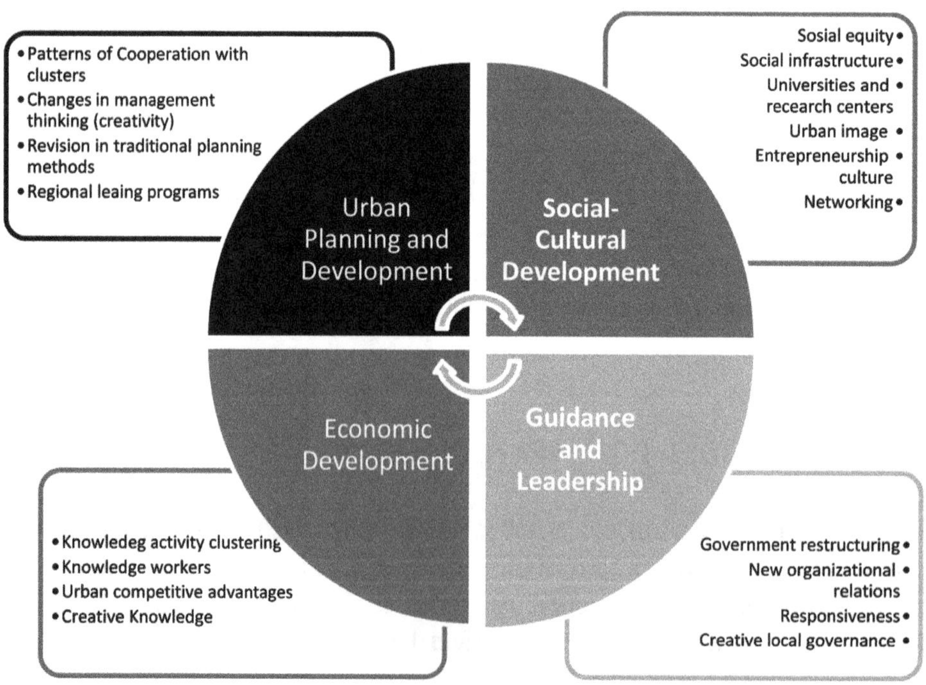

- In KE, economic development policy has been transformed from a linear project management to a holistic project in which the nature of leadership has changed and required guidance and participation of different interests. So, creativity in governance, responsiveness, new organizational relations and the essence of government restructuring are important elements in this process.

11. ANALYZING THE PROPOSED MODEL USING *ANP*[1] METHOD

Currently, in order to either test the reliability of the model or identifying the priorities of different factors in the proposed model, considering its network structure and inter-relation of different factors of the model, *ANP Method* has been used to prioritize the effective factors of development in order to finalize the model formulation. ANP method demonstrates the complex relations between among decision elements through considering the network structure of these items. So, a questionnaire has been designed for comparing every two elements of the model. These questionnaires are filled by all who were interviewed. In order to analyze the achieved data, *Super Decision* software (ver. 2.0.8) has been used. The final importance coefficient of every factor in relation with the goal of knowledge based urban development is achieved as shown in Table 1.

According to the results achieved from ANP analysis, two elements of urban image and regional superior plans are eliminated from the model (Figure 7).

12. CONCLUSION

According to theoretical studies it has revealed that KBUD have close relationship with sustainable de velopment and smart growth. Besides balanced and sustainable development, what makes it interested for urban planners is the connection it makes between planning theory and practice. Considering human and cultural aspects also got importance during last decades in planning theories. Knowledge based

Table 1. The final importance coefficients

Entrepreneurship culture	**Knowledge workers**	**Clustering**	**Creative knowledge**	**Competitive advantage**	**Responsiveness**	**New organizational relations**	**Government Restructuring**	**Creative local governance**	**Criterion**
0.32278	0.28346	0.44569	0.12934	0.14151	0.22457	0.08815	0.28382	0.40346	**Coefficient**
Superior regional plans	**revision in planning methods**	**Creativity for planners**	**Cooperation model**	**Universities**	**Social Infrastructure**	**Networking**	**Urban Image**	**Social equity**	**Criterion**
0.00000	0.03232	0.57917	0.38851	0.08975	0.31424	0.10586	0.00000	0.16736	**Coefficient**

Figure 7. The final conceptual model of affective factors on Isfahan knowledge-based urban development

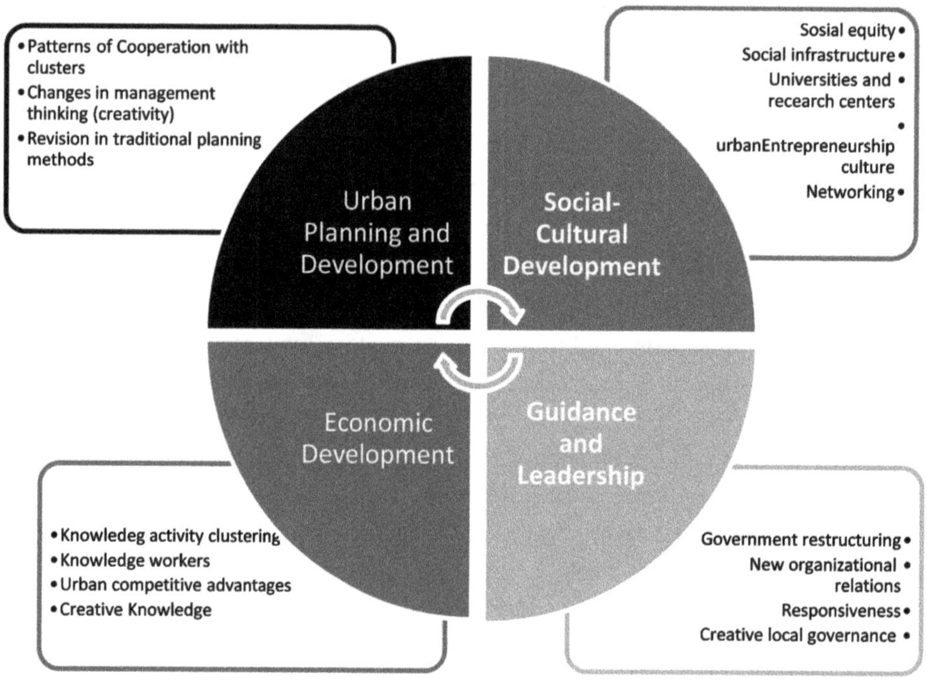

urban development concept is an end to positivist notions in urban planning and opens a new window to urban planners.

KBUD also introduces local and regional layers, as effective factors on competitiveness in KE, that make it possible for planners to get involved in economic issues. Joint proceeding between local knowledge-based system and local planning system will make Isfahan to benefit from knowledge synergies.

The effective factors for KBUD and their priorities are determined through the formulated conceptual model. The results show that the role of local and regional governments in planning is increasing, so government restructuring and creative local governance is essential. Therefore, a wide transition from hierarchical approach to network-based governance is needed.

REFERENCES

Baqir, M. N., & Kathawala, Y. (2004). Ba for knowledge cities: A futuristic technology model. *Journal of Knowledge Management*, *8*(5), 83–95. doi:10.1108/13673270410558828

Baum, S., Yigitcanlar, T., Horton, S., Velibeyoglu, K., & Gleeson, B. (2007). *The Role of Community and Lifestyle in the Making of a Knowledge City. Report*. Brisbane: Griffith University.

Berg, B. L. (2000). *Qualitative Research Methods for the Social Sciences (4th ed.)*. Allyn & Bacon.

Carrillo, F. (2004). Capital cities: A taxonomy of capital accounts for knowledge cities. *Journal of Knowledge Management*, *8*(5), 28–46. doi:10.1108/1367327041058738

Carrillo, F. J. (2002). Capital systems: Implications for a global knowledge agenda. *Journal of Knowledge Management, 6*(4), 379–399. doi:10.1108/13673270210440884

Carrillo, F. J. (2006). Introduction: the century of knowledge cities. In J. Carrillo (Ed.), *Knowledge Cities: Approaches, Experiences and Perspectives* (pp. xi–xv). Oxford, UK: Butterworth-Heinemann/Elsevier. doi:10.1016/B978-0-7506-7941-1.50003-8

Carrillo, F. J. (2009). Demarcation and levels of analysis in knowledge-based development. *Journal of Knowledge-Based Development, 13*(5), 208–213.

Charles, D. R., & Wray, F. (2008). *Science cities in the UK*. Available at www. D1074616.domain.com/worldcapitalinstitute/sites/default/files/

Chatzkel, J. (2004). Greater Phoenix as a knowledge capital. *Journal of Knowledge Management, 8*(5), 61–72. doi:10.1108/13673270410558783

Chen, S., & Choi, C. J. (2004). Creating a knowledge-based city: The example of Hsinchu Science Park. *Journal of Knowledge Management, 8*(5), 73–82. doi:10.1108/13673270410558792

Cheng, P., & Choi, C. (2004). Knowledge repositories in knowledge cities. *Journal of Knowledge Management, 8*(5), 96–106. doi:10.1108/13673270410558800

Corey, K., & Wilson, M. (2006). *Urban and regional technology planning: planning practice in the global knowledge economy*. New York: Routledge.

D. Evers H. (2002) *Knowledge Society and the Knowledge Gap*. Paper read at an International Conference, Globalisation, Culture and Inequalities, Kebansaan, Malaysia.

Dvir, R. (2006). Knowledge City, Seen as a Collage of Human Knowledge Moments. In F. J. Carrillo (Ed.), *Knowledge Cities: Approaches, Experiences, and Perspectives* (pp. 245–272). Amsterdam: Elsevier. doi:10.1016/B978-0-7506-7941-1.50022-1

Dvir, R., & Pasher, E. (2004). *Innovation Engines for Knowledge Cities: An Innovation Ecology Perspective*. Academic Press.

Edvinsson, L. (2003). *Introduction to Issues in Knowledge Management*. Oxfordshire, UK: Henley Knowledge Management Forum.

Ergazakis, E., Ergazakis, K., Metaxiotis, K., & Charalabidis, Y. (2009). Rethinking the development of successful knowledge cities: An advanced framework. *Journal of Knowledge Management, 13*(5), 214–227. doi:10.1108/13673270910988060

Ergazakis, K., Metaxiotis, K., & Psarras, J. (2004). Towards knowledge cities: Conceptual analysis and success stories. *Journal of Knowledge Management, 8*(5), 5–15. doi:10.1108/13673270410558747

Ergazakis, K., Metaxiotis, K., & Psarras, J. (2006a). An emerging pattern of successful knowledge cities' main features. In F. J. Carrillo (Ed.), *Knowledge Cities: Approaches, Experiences and Perspectives* (pp. 3–15). Oxford, UK: Butterworth-Heinemann/Elsevier. doi:10.1016/B978-0-7506-7941-1.50004-X

Ergazakis, K., Metaxiotis, K., & Psarras, J. (2006b). Knowledge cities: The answer to the needs of the knowledge-based development. *VINE. The Journal of Information and Knowledge Management Systems*, *36*(1), 67–81.

Evans, G. (2009). Creative city, Creative Spaces and Urban policies. *Urban Studies (Edinburgh, Scotland)*, *46*(5&6), 1003–1040. doi:10.1177/0042098009103853

Fernandez-Maldonado, A. M. (2012). Designing: combining design and high-tech in Eindhoven knowledge city. In T. Yigitcanlar, K. Metaxiotis & F. Carrillo (Eds.), Building prosperous knowledge cities: Policies, plans and metrics. Edward Elgar. doi:10.4337/9780857936042.00019

Fernandez-Maldonado, A. M., & Romein, A. (2008). A Knowledge-Base Urban Paradox:The Case of Delft. In T. Yigitcanlar, K. Velibeyoglu, & S. Baum (Eds.), *Knowledge-Based Urban Development Planning and Applications in the Information Era*. Hershey, PA: Information Science Reference. doi:10.4018/978-1-59904-720-1.ch013

Florida, R. (1995). Toward the Learning Region. *Futures*, *27*(5), 527–536. doi:10.1016/0016-3287(95)00021-N

Florida, R. (2000). *The Economic Geography of Talent*. Pittsburgh, PA: Carnegie Mellon University.

Florida, R. (2002). *The Rise of the Creative Class and How it's Transforming Work,L eisure, Community and Everyday Life*. New York: Basic Books.

Florida, R. (2008). *Who's Your City?* New York: Basic Books.

Franz, P. (2012). *Competing: important stimuli for knowledge cities to become prosperous. In Building Prosperous Knowledge Cities, Policies, Plans and Metrics*. Edward Elgar Publishing.

Friedmann, J. (2010). Place and place-making in cities: A global perspective. *Planning Theory & Practice*, *11*(2), 149–165. doi:10.1080/14649351003759573

Garcia, B. (2004). Developing futures: A knowledge-based capital for Manchester. *Journal of Knowledge Management*, *8*(5), 47–60. doi:10.1108/13673270410558774

Garrett-Jones, S. (2007). Knowledge and cooperation for regional development. *Prometheus*, *25*(1), 31–50. doi:10.1080/08109020601172886

Hall, P. (2004). Creativity, culture, knowledge and the city. *Built Environment*, *30*(3), 256–258. doi:10.2148/benv.30.3.256.54306

Information Society Commission. (2002). *Building the Knowledge Society*. Report to Government.

Kefela, G. T. (2010). Knowledge-based economy and society has become a vital commodity to countries. *International NGO Journal*, *5*(7), 160–166.

Knight, R. (1995). Knowledge-based development: Policy and planning implications for cities. *Urban Studies (Edinburgh, Scotland)*, *32*(2), 225–260. doi:10.1080/00420989550013068

Knight, R. (2008). Knowledge based development. In T. Yigitcanlar, K. Velibeyoglu, & S. Baum (Eds.), *Knowledge-based urban development* (pp. xiii–xviii). Hersey, PA: IGI Global.

Kunzmann, K. (2004). Culture, Creativity and Spatial Planning. *TPR, 75*(4), 383–404.

Kunzmann, K. (2008). Spatial dimensions of knowledge production. In T. Yigitcanlar, K. Velibeyoglu, & S. Baum (Eds.), *Knowledge-based urban development:Planning and application in the information era* (pp. 296–300). Hersey, PA: IGI Global.

Landry, C. (2000). *The Creative City: A Toolkit for Urban Innovators.* London: Earthscan Publications.

Laszlo, K. C., & Laszlo, A. (2002). Evolving Knowledge for Development: The Role of Knowledge Management in a Changing World. *Journal of Knowledge Management, 6*(4), 400–412. doi:10.1108/13673270210440893

Laszlo, K. C., & Laszlo, A. (2007). Fostering a Sustainable Learning Society through Knowledge-Based Development. *Systems Research and Behavioral Science, 24*(5), 493–503. doi:10.1002/sres.850

Maldonado, A., & Romein, A. (2010). The role of organisational capacity and knowledge-based development. *Int. J. Knowledge-Based Development, 1*(1), 79–96. doi:10.1504/IJKBD.2010.032587

Musterd, S. and Gritsai. (2012). The creative knowledge city in Europe: Structural conditions and urban policy strategies for competitive cities. *European Urban and Regional Studies*, (April): 1–17.

Ovalle, M., Marquez, J., & Salomon, S. (2004). A compilation of resources on knowledge cities and knowledge-based development. *Journal of Knowledge Management, 8*(5), 107–127. doi:10.1108/13673270410558819

Perry, B. (2008). Academic Knowledge and Urban Development: Theory, Policy, and Practice. In T. Yigitcanlar, K. Velibeyoglu, & S. Baum (Eds.), *Knowledge Based Urban Development: Planning and Applications in the Information Era*. Hershey, New York: IGI Global. doi:10.4018/978-1-59904-720-1.ch002

Perry, B., & May, T. (2010). Urban knowledge exchange: Devilish dichotomies and active intermediation. *International Journal of Knowledge-Based Development, 1*(1/2), 6–24. doi:10.1504/IJKBD.2010.032583

Porter, M. E. (2000). Location, Competition, and Economic Development: Local Clusters in a Global Economy. *Economic Development Quarterly, 14*(1), 15–34. doi:10.1177/089124240001400105

Romein, A., Fernandez-Maldonado, A., & Trip, J. (2011). Delft blues, *Int. J. Knowledge-Based Development, 2*(2), 148–165. doi:10.1504/IJKBD.2011.041245

Sanyal, B. (2000). Planning's three challenges. In L. Rodwin & B. Sanyal (Eds.), *The profession of city planning: changes, images, and challenges 1950-2000* (pp. 312–333). Rutgers: The State of New Jersey.

Sarimin, M., & Yigitcanlar, T. (2012). Towards a comprehensive and integrated knowledge-based urban development model. *International Journal of Knowledge Based Development, 3*(2), 175–192. doi:10.1504/IJKBD.2012.047035

UNESCO. (2005). *Towards Knowledge Society*. Paris: The United Nations Educational, Scientific, and Cultural Organisation.

van den Berg, L., Pol, P. M., Winden, W., & Woets, P. (2005). *European Cities in the Knowledge Economy: The Case of Amsterdam, Dortmund, Eindhoven, Helsinki, Manchester, Munich, Munster, Rutterdam and Zaragoza*. Hants, UK: Ashgate.

Van Winden, W. (2008). Urban governance in the knowledge-based economy: Challenges for different city types. *Innovation, Management. Policy & Practice*, *10*(2-3), 197–210. doi:10.5172/impp.453.10.2-3.197

Van Winden, W., Berg, W., van Den, L., & Peter, P. (2007). European cities in the knowledge economy. *Urban Studies (Edinburgh, Scotland)*, *44*(3), 525–549. doi:10.1080/00420980601131886

Van Winden, W., Carvalho, L. D., Van Tujil, E., Van Haaren, J., & Van Den Berg, L. (2010). *Creating Knowledge Locations in Cities: Innovation and Integration Challenges*. Rotterdam: Euricur.

Velibeyoglu, K., & Yigitcanlar, T. (2008). Understanding the supply side: ICT experience of Marmara region, Turkey. In T. Yigitcanlar, K. Velibeyoglu, & S. Baum (Eds.), *Creative Urban Regions*. Hershey, PA: Information Science Reference. doi:10.4018/978-1-59904-838-3.ch015

Yigitcanlar, T. (2003). *Bridging the Gap between Citizens and Local Authorities via e-government*. In *Symposium on E-government*, Muscat, Oman.

Yigitcanlar, T. (2007). The making of urban spaces for the knowledge economy: global practices. In I. Al-Furaih, A. Sahab, A. Hayajneh, A. Abdullah, M. Thalha, & M. Ibrahim (Eds.), *Knowledge Cities: Future of Cities in the Knowledge Economy* (pp. 73–97). Selangor, Malaysia: Scholar Press.

Yigitcanlar, T. (2010). Making space and place for the knowledge economy. *European Planning Studies*, *18*(11), 1769–1786. doi:10.1080/09654313.2010.512163

Yigitcanlar, T. (2011a). Redefining knowledge-based urban development. *International Journal of Knowledge Based Development*, *2*(4), 340–356. doi:10.1504/IJKBD.2011.044343

Yigitcanlar, T. (2011b). Moving towards a knowledge city? Brisbane's experience in knowledge-based urban development. *International Journal of Knowledge-Based Organizations*, *1*(3), 22–38. doi:10.4018/ijkbo.2011070102

Yigitcanlar, T. (2013). Building contemporary urban spaces of knowledge and innovation: Lessons from Australian practice. In *Proceedings of ICEIRD 2013*. Sehir University.

Yigitcanlar, T., Baum, S., & Horton, S. (2007). Attracting and retaining knowledge workers in knowledge cities. *Journal of Knowledge Management*, *11*(5), 6–17. doi:10.1108/13673270710819762

Yigitcanlar, T., & Lonnqvist, A. (2013). Benchmarking knowledge-based urban development performance. *Cities (London, England)*, *31*(1), 357–369. doi:10.1016/j.cities.2012.11.005

Yigitcanlar, T., Velibeyoglu, K., & Baum, S. (Eds.). (2008a). *Knowledge-based Urban Development: Planning and Applications in the Information Era*. Hershey, PA: IGI Global. doi:10.4018/978-1-59904-720-1

Yigitcanlar, T., Velibeyoglu, K., & Baum, S. (Eds.). (2008b). *Creative Urban Regions: Harnessing Urban Technologies to Support Knowledge City Initiatives*. Hershey, PA: IGI Global. doi:10.4018/978-1-59904-838-3

Yigitcanlar, T., Velibeyoughlu, K., & Martinez-Fernandez, C. (2008c). Rising Knowledge Cities:the role of urban knowledge precincts. *Journal of Knowledge Management*, *12*(5), 8–20. doi:10.1108/13673270810902902

Yin, R. K. (1994). *Case Study Research: Design and Methods*. Thousand Oaks, CA: Sage Publications.

ENDNOTE

1 Analytical network process.

Chapter 7
KBUD as an Alternative Approach for the Development of Cairo's Informal Settlements: Opportunities and Challenges

Ahmed Hassan Abayazeed
Independent Researcher, Egypt

ABSTRACT

This chapter investigates the opportunities and challenges related to KBUD found in Cairo's informal settlements. Also, it explores the ability of KBUD approach in dealing with the development of such settlements instead of the adopted approaches which failed in approaching the economic aspect within these communities. The chapter provides insights on the important role KBUD could play not only in the economic growth of richer and more prestigious contexts but also in poor communities which have a lot of hidden potentials. Accordingly, the chapter investigates Cairo's informal settlements, the policies and approaches used and applied, and the related defects and shortcomings. Then, it explores the theoretical framework of KBUD. Following this, opportunities and challenges related to KBUD in Cairo's informal settlements are discussed. By the end, the chapter sheds light on some points and concludes with recommendations for readapting KBUD approach when developing Cairo's informal settlements.

INTRODUCTION

Cairo is the largest city in the Middle-East and second-largest in Africa. As most of the mega cities in the Global South, Cairo has been expanding rapidly through the growth of informal settlements. According to the 2016 Egyptian Census, around 10% of the Egyptian population lives in Cairo (CAPMS, 2016). Around 40% of Cairo's population lives in informal settlements as estimated by the Ministry of Housing (Tadamun, 2014). Cairo gains its importance and attractive power because of its deep-rooted history as well as being the center of the country's political and economic life and most of the industrial activities. This leads to the centralization of jobs which attract rural populations to immigrate internally

DOI: 10.4018/978-1-5225-3734-2.ch007

Copyright © 2018, IGI Global. Copying or distributing in print or electronic forms without written permission of IGI Global is prohibited.

to work in Cairo and enhance their living situation (Kipper, 2009). This emphasizes what mentioned by Collier (2013), that migration, under ordinary circumstances, is usually motivated by escaping from insufficient social patterns towards other patterns offering them better economic conditions. Accordingly, the economic factor is considered the primary reason for the formation of these informal settlements.

Although adopting a range of policies and legislations by the Egyptian successive governments to slow down and limit the informal urban growth, and to upgrade and develop this kind of settlements starting from the 1990s till now, the economic and the financial issues are still the hardest part to approach especially because of economic challenges faced by Egypt as a developing society. This also depends on how the government and the policy makers see this kind of settlement. The government and the policymakers see informal settlements as a huge problem which should be treated as a temporary one that should eventually be demolished for building new housing projects or just raised to a standard and legalized state by providing basic services and infrastructure (Mostafa 2013). This kind of approach depends mainly on huge budgets which are usually not available.

This raises the importance of searching for alternative approaches to tackle the economic aspects seriously through activating them within the developing process of Cairo's informal settlements. This opens the door for rethinking the development approaches adopted by the policy makers when dealing with the development of these settlements. Most of these strategies are delayed and failed in achieving a great significance with the informality challenge facing Cairo. On the other hand, the extremely fast bounds in science and information are the main cause of the dramatic change from the 'information' era towards the 'knowledge' era (Yigitcanlar, 2008). This leads to the emergence of Knowledge-Based Urban Development (KBUD) which became known as a strategic development approach could be applied to human settlements and a promising strategy for sustainable development of cities (Yigitcanlar et al., 2008).

This chapter aims to examine the existing opportunities and challenges found in Cairo's informal settlements related to KBUD theoretical framework. Also, it sheds light on the extents to which KBUD approach could deal with the development of this kind of settlements. This research gains its importance from two points. The first one is the shortening of most the approaches and strategies dealing with the development and upgrading of Cairo's informal settlements in approaching the economic aspect as most of the plans broke down or were postponed because of the lack of funding. The second one is that the chapter provides fruitful discussion and insights on the important role KBUD could play in developing Cairo's informal settlements not only in the economic growth of richer and more prestigious contexts. To carry out this research, the chapter adopts a theoretical-based approach through a desktop research method to review the literature and examine different related studies and publications. Accordingly, This Chapter first sheds light on the evolution of Cairo's informal settlements, the main context, and the main reasons behind. The chapter, then, reviews the policies and approaches used and applied through the governmental and non-governmental efforts represented in some attempts and interventions done by donor agencies and civil society organizations. Following this, the chapter discusses the defects and shortcomings of these approaches represented in dealing with Cairo's informal settlements as just inadequate housing challenge and neglecting both of the economic component and community participation process within the development strategies. The chapter, then, explores the definition of KBUD, and investigates the theoretical framework of KBUD, and indicates clearly its domains and pillars. Following this, the existing opportunities and challenges related to KBUD in Cairo's Informal Settlements are discussed and reframed. By the end, the chapter reaches some points to be put into consideration when reframing KBUD approach in developing Cairo's informal settlements and concludes with recommendations which would help in avoiding obstacles related to the knowledge-based economic growth of such poor communities.

KBUD AND DEVELOPMENT OF CAIRO'S INFORMAL SETTLEMENTS

Emergence of Cairo's Informality

The informal growth phenomenon in Cairo began after the Second World War, due to the housing pressure caused by the migration from Upper Egypt and the Delta. The Economic development took place in Cairo plus the massive industrialization policy launched by President Nasser afterwards attracted the internal migrants to Cairo (Séjourné, 2009). The first migrants, mostly young men, stayed in rented and shared rooms and flats in central and historic districts. Later, after collecting some savings, some of them were able to buy and build on land on the fringes of the villages attached to the city where the land prices were cheaper than that in the central districts. In that period, the phenomenon of squatting on state-owned land started to appear mostly in the eastern part of Cairo. Some new informal districts appeared while others continued to grow. Poor families built houses on state-owned, which was almost desert land, through what is called *"Wada' al-yad"* (A phenomenon of squatting on a state-owned land through hand claim) as they could not afford to buy agricultural land. Thus, informal settlements, like Manshiet Nasser and Ezbet Al-Haggana, started to grow heavily on desert land (ibid). A new phase of informal urbanization started at the beginning of the 1970s as 84% of the new units built during this period were considered informal (ABT Associates et al. 1982). People invested in informal constructions during this period due to some factors. First, the oil booms in 1973 and 1979 which enriched the near oil producing countries like Libya, Saudi Arabia, and Iraq, which attracted the Egyptian manpower. Thus, this enables a big sector of the Egyptians to save money. Second, the insufficient and unaffordable housing supply proposed by the public sector. The third is the launching of the economic liberalization policy *"Infitah"* by Sadat in 1974 which enables Egyptians and goods to travel more freely. In 1977, a new town policy is introduced by Sadat. The goal was to solve the housing problem and the urban extension on agricultural land by relocating the demographic growth on the agricultural land into public housing on the desert fringes of the city. In the 1980s, the informal settlements in Greater Cairo slowed down in growth to some extent due to two reasons, the first one is the oil prices tumbling in 1983-1984 which caused decreasing the emigration of the Egyptian workers to oil countries, the second, Iran-Iraq War from 1980 till 1988 (Sims, n.d.). In the mid-1980s, the national demographic growth rates started to diminish and the migration from rural areas almost stopped (Bayat & Denis, 2000). In the 1990s, although the growth of the informal settlements didn't slow down, no new informal settlements appeared. In spite of the Military decrees (1 and 7) which forbid building on the agricultural land, informal settlements in Cairo continued to grow and extend. From 1986 till 1996, the construction growth rate of informal settlements reached 3.2% per year compared to 1.1% of growth in formal housing areas (Denis & Séjourné, 2002). During the past decades, the unsuccessful public housing policy adopted by the successive governments is one of the main reasons for the growth of informal settlements nowadays. This policy of producing housing units in the new towns failed because of the unaffordability for poor families with low income, and because of the accessibility problem as they are too far from Cairo city center where job opportunities are located, especially for poor people who could not afford to buy a private car

(Séjourné, 2009). In other words: *"Informality became the solution to the housing needs of the city's lower and middle classes."* (Piffero, 2009, pp.21). After going through the context of the emergence of Cairo's informal settlements, it is possible to conclude the main factors which are responsible for the existing and the growth of these settlements. According to Khalifa (2015), there are five main factors which are responsible for this phenomenon. The first factor is the imbalance between demand and supply of planned formal land to absorb the urban growth. The second factor is the absence of fair rent control regulations and laws. The third factor is successive wars faced by Egypt in the last six decades which absorb most of the national resources. The fourth factor is the internal migration from rural areas in the Delta and Upper Egypt to Cairo and other bigger cities. The last factor is the inequality between supply and demand of housing. It is important here to observe that economic component is the main common element among those factors and most of them are direct results of the economic insufficiency. In spite of the clarity of this fact, most of the adopted policies and approaches ignore it. This will be discussed in the next section.

Policies and Approaches Used and Applied

In order to face the informality challenge, a lot of efforts are made through policies and approaches which are adopted either by the government or civil society and other international cooperation actors. Accordingly, these efforts could be split into governmental and non-governmental efforts as follows:

1. Governmental Efforts

In the 1990s, the government started to pay attention to the growth of informal settlements as a result of security and humanitarian reasons (Khalifa, 2015). Accordingly, two successive programs for upgrading informal settlements were initiated. The first one was 'Informal Settlements Development Program' (ISDP) starting from 1994 till 2004. This program adopted an interventionist approach where the government intervenes through providing basic services and infrastructure like water supply, sewage systems and streets paving (ibid). Through this program, basic urban services were provided to about 325 informal areas and 13 areas of worse conditions were developed with a total cost of 3.2 Billion EGP (Algohary & El-faramawy, 2010). According to (Khalifa, 2015), the ISDP lacked the participation of the community and legalization through tenure security. It only focused on improving the physical conditions while ignoring the social and the economic aspects. The second program adopts a preventative approach, in which informal growth are limited through "*Tahzeem Al-Ashwai'at*" which means belting informal settlements by imposing UGB (urban growth boundaries), banning building on agricultural land, banning squatting on state-owned desert land, and using codes and regulations to prevent introducing new structures in these settlements (Khalifa, 2015; Tadamun, 2014; Algohary & El-faramawy, 2010). In 2008, Informal Settlements Development Facility (ISDF), following the Egyptian Cabinet, was established by presidential decree No. 305/2008 as a result of a rock fall over Duweiqa, one of Cairo's informal settlements located at the base of the Moqattam cliffs. Around 110 people were killed as a result of this catastrophe (Tadamun, 2014). The main target of ISDF is to contribute to ensuring safe housing and improve the quality of life of the residents in unsafe areas (Algohary & El-faramawy, 2010). Also, ISDF coordinates efforts and finance for the development of informal settlements. ISDF adopted new typology which categorized informal settlements into unplanned or unsafe areas. Grades from 1 to 4 are given to unsafe areas, where grade 1 includes areas threatened by the dangerous situations related to health and safety of its residents and Grade 4 includes areas exposed to the least dangerous situations (Tadamun, 2014). This clearly refers to the priority adopted by the ISDF and dealing with unsafe areas, which are in need to a quick intervention to improve the housing conditions, to prevent other catastrophes like Duweiqa rock fall from taking place again (ibid). The financial strategy adopted by ISDF is based on considering itself as a revolving fund seeking cost recovery and financial sources for focused grants providing a safe housing environment, market value compensation for properties, or their devaluation as a result of the development action (Khalifa, 2015). According to (Algohary & El-faramawy, 2010), ISDF's Resources of finance in 2010 were as follows:

- Part of the state budget with a total amount of 1.1 Billion EGP.
- A fund from The National Housing Program (NHP) for constructing of 25000 new units with total cost about 2.1 Billion EGP.
- The land-based finance from the Development of Governmental Lands (DGL) with a total cost recovery of 17 Billion EGP.
- The self-finance of the governmental authorities which own the lands with a total amount of 450 Million EGP.
- Funds from international development agencies, donor countries and financial institutions with a total amount of 300 Million EGP.

2. Non-Governmental Efforts

Besides the governmental efforts in developing Cairo's informal settlements, there were some attempts and interventions done by donor agencies, civil society organizations, and charities or religious institutions. According to (Abdelhalim, 2010), there are two main modes of these interventions. The first mode is 'upgrading' which include introducing services and upgrading sectors while maintaining most of the urban fabric and the physical structures. Upgrading of Hai Elsalam and Manshiet Nasser could be put under the umbrella of that mode. The second mode is 'redevelopment' which means demolishing the old physical settings and replacing it with new ones. In-Situ Zeinhum developed housing area, which depended on donations from businessmen under the follow-up of Cairo governorate, could be seen as an example of that mode. One of the initiatives that attempt to apply the community participation concept in upgrading informal settlements is the Participatory Development Program in Urban Areas (PDP) which is initiated by the German Development Cooperation (GIZ) and the Egyptian Ministry of Planning and International Cooperation (MoPIC). The PDP aims at the upgrading of informal settlements within Greater Cairo Region through adopting participatory methodologies for urban upgrading with the cooperation of local authorities and civil society organizations to improve services and enhance living conditions. Two pilot projects, focusing on upgrading infrastructure and community services, were implemented by the PDP in Manshiet Nasser and Boulaq el Dakrour (ibid).

Main Defects and Shortcomings of Applied Approaches

By moving through the previous discussed approaches and policies adopted, three main defects and shortcomings appear on the surface. They decrease their efficiency and inactivate reaching the development targets. The main defects could be stated as follows:

1. Seeing Cairo's Informal Settlements as Just an Inadequate Housing Challenge

The government and the policymakers' vision for Cairo's informal settlements is limited to seeing them as a huge problem of an inadequate housing of bad conditions. From their point of view, their main task is providing adequate housing for those poor inhabitants, who could not afford that. They don't see these settlements within more holistic and integrated development policies based on making use of the inhabitants' abilities and their real partnership.

2. Limiting the Economic Component to Just the Development Financing

In most of the discussed strategies and programs, the economic component is limited to providing huge financial sources for the development process even in introducing services and infrastructure or replacing the deteriorated structures by new ones. Accordingly, an important question raises itself, How to finance the development process of these settlements? In order to answer this question, the government has three key means. The first mean is through an allocated share of the public budget which was characterized by permanent inability in the last decades. This surely affects the other sectors of higher priorities like healthcare, education, etc. The second mean is very small grants provided by international entities and external bodies to finance small interventions related mainly to introducing one of infrastructure items, raising awareness and social development. These grants have insignificant impacts on the community compared to what is needed on the site because of their smallness. Also, this mean is neither sustainable nor continuous as it is usually dependable on plans of the donors and their financial state. The third mean is through small and limited donations of internal bodies and rich businessmen. In this mean, the political aspect plays an important role and financial state of these bodies as well. It is obvious that all the mentioned means are dealing with informal settlements and their residents as a resource absorbent rather than an economic partner which could participate in the cost recovery of the development process.

In fact, there were some approaches which tried to adopt some cost recovery strategies depending on the high price of the squatted state-owned land on which the informal settlement was established. It was believed that securing land tenure of informal settlements would improve the living conditions and could be a source of cost recovery through collecting taxes from the new legal owners of registered occupied land (Khalifa, 2015). Findings show that the land legalization is a time-consuming and expensive process as the dwellers usually face difficulties in paying their share because of their low income and their bad economic conditions (ibid). For that, in most cases, it hard to make use of the land value within applied strategies as it is considered as a permanent source of conflict between the government and the dwellers. In other words, the land value of most of these settlements is frozen in a way or another. With the exception of those frozen land value, most of Cairo's informal settlements suffer from lack of physical resources. Some existing initiatives aim at helping the inhabitants to enhance their economic conditions within social support programs. These initiatives include providing soft loans, affordable lending policies, and offering training programs for income generation. Although some of these initiations may have a strong impact on an individual basis, they are still ineffective on the community level.

3. Neglecting Real Community Participation Within the Development Strategies

Real and effective community participation is usually neglected within the strategies used. The existing participation level adopted is among the lowest ones which lie between informing and consultation according to Arnstein (1969) in his 'Ladder of Citizen Participation'. What is really missed, within these strategies, is a more advanced participation levels which should reach a real partnership making use of the abilities and sources of power the dwellers have. According to CAPMS (2016), around 50% of the Egyptian population is under 20. There are no clear demographic figures related to Egyptian informal settlements in particular, but this figure still could be considered as an indicator for how such young manpower is not utilized efficiently. Most of these strategies don't look at these dense settlements as a source of labor force and human resources which could be utilized within a holistic economic approach not just to integrate the existing primitive informal economy based mostly on unskilled labor within these settlements, but to reach more advanced economic activities through organized investments not depending on physical resources which are almost nonexistent. This pushes towards seeking an alternative approach filling the gaps within the existing approaches and policies.

Knowledge-Based Urban Development as an Alternative Approach

The rise of the knowledge-based economy as the key motivator of global and local economic development is seen clearly within the last few decades (Yigitcanlar, 2009). A shift from the age of ''information'' to ''knowledge'' is a direct result of that rise and the accelerated technological jumps in the fields of science, and information as well (Yigitcanlar, 2008). Accordingly, concepts of knowledge, innovation, and creativity became important key factors of development and production in this new age (Durmaz et al., 2008). This leads to the evolution of what is called 'Knowledge-Based Economies' which are defined according to (OECD, 1996, pp. 7) as "those economies which are directly based on the production, distribution, and use of knowledge and information". Consequently, ''Knowledge-Based Urban Development'' emerged and gained respect as a strategic development management approach could be applied to human settlements and a potent strategy for sustainable development of cities (Yigitcanlar et al., 2008). KBUD is not being fully theorized (Yigitcanlar, 2011). According to Rittgasszer (2013), KBUD has no one uniform definition. He argues that regions of different context with different conditions should build their own knowledge economy in different ways. For that reason, this research adopts the generic framework established by Yigitcanlar (2011) to conceptualize KBUD which could be a step towards generating a specific KBUD related to Cairo's informal settlements. Yigitcanlar (2011) states that KBUD could be seen as a strategy model built on four main pillars which are: economy, society, environment, and management. Accordingly, KBUD includes four main development domains which are: economic, socio-cultural, environmental-urban, and institutional development. These domains are discussed as follows:

The Domain of the Economic Development in KBUD

The KBUD sees the economic development as a process aiming to create knowledge economy based on producing, evaluating and using of knowledge to create economic benefits in high-technology businesses and services as well as education and R&D (Yigitcanlar, 2011). In order to reach successful local economic development, cities, and human settlements should have the ability to adapt to the knowledge economy requirements (Nguyen, 2010). These requirements are stated by Lever (2002) and Laszlo and Laszlo (2007) (cited in Yigitcanlar, 2011, p. 392-393) which are the

... technical knowledge for the innovation of products and services, market knowledge for understanding changes in consumer choices, financial knowledge to measure the inputs and outputs of production and development processes, and human knowledge in the form of skills and creativity.

The Domain of the Socio-Cultural Development in KBUD

The socio-cultural development with the KBUD's eyes seeks establishing a knowledge society where the economic, political and cultural activities are strongly related to the production, distribution, use and integration of knowledge and information. Within this development process, it is important to enhance the knowledge and the skills base of the inhabitants within a community development plan to invest in social and human capitals of the society (Gonzalez et. al., 2005; Frane et al., 2005).

The Domain of the Environmental-Urban Development in KBUD

This kind of development includes the development of both natural and built environments (Yigitcanlar, 2011). Within KBUD perspective, it aims to satisfy human needs without destroying the environment in the present and the future for the coming generations. This development process connects the social human challenges represented in urban development with the environmental systems in an ecological way.

The Domain of the Institutional Development in KBUD

One of the aims of this kind of development, within KBUD perspective, is to bring all the main actors, stakeholders and sources together for increasing the abilities of the community to regulate and facilitate necessary knowledge related activities and put a strategy for knowledge-based society (Yigitcanlar, 2009). According to Baum et al. (2007), there are some principles should be followed to achieve a successful institutional development which are: institutional leadership, good governance, strategic planning, achieving socio-economic and socio-politic equality and branding the society.

Although, according to Yigitcanlar et al. (2009), KBUD creates a secure economy within a sustainable human context and is developed mainly to deal and monitor prestigious cities within Global North, there no related coherent holistic model in the Global South cities where informality is the primary mode of construction. Of course, there are a lot of efforts should be done within applicable strategies and plans to reach what we can call it 'knowledge-based development of informal settlements'. Of course, dealing with these settlements will be different from developed knowledge cities in many ways.

The strategies within this KBUD approach may be more needed in these poor societies to break the bad cycle of poverty than that in more prestigious and richer communities. KBUD has a lot of values and principles to deliver to these poor communities, which suffer from very low quality of life, but at the same time, have a lot of potentials and opportunities which could help in formulating and reforming KBUD to be ready for applying within Cairo's informal settlements as they will be discussed in the next section.

Opportunities in Cairo's Informal Settlements Related to KBUD

In this section, main opportunities existing in Cairo's informal settlements related to the KBUD four main domains will be discussed. These opportunities could be a step on the way through making use of them and building on these chances and giving indicators on how KBUD could be adapted to match Cairo's informal communities and how they could help in enhancing the living conditions of the inhabitants.

1. Opportunities in Cairo's Informal Settlements Related to The Domain of the Economic Development in KBUD

a. The Existence of NGOs Working on Tiny Economic Initiatives

There are a lot of NGOs in Cairo working within economic related activities in informal settlements. They aim to create local development models to eliminate poverty, address the unemployment problem, enhance the inhabitants' living standard and promote for of human dignity. This is done by improving the capacity of young people through providing micro-loans and funding for small projects and small entrepreneurs and enabling training and workshops to develop the inhabitants' skills for enhancing their opportunities for employment. Alashanek Ya Balady, an association for sustainable development and Resala society are two examples of NGOs working on such kind of economic-related initiatives. These kinds of existing economic-related initiatives are considered as opportunities as more advanced plans and programs could build on. Inhabitants are familiar with such kind of cooperation between individuals and NGOs in Cairo's informal settlements which could be promising readiness for bigger collaborations.

b. The Existence of Informal Pattern of Economic Activities

Cairo's informal settlements are considered as a hub for informal economic activities because of the absence of local authorities, the need to services and also the harsh economic state of most of the residents. These settlements were converted gradually by the residents themselves into mixed-use settlements through introducing small shops and simple economic activities within residential streets. They sell some goods like vegetables, fruits, and domestic tools to their neighbors with affordable prices. Some cottage industries like handmade carpets are usually introduced by the NGOs working in the settlement or external partners who prefer to cooperate with inhabitants living in these settlements because of their low wages. These settlements are characterized by the proximity of work and house locations (Shehayeb, 2009). Bigger shops and cars maintenance workshops are usually located in main streets at the entrance of these settlements as they usually attract residents living in the surrounding formal districts (El Mouelhi, 2014). This leads to considering the urban economy as one of the main factors shaping these settlements where the income generation is the main trigger for most of the activities taking place (ibid). This pattern of informal economic activities forces most the inhabitants to be more familiar with simple and primary economic transactions and creates more powerful connections based on profits and trade. On introducing some training courses dealing with some more complex issues related to management and economic-related issues, they will be readier than others who are not exposed to such experiences.

2. Opportunities in Cairo's Informal Settlements Related to The Domain of the Socio-Cultural Development in KBUD

a. The Strong Social Solidarity in These Settlements

Within these settlements, different collective initiatives take place easily to compensate the absence of local authorities (Shehayeb, 2009). Services in the residential streets like garbage collection, street cleaning, introducing and maintaining street lighting, and public landscaping are all nearly controlled by the residents. Maintaining public order takes place to some extent. This is due the natural surveillance and self-policing adopted by the local residents as they are out on the streets most of the time (ibid). All the previous examples show how powerful social solidarity is which could be developed easily in cooperation in shared economic activities related to knowledge and skills within holistic programs.

b. The Existing Entrepreneurship Culture Within the Inhabitants of Cairo's Informal Settlements

Most of the inhabitants living in Cairo's informal settlements are forced to work in the private sector. Initiating simple micro-projects like selling goods, simple cottage industries like handmade tools and cooking sweets is common within these settlements. This builds Entrepreneurship culture which encourages creativity, initiating business, and facing risks which are among the bases for KBUD.

c. Believing in Education as a Mean for the Transition to Higher Social Classes

Unlike expected, education is fully respected within such communities. This may because of their harsh economic conditions and dealing with residents within formal and richer surrounding areas where the percentage of the educated people is higher with high living standard. They believe that education is may be the only way for the transition of their kids to higher social classes and a better life. The researcher found, among his field trips in these settlements, that most of the inhabitants he met are keen on sending their children to school if they have better living conditions and sufficient income. Jealousy between neighbors could not be ruled out as a motivator for caring about education in such contexts. Such belief in the importance of education among these communities is a great opportunity could be approached within KBUD strategies and programs.

3. Opportunities in Cairo's Informal Settlements Related to The Domain of the Environmental- Urban Development in KBUD

a. The Existing Sustainable and Environmental Principles in Cairo's Informal Settlements

Shehayeb (2009) argues that Cairo's informal settlements have some positive characteristics which are the exactly what city planners and sustainability and environmental agendas are calling for, such as self-financing housing mechanism, compact urban pattern offering shade in summer, low energy structures, walkable environment, availability of mixed uses, and work-home proximity. All these environmental qualities could be a good base when applying environment-related strategies in these communities and not start from scratch.

b. Most of the Building Structures are Built and Modified by the Inhabitants Themselves

Because of the absence of the local authorities and lack of building regulations, most of the building structure are built and modified and extended by the residents themselves. This strengthens self-reliance of the inhabitants could be a base for economic initiatives within holistic strategies for the developing these settlements.

c. Most of the Inhabitants are From Rural Background Which Means more Skills Related to Agriculture and Planting

As mentioned before, Most of the inhabitants living in Cairo's Informal Settlements have a rural origin. This means most of them, especially the older ones, have agricultural skills. As within rural Egyptian communities, most of the family members work in agricultural fields. It is common to see a tree or a shrub in front of one of the dwellings where the inhabitants take care of it. In the case of introducing soft scape elements within an environmental plan, the residents would interact easily with such elements.

4. Opportunities in Cairo's Informal Settlements Related to The Domain of the Institutional Development in KBUD

a. The Existence of Active Local NGOs

The existence of active NGOs working in the community and providing some services through cooperation with the residents within Cairo's informal settlements could be treated as one of the institutional anchors for KBUD especially when knowing that some of these NGOs were established by some residents belonging to powerful families. Putting some organization rules related to representing the whole inhabitants in the NGO's board could be a good start for the reformation.

b. The Existence of Powerful Key Person Within the Community

After the enhancement of the socio-economic conditions within the settlement phase in Cairo's informal settlements, the settlers bring their families and invite their relatives, living in rural areas, to join them in the settlement (Eldefrawi, 2015). Shehayeb & Eid (2007) argues that this social phenomenon is a result of the preference of moving in groups in the Egyptian culture and convincing relatives to live closer in the same area. This leads to the formation of strong social ties between the residents depending on the family ties (Eldefrawi, 2015). Accordingly, this complex social situation leads to the appearance of powerful persons in each family. This person usually is an old person who is treated as the main reference for all the family members. When conflicts take place, his words are usually respected. These kinds of persons are very important when developing such settlements. As dealing with them give their families that feeling of contentment and build trust with the inhabitants which, subsequently, facilitate the development processes.

Challenges in Cairo's Informal Settlements Related to KBUD

In this section, Challenges existing in Cairo's informal settlements related to the KBUD four main domains will be discussed. Facing and dealing with those challenges could be a step on the way of seeking for practical tools to approach the development of Cairo's informal settlements through KBUD.

1. Challenges in Cairo's Informal Settlements Related to The Domain of the Economic Development in KBUD

a. Concentration of Unskilled Labor Force

In the absence of any efforts for training programs except some initiatives provided by NGOs, most of the labor force in Cairo's Informal Settlements could be considered as unskilled labor. Most of the men work as street vendors selling cheap goods or working in primitive construction tasks, while women work in selling cheap goods in front of their dwellings or as maidservants in the surrounding rich formal districts.

b. The Difficulty of Integrating the Existing Informal Pattern of Economic Activities Into the Formal Ones

The lack of economic opportunities in rural areas leads to internal migration to Cairo which suffers from limited capacity of formal jobs. Subsequently, informal economic activities emerge especially in Cairo's informal settlements (Mehrem, 2014). In spite of the academic discussion about the importance of integrating such economic activities into the main formal economic stream, it is still a hard mission because of lack of a database for such activities, instability of most of those activities, and the complexity of the social networks on which some of these activities depend.

2. Challenges in Cairo's Informal Settlements Related to The Domain of the Socio-Cultural Development in KBUD

a. The Existence of Some Rural Habits

Rural-related habits like raising poultry and animals like goats in the streets in front of the dwellings and women gathering sitting in front of dwellings' entrances most of the day are mostly common in Cairo's informal settings El Mouelhi (2014). This kind of habits is not socially accepted within more advanced classes housing areas in Egyptian cities and does not fit with the urban life.

b. The Existence of a High Percentage of Drugs Dealers and Related Trade

As a direct result of marginalizing these settlements, and the lack of local authorities and governmental services in such contexts, the rate of activities against the law is high including selling and distributing drugs.

c. The Existence of a High Percentage of Illiteracy and School Dropout Especially Between Women and Girls

The harsh living conditions and lack of regular income push some of the inhabitants of Cairo's informal settlements to get their children out of school to help in generating money and save the education expenses. Also, some rural traditions, related to the inhabitants' origins, push families to prevent girls from education.

3. Challenges in Cairo's Informal Settlements Related to The Domain of the Environmental-Urban Development in KBUD

a. The Non-Existence of Environmental Awareness

As a result of the spread of illiteracy and school dropout, the environmental awareness is limited within these settlements. Although the efforts done by some NGOs in raising environmental awareness, some habits like throwing garbage in the streets, burning them as a way to get ride it and not caring about cleanliness are mostly common in these settlements.

b. Many of the Building Structures and the Urban Spaces Are Deteriorated

In general, the building structures are in bad conditions within Cairo's Informal Settlements. This is because of the high percentage of dilapidated structures as the residents don't invest more money in housing development due to the risk of eviction (Sims, 2003; Piffero, 2009).

4. Challenges in Cairo's Informal Settlements Related to The Domain of the Institutional Development in KBUD

a. Conflicts Among the Local NGOs

Usually, there are conflicts between different NGOs in such settlements because of several reasons. The first reason is the different interests. Some of them are interested more in capacity buildings and education for kids while others are more opened for different activities including physical interventions. The second reason is that they are all competing for attracting donations from the external fund bodies. For that each NGO tries to show that it is the best NGO working in the area with the best records. Some of them pretend that they participate in some projects in the area only for gaining credibility.

b. Conflicts of Interest Among the Families from Different Rural Tribes

In Cairo's informal settlements, it is easy to recognize that each family aims to strengthen their prestige in the area within a competition between the other families. The tribal traditions of rural areas especially in Upper Egypt – where most of the inhabitants are rooted – play an important role in such conflicts.

DISCUSSION AND CONCLUSION

Neglecting the financial component, within the strategies adopted by the successive Egyptian governments, was the main reason for the delay and postponing of most of the development projects in Cairo's informal settlements. This opens the door towards the questioning the old approaches and exploring KBUD as an alternative one. Although KBUD is developed mainly to deal with the more developed and prestigious contexts, it has the ability to be developed and modified, within its main and generic pillars and domains, to be applied in poor contexts. Cairo's informal settlements, as an example of those contexts, are urgently in need of more advanced strategies to break the destitution nasty cycle. Their need may be more urgent than contexts with a higher standard of living. The first step on the way of reforming KBUD to be more applicable to the development of Cairo's informal settlements is to understand their

Figure 1. KBUD framework pillars and domains with relation to the suggested main actors existing in Cairo's informal settlements
Source: Author based on (Yigitcanlar 2012)

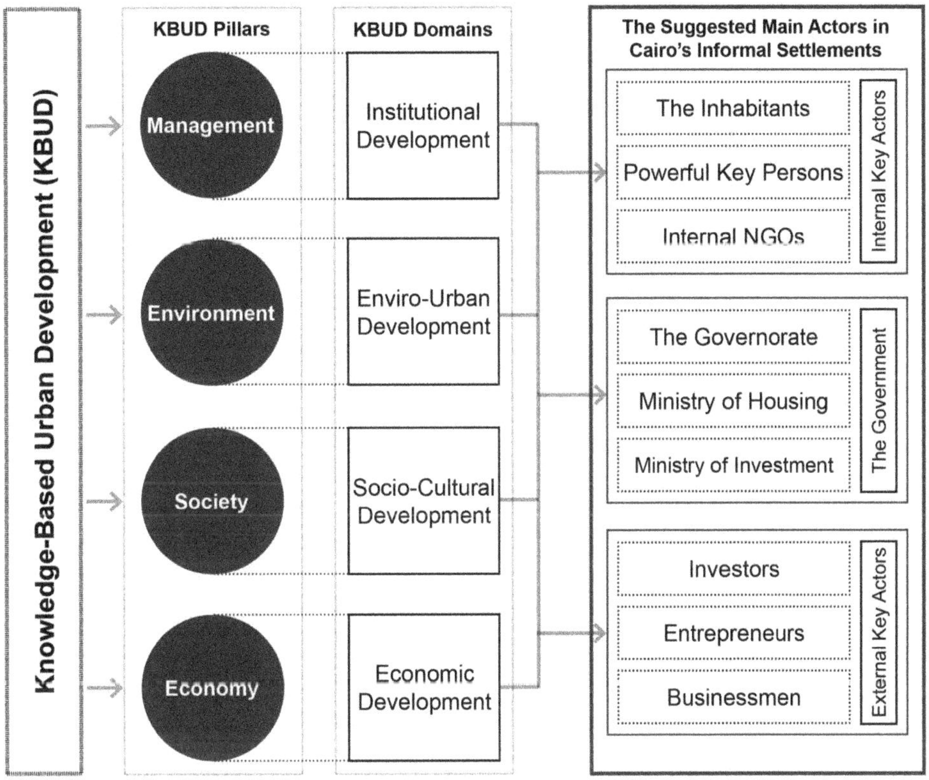

contexts and their main actors in light of KBUD's domains. This could be done through exploring related opportunities and challenges. It is also important to examine the main actors and stakeholders working behind those opportunities and challenges in order to approach them through convenient strategies and programs. These main actors could be split into three groups (see Figure 1).

The first group is the internal key actors which include the inhabitants, the powerful key persons, and the internal NGOs. This group is the most important one as they include the main beneficiaries who would fully cooperate within development processes. The second group is the government group which includes the local authority represented in Cairo governorate and both ministries of housing and investment which are the most related to KBUD domains. The importance of this group lies in its role in facilitating all the bureaucratic issues and providing all the legalization means. The third group is the external key actors, which includes the investors, businessmen, and the entrepreneurs. This group is the motivation group which is responsible for initiating and managing the projects through KBUD plans. Although KBUD framework is generic and adaptable and it holds a lot of values and qualities, a lot of efforts should be done in adapting KBUD to be applied in such poor contexts. For that reason, it is important to look at KBUD with open eyes as an alternative approach with more integrated and holistic means dealing with the economic component when developing Cairo's informal settlements and this chapter is a step on that long way.

REFERENCES

Abdelhalim, K. (2010). Participatory upgrading of informal areas: a decision-maker's guide of action. Cairo: Participatory Development Program in Urban Areas (PDP) in Egypt.

Algohary, S., & El-faramawy, A. (2010). *Egyptian Approach to Informal Settlements Development*. Informal Settlements Development Facilities. Available at: http://www.slideshare.net/GRFDavos/egypt-for-idrc-2-june-2010-finalpptx

Arnstein, S. (1969). A Ladder of Citizen Participation. *JAIP*, *35*(4), 216–224.

Associates, A. B. T. ADames and Moore, & GOHBPR. (1982). Informal Housing in Egypt. Cairo: U.S. Agency for International Development.

Baum, S., Yigitcanlar, T., Horton, S., Velibeyoglu, K., & Gleeson, B. (2007). *The role of community and lifestyle in the making of a knowledge city*. Brisbane: Griffith University.

Bayat, A., & Denis, E. (2000). Who is Afraid of Ashwaiyyat?: Urban Change and Politics in Egypt. *Environment and Urbanization*, *12*(2), 185–199.

CAPMS. (2016). Census. *Central Agency for Public Mobilization and Statistics*. Available at: http://www.capmas.gov.eg/

Collier, P. (2013). *Exodus: How Migration is Changing Our World*. New York: Oxford University Press.

Denis, E., & Séjourné, M. (2002). *ISIS: Information System for Informal Settlements*. Cairo: Ministry of Planning, GTZ, CEDEJ.

Durmaz, B., Yigitcanlar, T., & Velibeyoglu, K. (2008). Creative cities and the film industry. *The Open Urban Studies Journal*, *1*(1), 1–10. doi:10.2174/1874942900801010001

El Mouelhi, H. (2014). Culture and informal urban development - The case of Cairo's 'Ashwa'eyat (informal settlements). Berlin: German Academic Exchange Service (DAAD).

Eldefrawi, S. (2015). Community and Neighbourhood in Egyptian Context, case Formal and Informal Settlements - Cairo. *International Journal of Social Science and Humanity*, *5*(3), 281–286. doi:10.7763/IJSSH.2015.V5.467

Frane, A., Tomsic, M., Ronecevic, B., & Makarovic, M. (2005). *The challenges of sustained development: the role of socio-cultural factors in east-central Europe*. Budapest: Central European University Press.

Gonzalez, M., Alvarado, J., & Martinez, S. (2005). A compilation of resources on knowledge cities and knowledge-based development. *Journal of Knowledge Management*, *8*(5), 107–127.

Khalifa, M. (2015). Evolution of informal settlements upgrading strategies in Egypt: From negligence to participatory development. *Ain Shams Engineering Journal*, *6*(4), 1151–1159. doi:10.1016/j.asej.2015.04.008

Kipper, R. (2009). Cairo: a broader view. In R. Kipper & M. Fischer (Eds.), *Cairo's informal areas between urban challenges and hidden potentials* (pp. 12–15). Cairo: GTZ Egypt.

Mehrem, H. (2014). *What to do with Egypt's Informal Economy?* Available at: http://www.egypt-business.com/Paper/details/1448-What-to-do-with-Egypts-Informal-Economy/11368

Mostafa, M. (2013). Closing the loop: teaching what we have learned from learning from Cairo-an academic perspective. In B. Stryker, O. Nagati, & M. Mostafa (Eds.), *Learning from Cairo: global perspectives and future visions* (pp. 134–136). Cairo: Cluster.

Nguyen, T. (2010). *Knowledge economy and sustainable economic development: A critical review.* Munich: de Gruyter Saur.

OECD. (1996). *The Knowledge-Based Economy. Science, Technology and Industry Outlook 1996.* Paris: Organisation for Economic Co-operation and Development.

Piffero, E. (2009). Beyond rules and regulations: the growth of informal Cairo. In R. Kipper & M. Fischer (Eds.), *Cairo's informal areas between urban challenges and hidden potentials* (pp. 20–27). Cairo: GTZ Egypt.

Rittgasszer, I. (2013). Knowledge-based Urban Development, as a New Development Paradigm. In *Regional Growth, Development and Competitiveness.* Szeged: Doctoral School in Economics.

Séjourné, M. (2009). The history of informal settlements. In R. Kipper & M. Fischer (Eds.), *Cairo's informal areas between urban challenges and hidden potentials* (pp. 16–19). Cairo: GTZ Egypt.

Shehayeb, D. (2009). Advantages of Living in Informal Areas. In R. Kipper & M. Fischer (Eds.), *Cairo's informal areas between urban challenges and hidden potentials* (pp. 34–43). Cairo: GTZ Egypt.

Shehayeb, D., & Eid, Y. (2007). Neighbourhood Design and Community Building: A model of social interaction. In *The appropriate home: Can we design "appropriate" residential environments?* (pp. 129–144). Cairo: HBNRC.

Sims, D. (2003). *Cairo, Egypt - understanding slums: case studies for the global report 2003.* UN Habitat. Available from: http://www.ucl.ac.uk/dpu-projects/Global_Report/pdfs/ Cairo.pdf

Sims, D. (n.d.). *Library - analytical materials.* The Habitat International Coalition's specialized Member group: Housing and Land Rights Network (HIC-HLRN). Available at: http://www.landpedia.org/landdoc/Analytical_materials/Sims_Residential_Informality_in_Greater_Cairo. pdf

Tadamun. (2014). *Coming up short: Egyptian government approaches to informal areas.* The Tadamun Initiative. Available from: http://www.tadamun.info/

Yigitcanlar, T. (2008). *Knowledge-based development of creative urban regions. Knowledge International Week.* Manizales: Ibero-American Community for Knowledge Systems; doi:10.4018/978-1-59904-720-1

Yigitcanlar, T. (2009). Planning for knowledge-based urban development: Global perspectives. *Journal of Knowledge Management, 13*(5), 228–242. doi:10.1108/13673270910988079

Yigitcanlar, T. (2011). Knowledge-based urban development redefined: from theory to practice knowledge-based development of cities. In T. Yigitcanlar & C. Fachinelli (Eds.), *Summit Proceedings of the 4th Knowledge Cities World Summit.* The World Capital Institute and Ibero-American Community for Knowledge Systems, Bento Goncalves.

Yigitcanlar, T., & Velibeyoglu, K. (2008). Knowledge-based strategic planning. *3rd International Forum on Knowledge Asset Dynamics*, 296-306.

KEY TERMS AND DEFINITIONS

Cairo: The capital of Egypt and the largest city in the Middle East and second largest in Africa. It is a historic city located to the south of the Nile Delta, while its urban pattern is aligned to the East Bank of the Nile. Cairo gains its importance as it is the center of the country's political and economic life as well as most of the industrial activities.

Informal Economic Activities: Economic activities that take place without any governmental permission or registration.

Informal Settlement: An illegal, unplanned housing area that is built by the inhabitants themselves without any building or planning regulations.

Non-Governmental Organization (NGO): An organized voluntary group of inhabitants driven by a common interest that provides various services to its community.

Rural Tribe: A well-connected social group of people who often belong to one descent due to a higher grandfather or a tribal alliance and live in rural areas in the Delta and Upper Egypt.

Urban Upgrading of Informal Settlement: Providing the basic infrastructure and services to improve the wellbeing of the inhabitants and enhancing the settlement's physical settings in general.

Wada' Al-Yad: A phenomenon of occupying an abandoned land owned by the state through hand claim.

Chapter 8
Opportunities for and Constraints on the Transformation Into a Knowledge-Based Economy:
A Critical Analysis of Initiatives in Turkey

Zafer Kıyan
Ankara University, Turkey

Hakan Yüksel
Independent Researcher, Turkey

ABSTRACT

As information and communication technologies (ICTs) change economic and social activities creating a new economic paradigm based on the production and processing of knowledge, all aspects of human life are being transformed, including cities people live in. All around the world, countries are trying to adopt this new paradigm referred to as a knowledge-based economy (KBE) and organize their cities to possess a more competitive position in this new context. Turkey is one of these countries wishing to build KBE. The chapter analyzes Turkish efforts in building KBE and organizing its cities in this respect. It emphasizes that Turkey once had an important advantage in building KBE due to its developed telecommunication industry that offered the material infrastructure of KBE but lost this technological capacity owing to the implementation of inappropriate strategies. Turkey also conceptualizes KBE in such a narrow sense that leads to the adoption of other wrong policies effecting the country's economy, society, and cities.

DOI: 10.4018/978-1-5225-3734-2.ch008

Copyright © 2018, IGI Global. Copying or distributing in print or electronic forms without written permission of IGI Global is prohibited.

INTRODUCTION

In contemporary societies, the pace and scale of change are astonishing. Rapidly developing information and communication technologies (ICTs) have a significant effect on the social change in that they transform the conduct of economic and social activities in many ways. These technologies, making it possible to instantly transmit and process information and knowledge across the world, paves the way for new production patterns and means of social interaction. An important aspect of the change is the differentiation of development and urbanization paradigms due to the transformation in economies and societies. The Industrial Revolution brought about changes in production and social interaction through innovations in communication and technology, which subsequently initiated the growth of large metropolitan cities. This echoes the current development paradigm based on the production and process of knowledge by means of ICTs, which lead to the large-scale changes on the way people live.

This chapter explores Turkish efforts to implement the new development paradigm and plan cities within this framework. First, it examines how, after decades of development, Turkey lost its telecommunication technology production capacity due to the adoption and implementation of market-oriented neoliberal policies in the 1990s, abandoning State led protectionist policies. This investigation is especially important given that telecommunication constitutes the material infrastructure of the new paradigm. Such an examination is highly relevant for all developing countries wishing to establish the new development paradigm since it demonstrates that the dominant policies at international level may be in conflict with national aims.

The chapter also reveals that the narrow scope of Turkey's conceptualization of the new development paradigm and the policies generated from this perspective are far from fulfilling the anticipated changes. Another focus of this chapter is that this narrow conceptualization obstructs the efforts to build sustainable cities with better living conditions.

The new paradigm has been investigated widely in the literature using different concepts such as *information society, knowledge society, knowledge economy, knowledge-based economy* or *new economy.* All these concepts refer to the central role of producing and processing knowledge in conducting economic and social activities in developed countries as the result of the large-scale transformations since the 1970s; however, each emphasizes a different aspect of the process. In this chapter, the new paradigm is explored using the concept of knowledge-based economy (KBE) because it has a strong emphasis on the role of knowledge in socio-economic and urban development. Furthermore, KBE is more useful in understanding the new orientation in urbanization efforts that stresses the importance of knowledge for cities.

According to the OECD (1996), KBEs are "economies which are directly based on the production, distribution and use of knowledge and information" (p. 7). It would be wrong to assume that the concept does not refer to a complete transformation. In fact, KBE is an umbrella term (Madanipour, 2011, p. 207) and contains many other aspects, such as *knowledge management* and *knowledge-based development* (Ergazakis, Metaxiotis & Psarras, 2006). Another important aspect of KBE is *knowledge-based urban development*, which stresses the impact of the transformation on the development of cities (Yigitcanlar, Velibeyoglu & Martinez-Fernandez, 2008). In this respect, KBE opens possibilities for making investigations within the framework of the concept of *knowledge city* (KC), as will be explained in this chapter. Though Turkish policies for KBE do not emphasize the transformation into KCs, this has been adopted as a strategic aim in many countries around the world.

In this respect, this chapter initially explores the emergence of KBE in developed countries and its spatial impact on cities. Therefore, the first two sections of the chapter provide a theoretical framework for KBE and KC conceptualizations. The third section examines the development of the telecommunication industry in Turkey. The fourth section demonstrates that the neoliberal policies adopted after the 1990s played an important role in the loss of Turkish technological capacity in telecommunication. The fifth and sixth sections investigate the new KBE strategy of Turkey, and the conceptualization of cities, respectively. The last section presents a critical appraisal stressing that the narrow-scope of the Turkish conceptualization of KBE results in problematic policies and ineffective urbanization strategies.

The Rise of Knowledge-Based Economy

The remarkable economic growth of Western capitalist countries attained in the post-war period slowed down in the 1960s. At the beginning of the 1970s, the accumulation cycle of capital was so interrupted that it became common to speak in terms of a crisis. In order to overcome the problem, a comprehensive restructuration of economies and societies was initiated.

The crisis of the 1970s was clearly visible in the decrease of productivity and profit rates. As a solution, industrial production was transferred to developing countries where wages were low and environmental concerns were not considered important (Arrighi, 1996, pp. 1-2). In addition to production, demand also became global since companies began to scan world markets for potential demand. This restructuration of economic activities paved the way for the rise of the services sector (Harvey, 1992, pp. 156-157). The volume of services such as finance, insurance and logistic was amplified and designing, marketing, advertising and public relations became crucial in managing demand. Additionally, the media sector gained importance by reaching out to customers. In parallel with globalization, the telecommunication services connecting countries became one of the strategic sectors.

In the 1970s and early 1980s, theorists such as Daniel Bell (1973) and Alvin Toffler (1971; 1981) analyzed the transformation and announced the emergence of a new society. Their common emphasis is the outpouring of workers from industry into the services sector, creating a transformation as radical as the Industrial Revolution, which absorbed the labor released from agriculture in the 19th century (Bell, 1973, pp. 124-128; Toffler, 1971, pp. 13-15; Toffler, 1981, pp. 13-14). Furthermore, in their conception, the work of services sector workers is nothing but processing knowledge (Bell, 1973, pp. 116, 127-128; Toffler, 1971, p. 402). For example, those workers managing global production systems, analyzing market demand or designing new products are in fact processing knowledge.

After the 1990s, with the commercialization of the Internet, socio-economic activities on networks gained a new momentum. During this decade, while many developed and developing countries were preparing policy papers to facilitate the complete transformation into a KBE (Henten, Skouby, & Falch, 1996, p. 177), the theoretical efforts also multiplied. Manuel Castells is a leading figure in these efforts writing a trilogy of thousands of pages on the restructuration of Western capitalist societies and he became extremely influential in academic and policy circles in the 1990s and 2000s. According to Castells (2001), "A technological revolution, centered around information technologies, began to reshape, at accelerated pace, the material basis of society" (p. 1). He qualifies knowledge as "the main source of productivity" in today's advanced societies (Castells, 2001, p. 17), and claims that "For the first time in history, the human mind is a direct productive force, not just a decisive element of the production system" (p. 31). Similarly, Aubert (2005, p. 62) emphasizes the decrease of manufacturing activities is being reduced in

KBE, contrary to the rise of services. Gorz (2009) also stresses the domination of knowledge-intensive activities in contemporary capitalism.

According to Ampujo and Koivisto (2014), the works of Bell and Castells represent two different periods of the literature on KBE. Thus, it is possible to categorize the literature on KBE into two phases. It is also possible to argue that there is a strong emphasis on the deep impact of KBE on the spatial organization of societies in both phases. Before delving into this aspect of the restructuration, it is useful to briefly comment that there are also many theorists who interpret the restructuration from the perspective of historical continuity. Contrary to the theorists that argue for a new society constituting a break in history, they stress that the structural transformation is in accordance with capitalism that constantly changes its formation without shifting its basic principles (Beniger, 1986; Webster, 2006, pp. 6-7).

The Emergence of Knowledge Cities

The Industrial Revolution created large cities containing dirty factories and overcrowded neighborhoods. The first-phase theorists of KBE praised the fall of industrial production and heralded the rise of a more environmental, knowledge-based production. For example, Toffler (1981) stated that "Like rusty used cars, the most backward Second Wave industries are thus exported from the rich nations to the poor" (p. 181). However, these early theorists also underscore that the rise of KBE offers new opportunities for the Third World and the remote regions of the developed countries in that telecommunication and ICTs could establish the infrastructure of the new society by diffusing socio-economic activities instead of concentrating them in specific places (Toffler, 1971, p. 402; Toffler, 1981, p. 336-337). For instance, through distance learning and working, people living in isolated regions would be able to develop their skills and thus, benefit from more job opportunities. Due to the media network, they could receive information on the same basis as the inhabitants of cities, telemarketing would allow them access to good quality goods, and tele-medicine would be useful for maintaining their health.

According to Toffler (1981, pp. 336-337, 340-344), since the investment in processing knowledge is much lower than establishing gigantic factories, poor countries can leapfrog and reach the development level of rich ones. The fact that these poor countries have never experienced industrialism also constitutes an advantage in their transformation into a KBE because they are considered to be free of the defects of industrialism. For instance, their characteristics of environmental green energy and rural production are in line with KBE (Toffler, 1981, p. 336-337).

In Castells' theory, access to networks is even more vital because it paves the way for a prosperous society with the absence of access resulting in destitution and instability. He uses the categories of *space of flows* and *space of places* to explain the difference (Castells, 2001, pp. 407-459; Castells & Ince, 2003, pp. 55-58). Accordingly, knowledge workers in the center of contemporary capitalism living in cities like New York, London or Tokyo and the elite in the big cities of the Third World share the space of flows. These people have a common educational background and lifestyles even though they live thousands of kilometers apart. Contrary to their regular contact with each other through networks, their relation with the poor people of their cities is very limited. According to Castells, poor people, who are deprived of necessary skills for operating in networks, cannot access the space of flows and are trapped in the space of places qualified with lower living standards. Furthermore, countries, regions, cities or neighborhoods that do not have a solid access to networks are nothing but "black holes of human misery in the global economy" according to Castells (2001, p. 2).

There is a specific literature that analyzes the transformation of cities in the process of restructuration. In fact, Castells (1989) introduced the concept of the *informational city* even before his publications in the 1990s. It can be argued that the relationship between KBE and cities is one of the most vibrant topics discussed in today's academia. For instance, Stock (2011, p. 963) argues that a new type of city is rising in accordance with the advent of the knowledge in socio-economic activities. Additionally, Madanipour (2011, p. 65) comprehensively describes the changes in cities stating that "As manufacturing has been replaced by information processing, factories have been replaced by offices". As a result, "cities become increasingly entrepreneurial and competitive, investing in buildings and places that might distinguish them from their competitors". Madanipour adds that "Working-class neighborhoods are transformed for white-collar workers, places of learning find new economic priority, possibilities for new economies of scale are created through clustering knowledge-intensive activities and recreational spaces that would support them". Alraouf (2008, p. 241) also describes the transformation of cities and their pattern of physical development as a result of the rise of ICTs. He considers that as the nature of city development changes, the activities in the knowledge sector gain importance and require conditions and environments that are different from commodity-based manufacturing activities. Accordingly, back offices, customer service centers, and research and development laboratories have become widespread in cities.

The crucial concept behind all these scientific efforts on the relationship between cities and KBE is the *knowledge city* (KC) and Carillo (2006) describes the 21st century as a "century of knowledge cities" (p. xii). There are many theoretical works on KCs (Ergazakis, Metaxiotis, Psarras & Askounis, 2006; Martínez, 2006; Ergazakis, Metaxiotis & Psarras, 2004) in addition to empirical studies (Monnavarian, Mosakhani & Akbari, 2012; Méndez & Moral, 2010; Peyroux, Grossetti & Eckert, 2009; Wong, Choi & Millar, 2006; Azua, 2006; Chen & Choi, 2004). Additionally, there are international events related to KC, such as the Knowledge Cities World Summit held annually in different countries. There are cities around the world such as; Barcelona, Stockholm, Melbourne Montreal, Boston, Dublin and Delft preparing strategic plans through which they can identify themselves as KCs.

There are various definitions of a KC in the contemporary literature. According to Edvinson (2006), "a knowledge city is purposely designed for encouraging and nourishing the collective knowledge, i.e. intellectual capital, as capabilities to shape efficient and sustainable actions of welfare over time" (p. 7). On the other hand, Carillo (2004) describes KC "as permanent settlement of relatively higher rank in which the citizenship undertakes a deliberate, systematic attempt to identify and develop its capital system in a balanced sustainable manner" (p. 34). Ergazakis, Metaxiotis and Psarras (2004) proposed a generic definition of KC; in that it:

...is a city that aims at a knowledge-based development, by encouraging the continuous creation, sharing, evaluation, renewal and update of knowledge. This can be achieved through the continuous interaction between its citizens themselves and at the same time between them and other cities' citizens. The citizens' knowledge-sharing culture as well as the city's appropriate design, IT networks and infrastructure support these interactions. (p. 7)

The characteristics of a KC defined by the Latin American Knowledge Development Forum, Monterrey, Mexico (2003), and by the ENTOVATION 100, Barcelona, Spain (2004) may still be considered valid. Accordingly, a KC must:

- Have instruments to make knowledge accessible to citizens;
- Have a network of public libraries compatible with international standards;
- Provide all citizens with access to new communication technologies;
- Have cultural facilities and services with a central educational strategy;
- Have a high level of newspaper and book reading;
- Have a network of schools connected with artistic instruction throughout its territory;
- Respect the diversity of cultural practices of its citizens;
- Place streets at the service of culture;
- Simplify, through the provision of spaces and resources, the cultural activity of the community collectivities and associations;
- Have civic centers that are open to diversity and that foster face-to-face relations;
- Make available all the tools required for citizens from other territories to express themselves.

All these scientific investigations and efforts for transforming into a KC are for a vital cause. In today's KBE, it is extremely important to be a KC and connected to networks in order to possess competitive advantages and achieve a reasonable level of prosperity. In their study, focused on European cities, Van Winden, Van den Berg & Pol (2007) found that cities that benefit from the increased knowledge-intensity of economic processes manage to attract human resources and investment, create high-level jobs and demonstrate high growth rates and innovation levels. However, cities with economies, which are far from becoming more knowledge-intensive, face economic decline and degradation and lose vital human resources; thus, shifting toward a knowledge city is a necessity rather than an option for cities. However, even though Turkey had a considerable advantage in the potential to transform into a KBE and creating KCs, it has made no meaningful progress regarding this crucial matter.

The Development of Telecommunication in Turkey

As telecommunication constitutes the material basis of a KBE and in this respect establishes a precondition for any effort for creating KCs, it is useful to explore Turkey's experiences in this field. Due to its relatively developed telecommunication industry, in the 1990s, Turkey was considered as one of the few countries that could create KBE not just in its own territory but in its region (Hawkins, 1997, pp. 189-190). However, today, this potential of Turkey has not been realized.

In Turkish efforts for an advanced telecommunication, concerns over development and military efficiency played an important role, paving the way for the central position of the State. The first attempt to develop the telecommunication infrastructure of the country was initiated within the framework of American military assistance since Turkey is a NATO member with a common border with the Soviet Union (Başaran 2014, pp. 159-161; Geray, 2003, p. 143). In the early 1960s, Turkey achieved high rates of development through the application of a planned economic model but the telecommunication infrastructure of the country could not keep pace with the economic and social development, and the seemingly endless number of people waiting for a telephone line (Törenli, 2005, pp. 17-20).

In the face of the increasing demand for telecommunication, Turkey found a solution in a technological innovation supported by the long-term government policies. Turkey decided in the early 1970s to invest in the new digital technology, which offers a line capacity large enough to respond the enormous demand (Başaran 2014, pp. 171-172; Törenli, 2005, p. 21). Furthermore, the cost of establishing a digital telephone exchange was much lower than the earlier systems. Thus, the State-run PTT and the Scientific and Technological Research Council of Turkey (TÜBİTAK) signed an agreement to develop digital technology and the initiative for local production was begun under a foreign license. The determination of the Turkish authorities to install developed telecommunication technology was further reinforced by the country being subject to a military embargo after its intervention to Cyprus in 1974 (Başaran 2014, p. 171). Thus, Turkey founded ASELSAN in 1975, a company with military electronics and telecommunication expertise.

The priority accorded by Turkey for implementing up to date telecommunication technology for national development and security corresponded well with the global tendencies at that time. At the beginning of the 1980s, when the first locally produced digital systems became operational (Başaran 2014, p. 171; Törenli, 2005, p. 21), Turkey decided to restructure its economy and introduced export-oriented growth model instead of import substitution. In this critical period of integration with the world economy, the telecommunication systems made in Turkey established the required network and remained operational until the late 1990s (Törenli, 2005, p. 21).

The period between the 1970s and the 1990s, in which long-term State policies were based on investing in new technologies and generating local production capacity, can be considered as a kind of success story; however, after the 1990s, political and economic crises and short-term policies resulted in the loss of Turkish technological capacities. Thus, Turkey has failed to obtain the status of a producer country in relation to the Internet and mobile technologies that constitute a new stage in the process of technological innovation (Törenli, 2005, pp. 32-35).

In addition to crises in the country, globally, the dominant economic tendency of neoliberalism during the period was not in accordance with the policies that created the Turkish success in telecommunication. Neoliberalism prescribes the removal of the State from all economic domains; however, Turkey, as a country in crises that demanded international loans, could not resist the offers of international credit organizations such as International Monetary Fund (IMF) or the World Bank (WB) to support the liberalization of the telecommunication sector (Kıyan & Yüksel, 2011, pp. 56-62; Törenli, 2005, pp. 25-32; Geray, 2003, pp. 144-146, 199-210).

Turkish Policies for Knowledge-Based Economy

Until the middle of the 2000s, two different approaches on the development of KBE in Turkey were in conflict. Contrary to Turkish experts emphasizing the importance of local technological capacity and avoiding market-centered policies, the government chose to adopt the global neoliberal tendency. After a process, which was long and thorny due to social opposition and judicial battles, the Turkish Telecom Company (TT) was privatized in 2005, marking the triumph of neoliberalism.

The first report on KBE in Turkey was prepared in 1993 by the WB. The report, entitled *Turkey: Informatics and Economic Modernization*, was highly criticized by Turkish experts since it advised Turkey to relinquish its long-term efforts for technological capacity and adopt a cheaper option to import from developed countries which offer important subventions related to the global competitiveness of their companies (Geray, 2003, p. 145).

Against the dominant tendency, Turkish experts mobilized under auspices of TÜBİTAK and in 1999 presented the national strategy paper *Turkish National Information Infrastructure Master Plan* (TUENA) to protect the technological capacities of the country (Törenli, 2005, pp. 22-23; Geray, 2003, pp. 146-

151). However, at this time, Turkey was experiencing a deep economic crisis with major sociological repercussions and the government wanted to obtain an IMF loan, thus they ignored the document and also accelerated the process of the liberalization of the telecommunication sector.

Turkish experts (Kıyan & Yüksel, 2011, pp. 56-62; Törenli, 2005; Geray, 2003, pp. 198-210) offer a comprehensive account of the process of liberalization and the loss of technological capacities in telecommunication. In 1983, the PTT R&D Laboratory, which developed the digital telephone exchanges, was transformed into the private company, TELETAŞ. In the middle of the 1990s, while Turkey was about to sign a Customs Union Treaty with the European Union, TELETAŞ was sold to the French telecommunication giant Alcatel to ensure the support of France for the treaty (Törenli, 2005, p. 30; Kazgan, 2002, p. 241). Alcatel closed the R&D departments of TELETAŞ and used the company to market French products in Turkey. After a series of legal battles in the Constitutional Court, the government obtained the permission to separate the telephone division of PTT and in 1995 founded TT, which would later be privatized. After the economic crises in 1999 and 2001, as a part of the IMF restructuring package, in 2004, Turkey removed the state monopoly in telecommunication and privatized TT in 2005 by selling it to Oger Telecom, headquartered in Dubai.

In the late 1990s and the early 2000s, Turkey was abandoning the protectionist policy; however, Eastern Asian countries such as China or South Korea were benefiting hugely from the rise of the Internet and mobile technologies mostly because their governments considered these domains as strategic and should become an active actor (Harwit, 2008). Thus, Turkey missed out on adopting the new technological paradigm in telecommunication. One of the founders of PTT R&D Laboratory, Fikret Yücel, describes the negative effects of this policy change; in 1991, Turkey's telecommunication production was 669 million US dollar ($) and imports amounted to 189 million; however, in 2000, the volume of production decreased to 624 million US $ and importation increased to 2.463 billion (as cited in Saygı, 2002, p. 32).

The *Information Society Strategy (2006-2010)* plan, introduced in 2006, constitutes a milestone in Turkey's efforts towards a KBE. The plan was prepared as "the basic reference documents [...] for all segments of society" (State Planning Organization [SPO], 2006, p. 2). Its importance was further emphasized in the most recent Turkish policy paper concerning the development of a KBE, entitled *2015-2018 Information Society Strategy and Action Plan*, it was "a main policy document that would enable Turkey to achieve its information society goals" (Ministry of Development [MoD], 2015, p. 10).

The document of 2006 emphasizes the following seven specific strategic priorities for the transformation of Turkey into a KBE (SPO, 2006, p. 20):

- Social Transformation;
- ICT Adoption Businesses;
- Citizen-focused Service Transformation;
- Modernization in Public Administration;
- A Globally Competitive IT Sector;
- Competitive, Widespread and Affordable Telecommunications Infrastructure and Services;
- Improvement of R&D and Innovation.

According to the simplistic logic of the document, in order to establish KBE, citizens and businesses, especially SMEs, must use ICTs. Thus, they must have an awareness of these technologies and access to networks. These points are particularly highlighted with the first two priorities (SPO, 2006, pp. 22-28). The third and the fourth priorities concern the transformation of public services and establishing e-government in Turkey (SPO, 2006, pp. 29-37). Accordingly, offering public services through networks would be productive for the government, citizens and businesses. Furthermore, this would mobilize citizens and businesses to use ICTs, which is a sine qua non for KBE. According to the fifth priority (SPO, 2006, pp. 37-39), the transformation into a KBE and public investment for that purpose would create a demand for the information technology (IT) sector that would lead the development of more local companies. With their experience in the local markets, Turkish IT companies would have competitive advantages in global markets. The sixth priority on telecommunication is to ensure the material basis of these projections (SPO, 2006, pp. 40-43). Accordingly, widespread use of ICTs is only possible with competition existing in telecommunication market that would offer a developed infrastructure and ensure costs were affordable. In this section, the reduction of taxes in telecommunication and the development of broadband access are also emphasized. The last priority section stresses the importance of R&D for technological production (SPO, 2006, pp. 43-44).

Thus, according to the document, once people and businesses start using ICTs, the transformation into a KBE would be automatic. In order to trigger the massive use of the technologies, competition in telecommunication sector and e-government are required and thus, Turkey would have a competitive IT sector.

Nearly, a decade later, the most recent Turkish policy paper presents the catastrophic results of this simplistic approach. The document emphasizes eight areas as pillars of the new Turkish strategy for KBE (MoD, 2015, pp. 13-14). Before explaining specific actions for each of these areas, a summary of Turkey's current situation is presented below:

- Information Technologies Sector (MoD, 2015, pp. 36-39):
  - Considerably small market with insufficient expenditure;
  - Demand concentration on imported hardware;
  - Low value-added assembly processes in local production;
  - Low market share of software and IT services;
- Broadband Infrastructure and Competition (MoD, 2015, pp. 39-41):
  - Concentration of fixed broadband access in DSL technologies;
  - Low share of fiber and cable infrastructure in fixed broadband access;
  - Lack of competition in the DSL and cable market;
  - Rapidly increasing but still small share of fiber connections due to competition;
  - Prevalence of a mobile infrastructure in broadband access;
  - High cost of access to fixed broadband due to high taxes and lack of competition;
  - Geographical differences in access quality;
- Qualified Human Resources and Employment (MoD, 2015, pp. 41-45):
  - Steady share of employment in ICTs;
  - Quality gap between labor offers and demand;
- Diffusion of ICT into Society (MoD, 2015, pp. 45-50):
  - Low diffusion and use of ICTs;
  - Insufficient digital content in Turkish;
  - High cost of access and devices due to taxation;
  - Low ICTs awareness and skills of citizens;
  - Digital gap among citizens;

- Information Security and User Trust (MoD, 2015, pp. 50-51):
    - Incomplete legal regulation;
    - Increasing cyber-crime;
    - Lack of cooperation between authorities;
- ICT-Supported Innovative Solutions (MoD, 2015, pp. 51-53):
    - Lack of guidance and standards in smart city applications;
    - Limited practice of smart city and smart building applications;
    - Low diffusion and regulation problems concerning telemedicine;
    - Limited big data applications;
- Internet Entrepreneurship and e-Commerce (MoD, 2015, pp. 54-56):
    - Insufficient demand for the Internet and e-commerce;
    - Lack of funding for startups;
    - Difficulties in obtaining State support;
    - Lack of orientation and education;
    - Difficulties in starting up and closing down a business;
    - Security and privacy concerns;
- User-Centric and Effective Public Services (MoD, 2015, pp. 56-60):
    - Insufficient integration and cooperation of institutions;
    - Service quality and participation problems related to institutions;
    - Poor working conditions of ICT experts;
    - Problems in sharing public data for the creation of added-value.

It is obvious that Turkish policies conducted between 2006 and 2015 failed. According to the latest document, there was not sufficient local production and most of the IT spending was spent on imported hardware, creating a trade deficit. The competition in fixed broadband access was not at a satisfactory level given that in the DSL and cable access markets alternative operators were in marginal position. Furthermore, the country was highly dependent on the old infrastructure established before privatization because the share of DSL technologies delivered over the copper infrastructure in fixed broadband access was 78.4 percent as of March 2014, with 6.67 million subscribers (MoD, 2015, p. 39). There was competition in the fiber access market, which increased the number of subscribers but this should also be questioned given that different operators were establishing their own networks of fiber infrastructure instead of sharing the already existed infrastructure and resulting in a waste of resources. According to the latest document, there were 52 million 3G and 26.4 million mobile broadband subscribers as of March 2014 (MoD, 2015, p. 41), and competition was working well in mobile broadband access sector. However, the mobile access market had difficulties in keeping up with the new technologies according to the initial Turkish version of the last strategy document, which contains more detailed information (MoD, 2014, pp. 44, 105-106). 3G technology was available in many countries in the early 2000s however, Turkey organized the tender for the introduction of the same technology in 2008, the year first 4G networks became operational. In 2015, Turkey tendered for 4G licenses. It can be also argued that the government considers telecommunication sector as a milk cow because of high taxation. This may be useful to cover budget deficits but it is in contradiction with the aim of establishing KBE.

The 2006 document does not offer an insight on the relationship between the development of KBE and the organization of cities. It only refers to the use of new technologies for an effective transportation system and the electronic services provided by local administrations that would also reinforce e-democracy in the country (SPO, 2006, p. 33). In this respect, the 2015 document offers more insight into the issue but it is difficult to presume that it does not suffer from a narrow perspective, as will be elaborated in the following sections.

The New Policy Framework

In the light of the critical appraisal of previous policies, the latest strategy document on KBE offers more concrete projects for each of the eight pillars. It can be argued that Turkey once again understood the importance of local production and the crucial role of the State in developing the technological capacity. However, it has to be admitted that Turkey lost precious time in the transformation into a KBE. In order to catch up with the developed nations, Turkey decided to determine and then focus on the most promising technologies and services, as it had done in the 1970s.

In this respect, the 2015 document contained several important measures (MoD, 2015, pp. 61-62) such as cloud computing, digital games, security, defense, healthcare, telecommunication, business practices and education, which were especially emphasized as promising domains. Furthermore, the importance of R&D, innovation and export incentives associated with ICTs was highlighted. The document reveals the importance of attracting the attention of large IT companies in order for the country to be a part of the global value chain. However, the core of the new policies for developing IT sector in Turkey is the Movement of Enhancing Opportunities and Improving Technology (FATİH) project (MoD, 2015, pp. 17, 38, 49-50, 61). Within the scope of FATIH, all schools will be equipped with smart blackboards, 10.6 million tablet computers will distributed to students and teachers, which will be renewed every four years. Furthermore, e-content for education will also be promoted. The project is expected to would contribute to the growth of software, services, digital content and mobile applications markets as well as increasing domestic value-added in hardware production, due to the scale and continuing nature of the scheme. Moreover, in the original Turkish version of the document, two points are also emphasized (MoD, 2014, p. 95). Firstly, the FATİH project would have a role in attracting foreign firms to engage in production in Turkey. Secondly, priority being given to tablet computers would facilitate the future production of smart phones.

The Turkish version of the document considers Turkey as an important market for smart devices and emphasizes local production in this field (MoD, 2014, p. 95). In order to close the technological gap between Turkey and the developed countries, the document underscores the importance of local production for 4G mobile equipment and R&D for 5G mobile technology (MoD, 2014, pp. 106-108).

Thus, according to the new policy framework, the production of new generation smart devices such as tablets and smart phones is a priority and given a high level of State support. The rationality of this is explained as follows: "65-70 percent of global hardware market is under the control of 5-10 global firms. Access to market is rather challenging due to reasons like importance of technologies with patent protection, first mover advantage and economies of scale. Hence, determining technologies that will be in demand in the future and channeling R&D activities to these areas are essential for gaining technological competitive advantage" (MoD, 2015, p. 38). However, it is also indicated that "[a]lthough global demand for hardware is increasing, due to high productivity levels and fierce competition, prices are decreasing and share of hardware sector in global economy is getting lower" (MoD, 2015, p. 19). Thus, there are concerns over the future importance of hardware production.

In the section of the 2015 document that contains new policy priorities of Turkey (MoD, 2015, pp. 61-71), there are also other measures. The diffusion of the new generation of access infrastructures such as fiber networks and establishing competition in access markets are still targets to be achieved. Moreover, the necessity to decrease the current high taxes, the diffusion spread of ICTs among citizens, increased awareness and development of skills of citizens concerning ICTs, together with the importance of e-commerce are important aims given in the new document.

Cities in Turkish Policy Framework

As mentioned above, the strategy document of 2006 gives limited information about KCs. Though the 2015 strategy document partially explores the relationship between KBE and organization of cities, it does not offer an in-depth insight.

The latest document deals with the issue under the sixth pillar of the new policy framework, entitled *ICT-Supported Innovative Solutions*. First, an analysis of the contemporary situation at the global level (MoD, 2015, pp. 28-31) is presented. In this section, the benefits of ICTs for providing city services and protecting the environment are particularly emphasized. According to the document, "[t]oday, 52 percent of the world population, which is about 7 billion, lives in urban areas. The rate of urbanization tends to increase all around the world. Fast pace of urbanization makes it difficult to provide sustainable and quality services in housing, infrastructure, transport, education, health and security. Developed countries have launched GIS [Geographic Information Systems] based smart city applications that facilitate provision, monitoring and improvement of various city services and enable decision making based on real-time information" (MoD, 2015, p. 29). The use of ICTs by cities is further emphasized by underscoring the concept of *smart cities* (SC) multiple times but without giving further explanation. Moreover, it is indicated that in face of the global gas emission problem, SCs offer considerable benefits for the protection of environment since smart grids and smart building of these cities provide an enormous energy saving. An emphasis on the *green ICT* concept complements this environmental approach. The document describes green ICT as a key sector in fighting climate change and improving energy efficiency.

Thus, ICTs, which render the transition into a KBE possible, are also useful tools for creating better cities with more effective services and a cleaner environment. On the other hand, according to the document, cities are also tools for developing ICTs. In the same section on global tendencies, there is an emphasis on *Living Laboratories* described as follows; "[The] [l] labs approach, within which the needs of citizens are identified through more effective channels, ICT goods and services are developed in accordance with these needs and these goods and services are tested by people in real life, is widely used in smart city applications" (MoD, 2015, p. 29).

Then, the document provides a description of the context in Turkey (MoD, 2015, pp. 51-53) and principally problematizes the lack of efficient SC applications in face of increasing problems. Industrialization and urbanization in Turkey accelerated after 2000, and Turkey experienced the most rapid energy demand growth over the past 10 years among the OECD countries resulting in major environmental concerns. Furthermore, according to the document, there are difficulties in providing services such as transportation, water, health and safety in increasingly crowded Turkish cities.

Against these challenges, Turkey must benefit from ICTs but there is a lack of awareness, orientation and cooperation, which obstructs finding solutions based on new technologies. In this respect, particularly important is the establishment of a GIS infrastructure "as a base for smart urban planning" (p. 52) but according to an official survey conducted in 2011, only 3 percent of municipalities have completed GIS work. The results of another survey on the SC applications of municipalities conducted in 2013 in 40 municipalities shown in Table 1 reveal not only the situation in Turkey but also on the conceptualization of the issue.

In Table 1 it is not the results obtained from municipalities that are essentially important; rather, it is the categories created for the survey as the indicators of SC. Thus, SC conceptualization depends on mostly the use of ICTs and it is, in this respect, a very narrow concept when compared with KC.

With the information given on the situation in Turkey in the 2015 document, it is also understood that green ICT is the tool for procuring SC applications because as stated in the document "[a] [s]mart grid is one of the areas where green ICT can be used most effectively" (MoD, 2015, p. 53). According to the document, another important aspect of green ICT is the reduction of e-waste. In this respect, building SCs and developing green ICT with particular reference to GIS and smart transportation, are cited among the new policy objectives of Turkey, together with the adoption of the living labs approach (MoD, 2015, pp. 67-68). After engaging in all these efforts, using ICTs in cities would offer time and cost savings in the design and management of urban transformation and facilitate the participation of citizens in this process (MoD, 2015, p. 52). Moreover, cities will gain economic, social and environmental benefits and an improved quality of life (MoD, 2015, p. 67). According to the original Turkish version of the document, this process would also increase brand value and competitive power of Turkish cities (MoD, 2014, p. 146) and explains that this is why an index of SC is required for measuring the transformation of Turkish cities (MoD, 2014, p. 145).

The longer Turkish version of the 2015 strategy document, which explains more comprehensively the actions that will be initiated, explores another important aspect of KBE and urban organization (MoD, 2014, pp. 93-94). Since the 2000s, Turkey has established several important Technology Development Zones in order to create its own version of Silicon Valley. These zones are usually called *Teknoparks* and are generally established in university campuses, which is an environment that offers easier access to the required cooperation with the academia to conduct efficient R&D activities. IT companies operating in these zones can benefit from important tax incentives. Furthermore, the availability of skilled human resources and proximity to markets have also driven IT companies to operate in these zones. Currently, although these *teknoparks* are operating at 100 percent capacity they are only located in large cities. The new document emphasizes the necessity to introduce location-independent support for software companies, constituting a new approach, which geographically spreads the benefits of KBE.

Table 1. Smart city application of 40 municipalities surveyed in 2013 (MoD, 2015, p. 52)

	List of Smart City Applications	Completed	In Planning	Unbegun
Energy	• Intelligent street lighting. • Building energy management. • Smart metering. • Smart grids.	4 3 2 1	6 3 2 2	30 34 36 37
Water	• Smart metering and demand management. • Leakage detection and preventive maintenance.	4 2	9 7	27 31
Transport	• Smart parking meters and pricing. • Fleet management. • Integrated public transport fare system.	6 23 15	6 0 4	28 17 21
Urban Services	• Cultural and touristic services. • Accessing services through electronic channels. • Emergency action and disaster management. • Monitoring air quality.	13 31 9 12	12 4 12 2	15 5 19 26

An Appraisal of the Turkish Approach to Knowledge-Based Economy

It can be argued that Turkey developed an effective telecommunication infrastructure through the protectionist policies applied after the 1970s but lost its technological capacity after the 1990s with the rise of neoliberal policies, which emphasized the supremacy of market and requiring the removal of the State from economic domain. In this respect, the latest strategy document dated 2015 represents a policy change because it underscores the technological production capacity supported by State policies.

It is also possible to argue that Turkey has neither fully understood the importance of KBE nor managed to overcome the development paradigm based on industrialism. Its conceptualization of KBE is highly marked by industrialism given the prioritization of the mass production of hardware and the establishment of a developed infrastructure. These are the tangible dimensions of KBE; however, there are also intangible dimensions ignored by Turkey.

Achieving a high capacity for technological production was an important aim for Turkey, it is unfortunate that the capacity that was achieved was mostly lost. With the new strategy, the ability to obtain a good level of technological production is, once again, an important target. For that purpose, foreign companies are being invited to set up operations in Turkey; however, the same policy paper indicates that the total share of the hardware sector in global economy is decreasing, raising questions over Turkey's efforts towards technological production.

In the same manner, a developed telecommunication infrastructure is necessary for building KBE, especially taking into account the increasing amount of data transfer. Turkey appears determined to focus on that the infrastructure issue but the 2015 document comments that the revenue of infrastructure operators and investors is not increasing (MoD, 2015, p. 23). Thus, it is necessary to critically reassess Turkey's aim in relation to this requirement though it is impossible to deny the importance of a developed infrastructure.

In the light of the information given in the latest strategy document, when compared with hardware production and infrastructure operation, software development and IT services are more promising aspects of KBE. However, because they are intangible aspects of KBE, they do not fit the Turkish conception of KBE, which is marked by industrialism. Therefore, these intangible aspects do not become prioritized and Turkey puts an emphasis on hardware produced in factories and huge networks instead of the knowledge flowing through networks.

Another concern over Turkey policies for KBE is that the strategy document covering the period from 2010 to 2014 was never prepared. Turkey adopts the transformation into a KBE as a strategic aim but it fails to prepare the required strategy document, which creates reservations about the determination of the political power.

Contrary to its ambiguous position related to KBE, the government depicts a strong determination for multi-million dollar construction and energy projects. Ignoring environmental concerns, the government organized international tenders for the construction of two nuclear power plants and ordered the building of numerous hydropower plants that will have a serious effect on the natural environment in many regions of the country (Gibbons & Moore, 2011). According to the General Directorate of State Hydraulic Works (2015, p. 29) at the end of 2015, there were 562 hydropower plants in Turkey. Similarly, the State issued licenses for mining activities in the most important natural sites of Turkey, such as the Kaz Mountains and Cerattepe. While the declared objective for these actions is that development is necessary, those who raise objections citing the protection of the environment are being categorized by government sources as reactionaries opposing development.

This approach to development also threatens the future of Turkish cities. This can be best observed in Istanbul, the largest city and economic powerhouse of Turkey. In recent years, accelerated projects have been undertaken; a new suspension bridge was constructed across the Bosporus, and the construction of a new tunnel under the Marmara Sea and a third airport in the city, which would be one of the biggest in the world, is underway. The building of new highways linking the new bridge and new airport to the existing road network are destroying northern forests of the city (Uzunçarşılı Baysal, 2016). Through these huge projects, Istanbul is testing the limits of the industrial development paradigm. Rather than development in other regions of Turkey, this construction is concentrated on Istanbul and brings with it a boom in housing projects, rendering the city more crowded. According to the Turkish Statistical Institute (TUİK) (2016), there were 114,751 house sales in Turkey in August 2016, constituting a 2 percent increase in comparison with the same month in 2015. Of the total sales, Istanbul had the biggest share with 15.3 percent. The concentration of such a development in Istanbul also results in traffic congestion and noise pollution. As Rosenberg (2016) comments, "With urbanization comes numerous problems, such as finding housing, employment and transport solutions for growing cities. Yet one particular problem flies under the radar, although it affects a great many people: noise" (p. 190).

Industrial development seems to be more prone to be transformed into electoral support, constituting an important political motivation. Thus, the government inaugurates every construction project with a large prestigious event ("President Erdoğan Inaugurates," 2016). In addition to concerns over sustainability, it is also very simple to see problems of productivity in this conceptualization of development. For example, in 2012, Facebook paid 1 billion US $ for the photo sharing company Instagram that had been in operation for less than two years (Upbin, 2012). However, Turkey privatized 55 percent of TT in 2005 for a sum of 6.55 billion US $ ("Saudi Arabian Consortium," 2005). Similarly, the Candy Crush game appeared first in April 2012 and after being downloaded on more than 500 million mobile devices was sold in 2015 for 5.9 billion US $, a sum that would be enough to build two suspension bridges over the Bosporus (Şenerdem, 2015).

Once the industrial paradigm is accepted as the path to development, it becomes inevitable that more energy will be consumed and this paves the way for the large energy projects. Under these circumstances, media companies, which are supposed to be major actors of KBE by producing content for networks, invest heavily in the energy sector in Turkey. For example, Doğan Holding, the biggest Turkish media conglomerate, gains 46 percent of its profit from energy with the income from the media division being 38 percent (Doğan Şirketler Grubu Holding A.Ş., 2015, p. 21). Similarly, the Ciner Group also operates in different sectors, such as energy, mining, chemicals and media (http://www.cinergroup.com.tr/en). It is interesting to note that these companies became involved in the energy business in the 2000s, after initiating their media operations.

Thus, it is not surprising that Turkey emphasizes the concept of SC, based on the use of ICTs for delivering public services and protecting the environment, instead of KC in its efforts for KBE. The concept of KC requires an in-depth insight into KBE and more comprehensive planning and commitment; however, Turkey suffers from a superficial approach to the issue.

CONCLUSION

Turkey's failure in the transformation process into a KBE is not only limited to the loss of its telecommunication technology production capacity which had led to the construction of a developed digital network until the 1990s. It has also failed to fully understand the essential elements of KBE with all its different aspects, tangible or intangible. This is why Turkey is also very far from developing KCs and this is clearly indicated by the actions of all the fundamental actors of the process.

Ergazakis, Metaxiotis & Psarras (2006, p. 4) stated that "The process of developing a knowledge city is neither quick nor simple. Consequently, any effort to develop a knowledge city should have assured the active support of the entire society, i.e., local government, citizens, private sector, organizations, universities, etc." However, in the Turkish context, even the support and guidance of the foremost authority, the State, is problematic. According to Monnavarian, Mosakhani & Akbari (2012), it is impossible to build KBE or KCs in the absence of the strategic participation of the State in the process, and "creating a KC does not happen overnight or without planning" (p. 170). The authors emphasize that "two factors have the highest priority: human-legal infrastructure and strategic approach" (Monnavarian, Mosakhani & Akbari, 2012, p.170). Local municipalities can take the preliminary steps in the absence of State support to initiate the transformation process and Shagrah (2014) underscores their importance in that process. Unfortunately, Turkish municipalities also suffer from an incomplete comprehension of the importance of KBE and KC.

In addition to the State and municipalities, other actors of the process in Turkey such as universities and companies also have problems. In establishing KBE, the interaction between universities and private sector is crucial for building KCs (Van Winden, Van den Berg & Pol, 2007). In order to provide a better interaction, Turkey has founded *teknoparks* but this initiative did not produce the expected results since being installed in the university campuses of big cities constrained the development in a narrow space instead of spreading the idea across the country.

As Stock (2011, p. 971) emphasizes, "Knowledge originates not only from science and technology but also from everyday life". Therefore, the public support can make a difference in face of most problems. For example, the Internet, social media, theatres, museums, libraries etc. have an important role to play in the process transformation into KCs and KBE. Confirming this argument, Ergazakis, Ergazakis, Metaxiotis & Charalabidis (2009) show that successful KCs have a network of public libraries and indicates that KCs offer citizens the possibility of access to the bulk of the libraries' available material online. Contrary to this perspective, Turkish authorities do not take necessary steps given that their strategy mostly rely on the use of new technologies, ignoring cultural and social aspects. As a result, public support for the transformation is lacking.

It can be concluded that the industrial paradigm of development is still powerful in Turkey, creating the conceptualization of KBE in such a way that prioritizes mass production of technological goods and establishment of a developed infrastructure. In this framework, the adopted aim at political level for cities is not based on KCs but on SCs, which is a rather narrow conceptualization for the future. More importantly, this problematic approach is prevalent among all the key actors of society, hampering the anticipated transition.

REFERENCES

Alraouf, A. A. (2008). Emerging Middle Eastern Knowledge Cities: The Unfolding Story. In T. Yigitcanlar, K. Velibeyoglu, & S. Baum (Eds.), *Knowledge-Based Urban Development: Planning and Applications in the Information Era* (pp. 240–259). New York: Information Science Reference. doi:10.4018/978-1-59904-720-1.ch014

Ampujo, M., & Koivisto, J. (2014). From 'Post-Industrial' to 'Network Society' and Beyond: The Political Conjunctures and Current Crises of Information Society Theory. *TripleC, 12*(2), 447–463.

Arrighi, G. (1996). *The Long Twentieth Century: Money, Power, and the Origins of Our Times*. London: Verso.

Aubert, E. J. (2005). Knowledge Economies: A Global Perspective. In A. Bounfour & L. Edvinsson (Eds.), *Intellectual Capital for Communities: Nations, Regions, and Cities* (pp. 61–69). Burlington, MA: Elsevier Butterworth-Heinemann. doi:10.1016/B978-0-7506-7773-8.50007-8

Azua, J. (2006). Bilbao: From the Guggenheim to the Knowledge City. In F. J. Carrillo (Ed.), *Knowledge Cities: Approaches, Experiences and Perspectives* (pp. 97–112). Burlington, MA: Elsevier Butterworth-Heinemann. doi:10.1016/B978-0-7506-7941-1.50011-7

Başaran, F. (2014). *İletişim ve Emperyalizm: Türkiye'de Telekomünikasyonun Ekonomi Politiği*. Ankara: Ütopya.

Bell, D. (1973). *The Coming of Post Industrial Society*. New York: Basic Books.

Beniger, J. (1986). *The Control Revolution: Technological and Economic Origins of the Information Society*. Cambridge, MA: Harvard University Press.

Carrillo, F. J. (2004). Capital cities: A Taxonomy of Capital Accounts for Knowledge Cities. *Journal of Knowledge Management, 8*(5), 28–46. doi:10.1108/13673270410558738

Carrillo, J. F. (2006). Introduction: The Century of Knowledge Cities. In F. J. Carrillo (Ed.), *Knowledge Cities: Approaches, Experiences and Perspectives* (pp. XI–XV). Burlington, MA: Elsevier Butterworth-Heinemann. doi:10.1016/B978-0-7506-7941-1.50003-8

Castells, M. (1989). *The Informational City: Information Technology, Economic Restructuring, and the Urban-Regional Process*. Oxford, UK: Blackwell.

Castells, M. (2001). *The Rise of the Network Society*. Oxford, UK: Blackwell.

Castells, M., & Ince, M. (2003). *Conversations with Manuel Castells*. Cambridge, UK: Polity.

Chen, S., & Choi, C. J. (2004). Creating a Knowledge-Based City: The Example of Hsinchu Science Park. *Journal of Knowledge Management, 8*(5), 73–82. doi:10.1108/13673270410558792

Doğan Şirketler Grubu Holding, A. Ş. (2015). *Moving Forward… Moving Beyond…* Retrieved October 21, 2016 from http://www.doganholding.com.tr/_files/en/annual-report/DOHOL_2015_Annual_Report.pdf

Edvinsson, L. (2006). Aspects on the City as a Knowledge Tool. *Journal of Knowledge Management, 10*(5), 6–13. doi:10.1108/13673270610691134

ENTOVATION 100. (2003). *The Latin American knowledge development forum*, Monterrey, Mexico.

ENTOVATION 100. (2004). *Roundtable*. Barcelona, Spain.

Ergazakis, E., Ergazakis, K., Metaxiotis, K., & Charalabidis, Y. (2009). Rethinking the Development of Successful Knowledge Cities: An Advanced Framework. *Journal of Knowledge Management, 13*(5), 214–227. doi:10.1108/13673270910988060

Ergazakis, K., Metaxiotis, K., & Psarras, J. (2004). Towards Knowledge Cities: Conceptual Analysis and Success Stories. *Journal of Knowledge Management*, *8*(5), 5–15. doi:10.1108/13673270410558747

Ergazakis, K., Metaxiotis, K., & Psarras, J. (2006). An Emerging Pattern of Successful Knowledge Cities' Main Features. In F. J. Carrillo (Ed.), *Knowledge Cities: Approaches, Experiences and Perspectives* (pp. 3–15). Burlington, MA: Elsevier Butterworth-Heinemann. doi:10.1016/B978-0-7506-7941-1.50004-X

Ergazakis, K., Metaxiotis, K., Psarras, J., & Askounis, D. (2006). A Unified Methodological Approach for the Development of Knowledge Cities. *Journal of Knowledge Management*, *10*(5), 65–78. doi:10.1108/13673270610691189

General Directorate of State Hydraulic Works. (2015). *Devlet Su İşleri Genel Müdürlüğü 2015 Yılı Faaliyet Raporu*. Ankara: DSİ.

Geray, H. (2003). *İletişim ve Teknoloji: Uluslararası Birikim Düzeninde Yeni Medya Politikaları*. Ankara: Ütopya.

Gibbons, F., & Moore, L. (2011). Turkey's Great Leap Forward risks cultural and environmental bankruptcy. *The Guardian*. Retrieved October 21, 2016 from https://www.theguardian.com/world/2011/may/29/turkey-nuclear-hydro-power-development

Gorz, A. (2009). *The Immaterial: Knowledge, Value and Capital*. London: Seagull Books.

Harvey, D. (1992). *The Condition of Postmodernity: An Enquiry into the Origins of Cultural Change*. Oxford, UK: Blackwell.

Harwit, E. (2008). *China's Telecommunications Revolution*. Oxford, UK: Oxford University Press. doi:10.1093/acprof:oso/9780199233748.001.0001

Hawkins, R. (1997). Prospect for a Global Communication Infrastructure in the 21st Century: Institutional Restructuring and Network Development. In A. Sreberny-Mohammadi, D. Winseck, J. McKenna, & O. Boyd-Barrett (Eds.), *Media in Global Context: A Reader* (pp. 177–193). London: Arnold.

Henten, A., Skouby, K. E., & Falch, M. (1996). European Planning for an Information Society. *Telematics and Informatics*, *13*(2-3), 177–190. doi:10.1016/S0736-5853(96)00010-X

Kazgan, G. (2002). *Tanzimat'tan 21. Yüzyıla Türkiye Ekonomisi: Birinci Küreselleşmeden İkinci Küreselleşmeye*. İstanbul: İstanbul Bilgi Üniversitesi Yayınları.

Kıyan, Z., & Yüksel, H. (2011). The GATS and the Globalizing Public Services: The Case of Turkey and Türk Telekom. *AİD TODAİE's Review of Public Administration*, *5*(1), 35–68.

Madanipour, A. (2011). *Knowledge Economy and the City: Spaces of Knowledge*. New York: Routledge.

Martínez, D. S. (2006). A Comparative Framework for Knowledge Cities. In F. J. Carrillo (Ed.), *Knowledge Cities: Approaches, Experiences and Perspectives* (pp. 17–30). Burlington, MA: Elsevier Butterworth-Heinemann. doi:10.1016/B978-0-7506-7941-1.50005-1

Méndez, R., & Moral, S. S. (2010). Spanish Cities in the Knowledge Economy: Theoretical Debates and Empirical Evidence. *European Urban and Regional Studies*, *18*(2), 136–155. doi:10.1177/0969776410381039

Ministry of Development. (2014). *2015-2018 Bilgi Toplumu Stratejisi ve Eylem Planı*. Ankara: MoD. Retrieved October 21, 2016 from http://www.telkoder.org.tr/docDownload.php?docID=2287

Ministry of Development. (2015). *2015-2018 Information Society Strategy and Action Plan*. Ankara: MoD. Retrieved October 21, 2016 from http://www.bilgitoplumu.gov.tr/en/wp-content/uploads/2016/03/Information_Society_Strategy_and_Action_Plan_2015-2018.pdf

Monnavarian, A., Mosakhani, M., & Akbari, M. (2012). Is Tehran a knowledge city? *Journal of Place Management and Development*, *5*(2), 158–173. doi:10.1108/17538331211250053

OECD. (1996). *The knowledge-based economy*. Paris: OECD. Retrieved October 22, 2016 from https://www.oecd.org/sti/sci-tech/1913021.pdf

Peyroux, E., Grossetti, M., & Eckert, D. (2009). Becoming a Knowledge City: The Example of Toulouse. *Built Environment*, *35*(2), 196–203. doi:10.2148/benv.35.2.196

President Erdoğan Inaugurates Osmangazi Bridge. (2016, June 30). Retrieved October 21, 2016 from http://www.tccb.gov.tr/en/news/542/45570/president-erdogan-inaugurates-osmangazi-bridge.html

Rosenberg, B. C. (2016). Shhh! Noisy Cities, Anti-Noise Groups and Neoliberal Citizenship. *Journal of Sociology (Melbourne, Vic.)*, *52*(2), 190–203. doi:10.1177/1440783313507493

Saudi Arabian Consortium win Turk Telecom privatization tender. (2005, July 2). Retrieved October 21, 2016 from http://www.hurriyet.com.tr/saudi-arabian-consortium-win-turk-telecom-privatization-tender-331772

Saygı, N. (2002). Telekomünikasyon ve Bilgi Teknolojileri Pazarı: Mevcut Durum ve 10 Yıllık Perspektif. *Telekomünikasyon Ekseni*, *4*, 17–34.

Şenerdem, E. (2015, November 3). Bir Candy Crush nelere bedel? *BBC Türkçe*. Retrieved October 21, 2016 from http://www.bbc.com/turkce/ekonomi/2015/11/151103_candy_crush_nelere_bedel

Shaqrah, A. (2014). The Role of Greater Amman Municipality in the Making of a Knowledge City. *European Scientific Journal*, *10*(28), 448–456. Retrieved from http://www.eujournal.org/index.php/esj/article/view/4410

State Planning Organization. (2006). *Information Society Strategy (2006-2010)*. Ankara: SPO. Retrieved from http://www.bilgitoplumu.gov.tr/Documents/5/Documents/Information_Society_Strategy.pdf

Stock, G. W. (2011). Informational Cities: Analysis and Construction of Cities in the Knowledge Society. *Journal of the American Society for Information Science and Technology*, *62*(5), 963–986. doi:10.1002/asi.21506

Toffler, A. (1971). *Future Shock*. New York: Bantam Books.

Toffler, A. (1981). *The Third Wave*. New York: Bantam Books.

Törenli, N. (2005). Türkiye'de Telefon Haberleşmesi Alanında Yaşanan Dönüşüm: Neo-liberal Politikalar Eşliğinde Ulus Devletin Elinden Alınan Politika Araçları. *Kültür ve İletişim*, *8*(1), 11–40.

Turkish Statistical Institute. (2016). *Konut Satış İstatistikleri, Ağustos 2016*. Retrieved October 21, 2016 from http://www.tuik.gov.tr/PreHaberBultenleri.do?id=21716

Upbin, B. (2012). Facebook Buys Instagram for $1 Billion. Smart Arbitrage. *Forbes*. Retrieved October 21, 2016 from http://www.forbes.com/sites/bruceupbin/2012/04/09/facebook-buys-instagram-for-1-billion-wheres-the-revenue/#553c1ebe447f

Uzunçarşılı Baysal, C. (2016, February 7). *Probing the 3rd Airport Project vis-a-vis Life, Nature, Environment and People*. Retrieved October 21, 2016 from http://www.kuzeyormanlari.org/2016/02/07/probing-the-3rd-airport-project-vis-a-vis-life-nature-environment-and-people/

Van Winden, W., Van den Berg, L., & Pol, P. (2007). European cities in the Knowledge Economy: Towards a Typology. *Urban Studies (Edinburgh, Scotland)*, *44*(3), 525–549. doi:10.1080/00420980601131886

Webster, F. (2006). *Theories of Information Society*. London: Routledge.

Wong, C. Y. L., Choi, C. J., & Millar, C. C. J. M. (2006). The Case of Singapore as a Knowledge-Based City. In F. J. Carrillo (Ed.), *Knowledge Cities: Approaches, Experiences and Perspectives* (pp. 87–96). Burlington, MA: Elsevier Butterworth-Heinemann. doi:10.1016/B978-0-7506-7941-1.50010-5

Yigitcanlar, T., Velibeyoglu, K., & Martinez-Fernandez, C. (2008). Rising knowledge cities: The role of urban knowledge precincts. *Journal of Knowledge Management*, *12*(5), 8–20. doi:10.1108/13673270810902902

KEY TERMS AND DEFINITIONS

Information and Communication Technologies: Technologies that make information and knowledge production and processing possible.

Knowledge City: A contemporary type of city prioritizing knowledge production and processing in the conduct of social activities and through this tries to become competitive in the global economy.

Knowledge-Based Economy: An economy paradigm that prioritizes the production, distribution, and use of knowledge and information.

Neoliberalism: An economic approach that prioritizes the supremacy of market and imposes the removal of the state from all economic domains.

Services Sector: The third sector of economy in addition to agriculture and industry. Its volume in the economy has been increasingly expanding since the 1970s.

Smart City: A contemporary type of city that puts an emphasis on the use of ICTs in implementing urban services and activities.

Telecommunication: The basic infrastructure of knowledge based economies that renders ICTs operational.

Chapter 9
Creative Cities and Knowledge Capital:
The Case of Dubai (UAE)

Aly Abdel Razek Galaby
Alexandria University, Egypt

ABSTRACT

Many nations of the world are responding to the shift from development policies that rely on intensified labor and capital into alternative policies that build on the intensification of knowledge. The trend towards knowledge-based development has received increasing attention from academics and policy makers in the world. Innovative development paradigms of existing urban models (cities of knowledge, creative cities, and local circles of the knowledge society [precincts]) have opened up alternative prospects for development to the nations of the world. The Emirate of Dubai was among the Arab countries that absorbed this lesson and took the initiative of transforming its economy into a knowledge economy, building their development policies on the intensification of knowledge, embarked on the creation of the creative city and the formation of a knowledge capital, and stopping to understand this experience and explain its constraints; perhaps the research findings would support this effort.

INTRODUCTION

Globalization has become familiar to all of us, along with the repercussions of its structural nature, which have outstripped the limits of time and place. Foreign investments and the free movement of goods, capital and labor have increased, and the countries of the Western world have found new markets and opportunities for investment abroad. With globalization, new players have come to compete with the highly advanced Western economies, especially those where labor costs are low, Such as North-east Asia, Eastern Europe and Latin America. It has become clear that it is no longer sufficient for developed countries to compete on the basis of low costs but they had to revitalize their competitive returns from intensifying knowledge and high-quality innovations. Cities have begun to wonder how they can compete in a more intelligent way in the shadow of all these global transformations (Hospers, 2014).

DOI: 10.4018/978-1-5225-3734-2.ch009

Copyright © 2018, IGI Global. Copying or distributing in print or electronic forms without written permission of IGI Global is prohibited.

Many nations of the world are responding to the shift from development policies that rely on intensified labor and capital into alternative policies that build on the intensification of knowledge. The trend towards knowledge-based development has received increasing attention from academics and policy makers in the world. Innovative development paradigms of existing urban models: Cities of knowledge, creative cities and local circles of the knowledge society (precincts) have opened up alternative prospects for development to the nations of the world.

The Emirate of Dubai was among the Arab countries that absorbed this lesson and tried to overcome the development dilemma it faced during the financial crisis through the first decade of the 21st century, and took the initiative of transforming its economy into a knowledge economy, building their development policies on the intensification of knowledge, embarked on the creation of the creative city and the formation of a knowledge capital, and it was important to stop to understanding this experience and explaining its constraints, perhaps the research findings would support this effort.

METHODOLOGY

The Conceptualization of the Relationship Between Creative Cities and the Knowledge Economy

Knowledge-based development, knowledge economy, knowledge-based urban development and knowledge precincts literature had reviewed in a previous study (Galaby, 2013), we focus here on revising the literature on the concepts of creative cities and knowledge capital, and those that analysis of issues: models of creative cities and their structure, the objectives of creative cities and the formation of knowledge capital, globalization and the knowledge economy.

Models and Structure of Creative Cities

The creative city is a phenomenon that belongs to every age, and there is no particular urban environment that always demonstrates creativity. History is replete with different models of creative cities, some of which are technological regeneration cities, the second is cultural intellectual cities, and the third are cultural technological and the fourth is technological organizational cities. In this regard, Hospers is reminded that in the past we have seen many examples of the cities of technological-innovative, which have contributed to generating new technological developments. One example is the city of Detroit, the automotive industry in America around 1900 and Manchester City, famous for the 19th century in the textile industry, and the cities of the Rhine Ruhr, which are renowned for the coal and steel industry. As for the modern-day, we can cite the Silicon Valley, San Francisco in America, Oxford and Cambridge in the United Kingdom. These technological poles represent the technology's models in the world and are targets for many cities and urban areas that wish to imitate (Hospers, 2014).

Cultural and intellectual cities was concerned with culture, science and performing arts has flourished in periods where tension has occurred between the old conservative system and among small groups of radicals, with brains renewed, such as artists, philosophers and thinkers, who were seeing in such cities as places that would allow them to unleash their talents. In ancient times, Athens is home to democracy, and Florence was the city of art during the Age of Enlightenment. The thriving university cities of Cambridge (in the United Kingdom and the United States), Boston, Toulouse and Heidelberg can be regarded as contemporary examples of that kind of creative city (Hospers, 2014).

The cities of technology and culture in the past we have seen cities concerned with cultural industries, like the Hollywood Film Industry (1920), the music in Memphis, and the fashion in Paris and Milan. This type of creative cities in the modern era are Toronto, the multimedia industry, Austin, the live music scene, Manchester, New Wave music, and Hamburg where the new media and the entertainment industry. Technological and cultural elements have emerged in German cities such as Amsterdam and Rotrodam, which was chosen as the European Capital for Culture in 2001 due to the cinema and Architecture Festival. Hal (1998) and Scott (2000) predicted multimedia, and display culture intelligently, in the form of virtual visits to museums. The cities of organization and Technology offer creative and authentic solutions to the worsening problems in bustling urban life, such as the provision of clean water to the population, the establishment of infrastructure, the provision of appropriate transportation and safe housing. One example is the city of Rome under the rule of Caesar, London in the 19th century, Paris and the means of transport of tunnels, and New York in 1900 and Stockholm after the war, where dual housing systems. Residential cities in the United States and Europe are still demonstrating organizational and technological innovation (Hospers, 2014).

When we questioned about the fundamentals of creative cities and their structure elements, we found Hospers adds in this regard: all these models of creative cities are compatible with each other as a place to create creativity to think that the creator can with others build a creative city with a knowledge density that can contribute to the Urban knowledge economy, but rather a combination of elements or conditions that bring together in the city, increase opportunities for urban innovation, which can be limited to: intensity of interactions, diversity and challenges (Hospers, 2014):

- **Intensity of Interactions and Concentration:** Creativity, knowledge and innovation are the work of human beings, in the sense that the city itself is not the source in this regard, as its inhabitants are the ones who do the renovation. Because the presence of enough people and their concentration in a particular location is an essential catalyst for urban innovation, where they have the opportunity for human interaction and communication. This means that the concentration of the population depends not only on the population, but on the intensity of the interaction between them, where frequent encounters and intensive communication, helps to create new ideas and innovations (Hospers, 2014);
- **Diversity:** Here we mean diversity of the population in their knowledge, skills and activities and of their perceptions of the city's enterprises, buildings and projects. This reminds us of Jacobs (1969) idea of diversity as a breeding ground for creativity in cities, and the city with population diversity, which includes entrepreneurs, artists, immigrants, the elderly, students and families... etc., their differing skills and abilities, and the opportunities to meet can exchange knowledge, and to put forward new ideas and offer their renovation, while in the presence of offices, shops, clubs, places of worship, restaurants, cafes, etc. (Hospers, 2014);
- **Challenges:** If we go back to the past, we note that in times of crisis, the more creative the city faces, the more challenging and unstable it has shown. This happened in Amsterdam about 1600, and in London, Paris, as well as Berlin during the two world wars. They are all far from being sta-

> ble cities, and in the view of some, this instability is an additional circumstance in favor of urban innovation. When the city finds itself in a situation that may expose it to a fall, it may invite it to creativity. Some small events or opportunities such as meeting some creators with entrepreneurs can affect the way in which the city grows in the future (Hospers, 2014).

Our agreement with the Hospers analyses of creative city models and their structure due to use the concept of creative cities although the literature reported to use concepts such as City of Knowledge, Oasis of technology, Smart city and City of education in describing these models of cities—Adding to that Yigitcnta assumed, that in the past few years, both knowledge and cities have become prominent roles, where knowledge has been replaced the physical factors and capital. The cities have become important platforms for shaping and raising human capital and turning it into a knowledge capital, that Which is one of the primary detonators for the production of knowledge and innovation; those that create opportunities for employment, wealth and sustainable economic growth (Yigitcnta, 2013).

Objectives of Creative Cities and Knowledge Capital

Gertler argues that these cities play an important role in enhancing the resilience and competitiveness of the national economy, by supporting the state of innovation between employees and between firms or other organizations that make up urban territory, as they become with the broader transformation to knowledge-based economy key create a value by supporting innovation, adaptation and quality promotion. Creative cities have the potential to enhance the quality of life and opportunities in front of a large section of citizens. Creative cities are also working to achieve social inclusion among citizens, with the goal of quality of place, as a combination of economic resilience and a better life for the urban population. It is appropriate to link the objectives of creative cities not only to the objectives of the knowledge economy, but also to the objectives of knowledge-based development (Gertler, 2004). Because there are four pillars that define this type of economy and the knowledge-based development:

1. An economic and institutional system that provides incentives for the efficient use of existing knowledge and creates new knowledge and entrepreneurial leadership;
2. Educated people with skills that enable them to create and use knowledge;
3. Information-based infrastructure that can facilitate effective communication and disseminate and rotate information;
4. A system of research centers, universities, think-tanks, consultancies, companies and organizations that can open up to the growing Cosmic knowledge repository, works to reconcile and adapt to the local needs and creates new knowledge. Different models of knowledge cities can achieve these objectives (Winden, 2007). Lazlo identified three objectives of knowledge-based development as first a strong strategy for economic growth, urban upgrading and states to participate in the knowledge economy, second to support sustainable human development and third to the perspective of an environmentally and socially sustainable learning society in the future. Instead of thinking about different strategies, economically, financially, socially and culturally environmentally responsible, as separate from each other, it has confirmed in the recent years that better to thinking in the light of a unified strategy focused on the development of its goal of generating (10) Types of capital (Lazlo, 2004).

Natural capital, the manufactured capital, the technological capital, monetary capital, the know how capital, human capital, social capital, cultural capital, the eco-system, the evolutionary capital. These ten types of capital are, in fact, intertwined, as occurs when the patent is manufactured and transformed from a knowledge and intellectual capital to a manufactured capital, a technological capital, and a monetary capital... etc. each time an exchange and creation of values takes place, the capital is transformed from a tangible and visible form to another just and intangible and vice versa (Lazlo, 2004).

And here I may ask a few questions, what about the knowledge capital? And from what consists? How do creative cities contribute to the formation of knowledge capital as a necessary requirement for a transition to a knowledge economy?

Florida related contributions of creative class have helped us to answer these questions, because it has set off in its analyses an critique of human capital theory, and considered the creative population as the driving force in regional economic growth and that economic growth accordingly will occur in places where there is a high level of population in education. But the main question still needs to be answered according to Florida; why does the creative population gather in certain places, in a world where the population is moving so high? Why would they choose some cities without others? What are the reasons? Florida was of the view that creative populations preferred places characterized by diversity, innovation and tolerance (Florida, 2009).

The knowledge capital is mainly composed of the creative class people, whose members participate in the work whose job is to create and invent new meaningful forms, including scientists, engineers, university professors, poets and writers novel artists, actors, designers, architects, leaders of thought in society, writers and editors, cultural personalities and researchers in strategic centers think tank, analysts and other opinion makers. This super creative core produces new forms or designs that can already be translated for the wider use, such as a product design that can be manufactured, sell and use it on a worldwide scale or come up with theories and strategies that can be applied in many cases or to form music that can be performed times and times. Added to this is the Creative professionals segment especially those who work in the range of knowledge-based professions in the advanced technology and services sectors finance, legal professions and health care, and what they need to do regularly is to think and experience new ideas and innovations. The creative class is therefore moving to creative centers because they want to live in places that provide an integrated and home-based environment for all artistic, cultural, technological and economic creations. What the creative class of these communities are looking for is the abundance of high quality and openness to diversity of all kinds, and above all the opportunity for the credibility of their identities as creative people (Florida, 2003).

Bradford illustrates how creative activity can support the economic vitality of the city's territory, when he highlighted the contributions of design and creative skills within the Ontario economy in Canada. He stressed that the design task force, which includes graphic designers, industrial designers, theatre and fashion, architects and engineers has grown rapidly, up from 4 to 5 times the overall labor force growth in Canada and Ontario between 1991 – 2001. Other research showed how the design enabled companies in other industries such as construction, furniture, toys and food products, to produce new products that are more environmentally sustainable, with the design of an increasingly valuable input to the production of the innovation process (Hospers, 2014).

Markus and King's work have recently documented the impact of arts workers throughout the United States economy, and they have identified this category in painters, photographers, sculptors, writers, musicians, composers, ballet dancers, actors and directors. They concluded that artists have raised overall productivity and gains in the regional economy over the last five years by exporting their businesses and selling their products and services in foreign markets. Artists added more money to the territory, using their creative abilities to promote the products and services of others in different sectors within the local economy, by purchasing specialized services and inputs from analysts suppliers, and helping workers across the regional economy to employ talent, and by promoting a culture of entrepreneurship, as long as many artists are self-employed. It is precisely because successful artists are the ones who take the risk (Hospers, 2014).

Narula (2003) addresses knowledge Capital in the context of his study of innovation patterns in developed and developing countries and how there is a strong interest on the part of national governments in the ability of companies to carry out activities promotes competitiveness through the generation and improvement of the quality of knowledge and human capital as one of the basic determinants behind technological accumulation and the ability to acquire and absorb knowledge, monitor the development of knowledge and assess its suitability. The more skilled the workforce, the higher the level of education, and the chances good training, which could be used for research and development activities, and where market imperfections and distortions can be minimized. Hence, national Governments attach great importance to the creation and diffusion of knowledge capital, which has been seen as a fundamental basis for economic prosperity and competition in developed industrial countries (Narula, 2003).

Globalization and the Knowledge Economy

Scott believes that in the context of the economic history of capitalism and its attachment to certain forms of urban development and the remarkable transformation of the present, a new method of work, production and urban life called by some the post-industrial community constituted on the way in which the growth and innovation of the modern economy and urban life can be said to be made through new labor and production sectors such as advanced technology industries, new art manufacturing, money and business services, and cultural products industries. These sectors as a whole are what is known as the new economy (Scott, 2006).

Several important characteristics of this economy have emerged, firstly: production work typically takes the form of an expanding network of companies, which in many cases is dominated by entities large integrated, but also disjointed in the form of subsidiaries of small companies operating in a flexible specialty mode in which production is concentrated on one type of product, where the product design specification is constantly changing. Second, labor markets associated with these sectors tend to be highly competitive and flexible, with many individuals taking part-time and independent forms of work duties, and the coordination of business practices in subsidiary companies is done through a creative workforce and a temporary working group to handle the project. Third: As a result of the decentralization of both flexible specialization and the complexity of consumer markets, the end product competes with one another not only on the basis of costs but also on the basis of its increasingly qualitative characteristics. Fourthly, an emerging characteristic of many sectors of this new economy is their marked tendency to be geographically concentrated in the form of clusters conglomerates, e.g. Silicon Valley, Hollywood, City of London, and Civeer in Paris and the industrial district of Italy. Indeed, the sectors of this kind are not confined to the most industrialized countries alone, but we find many different sections of the new economy and the conglomerate in various parts of Asia and Latin America, handicraft industries in South China, and advanced electronics in Beijing Bangladesh Bangalore and the telephone production pools in Bogota, Caracas, Mexico City and São Paulo (Scott, 2006).

There may have been repercussions of globalization on contemporary urban development in general and on creative cities in particular, following the expansion of many cities and extending beyond direct national borders. Cities with sectors and industries of the new economy have been associated with the process of globalization through four distinct scenes, despite their association. First, with the expansion of markets due to globalization, the trend towards urban agglomeration has actually increased across many sectors of the new economy, and the modern world order has been partly described as an integrated and competitive regional Economics group (Gertler, 2004).

Secondly, the forms and images of economic rivalry between different creative cities, tend to diversify according what is known as monopolistic competition, and competition of this kind may affect the characteristics of cities with distinct creative capabilities. If there is a claim that the modern world is often moving in the direction of uniform patterns of cultural consumption that was fuelled by the dream of Hollywood factories, for example, there is an opposite and reasonable claim that there are alternative centers of cultural production in general and film production in particular can be shared by Hollywood, so that these alternative centers should be able to increase the amount of effective systems of commercial promotion and distribution of their products (Gertler, 2004).

Third, many creative city companies around the world have been involved in building international networks of creative partnership with each other, in the form of joint deals, strategic alliances, joint production and so on. these arrangements reflect the forms of cooperation that can be achieved by being together and bringing in unique groups of talents, ideas and skills are available in different clusters, with diverse traditions, cultural origins and multiple creative abilities. From this perspective, the cities with a cosmic mosaic offer many and undoubtedly, rapid opportunities for these complementary interactions (Gertler, 2004).

Fourthly, despite the trend towards strengthening clusters and groupings in the context of globalization, there is a reverse trend towards decentralization that is also evident in certain sections of the new economy. As transport and communication costs continue to decline as a result of globalization, it is becoming clear that producers in creative cities share the achievement of certain types of duties and tasks or packages of work, to production centers where the conditions of production have their distinctive characteristics. These functions are part of more skilled and innovative processes that remain concentrated in major clusters and can be easily dismantled to be completed in other low-cost localities. For example, garment industries in cities such as New York, Los Angeles, London and Paris have now been deeply associated with the relationships between this type of manufacturing and sub-contracting with different sectors of Latin America, Asia and North Africa. Globalization is thus replete with opportunities and risks for creative cities, and policy makers need to be sensitive to actions and works that may allow them to avoid risks and increase opportunities (Gertler, 2004).

Methodological Procedures for Studying the Relationship Between Creative Cities and Knowledge Capital (Case of Dubai)

The definition of the concepts of creative city, knowledge capital, knowledge economy and knowledge-based development has been reported by the previous analyses of the writings of Hospers, Yigitcnta, Gertler, Winden, Laszlo, Florida, Bradford, Narula and Scott. They also highlighted the issues of the relationship between the city's creative structure and the components of knowledge capital, the city's creative objectives (quality of life and education), the formation of a knowledge capital, and how it contributes to the transition towards a knowledge economy. These analyses have helped to crystallize the current research problem in the hypothesis test "the structure of creativity city contributes to the growth of a knowledge capital necessary for the transition to a knowledge economy". They have been formulated in a set of specific questions, which, tested through a variety of methodological procedures, the use of the reanalysis approach, and the case study method of the Emirate of Dubai. Where the Re-analysis method helped to re-read the results of past research and related literature and dismantle its elements and its reinstallation to provide material and data to shed light on the mentioned issues, and the way in which the case of the Emirate of Dubai is studied achieved through analyze the statistical data, records, plans, strategies and conferences that are available about the Emirate structure of Dubai; knowledge capital, transformation towards the knowledge economy and other necessary variables in the hypothesis statement. The research carried out its analyses at different levels, cosmic compared to the world's creative cities, and then at an mezzo level focused on the city's creative structure in Dubai, especially quality of life and education.

In fact, the choice of Dubai as a model for creative cities in developing countries and the Arabic world has not been done in a vacuum because there are signs of this paradigm:

1. The literature associated with knowledge cities and knowledge-based development has referred to models of knowledge cities; global like Barcelona, Manchester and Melbourne and other cities that managed to skip the planning stage to the reality of the application and practice, as indicated some regional models of cities of knowledge such as Singapore, Malaysia and Monterrey. Some Arab models of knowledge cities reported such as the City of knowledge of the Medina and Dubai city, which is still at the beginning of the road and awaiting various efforts to support it (Carrillo, 2011);
2. The Emirate of Dubai, is one of the most developed Arab and Gulf cities, and has turned from a small village of hunters with a ruthless desert player to a dynamic urban fantasia grow vertically and horizontally and transform the contemporary landscape of the city into a set of investment projects of investment: commercial, residential, amusement parks and skyscrapers dedicated to giants firms. In a short period, Dubai turned an urban brand that has raced Gulf cities and other Arab and Asian cities to try to imitate this cosmic model (Abdel Raouf, 2014);
3. Dubai has undergone rapid shifts during the period between 1990 and 2010 in search of non-oil revenues from trade between ports to trade, which has made it a hub Logistics for real industries through the free Zone (Jebel Ali) and finally to build a knowledge economy (Dubai from sand to silicon, 2014).

CITY OF TECHNOLOGY, CULTURE AND QUALITY OF LIFE IN DUBAI

Based on a strategic vision of the political leadership in Dubai, there has been a shift from trade to services to new areas based on the knowledge economy, an economy based on research and development, technology, information, education, communication and services in the sense that it is an economy that combines technology and culture and approaches the model of creative cities that we have given examples of in ancient and contemporary history, which we will elaborate on when we talk about Dubai's transformation into a knowledge economy. We turn directly to the answer to the question: what is the interaction and dimensions of diversity and the most important challenges facing the Emirate of Dubai? What are their potential to enhance the quality of life and opportunities for their people?

The Fundamentals of the City of Technology and Culture in Dubai

Intensity of Interaction in Dubai

Although the total size of Dubai's population is only 2.156 Million and the people active during the day 3.149 Million, the opportunities for interaction among the population varied from the diversity of sites housing; the number of buildings completed was 2.421 Million, and transport and air transportation were numerous (arrivals were 28.457) the Navy (where the arrivals were 124.511) and the wilderness (the number of bus passengers was 107.792) and the either Metro Dubai (the number was 71.915 (red Line) and 19.917 (Green Line), and the number of hotel guests (7.823.117). The number of guests in the Hotel apartments (2.134.044). Opportunities for interaction between the population in Dubai have increased through telephone and facsimile lines (453.442) and mobile lines (3.724.092), the number of Internet lines (332.846) (Dubai center for statistics, 2012).

Dubai organizes festivals and events to increase the chances of interacting in the city, with the famous Dubai Shopping festival held every year from 1996 onwards. Dubai has many shopping malls and tourist facilities, and the total number of Arab tourists to Dubai (3.2 million), of whom 1.5 million are from the Arab Gulf states, while the number of Asian inmates has been from the Far East and South Asia (3.1 million), from Europe (2.3) million from the Russia-Baltic region (510) thousand, from the Americas (622), from Australia and the Pacific (222) thousand (Dubai center for statistics, 2012).

Cultural and Economic Diversity in Dubai

Dubai Society is also characterized by cultural diversity, both in terms of nationalities and breeds, or religions. In 2013, there were 10-15% of the Emirati population, and approximately 80-85% of the resident strangers. The predominant proportion of residents were Asian nationalities and descendants, 51% of India 16% Pakistan, 9% Bangladesh, 3% the Philippines and about 300,000 Somalis, as well as other national groups. A quarter of the UAE's population is traced back to Iran, and there are approximately 100,000 British in Dubai as the largest Western group in the city (Wikipedia, Dubai, 2014).

Dubai's diversity has expanded to the economy after the government of Dubai has recognized the need to reduce its dependence on oil and gas exports and has built up its advanced trade infrastructure and industrial and agricultural, the creation of a giant export system and "free zones" investments to host foreign companies along with their foundation for tourism, recreation and real estate. In parallel to the free Zone strategy, Dubai has also committed itself to building the international tourism industry and by the Year (2008) with hundreds of hotels, the Emirates hosts more than 6 million tourists annually. Dubai has succeeded in diversifying its economy, with non-oil sectors accounting for more than 95% of total GDP (Kristofer, 2012).

Dubai and Dealing With Challenges and Crises

The Dubai model, originally founded on trade and certain services, as well as free zones, has already achieved some successes by the beginning of the third millennium. However, it then took a negative turn marked by an unjustified real-estate boom fueled by the increase in oil prices, as well as by the flow of speculative foreign funds. This paradigm has thus shifted from a scalable and imitated model in the region to one that marginalizes the economic role of the citizen. It then became a burden for the state, especially when the real estate bubble exploded and showed the magnitude of the indebtedness of the Emirate of Dubai and its repercussions on the stability and prosperity of the country in the years to come. But this does not mean that the recent financial crisis at his home is a knockout of the Dubai model, there are strengths in this model such as trade and services, Port management, Emirates flight, and some industries such as aluminum, which have not been affected much during this crisis (Al- yousef, 2013).

Linked to the financial crisis in Dubai, another challenge is that the Dubai model, which is based on image, format and visual marketing more from its reliance on sustainable development concepts, it caused a clear flaw in what happened in the Gulf city in the early years of the twenty-first century especially in what is related to superficial virtual interpretations of the theses of globalization and cortical dealings with the sculptant values and what follows of citizenship and identity issues, which made some believe that Dubai lost the spirit of the Arab Gulf city and turned into a lab Open to test and apply exotic architectural styles and models to strengthen their new identity as a global city. It thus created an architectural and physical environment filled with illusions and fantasyland that are radically separated from the spatial or culture of Dubai (Abdel Raouf, 2014).

Despite the development in the Gulf, the measurements of global environmental organizations reflect a catastrophic reality in energy consumption rates water and carbon emissions in the six Gulf states, for example, the city of Dubai, has an emission carbon per person second place after the United States of America, and the rate of consumption of the UAE's energy population is more than double that of the global average, marine beaches have also been subject to abuses that are not addressed by real estate and hotel development projects and organized work to bridge the Gulf (Abdel Raouf, 2014).

The Smart City and Quality of Life in Dubai

Quality of Life in Dubai

Dubai has developed a strategic plan that it considers a programme of action outlining future directions and strategic goals, focusing on five main themes, including areas of development and life, e.g. economic and social development, the environment, security, justice and all government excellence include the sustainability of growth and prosperity, quality of life for citizens and residents. One of the most important strategic criteria through which the goals of economic development will be achieved is to ensure that the workforce in Dubai is distinguished and integrated with the economic orientation by attracting and maintaining highly skilled labor, improving the efficiency of citizens and increasing their motivation. Also, by taking care of science, technology and innovation and transforming Dubai into a scientific and technical center, as well as addressing the high cost of living, this is in addition to improving the quality of life and making Dubai a favorite destination for current and prospective residents by improving the well-being of citizens and residents and helping them to live a better life rich in opportunities and choices (Features of Dubai strategic plan, 2014).

Dubai Smart City

Dubai has also developed its vision to become the smartest city in the world over the last three years and has set up its plan based on six columns, intelligent life, transportation, Society, economy, government and environment. In (15) September 2014 Dubai organized the City of intelligent life Conference. The agenda of the Conference included several issues: Creating a smart economic system. Connect all public and private sectors, education, business and entrepreneurship, Large data and information and smart government solutions, urban development, technology, management and smart people transport and movement the water issue, electricity the future of education, creating a hub for innovation and the work between the organizations on the network. etc. (Smart living city, 2014).

The smart city uses integrated and connected electronic data through information systems and simultaneous networks to regulate city matters by relying on computers and special programmes through the Internet and cloud computing technology, to manage the city, its municipal affairs, education and health care, public security and facilities, as used by devices and sensors distributed in all vital locations and the emirate to provide more efficient services, information and services in an intangible and highly accurate manner and link the population to their city. The smart city provides information to its residents about what affects their life affairs, such as weather, traffic, transport and emergency and intelligent services in education and health, as well as the provision of recreational and touristic services, such as smart restaurants and airline and traffic services, as well as the city's interest in managing economic services to investors businessmen are intelligent and interconnected, such as intelligent Exchange services, ports, smart customs and others. Dubai Smart Government announced its launch of the updated version of the Mpay smart phone payment application, which is shared by four government agencies, the Electricity and Water Authority Dubai, Road and Transportation Authority, Dubai Police and Dubai Telecom, allowing them to perform a single, basic government service is to pay invoices, ship and recharge and pay for traffic tickets. The application of smart phone payment has seen increasing rates of individuals and institutions, and the amounts received through this application have reached 15.5 DHS million during the period from January to October 2013, several banks in Dubai participate in this application and discount from the customer account and credit cards... etc. (The intelligent change is coming, 2014).

It can therefore be said that in Dubai, as an innovative city, the hard component and the environment for learning and knowledge creation are available. There remains a question about the soft component, the learning community, the culture of learning, creativity and innovation, and linking Dubai to the goals of development based on knowledge and adoption of the unified strategic direction that generates these different types of capital and, above all, the knowledge capital?

QUALITY OF HIGHER EDUCATION IN DUBAI AND THE GROWTH OF KNOWLEDGE CAPITAL

Dubai Knowledge Capital

There are 3,800 companies in the Emirate of Dubai that have taken up positions in the free zone of technology and information, and there is a network of relationships between about 1,200 companies, and these companies are using 15,000 workers in innovation, a host of major events in the areas of information, communication technology and knowledge are working to spawn talents and creative projects. (Dubai from sand to silicon, 2014). These occupational slides form a large part of Dubai's knowledge capital, which relies on the experience of the expatriate. It may include segments of the creative class of scientists, engineers, university professors, poets, writers, artists, actors and architects, thought leaders, cultural personalities, researchers in strategic centers and a lot of professionals based on knowledge in the high-tech sectors and financial services, added to them are the owners of design and graphic skills and designers industrialists and professionals in the fields of art such as painters and photographers, workers in research and development activities and others. But what about the learning community and the culture of learning, creativity and innovation in Dubai? What contribution does Dubai education make to enhancing knowledge capital?

Quality of Higher Education in Dubai

Dubai has realized the need to change its investment strategies that lead to growth and the development of a knowledge-based economy in the short and long term. The knowledge-based economy is based on education, and its success depends to a large extent on its ability to educate and train the workforce that the growing demand for markets needs, and its productivity and competitiveness are determined by the existence of sophisticated formal educational entities, labor markets and intra-corporate and business training. In fact, education in Dubai has developed remarkably rapidly in the last three decades. In less than 30 years, Dubai has transformed its education sector from a vulnerable group of schools into a dynamic educational sector. Although access to education has visibly increased, the quality of education has not progressed at the same pace. The federal government has begun to pay attention to addressing severe restrictions in public education and national universities. (Soto, 2012). We may have to stop in front of the quality of higher education in the Emirate of Dubai, especially since the Universities of Dubai and the United Arab Emirates, have been given a prominent role by the government as a cornerstone of the knowledge-based economy. Although acceptance of higher education has been significantly expanded in recent decades in Dubai to a clear effort by society to strengthen human capital, however, acceptance rates remain below international standards and the requirements of a knowledge-based economy. Although acceptance rates have increased from 17% (1999) to 25% (2008), they are less than developed and developing countries like Latin America, which was 50% and 35% respectively, taking into account the fact that the size of the Dubai population doubled in the same time period. Enrolment among citizens was also heterogeneous in 2010, with a female ratio of 70% and among males about 25%. While it is important to expand acceptance, quality has not improved at the same rate. According to international standards, Dubai universities are lagging behind universities in other Arab countries such as Saudi Arabia, Egypt and Tunisia. There is no one university in Dubai that appeared among the top 500 universities in the world, the United Arab Emirates University in Al Ain has reached 372 in order to reach the number of 400 universities according to the QS survey in the rankings of the world's universities. An alternative measure of quality of research is based on the number of researches published in scientific journals and according to the latest Arab reports of knowledge issued in 2009 by (UNDP), which indicated that the Arab Emirates had lagged behind most countries in the region, although they have revealed a positive trend, with a yearly publication of scientific work by researchers in United Arab Emirates (500) article between 1992 and 2002, and increased to (2000) an article between the period 2008 – 2009). (Soto, 2012). The quality of research in Dubai universities is not appropriate, according to the Scientific Quotations Index (ISI). Under these performance indicators, the higher education system in Dubai does not appear to be genuinely competitive in accordance with international standards, and there are many reasons why the most important is that Dubai universities are still relatively young, especially the branches of international universities that have recently begun their educational activity in Dubai. Because most of these universities often focus on teaching for first degree levels. Research and networking with industry have been limited to small roles and in insignificant dimensions. The result is that it is not surprising that research and innovation do not have a noticeable presence (Soto, 2012).

Another worrying issue related to the performance of universities in Dubai is the exclusive focus on business management, religion and information technology where there was according to the 2010 statistics, 55% of all graduates in Dubai specialize in business management, while 25% are divided evenly between the field of religious studies and information technology. Less than 1% specialize in nature sciences, physics or medicine. And more, because admission and registration costs are not low, universities tend to focus on low-cost programs and avoid intellectual systems (science) requires a heavy investment (e.g. hospitals needed by medical colleges, or laboratories required by the natural sciences). In fact, Dubai has only very few research programs that provide a showcase of skilled researchers and scientists for the transition to a knowledge-based economy, and the newly established institutes are unlikely to provide such degrees in the future. Therefore, Dubai will continue to rely on imported expertise to support its research and development capabilities for the foreseeable future. While the average performance of the United Arab Emirates has surpassed economic incentives and communication and information technology, it has achieved marginal superiority in education and has declined in innovation, these results are likely to be the outcome of the Government's efforts in providing the business environment and improving the information and communication infrastructure. The relative weakness of education and innovation indicators is compatible with the low quality of education (Soto, 2012).

DUBAI AND THE TRANSITION TOWARDS A KNOWLEDGE ECONOMY

What about Dubai's orientation towards the knowledge economy? How is this economy shaping up? How widespread are the technological and cultural industries? To what extent has it been driven by innovation and interested in building clusters through international networks?

The Knowledge Economy and the Diffusion of the Technological and Cultural Industries in Dubai

Dubai has decided to move towards a knowledge economy for about a decade, a strategic orientation supported by the leadership of the ruling family, as a reaction to the gradual liberalization of the oil economy and the initiation of a policy of economic diversification (Abdel Raouf, 2014).

Dubai has established three major projects, Dubai Media City, Dubai Internet City and Knowledge Village, all located within the Dubai free technology and media zone. In its strategy, the Dubai Media City (DMC) focuses on specific sections of media activity such as satellite channels, public relations companies, marketing research and trade, and supported the city with major publishing companies and Arab newspapers stationed outside the Arab nation, and moved to it some Arabic satellite channels like MBC, a branch of the CNN news channel and the Reuters news agency Middle East, the city focuses on digital media and film production. (Abdel Raouf, 2014). It has been interested in advertising and art, design, cinema, video, photography, computer programs, electronic games, music, performances, publishing, television and radio. (Dubai from Sand to Silicon, 2014). The Dubai Internet City is aimed at attracting new ideas in the Internet world, outstanding projects and their financing, to interact with the minds local, where Microsoft transferred the Arabization unit from Seattle to Dubai, a unit of approximately 200 translators and programmers, and hosted sites electronic and space publishing and Internet services, as well as complementary activities such as restaurants, banks, travel agencies, car rentals, pharmacies, clinics, supermarkets, and jamanday, and beauty salons, in a way that facilitates the lives of people belonging to the city. (Abdel Raouf, 2014). Dubai Internet city has been active in the areas of computer software production, electronic gaming and electronic publishing. The Knowledge Village (KV) aims to build an integrated knowledge society capable of enriching the learning process by building a sophisticated learning base with the aim of achieving a strategic goal of refining creative energies and increasing the numbers of knowledge specialists. The project began in 2002 and included the Information Academy, university campuses, foreign institutes, the Creativity Centre, the e-learning Centre and the institutions Research, multimedia libraries, training and educational centers for information technology companies and scientific and artistic societies. (Abdel Raouf, 2014). The knowledge Village includes creative industries in the field of communication and information technology such as marketing, media, radio and film Services, new media, computer software, e-commerce, web design, telephony and multimedia, consulting and creative industries in the field of knowledge such as e-learning, management development and training in information technology, centers of innovation, research and development, and academic infrastructure. etc. (Dubai from sand to silicon, 2014).

The Dubai Knowledge Village currently hosts 200 companies, including global universities, American College of Dubai, Australian University of Wellington, Mira Institute of Science and Technology, University of Purcell, University of Heroati, University Azad Islamic, Mahatma Gandhi University, University of Medellin, University of Neubransuik, Santi Peterberg State University for Economics and the British University, Financial Management Academy, Eaton Institute Education (Knowledge village in Dubai, 2015).

Innovation, Clustering and International Partnership in Dubai Economy

As for innovation and clustering, Dubai has been attracting huge investments in both concrete and intangible infrastructure (hard and soft). The next step was to shift from an investment-driven economy to an innovation-driven economy. Innovation includes the development and wide use of new products, processes, strategies and organizational forms. Major innovations have huge economic consequences, and it is therefore important for the state of Dubai to begin generating its own creativity stream and to make it commercially tradable in and out of the country. Recent writings focus on innovation through partnership between firms, on the one hand, and between companies and all those who use their innovations on the other hand, based on the fact that knowledge is widely distributed, and companies interested in innovation interact with the surrounding business environment, which includes cosmic markets and agglomeration conglomerates. New ideas, products and processes, which are already successful in markets, are often the result of a continuous process of interaction between firms and other bodies in the local and regional business environment, the most important of which are gatherings in the city, such as what we observe in Dubai, the diversity it expresses, and the cartels that include industries associated with each other, and organizations, such as in Hollywood and Silicon Valley. In this type of conglomerate, companies have extensive cooperation and close ties to academic and other organizations within a conglomerate innovation where high-tech innovations tend to establish close cooperation with universities and other scientific bodies (Solevell, 2009).

With regard to cluster development and customer inclusion, there is a crew or service support group for business activities that includes the development and networking of the relationship between this activity and development of business leaders, talent galleries, business activities, information systems, communication and feedback, social issues and events (Dubai from Sand to Silicon, 2014).

There are also examples of the linkage of the new economy sectors and industries to the cosmic economy through international networks, creative partnership and transactions alliances and co-production can be mentioned, to name but a few; partnership between the Dubai International Film Festival and the Sharjah Foundation for the Art of Dubai, a partnership that combines one of the most important cinematographic platforms (the Dubai International Film Festival) with the largest institutions of culture and arts is effective in the region (Sharjah Arts Foundation), where the "Moving Images" initiative, dedicated to artistic films and the art of film makers, takes the long-term nature of the partnership between the entities mentioned and includes a series of cinematic performances and dialogues leading to the exchange of experiences and ideas (New partnership, pictures move, 2014).

The RTEX robot Technology exhibition was brought together by various industry partners (International Association of Motorized Transport Systems) AUVSI and local universities; the University of Wellington as well as other supporting bodies such as the media and Events Expo 2020 and others. As the government of Dubai aspires to invest in the latest creations and scientific innovations, support new ideas and move towards a knowledge economy, the RTEX Dubai Fair brings knowledge and technology from all over the world in this event featuring a showcase of the latest innovations in Android and Automation offers a distinctive opportunity for companies and investors to turn into a new market for science and technology (RTEX EXHIPTION, 2014).

CONCLUSION: GENERAL RESULTS AND OPTIONS FOR THE FUTURE

1. Dubai is approaching the creative city model, especially the third model of the cities of technology and culture, as it was transformed in a short period into an urban sign that raced the Gulf cities and others on its tradition and access to the cosmic model, this is in addition to creating a knowledge economy based on research and development, technology, information, education, communication and services;
2. The model of the city of Technology and Culture in Dubai was founded on the creative features of the city, from interaction, diversity and challenges. With the small size of the population in Dubai, as the opportunities for interaction between them have varied and diversified, in terms of housing locations, and transport and transportation between the sea and land and air, communications (telephone, fax, Internet), as well as numerous events and festivals, whether for marketing, trade, tourism, media, culture, cinema, etc. The City of Dubai has also been characterized by cultural diversity, bringing together different nationalities and breeds, Asian, European, Arab and other, and the diversity in Dubai has expanded to the economy, trade, industry, agriculture, tourism and real estate, as well as oil production, account for the non-oil sectors accounting for 95% (GDP).

Nor was the financial crisis a fatal blow, because there were strengths in this model, such as trade, services and some industries that were not much affected by this crisis, namely areas in which previous studies recommend interest, and make use its value added under a federal model that is consistent with Gulf development efforts. Another challenge associated with the financial crisis was the adoption of the Dubai model to the optical marketing message rather than its reliance on sustainable development concepts, and the defect of making Dubai lose the spirit of the Gulf city, it is transformed into an open laboratory for the application of exotic architectural topics and models, and the strengthening of its new identity as a global city, at the expense of local values of citizenship and identity. In view of the importance of relying on the concepts of sustainable development, we may agree with the proposals of previous studies to ensure that Arab and Islamic values and the rights of citizenship and the Arab-Muslim identity are overcome (Abdel Raouf, 2014).

3. Dubai translated the goal of improving the quality of life on the ground and turned into a preferred city for current residents and are expected to improve the well-being of citizens and residents and help them to live a better life rich in opportunities and choices. and implemented its vision to become the smartest city in the world based on six pillars; smart life, intelligent transportation, society, government and environment apart from the smart economy, according to Winden and his colleagues with regard to the pillars of the economy and knowledge-based development. (Windens, 2007). The updated version of the smart-phone payment application involving four government agencies, the Dubai Electricity and Water Authority, and the roads, transportation, Dubai police and communications; one-step implementation of five basic government services from payment for invoices, shipping and balance packing and pay for traffic violations this application has seen increasing rates of individuals and institutions, and several banks in Dubai are involved in this application for discount route from customer account and credit cards, Dubai model represent the key to creating economic value, they are working to support innovation, they have the quality of life and opportunities can be enhanced in front of a large section of the population, helping to attract and maintain knowledge capital as indicated by Florida (Florida, 2003);
4. Education in Dubai has developed at a remarkable pace in recent years, and acceptance has expanded at all levels, regardless of the student's nationality. This attests to the commitment of the Government of Dubai to form human capital, but although access to education has increased, the quality of education has not progressed at the same speed, the government appointed Dubai and UAE universities a prominent role as a cornerstone of the existing economy on knowledge. Consequently, acceptance of higher education has been expanded, but the rate is still lower than international standards and the requirements of a knowledge-based economy. If universities play a key role in contributing to innovation and knowledge, not a single university in Dubai shows the world's top 500 universities according to AAWR.

The data revealed a positive trend, with an increase in the annual scientific work published by researchers in the United Arab Emirates from 500 articles in 1992 to 2000 in 2009. Research and networking with industry have been limited to small and insignificant roles. The majority of universities in Dubai offer one or two programs in business or IT management, and the result is that it is not surprising that research and innovation have no apparent existence. Dubai has only very few research programs that provide a showcase of skilled researchers and scientists who need to switch to the knowledge-based economy, the newly created institutes are unlikely to provide these degrees in the future, so if Dubai adopts in its knowledge capital on imported expertise to support its current R & D, they will continue to move in that direction in the foreseeable future, which may be aided by its diversity and its interest in quality of life, according to Florida's view that the creative class prefers places that are characterized by diversity, innovation and tolerance. (Florida, 2003). Previous studies in this regard recommend that Dubai should not stop revising its educational policies, as the system of education not only adversely affects the transition to a knowledge-based economy but also reflects economic growth. (Soto, 2013). Priority should be given to the branches of basic and Applied natural science in university education programmes.

5. The Emirate of Dubai has established its new economy in accordance with the innovation-driven model and has been interested in strengthening the clusters and continuous interactions between companies and other bodies in local and regional business environment, inter-firm partnerships and intensive collaboration with academic organizations and universities have emerged, as has a network of relationships between 1200 companies.

Dubai has sought to develop clusters through the service support package for business activities, using the means to develop and link the relationship between these activities and programmes to develop the business personality, It is time for Dubai to develop policies that help build new blocs or contribute to the growth and prosperity of clusters. Dubai must establish a future agenda that takes into account the realities of modern innovation processes and a modern understanding of bloc dynamics; innovation is an open process through which many bodies can collaborate through a non-linear approach, because the traditional linear model that sets clear roles for basic research at the University and applied research in research and development centers in companies no longer bear fruit, and because ideas move across institutional boundaries on a More frequent. Innovation benefits from a spatial proximity that enables the flow of intangible tacit knowledge and unplanned interactions that represent important parts of the process of innovation, because more investment in science and research and development is no longer conducive to the future of innovation and the formation of a new company. The main clusters of the modern innovation process, specifically defined as the co-location between production and provider the service, financial institutions, research and educational institutes and other governmental and private institutions that are linked through Links of different types-represent two important elements in building a sustainable Dubai future (Solvell, 2009).

6. The outcome of the answer to research questions may prove that the premise that "the creative city structure contributes to the growth of a knowledge capital necessary for the transition to a knowledge economy" has been achieved partly because the growth of the knowledge capital is a result of attracting quality of life in the city of Dubai to workers in the fields of creativity rather than to the quality of higher education that builds the capacity of citizens to work in the knowledge professions. In addition, the transformation of Dubai into a knowledge economy have to overcome the challenges of innovation development, and supporting clusters between firms, universities and strategic centers, and strengthening regional international partnerships.

REFERENCES

Al-Yousef. (2013). *Yusuf Kalifa, United Arab Emirates at a Crossroads, Arab future, 12th and 400.* Beirut: Centre for Arab Unity Studies.

Android Technology Fair, R. T. E. X. (2014). *Exhibitors Handbook.* Retrieved from http://www.rt-exhiption.com

Carrillo, F. (2011). *knowledge cities, entrances, experiences and visions* [Arabic translation]. Khalid Ali Yusuf.

Dubai from Sand to Silicon, Growth of Creative Industries, The Dubai Experience. (n.d.). Retrieved from http://www definitely dubai.com

Dubai Statistics Centre. (2012). Dubai, UAE: Dubai in Figures.

Emirate of Dubai. (n.d.). In *Wikipedia, the free encyclopedia*. Retrieved from http://www.wikipedia, org/wiki

Features Dubai Strategic Plan. (2015). *Dubai where the future begins: The official website of the secretariat of the Executive Council of the Emirate of Dubai*. Retrieved from http://WWW.TEC.GOVE.AE/TEC/IMAGES/PDF/DSP

Galaby & Abdrabo. (2013). Knowledge-based development, an Alternative Development Policy: Analysis of the Discourse of knowledge precincts in Egypt. *Egyptian Journal for Development and Planning, 21*(1).

Gertler, M. (2004). *Creative Cities, What are they for? How do they work? And what do Build them?* Back ground Paper (f 48), Canadian Policy Research Network. Retrieved from http://www. cprn. Org

Hospers, G-J. (2014). *Creative Cities: Breeding Places in Knowledge Economy*. Back Ground Paper (f/48, Auges dt 20904). Retrieved from http://www.cpth.org

Knowledge Village in Dubai. (n.d.). In *Wikipedia, the free encyclopedia*. Retrieved from http: www. wikipedia, org/wiki

Kristofer, D. (2012). *Dubai model; Diversification and slowdown in the political economy of the Gulf region. Centre for Regional and International Studies*. Qatar: Faculty of International Affairs, Georgetown University.

Lazlo & Lazlo. (2009). Fostering Sustainable Learning Society Through Knowledge Based Development. *System Research & Behavioral Science*, (24).

Narula, R. (2003). *Globlization & Technology; Interdependence, Innovation systems and Industrial policy*. MPC Book LTD.

Overall Intelligent Change Coming. (n.d.). *Tech Magazine for All C4 No. 121*. Retrieved from http://www.dsg.gov.ae

Abdel Raouf, A. (2014). Social inclusion between identity dilemmas and the trap of globalization: The challenges and transformations of the modern Gulf city of Amran. In *The Dialectic of social inclusion, state and nation-building in the Arab nation*. Arab Centre for Research and Policy Study.

Scott, A. J. (2006). Creative Cities; Conceptual Issues and Policy Questions. *Journal of Urban Affairs, 28*(1).

Smart Living City Dubai. (2014). Retrieved from http: //www.smart Living city. Com

Solvell, O. (2009). *Along-term Strategy for Dubai Bulding On Innovation and Clusters*. Dubia Economic Council.

Soto, R. (2013). Education in Dubai From Quantity to Quality. Dubai Economic Council.

Winden, W.V., Denberg, L.V., & Pol, P. (2007). European Cities In the knowledge Economy: Toward A Typology. *Urban Studies, 44*(3), 525-549.

Yigitcanta, T. (2010, November). Making Spaces and Places for the knowledge Based Development- Australian Cities. *European Planning Studies, 18*(11), 1770–1786.

APPENDIX: FIGURES

Figure 1.

Figure 2.

Figure 3.

Figure 4.

Figure 5.

Figure 6.

Figure 7.

Figure 8.

Figure 9.

Figure 10.

Figure 11.

Figure 12.

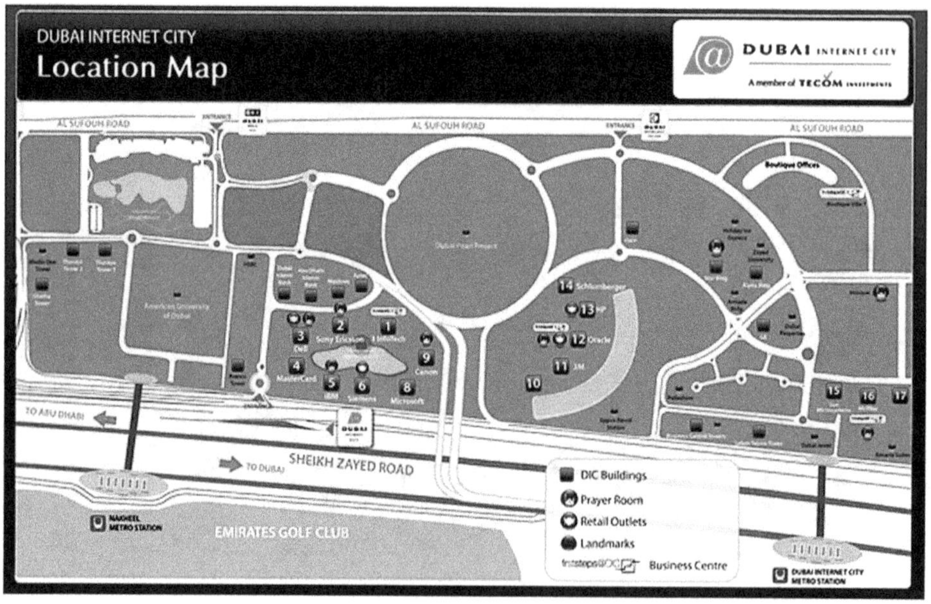

Figure 13.

Figure 14.

Figure 15.

Figure 16.

Section 3
Transformations and Trends

Chapter 10
Kuwait Urban App:
The Application of Knowledge-Based Urban Development in Kuwait

Robert H. Gurney III
Kuwait University, Kuwait

Anas Alomaim
Kuwait University, Kuwait

Jawaher Al-Bader
Kuwait University, Kuwait

ABSTRACT

Through an investigation of social media and contemporary smart phone applications, the urban landscape of Kuwait is analyzed to propose a method for knowledge-based urban development (KBUD). Historically speaking, urban planning and design have been dominated by a formalized methodology that seeks to reinforce existing power structures. The promise of KBUD is a more balanced approach towards development, considering economic, social, environmental, and cultural factors. The chapter suggests an up-to-date method of research that consists of three overlapping stages, starting with collecting big data through cellphone software applications, followed by a set of interviews with several entities and ending with a method of behavioral mapping and space syntax. This cross-referenced research process encapsulates the multifaceted approach of KBUD that would produce a complex adaptive system and an underlying framework to help understand the non-linear interactions between the local populations in Kuwait.

INTRODUCTION

In this chapter, we will discuss alternative ways to utilize KBUD in Kuwait. The focus will be on analyzing the contemporary needs of city dwellers by investigating their use of smartphone applications, which is software most commonly developed for portable devices.

DOI: 10.4018/978-1-5225-3734-2.ch010

Copyright © 2018, IGI Global. Copying or distributing in print or electronic forms without written permission of IGI Global is prohibited.

The case of Kuwait holds both global and regional relevance. The sudden oil wealth, as well as the abundant availability of domestic and physical comforts, has expedited much of the technological development of the country (Al-Bader, 2012, pg. 17–20). With the accessibility of the latest technologies, smartphones have been integrated into the daily lives of people. This produced a technologically savvy population who are best described by Jameson as *postmodern* and are *late capitalists*, who are "alienated from everyday events, with a servant or service to fill every need" (Jameson, 2003; Al-Bader, 2012, pg. 17). Smartphone applications have become a daily part of people's lives. For example, David Pogue reviewed "apps that remind you to take your pills," showcasing the popularity of applications to support everyday habits (Pogue, 2017). Hence, smartphone applications have opened a new market (Baker, 2005). The vacuum that has been created with late capitalism has been filled with anything that is bought with money. In this chapter, we are viewing smartphone applications as a manifestation of individual agency (Luhmann, 2012).

On the one hand, like many locations in the global south, Kuwait has changed very fast, but as it moves toward urban sustainability, Kuwait still faces many challenges such as resource management, traffic congestion, and uneven access to city services as shown in Figure 1. On the other hand, the use of smartphones has transformed everyday life in Kuwait, the Gulf, and Arabic countries in a more general way. Smartphone penetration, especially social media and navigating tools, is significant in the Gulf States, having reshaped social and physical interactions (Northwestern University Qatar, 2014).

Although such services were invented in the West, the way the Kuwaiti population and its residents use them has changed the local lifestyle drastically seen in Figure 2. Due to the unique cultural and social milieu of the contemporary Kuwaiti society the use of these applications has become an important, if not vital set of data for researchers, theorists, urban planners, and architects to better understand the urban behavior and needs of the future Kuwaiti population. It connects Kuwaitis with each other, their food,

Figure 1. A view from Khalid Ibn Al Waleed St., one of the main entries from the suburbs into the commercial center of Kuwait City
Source: Photo credit Jawaher Al-Bader

Figure 2. An existing contrast between the old (dhows) and the new (towers) in Kuwait City
Source: https://upload.wikimedia.org/wikipedia/commons/b/b4/Kuwait_city_skyline.jpg

transportation, and the urbanized environment displayed in Figure 3. Such social networks are imbedded within the local culture and the vernacular social network of Kuwait (Al-Nakib, 2016). The ability of social media to intensify the local social network with a sense of anonymity connects well with the social nature of the Kuwaiti, both private and social.[1] Analyzing the data from smartphone applications is a vital way to produce Knowledge Based Urban Development (KBUD) for Kuwait and the Gulf Region. Thus, a study of smartphone application use in Kuwait will produce an important set of data for

Figure 3. An aerial image revealing the voids and disconnections within the contemporary urban landscape of Kuwait
Source: Photo credit Jawaher Al-Bader

researchers, urban planners, and architects, supporting them to better understand complex, diverse, and unequal urban societies in the process of transformation and digital change.

Collecting data through geo-tagging in social media can be used to determine areas, paths, and destinations of popular interest and interaction. Understanding movement and gathering places in cities can help activate or re-active public balance. When combining location data over time, we can better understand sites where people congregate, referred to by Lynch as *nodes* (Lynch, 1960). These locations can be investigated through the lens of "social system" thinking, as outlined by Niklas Luhmann, as each smartphone application is representative of different aspects of Kuwait's cultural and social scene (Luhmann, 2012). This information will provide urban planners with a perspective on the urban environment as a collection of moments, where people gather, allowing more support for social and civic functions (Whyte, 1998). The social-civic realm, as one of the four pillars of KBUD, is a cosmopolitan atmosphere where the quality of life intertwines with the development of cultural and aesthetic values (Yigitcanlar, 2010). By collecting specific data that records behavior and location within a timeframe, a glimpse of how people function within the environment can be considered in the convergence of the digital and physical world. This is a rich source of data, bridging a relationship between embodied spaces within the contemporary rhythms and trends of the city (Netto, 2017).

Through a more complete understanding of the social organization of the urban landscape, a better understanding of their flows and desires can be determined (Batty, 2007). How can we integrate these newly purposed spaces into an existing infrastructure and the social media that activates them?

Thinking of cities as complex adaptive systems challenges us to review and revise our current planning, engineering, and design methodologies, which in most cases reflect a more linear, Newtonian worldview. In undertaking such a review, we need to ask ourselves: First, which methods recognize the properties of complex adaptive systems? Second, what kind of knowledge about the system is provided by the method? (Sanders, 2008, pp. 276)

A complex adaptive system provides an underlying framework to help understand the non-linear interactions and connection of cities and communities and encapsulates multifaceted approach of KBUD.

BACKGROUND

Kuwait's current urban planning follows the initial strategies that were implemented during the 1950s. The British firm Minoprio, Spencely, and Macfarlane designed Kuwait's first modern urban plan in 1952 shown in Figure 4. Their methods incorporated a complete urban renewal and a city design based on a radial grid protected by a Green Belt see Figure 5. Their new master plan demanded the relocation of residential areas from old Kuwait City to the new suburbs placed outside of the city's old borders. The new residential areas comprised of self-dependent neighborhoods. This method clearly follows the urban theories of Ebenezer Howard's urban planning methods of the 19th century. Howard's methods stemmed from the need to design the industrial cities in Europe, which has almost no similarity to Kuwait. During the 1960s, urban planners and other specialists realized that the plans of 1952 erased the vernacular fabric of Kuwait thus causing a disconnection between the Kuwaiti population and their newly built environment seen in Figures 6 and 7.

Figure 4. Kuwait's first master plan by Minoprio & Spencely and Macfarlane (1952) showing the new residential neighborhood (in orange) outside of old Kuwait City
Source: Courtesy of Kuwait Municipality Archives

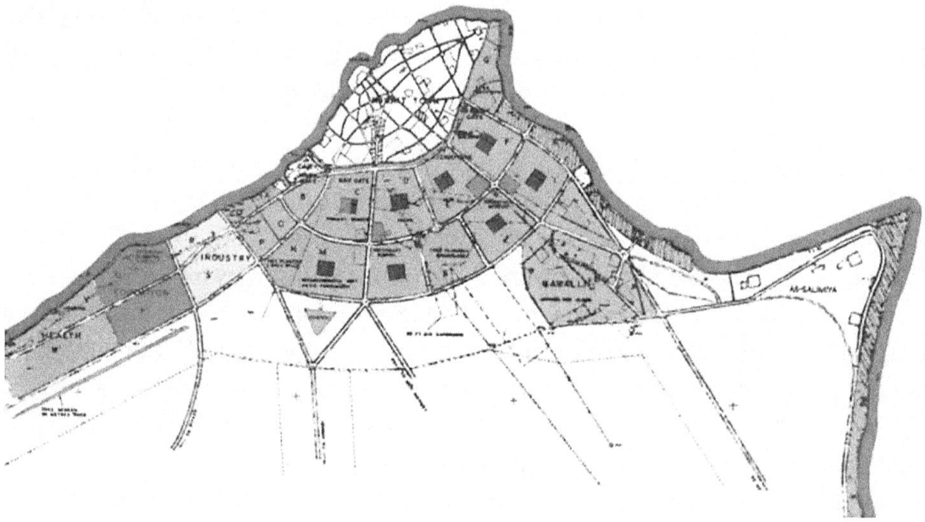

Figure 5. Diagram highlighting the radial grid and its center (the Seif Palace)
Source: Diagram credit Anas Alomaim and base map Courtesy of Kuwait Municipality Archives

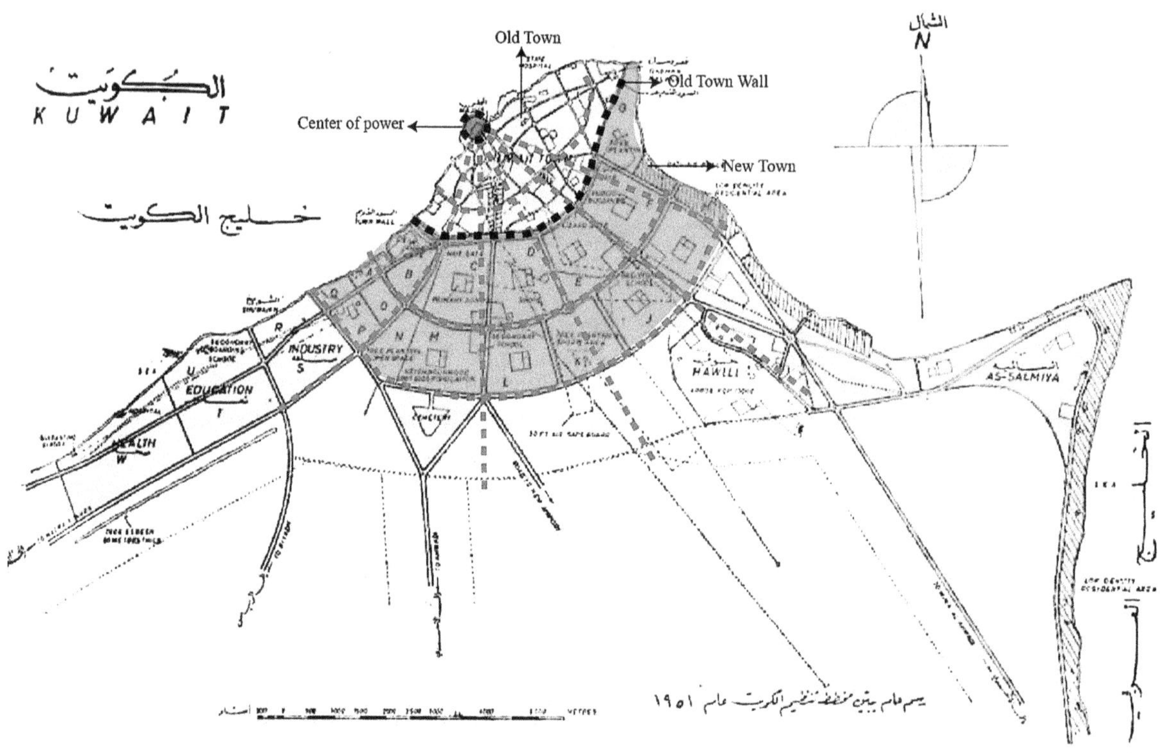

Figure 6. A close-up of an aerial photograph showing the old vernacular fabric of Kuwait before its demolishment
Source: Courtesy of Kuwait Oil Company

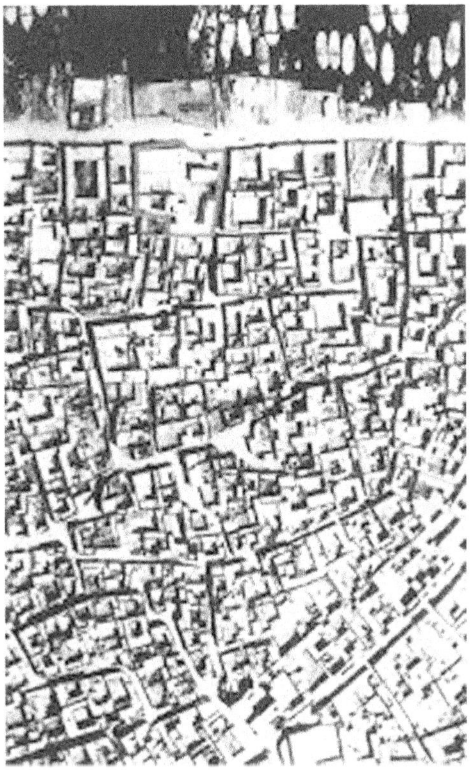

Further urban development that occurred in the following decades aimed to salvage the situation by commissioning architects, urban planners, and consultants to design a modern environment, suitable for a modern Kuwaiti society. For this reason, the Kuwaiti government hired Colin Buchanan and Partners (CBP) to develop the second master plan for Kuwait. CBP's aim was to find a more comprehensive master plan that included both a short and a long-term solution that would help in producing a more organized urban development (Al-Nakib, 2016). Simultaneously four international architectural firms were invited to investigate the possibility to realize CBP's vision for Kuwait City through urban projects with an architectural details; they were Alison and Peter Smithson from England, Georges Candilis from Greece, Reima and Raili Pietilä from Finland, and the Italian firm Banfi, Belgiojoso, Peressutti, and Rogers. Although none of these projects were realized, the proposals of these firms directed the architectural approach in Kuwait in the following years (Alomaim, 2016; Al-Nakib, 2016). During this phase of Kuwait's urban development and throughout the 1970s Kuwait government, with the help of Saba Shiber, a Palestinian American urban planning consultant hired by the United Nations, further developed their plans by establishing an advisory Planning Committee (APC) to start a phase of nation-building in Kuwait (Alomaim 2016).[2, 3] The aim was to construct urban and architectural plans suitable for the local population.

Hitherto all of the projects and urban development were designed and constructed by Western professionals (Alomaim, 2016). Until today these urban planning methods were working for Kuwait, but they

Figure 7. A series of aerial photographs of the progress of the urban fabric of Kuwait from organic/ vernacular to modern radial grid allowing for wider streets for automobiles
Source: Source: Courtesy of Kuwait Oil Company

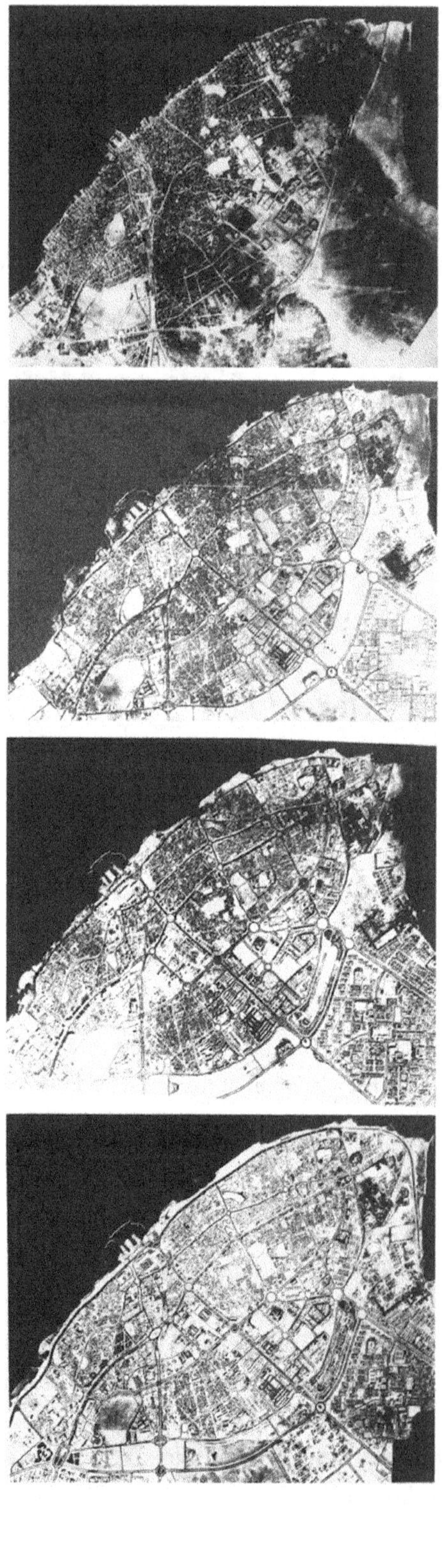

remain stagnant, without taking into consideration the contemporary need of Kuwaiti society, leading to deterioration of the urban environment, excessive congestion, and the obstruction of proper development to urban public spaces.

As reviewed by Anderson and Al-Bader in 2006, the strife that existed between Arab regionalism and globalization has developed as a process of building an image for Kuwait. Many forces have shaped the design and construction of buildings since Kuwait's independence. "[H]uman values, social structures, livelihood, and cultural changes are frequently manifested in the built environment" (Anderson & Al-Bader, 2006, pg. 135). In this review, global influences were looked at on the local level, as pieces of a larger puzzle. By using multiple sources of qualitative and quantitative data, we are attempting to develop a complex, multi-layered method to provide a holistic approach to KBUD.

PHONE APPS AS A RESEARCH MECHANISM

The purpose of this investigation is to create a mechanism that helps designers and urban planners to better develop a sustainable urban fabric. With data at multiple levels providing a comprehensive view of the urban environment, a more complete picture of development can be envisioned, and outcomes of potential interventions can be discerned before implementation.

These multiple layers of data will be triangulated in a search for overlaps, intersections, and interactions, which could provide insights on how the space is used. The Big Data from the smartphone applications can be further studied in conjunction with more traditional data.[4] The goal is to understand the different ways in which life in the city (1) is experienced by locals, expats, and migrants, through different digital practices; (2) encompasses various kinds of digital connections, which differ amongst urban dwellers/urban groups or classes, who might be enjoying or losing out from digital connections.[5]

The SPIN Unit is a good example of the work we are introducing in this chapter (Orzan, 2014). The SPIN Unit is an international network of scholars and practitioners that works through innovative forms of research, to analyze cities, urban planning social behavior and interactions, to meet the contemporary needs of the public.

Questions that this research hopes to answer:

- How do these apps impact gathering places and routes chosen by users?
- What other social applications are used in conjunction?
- Does social media affect the idea of citizenship?
- How does the use of social media by various groups alter the urban environment?

Methodology

This method is a dialogic post-structural approach, grounded in sociology and anthropological disciplines (Sullivan, 2012).[6] We are adapting tools from multiple disciplines to form a holistic interdisciplinary approach that documents a variety of sensitive data produced by the users of the urban landscape. This is a research approach that includes data application, interviews with citizens and residents of the city, and behavior mapping. The approach we are suggesting in this chapter will be organized in three layers: 1) Macro 2) Mezzo and 3) Micro.

Macro Layer: Collecting Big Data

We are beginning the research process with the Macro layer, which focuses on studying several cellphone applications: Talabat, Carriage, WhatsApp, Instagram, Snapchat, Uber, Careem, PayLe, Tap, and MyFatoora. We will investigate the data provided by these applications, the number of users, the type of users, the physical outcome of these applications and finally how they could help in producing KBUD in Kuwait.[7] This will inevitably create a layer of data that has not yet been taken into consideration by urban planners and designers in Kuwait. This will also involve many disciplines and experts to analyze such Big Data.

Today a new structure is coalescing, one based on the interaction of individuals through social media (e.g., Instagram, Snapchat and the geo-tagging technology) that supports these applications. The proliferation of social media applications in Kuwait covers a wide range of the population, providing insight towards the contemporary urban environment. These methods for social communication, and social cohesions, are crucial in our understanding of the current active spaces (Al-Nakib, 2016). The contemporary concept of the Fareej in Kuwait, as a space revived by social media technologies (Al-Bader, 2017).[8] Smartphone information will provide a deeper understanding about the users of the urban landscape. Data from applications can become mainstream data sourced for designers facilitating designs, that meet the needs of the public use of space. Research conducted in design offices responds to cultural norms in basic, if not superficial, ways. This basic information when translated into design solutions does not meet the actual needs of the users.

Important apps used in Kuwait are placed under 3 categories, that investigate the different aspects of each:

1. Delivery and Transportation services (e.g., Talabat, Carriage, Careem);
2. Social media apps with Geo-tagging (e.g., Facebook, Instagram, Snapchat);
3. Payment services (e.g., PayLe, Tap, MyFatoora).

Delivery and Transportation Services

Kuwait transportation services are not popular due to the use of personal methods of transportation. Other applications under the same category could define the delivery location and therefore allow us to understand vehicular movement during hours, along their way direction and concentration, allowing a more thorough understanding of the connections between various areas, and their effect on traffic congestion. *Data collected* will include: area of origin, route, destination, and time of travel.

Food delivery has taken on a new dimension with the advent of smartphone apps like Carriage and Talabat. Ordering from any restaurant in Kuwait through these platforms turns any home or office into a one-stop shopping location for the hungry masses. The design of these apps allows you to specify your location and discover available restaurants that delivers to that area:

1. **Areas**
    a. **Location:** This relates to the origin of the service, the individual neighborhoods, and the community that support a service. Groups find the service appealing due to their proximity. Order frequency shows the distribution of various types of food to different users across the

urban landscape. The concentration of food categories in each neighborhood defines a cultural enclave and their tastes;

   b. **Destination:** Services can be localized or specialty ordered from outside of the community. The amount of delivery that is taken to different locations adds to the traffic, especially when food travels outside of a neighborhood. Restaurants that are not based in the local community add to the pollution and environmental costs;

2. **Travel**
   a. **Time:** The rhythm and trends of the city are services in demand, and the time is more valuable during rush hour and meal times. As more food is delivered across Kuwait, it adds to the traffic congestion;
   b. **Distance Traveled:** The length a delivery must go from one area can be calculated by tracking the food from pickup to delivery. The use of GPS tracker on many of the phone apps provides a simple way to check the traffic flow and speed from one location to the next, illustrating the flow of commercial vehicles on the streets;
3. **Tastes**
   a. **Company Profile:** They aim to accommodate social group's tastes and existing menus, marketing the restaurant's commercial image through apps, often with a minimum purchase amount and/or delivery fee required. All these pieces help us to understand the social, cultural, and economic means of the purchasers;
   b. **Popularity:** The food delivery apps provide detailed information of the age and gender of each account user. The users' frequency of ordering and restaurant preferences provide insight into the trends and rhythm of food consumption by local residents, showing the trends in popular choices.

Social Media Apps with Geo-Tagging

The Kuwaiti population and residents converge around cultural sites/buildings in patterns depending on the date and time. For example, on weekends residents congregate in malls, beaches, homes, or even travel to an international destination. Through Geo-tagging we may be able to understand the urban concentration of certain categories (Batty, 2005). *Data collected* should include location, zone, building type, time, and date.

Instagram has become one of the most used cellphone applications in Kuwait. The app is not only used as a social media platform, but also as a contact directory, a marketing tool, and an entertainment media source. The function and features available on Instagram allow us to investigate the urban behavior of local citizens and residents in Kuwait through different features. The following is a categorization of the different ways researchers could potentially use to analyze data:

1. **Geo-Tagging:** Instagram offers the function of Geo-Tagging on shared videos and photos. This is perhaps one of the most important functions based on a complex algorithm that would help urban planners in their task to design better environments for the Kuwaiti population. There are various ways to utilize this function, to collect and analyze traffic patterns and preferences by demographic. Following the location link on top, the user is taken from a single posted image to all images posted at the same location. Therefore, analyzing the photos under each location allows us:

   a. To better understand the importance of the location by simply counting the number of photographs taken there;
   b. To understand the demographics of individuals visiting this location by analyzing the profiles of people listing the images taken there;
   c. To better understand the geographical links and routes of movement by overlaying the studied location with the location of the individuals who took photos there;
2. **Profile Connected Algorithms:** Creating a profile and linking it strictly to certain business profiles, or the profiles of civic institutions:
   a. **Explore:** Upon creating a profile, the public browser with its complex algorithm would connect the created profile to other related profiles. For example, following Kuwait Municipality, Kuwait Projects, and the Ministry of Youth would reveal the importance of the Diwan Amiri;
   b. **Survey:** This specially created profile can be used as a survey tool;
   c. **Suggestion and Updates:** Instagram constantly updates a user's feed with suggestions to follow individuals, institutions, or business. The new profiles that are suggested work as updates for the researchers to add more current data about a geographical location;
3. **Insta-Stories and Live-Videos:** See below:
   a. Insta stories are the contemporary platform of information. The live feed acts as empirical evidence to happenings. For example, a profile called @Kuwait_projects is a profile by an individual sponsored by the government to keep the public updated with the latest news and problems on the current situation of various development projects. The live feedback of the profile's followers is an unedited platform of the public reactions on the development on any given project. This function of Instagram has great potential in understanding the needs of Kuwaiti citizens and residents in what could be termed as "democratic and unedited data;"
   b. Live-videos facilitate a spontaneous conversation between the owner of the profile creating the live-video and other app users, through the live chat function. This is a live survey of data and access for the researcher to better understand the contemporary needs of any urban setting as people traverse it;
   c. **Filters**
      i. **Facebook:** Facebook was initiated as a social networking platform for students. Since Facebook is now connected to Instagram and other apps, Facebook's main features revolve around providing more personal information about the owners of the accounts;
      ii. **Snapchat:** Snapchat functions in similar ways to Instagram stories. Snapchat features are the origin of Instagram's story. To understand how Snapchat could potentially be used in KBUP please refer to the benefits listed above for Insta-stories.

Payment Services

The third category of smartphone apps allows us to understand socioeconomic patterns by using the apps PayLe, My Fatoorah, and TAP. For example, by analyzing data we will be able to understand not only potential physical movements of goods, but also the commercial and capital movement. *Data collected* should include clients' demographics, purchase company, amount, type, and source of goods:

1. **Location**
    a. **Business Location:** This includes the areas that are popularly used by both well-established traditional companies, as well as services that have less frequent transactions such as startups and home business. Detailed information regarding merchant, customer location, and purchasing habits can be collected. Transaction data can provide insight into the influence of location on commercial activity. The distribution of small businesses in communities across Kuwait and their level of commercial interaction can also be analyzed;
    b. **Delivery Location:** The information can help understand the communities that are supporting these initiatives and the urban environments that are fostering these local commercial events, such as the pop up markets, art fairs, and farmers markets. It also provides information on where the services are originating and who the primary users are for each payment services app;
2. **Material**
    a. **Service:** Any business or individual can use these apps as a paperless money transfer service between two parties, using credit or debit card data in a secure method. This allows the quick transfer of funds from customer to merchant without cash or a credit card machine;
    b. **Material Product:** Apps enable data collection to track the type and cost of a given product from shoes to handbags, to cakes and music lessons. That information can be analyzed to understand what people are paying for products that are not commercially available in the existing shopping centers and chain stores;
3. **Type**
    a. **Hidden:** This data would provide insight into the hidden economies of Kuwait, those not using the conventional business model. With the recent legislation supporting the legitimization of these businesses, there has been an increase in small home kitchen and craft services;
    b. **Mainstream:** Conventional chain stores are providing basic services that meet the needs of many consumers.

Big Data Analysis

After the collection of the smartphone app data sets, a process of data mining will search for patterns, connectivity, and intersections. This will provide insight into emergent trends in the urban environment. The analysis of this information will guide the second layer of investigation. By looking at the connectivity and intersection, clusters of various data sets to determine the location of these clusters or areas, that will be the site of interviews and case studies in the mezzo layer.

Mezzo Layer: Participatory/ Social Activism

This layer involves continuous data analysis using visual images and geo-tags (Fram & Margolis, 2001). Based on the analysis of the smartphone data, specific 'types' of areas will be identified, and approached for ethnographic interviews and case studies. Based on the quality of the data received, we will concentrate on three specific areas in Kuwait, where there was heightened activity, that can be compared with existing census data determining the general population information (ethnicity, religion, economic status). This will lead to a series of interviews conducted for a multi-sited ethnographic investigation, using a network of cultural insiders to understand the level of smartphone penetration into areas and individual families (Marcus, 1995). This is action-based research (Valverde, 2012). Architects, urban planners, real estate owners, municipality employers will be part of focus group discussions related to social activity (Kamberelis, 2010):

Stage One - Analyze Data for Emergent Themes: Location data in the apps section will be the source for physical areas where further research can be conducted. The census data from these areas will provide basic information on ethnic, religious and economic backgrounds. Considering Pierre Bourdieu's idea of Cultural Capital within a community, what is the social significance of the app and its usage within a community (Bourdieu, 1984)? Three case studies will be identified based on different locales of the city where digital communication activity is intense and where app usage is associated with the physical space. These areas will then be the site for interviews and further investigations to better understand how the apps are viewed within a community.

Stage Two - Interview Users, Policy Makers, and People From Multiple Age Groups: For each case study, ethnographic research will be conducted, including interviews and data collection for visual analysis. This step will investigate selected communities, specifically to understand how networks are shaped and changed based on digital communications. Interview data will be analyzed, seeking to bridge the gap between the digital and physical networks, while defining the role of digital communications in the communities. The case studies will provide a framework to understand the significance of smartphone's usage in relation to social class, economic status, and taste.

Stage Three - Conduct Focus Groups With 'Like' Users: The goal of these interviews is to understand public use of these applications. Areas of interest include social status and acceptance with peer groups and family, along with location, frequency, tastes, and nature of use. The various connection points between users in apps can create a picture of the closeness or separation of family and friends through different social media platforms. These focus groups can also highlight the economic, cultural, and social divides between application users.

Stage Four - Hold Focus Groups With Multiple Users: Focus groups will be conducted within a collective that will be determined through interviews. Groups that have a combination of the users (e.g., children, youth, elderly, expatriates) will be cued using visual artifacts from the site. We will investigate the question: does their app usage imbue a status within the community, or does it carry a stigma? Apps may allow users to increase their social importance with a given group.

Micro: Space Syntax

The last suggested layer of research demonstrated in this chapter is the Micro scale. Through a method of behavioral mapping and space syntax, these nodes that gather space can be studied to see their importance with the community on the social and cultural level (Moore & Cosco, 2010). These methods look at the frequency and use of the space, while also measuring the level of interaction within each location. This data should provide a guide to areas of concentration: gathering spaces such as malls, public monuments, community centers, places of worship, etc. These nodes can be correlated with time and frequency of use, allowing for a more thorough understanding of the people's movements and rhythms. This analysis may provide a rough guide to work and leisure gathering, helping researchers understand the various forms of social gathering.

Where is activity concentrated both in the physical and virtual spaces, and what is the place and time of such gatherings?

1. **Locating a Specific Place:** The interviews will serve to gather information about areas of interaction and clustering, the spaces of social significance to communities and social groups. Where do people gather and for what purpose? Does the urban environment facilitate moments of connection (i.e., social, physical, virtual)?
2. **Choosing a Specific Location From App Data and Interviews:** The intersection of these two data sources will provide a starting point for a closer look at urban spaces; as defined by the community or social group to have social significance. These spaces (i.e. plazas, shopping centers, domestic dwellings community centers, places of worship) in each clustered area will then be investigated;
3. **Investigation:** The space will be investigated via behavior mapping, by studying the physical relationship of people's interaction with the space (Moore & Cosco, 2010). Through a series of detailed mappings, the relationship between physical interaction and the social relevance of the space can be discerned, both in its physical quality and its virtual presence (Nickerson, 1993). This can be followed with a study of space syntax, the measuring of lines of connection and pathways, building a map of connectivity between spaces to detail their amount of intersection. This will include the number of people that activate the space at given times, their social or economic status, and the level of interaction between people at the chosen location. Data will also be collected to consider the interaction that happens across economic and cultural boundaries;
4. **Intervention:** This information can provide a framework to use more specific and accurate techniques such as Tactical Urbanism—as defined in the early 2000 as short-term action to bring about long-term change—helping in the development of social capital between citizen and organizations at the scale of block, street, or building (Pfeifer, 2013). These interventions, a product of a multilayer analysis, would provide a more complete response to the needs of the city in each location, thus leaving less to chance as urban environments are now the primary habitat of humanity. An example of tactical urbanism can be found in Kuwait in the revitalization of a small area in the old shopping Souq called SoMu (South of Mubarikiya), that has helped reengage the public in the traditional Souq, but with a modern gentrified flair. Interventions will address the need to create more complete urban environments that respond to the increasing complex multicultural population of global cities;
5. **Post Occupancy Study:** Following such interventions, a post occupancy study would be conducted, comparing all the data gathered, social media actives, interviews, and behavior mapping with new data collected following the completion of the intervention. This post occupancy study would reflect the effect of the changes on the urban population, while providing information for the future alteration and adjustment of the spaces. The apps' ongoing data collection provides a constant feedback loop, allowing for the adjustment to services that are needed by the local population.

FUTURE RESEARCH DIRECTIONS

The methodological approach proposed here facilitates insight into the social aspects of the city. This method quantifies the interaction between individuals, services, and community. These are element of the city which are normally obscured by cultural conventions. This approach makes this hidden dimension more accessible when collected and analyzed. All the data collected is linked back to all the users who are engaged in the use of their smartphone application. This method will begin to include parts of the community that are marginalized or are invisible in traditional planning processes. As the urban fabric of our cities become more cosmopolitan, planners must look toward methods of inclusive integration of various cultures in the urban environment (Georgiou, 2013). This method provides a more balanced approach to cultural inclusion in the urban environment by looking at all the users.

The ability to quickly understand the movement of people within spaces and their interactions, in the work place, around food and leisure services, or when they are at home, will facilitate a more complete understanding of the urban landscape (Whyte, 1998). This multi-layered process will allow the Urban Planner to be a proactive agent in the design of future cities. This complex, multifaceted method that includes information gathering such as interviews, behavioral mapping, and space syntax, as outlined here, can provide a more holistic understanding of the urban environment. Consequently, the city will be viewed a complex adaptive system rather than a random collection of streets, buildings, and people.

Such a rich information bank can be used to interrogate multiple issues including verifying the effects of policy decisions and their implementation, quantifying the effectiveness of policies and urban interventions, and providing planners almost immediate feedback on their decisions. This continuous cycle of reflection is a self-reinforcing feedback loop that can bring about a constant incremental improvement to the urban fabric. The concept of "designing cities" will no longer be the dominating paradigm for our urban environments; instead the different aspects will be facilitated by the users to build a more efficient environment in which needs of the public are met. The users' physical interaction with the environment, becomes the most powerful tool, shaping it based on their actions. The design mechanism can be a silent observer to the already existing collection of behaviors, crafting space to the needs of the users.

CONCLUSION

Smartphone Apps are an intrinsic part of the contemporary life in Kuwait, for all its residents. The level of cell phone integration provides a continuous stream of data which intersects various social and economic classes within the occupied spaces, both, in the physical and digital world. Gathering and analyzing the data provided by such smartphone applications is one of the most important ways to establish any new research concerning the future development of urban planning in Kuwait.

The implications of such a KBUD is the transparency of the process of design. Decisions will be made based on the visible needs of public. This may threaten the dominant economical forces, contracting companies, individual businesses, and those in power—a shift that provides a voice to all. The building of Central Park, NYC, which provided a much-needed green space in a dense urban environment, came with a cost to the displaced residents of Seneca Village. More recently, a similar cost was felt by the residents of the villages of Imwas, Yalo, and Beit Nouva in Israel, who were displaced for the creation of Ayalon Park south of Tel Aviv (Al-Bahar, 2016). The displaced of residents is a common theme in urban development. Whereas now concerns of marginalized communities are not addressed by urban planning, a more thorough understanding of all residents would create a more nuanced approach, helping to provide a real picture of use.

Smartphone data is the new starting point for investigation of Knowledge Based Urban Development. In this way, the city is not designed but rather *facilitated* based on the data received. This approach would change the nature of urban education, focusing more on human-driven design and policies, turning to data for guidance when developing and implementing programs within cities.

REFERENCES

Al-Bader, J. (2012). *Visual Ethnography in Three Preschools in Kuwait (Middle East). Arizona State University*. ProQuest.

Al-Bader, J. (2017). Spaces for reviving traditions: Vol. 282. *Legitimating Tradition, Kuwait, 2016*. Berkley, CA: The International Association for the Study of Traditional.

Al-Bahar, S. (2017). Brownfield Remediation and Recovery: A Non-Militaristic Tactic to Territorial Acquisition: Vol. 285. *Legitimating Tradition, Kuwait, 2016*. Berkley, CA: The International Association for the Study of Traditional.

Al-Nakib, F. (2016). *Kuwait transformed: a history of oil and urban life*. Stanford, CA: Stanford University Press.

Alomaim, A. (2016). *Nation Building in Kuwait 1961–1991. University of California Los Angeles*. ProQuest.

Anderson, R., & Al-Bader, J. (2006). Recent Kuwaiti architecture: Regionalism vs. globalization. *Journal of Architectural and Planning Research*, *23*(2), 134–146.

Baker, C. (2005). *Cultural Studies: Theory and Practice*. London: Sage.

Batty, M. (2007). *Cities and Complexity: Understanding Cities with Cellular Automata, Agent-based Models, and Fractals*. Boston: MIT Press.

Becker, R., Caceres, H., Hanson, K., Loh, J. M., Urbanek, S., Varshavsky, A., & Volinsky, C. (2011). A Talc of Onc City: Using Ccllular Nctwork Data for Urban Planning. IEEE Pervasive Computing.

Bourdieu, P. (1984). *Distinction: A social critiques of the judgement if taste*. Harvard University Press.

Fram, S., & Margolis, E. (2001). Architectural and build environment discourses in an educational context: The Gottscho and Schleisner collection. *Visual Studies*, *26*(3), 229–243. doi:10.1080/1472586X.2011.610946

Georgiou, M. (2013). *Media and the City: Cosmopolitanism and Difference*. Cambridge, UK: Polity Press.

Jameson, F. (2003). *Postmodern, or cultural logic of late capitalism*. Durham, NC: Duke University Press.

Kamberelis, G. (2010). Focus Groups: Contingent Articulations of Pedagogy, Politics, and Inquiry. *Collecting and Interpreting Qualitative Materials*, *3*, 1–17.

Luhmann, N. (2012). *Theory of Society*. Stanford, CA: Stanford University Press.

Lynch, K. (1960). *The Image of the City*. Boston: The MIT Press.

Marcus, G. (1995). Ethnography in/of the world system: The emergence of multisite ethnography. *Annual Review of Anthropology*, *24*(1), 95–117. doi:10.1146/annurev.an.24.100195.000523

Moore, R. C., & Cosco, N. G. (2010). Using behavior mapping to investigate healthy outdoor environments for children and families. In C. W. Thompson, P. Aspinall, & S. Bell (Eds.), Innovative Approaches to Researching Landscape and Health: Open Space: People Space 2 (pp. 33–72). Taylor & Francis.

Netto, V. M. (2017). *The Social Fabric of Cites (Design and the Built Environment)*. New York: Routledge.

Nickerson, N. P. (1993). Understanding your consumers through behavioral mapping. *Parks & Recreation*.

Northwestern University Qatar. (2014). *Social media ubiquiitous, more used than email*. Retrieved September 2017, from http://www.mideastmedia.org/survey/2015/chapter/social-media.html#subchapter4

Orzan, S. (2014.) *An Interview with Damiano Cerrone, Co-Founder of SPIN Unit*. Retrieved September 2017, from http://www.startuberlin.com/spin-unit-damiano-cerrone-interview/

Pfeifer, L. (2013) *The Planner's Guide to Tactical Urbanism*. Montreal: McGill. Pogue, D. *David Pogue tested 47 pill-reminder apps to find the best*. Retrieved September 2017, from https://finance.yahoo.com/news/david-pogue-tested-47-pill-reminder-apps-to-find-the-best-154017023.html

Reades, J., Calabrese, F., Sevtsuk, A., & Ratti, C. (2007). Cellular Census: Explorations in Urban Data Collection. IEEE Pervasive Computing.

Sanders, T. I. (2008). Complex system thinking and new urbanism. In *New Urbanism and Beyond designing cities for the future* (pp. 275–279). New York, NY: Rizzoli.

Sullivan, P. (2012). *Qualitative Data Analysis: Using a dialogic approach*. Los Angeles: SAGE Publications Ltd. doi:10.4135/9781446268391

Valverde, M. (2012). *Everyday Law on the Street: City Governance in an Age of Diversity (Chicago Series in Law and Society)*. The University of Chicago Press. doi:10.7208/chicago/9780226921914.001.0001

Whyte, W. H. (1980). *The Social Life of Small Urban Spaces*. Ann Arbor, MI: Edwards Brothers, Inc.

Yigitcanlar, T. (2010). Knowledge-based devlopemnt of cities: a myth or reality? *Proceedings of REvive MTY forum 2010*, 3–4.

ADDITIONAL READING

Bakhtin, M. (1981). *The Dialogic Imagination: Four Essays by M.M. Bakhtin* (M. Holquist, Ed., C. Emerson & M. Holquist, Trans.). Austin: University of Texas Press.

Camagni, R. (1998). Sustainable urban development: Definition and reasons for a research program. *International Journal of Environment and Pollution*, *10*(1), 6–27. doi:10.1504/IJEP.1998.002228

Dandekar, H. (1998) Global spaces meets local space in the twenty-first century. In H Dandekar (Ed.), *City, space, and globalization: An international perspective (Proceedings of an International Symposium in the College of Architecture and Urban Planning)*. Ann Arbor: University of Michigan Press, pp.20–25.

Lerner, J. (2016). *Urban Acupuncture*. Island Press.

Thrift, N. (1996). Spatial Formations (Published in association with Theory, Culture & Society. SAGE Publications Ltd. Tuan, Y.-F. (1977). Space and Place: The Perspective of Experience. University of Minnesota Press.

Wittgenstein, L. (1953). *Philosophical Investigations*. MacMillan Publishing Company.

ENDNOTES

1 There is an apparent increase in use of social media in Kuwait. We argue that the reason behind this is the nature of Kuwaiti culture, being private and at the same time very social. There isn't any in-depth research that explains the reason behind this intense use, and since it is not the aim behind this research, it suffices to say that one quarter of the population is actively using cellphone applications such as Instagram, which is the same percentage of users in the United Kingdom or the United States.

2 The committee comprised of Sir Leslie Martin, Omar Azzam, Franco Albini, and Hamed Shuaib (Alomaim, 2016).

3 In 1977, the firm Shakland and Cox proposed the construction of two new cities for the future expansion and growth of Kuwait.

4 Big Data refers to extremely large data sets that are analyzed for rhythms, patterns and trends.

5 For previous studies using similar approaches see (Reades, Calabrese, Sevtsuk, & Ratti, 2007) and (Becker et al., 2011).

6 This term is rooted in Mikhail from Baktin's (1981) ideas of heteroglossia, and multiple points of view.

7 Analysis of the data will be approached individually based on nature of this data. If the data from Instagram is a photograph, then it will be analyzed using visual analysis tools.

8 This refers to a group of family homes that are clustered around a courtyard, or a public space. Fareej could also mean a group of houses that share a street or a neighborhood.

Chapter 11
Knowledge-Based Urban Design in the Architectural Academic Field

Hisham G. Abusaada
Housing and Building National Research Center, Egypt

Abeer Elshater
Ain Shams University, Egypt

ABSTRACT

This chapter focuses on the theory of knowledge-based urban design as a tool for intellectual literacy in architecture schools. It explores the extent of the current knowledge effects in the educational process by knowing the experience gained by the students during the current learning plans, as opposed to what the urban designer should know. The dilemma is what could happen if the experts in the relevant disciplines of urban design do not accept such a paradigm shift or even recognize that there is intellectual illiteracy in a particular discipline and closely relevant fields by discussing some features of intellectual illiteracy in the academe of some developing countries. These features could provide a ground for accepting this theory. Furthermore, the chapter helps to present what can reduce the alleged intellectual illiteracy. In conclusion, this chapter provides an experimental attempt to explore the relationship between illiteracy of thought and mental ability among professionals in the field of urban design to raise their intellectual and cognitive competence.

THE ROLE OF KNOWLEDGE IN TEACHING AND LEARNING

Generally speaking, all people by nature are interested in knowledge. And, it is widely recognized that knowledge has become the key source of wealth in advanced economies. In this matter, Brontis (1998, p. 63) cited from Aristotle who was inspired from Plato's common definition for knowledge. They all agreed that it is the true justification or pretext powered belief ideological belief (Plato, 1935, p. 140). Andrew Leach notes, quoting Michel Foucault that knowledge does not exist for something basic or specific meaning behind things, and therefore everything can be judged according to the framework

DOI: 10.4018/978-1-5225-3734-2.ch011

Copyright © 2018, IGI Global. Copying or distributing in print or electronic forms without written permission of IGI Global is prohibited.

of knowledge that always change (Leach, 2006, p. 329). According to the theoretical platform of how people learn in the traditional methods of education, it is important to say that learning is a process of remembering what person gets by his five senses, and knowledge consists of what is interpreting through various skills and is affected by what they believe (D. Bransford, L. Brown, & R. Cocking, 2000, p. 10). This could lead to the search for the concise of knowledge for being a holistic icon gets in touch with all that student gains in the academic learning and could be transferred to others and be seen in their intended learning outcomes (various assignments and study projects). This could give them the ability which enables them to present their work in a distinctive way reflecting their theoretical base. Whenever we fought in tracking the dialectic of knowledge to understand, it was possible to be developed to be a gateway to learn. Thus, each individual in the field of competence of the Architecture and urban studies, in particular, accurately represents the intellectual capital for the field of his/her professional practice. Following to this, the presence of each person will play an important role in future of the affiliated institution which is affected by/on the whole society (Starovic & Marr, 2003, p. 26). This process takes into consideration what happen earlier through learning procedures and afterward steps of the early career. Albert Einstein mentioned that the main driving factors in person's work are not in the knowledge gained from the school rather from the experience of life and this can be seen in his/her appropriateness of the outcomes which reflect with benefits on local/ global communities (Einstein, 1954, p. 62). On another word, the knowledge in the field of Architecture is directly linked to the quality and value of the outcomes products constructed features. This indented quality is not only the quality of the building but also the one which targeting a certain level of standards of fluffing the users' requirement (Volker & Prins, 2006, pp. 900, 902). Therefore, one of the most urgent questions in this chapter is the students' qualification that should be covered to make the student qualified at the level of Bachelor and how they gained knowledge to be used in the early career in a useful way gets its befits to their community. Also, this may need a better understanding of the meaning of the word 'intellectual illiteracy.' The development of the intellectual skills are usually related to the social interaction between the tacit and explicit knowledge through a framework consist of four main factors (SECI) (Nonaka & Takeuchi, 1995, pp. 60-62). The first is creating knowledge which begins by socialization (S). The second is continuous with externalization (E). The third and fourth are a combination (C) and intellectualization (I). Then, the process returns back to socialization but at new level due to the metaphor of spiral of knowledge (Figure 1).

Also, Volker and Prins (2006, pp. 900, 902) mansion that knowledge is directly connected with quality in the field of Architecture. Whereby, they described that the value of the urban context is related to the quality and value of the outcomes of the constructed environment to fitful the assigned needs or what could be in term of the adaptation between the needs and the product which can be judged by its value. In implementing management in design, the premise is frequently presented a fluent, effective and efficient process that will influence the value of the outcome (Volker, Deciding about Design Quality, 2010). According to literature, the values in architecture are the principles, standards, and qualities by which we live and guide our actions (Thomson, Austin, Devine-Wright, & Mills, 2003) (Le Dantec & Y-Luen Do, 2009), (Volker, 2010). Previously to this, Rokeach (1973) has defined two types of value terminal values (end goals) and instrumental values (means to reach goals). In a similar way, the School of Management, Canfield University (2006) describes the knowledge in a tangible way to have a judgment as a sequenced hierarchy of assets of knowledge. In addition, the value in the field of knowledge management can deal with students collectively as the gateway to a group of processes and practices that are used by organizations to increase the value by improving the effectiveness of the generation

Figure 1. Tacit an implicit knowledge

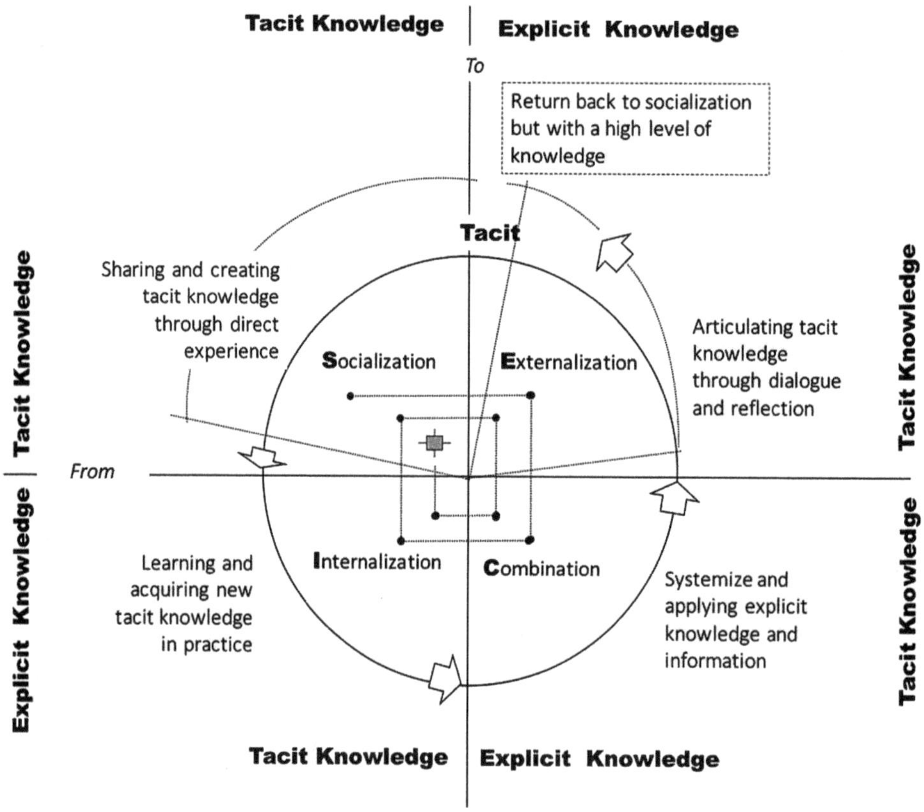

and application of intellectual capital through a structured process. In the process, Nonaka (1994, p. 14) calls for a paradigm shift where any organization that dynamically deals with a changing environment should not only deal with the process of handling the knowledge through a certain information but also, should create it through a sufficient environment.

On the other side, literature by Winden (2011) describes the knowledge as one particular way to promote the urban knowledge economy through creating knowledge 'hotspots.' He recommends making the hotspots attractive places (Winden, 2011, p. 3). Whereby the talented people are the key drivers for innovation, especially higher educated, entrepreneurial and creative people. Places that manage to attract/retain these people are successful in the knowledge economy. A sound knowledge hotspot has at least four features illustrated in (Figure 2).

Thus, it could be said that the human capital (Table 1) is the heart of the intellectual capital as the latter is a common topic in the field of human resources, a new millennium currency is used wisely key to success in the age of knowledge, in which knowledge transformed into value. Meanwhile, while the usage of all the material, intellectual property, and information to create wealth with a view to doubling the output of the physical assets gains a competitive advantage and/or enhances the value of other types of capital. And through the individuals who have experience and knowledge, abilities and skills and communicate with others, mind resources determine the value of the particular institution and the competitiveness of this institution which could be measured by the ability to use knowledge.

Figure 2. Knowledge assets (School of Management, Granfeild University, 2006, p. 9), (Winden, 2011, p. 3)

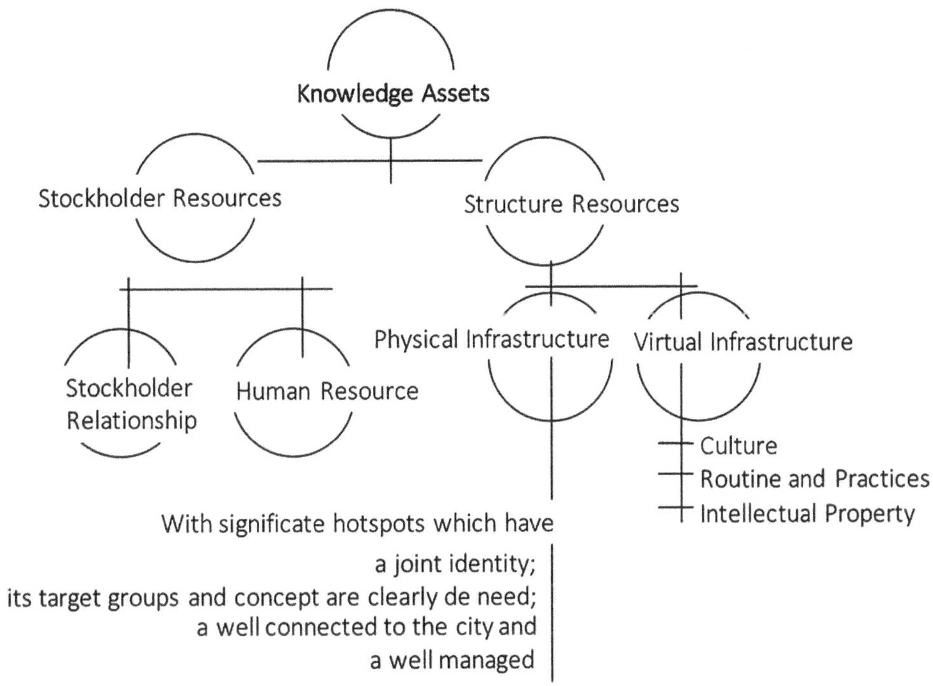

Table 1. Some comments about human capital

The Commentators	Year	The Concepts	Citation
Alfred Marshall	1890	Investment in human is the most valuable of all capital	(Marshall A., 1890, p. 564)
Gary S. Becker	1962	The total capacity, experience, and knowledge, which refers to the role of individuals as producers of the value in the economy.	(Becker, 1962, pp. 45-46)
Thomas Kuhn	1970	Investment in human is the most valuable thing in this world Collective knowledge is of intangible assets, a cognitive dimension.	(Kuhn, 1970, p. 51)
Ken Robinson	1999	The human capital which is a vital investment in itself, and the ability to create and take advantage of them became represent high human value based on economic behavior.	(Robinson, National Advisory Committee on Creative and Cultural Education, All Our Futures: Creativity, Culture and Education, 1999, p. 5)
Danka Starovic; Bernard Marr	2003	Unique knowledge or general skills and experience of staff that they take with them when leaving examples include the ability to innovation and creativity, expertise and past experience, the ability to teamwork, flexibility, tolerance for ambiguity, motivation, satisfaction and learning ability, loyalty, and formal educational training	(Starovic & Marr, Understanding Corporate Value: managing and reporting intellectual capital, 2003, p. 5)
David Alexander Clark	2006	Investigation in knowledge is the best	(Clark, 2006, p. 245)
Cindy Eggs	2012	Collective knowledge (whether documented or not documented) by individuals in the organization or community is the dimension of knowledge.	(Eggs, 22-23 April 2012, p. 173)
Payam Mojtahedi	2013	Knowledge is the main factor of the inhuman capital	(Mojtahedi, 2013, p. 535)

Often knowledge management is the aim of creating the human and intellectual capital (Table 2), where they become closely linked to economic interests. Knowledge is always economic development axes Where the economy is based on knowledge taken the concept figuratively as a big place in the dissemination and use and create information and knowledge (Organization for Economic Co-Operation, 1996, pp. 9, 14). It is important to transform knowledge into valuable assets (Kok, 2007, p. 184). The assets respect over a very colossal human knowledge in the present day. In addition to this, the value of this knowledge increases when making decisions in confronting the problems of design, even if it seemed to us that knowledge arises from experience but the result is to flourish and evolve through thinking and reasoning (Audi, 2003, p. 220).

The theory of knowledge (epistemology) is of the primary branches of philosophy; it is the theory of knowledge and justification (Audi, 2003, p. X) where the form of knowledge as a force in the developed world today is a kind of world system (Kuwayama & Bremen, 26-27 September 1997, p. 54). Knowledge is a tool to understand facts as an essential tool for human progress (Coulby & Jones, 1995, p. 25). Thus, the progress of any institution depends on the people stacked to it to whom represent the real capital of it (Nonaka & Takeuchi, 1995, p. 7). But what has concerned us through shed light on the knowledge here as a global subject that can be acquired by students of architecture and urbanism during the period of their undergraduate studies. Additionally, knowledge is a process for handling

Table 2. Intellectual capital

The Commentators	Year	The Concepts	Citation
John Kenneth Galbraith	1969	Knowledge power is the common topic in the field of human resources. The knowledge is not only the most important interests but also with the experience, skill, and communication with others.	(Feiwel, 1975) (Kaya, Sahin, & Gurson, Intellectual Capital in Organizations, 2010, p. 154) (Bontis, Intellectual capital: an exploratory study that develops measures and models, 1998, p. 67)
Leif Edvinsson; Patrick Sullivan	1996	The usage of knowledge to be transformed into value	(Edvinsson & Sullivan, 1996, p. 358)
Thomas A. Stewart	1887	Intellectual materials, information, and intellectual property could be managed to create wealth.	(Stewart, 1997, p. Foreword XX)
Andrew Kok	2007	Identify elements of knowledge and procedures of value come across three continents which are the expertise the know-how, capabilities and human skills.	(Kok, 2007, p. 185)
Nick Bontis; William Chua Chong Keow; Stanley Richardso	2008	The knowledge is the currency of the new millennium and were used wisely as the key to success in the knowledge age.	(Bontis, Keow, & Richardson, Intellectual Capital and Business Performance in Malaysian Industries, 2000, p. 85)
Donna M. Nickitas; Donna J. Middaugh; Nancy Aries	2011	It uses knowledge to produce wealth and doubling the output of the physical assets and gain a competitive advantage and / or to enhance the value of other types of capital.	(Nickitas, Middaugh, & Aries, 2011, p. 264)
Bob Barret	2012	It is all materials that determine the value of the particular institution and the competitiveness of this institution.	(Barret, 29-30 March 2010, p. 70)
Keng-Sheng Ting		The key for competitiveness and the ability to use knowledge.	(Ting, 2012, pp. 60, 61)
Samah Souleh	2014	It represents the intellectual capacity of the individual and is a factor of value to create wealth.	(Souleh, 2014, pp. 82-83)

those gains and applying the indented outcomes in their projects tuition. Thus, those consists have the experience to help them take out their projects, status differentiation of knowledge, the more fought in tracking the dialectic of knowledge to understand the form of knowledge. It was possible to develop it to be a gateway to learning. The solid base of learning can formulate the intended learning outcomes in a way reflect the quality and value of constructed environment. In other words, knowledge is the quality determines how we can produce a good service, a think-tank material that can be put to use in order to create wealth. It is illustrative of the ability to act and deed, a dynamic humanitarian of operation as part of the aspiration of the truth.

Accordingly, knowledge comes in the philosophical and scientific literature to be a specified entity that appears in the form of ideas which rises from understandings the specification and principles to a subject. It can be for this entity achieving its objectives, where knowledge is recognized as the outcome of the economic value of the graduate as a product through the input process. The indented outputs are considered in the facts, information, and skills which are acquired through accumulative experiences or education. It is also considered the theoretical or practical understanding of a subject (Fowler, Fowler, & Sykes, 1976, p. 598), (Australia's National Dictionary, 1981, p. 978). The specific things create the knowledge and are gotten through the experience and the production of meanings. The knowledge comes in philosophy from the experience and justification practices or innate ability to think (Audi, 2003, pp. 207-208). Bennet & Benne (2014, pp. 13-16) considered knowledge as a comprised of two parts; information and proceeding. The first calls for the meanings, visions, expectations, intuition, theories and principles. It also looks for understanding and supporting or leadership to effective action. The second concerns the process of handling of information access and exchange (Bennet & Bennet, 2014, pp. 12-13) (Table 3).

Manuel Castle has defined the information as a tool to produce knowledge and could be used to communicate with others. Additionally, The Oxford English Dictionary (1989, p. 944) mentions through literature that the concept of knowledge is seen from two sides: *to know* which depends on the information and facts and *to whom* which concerns the ability to do something based on the *to know.* Meanwhile, the management of knowledge is controlled through the distinguished perceiving subjects (Lytras, Russ, Maier, & Naeve, 2000, p. 223).

The term 'knowledge creation' is the production of the new ideas (Blakeley, Lewis, & Mills, 2005, p. 8). Figure (1) shows the process of creating knowledge that has been developed by Aakojiro Nonaka. Moreover, the interested absorb knowledge is an acquisition of knowledge based on the concept that raised outside the company process (Blakeley, Lewis, & Mills, 2005, p. 9), while the process of using knowledge to accumulated knowledge followed by creating value in the application procedure. The human resources lose the power without knowledge which makes finding the combinative method to come over the intellectual illiteracy.

THE ROLE OF KNOWLEDGE IN INTELLECTUAL ILLITERACY

The term of Illiteracy in the field of information technology comes to describe the person's ability to preserve the knowledge and have the ability to determine and evaluate the effective use of the information needed. It is also a set of core competencies that should be used by everyone, which is efficient for the effective information system and ethical manner. It is also a set of core competencies that should be used by everyone, which is efficient for effective information system and ethical manner (Virkus, 2013).

Table 3. The forms of knowledge

Forms of Knowledge	Adventive Concepts	Cited Works
Convincing, general, scientific and reasonable	Subject that could be transforming and modified	(Hayek, 1945, p. 521)
The knowledge could be gained through the syntax and synchronize process	Explicit	(Goldman, 1967, p. 360)
At the first level of intellectual literacy, the persons are the ones who establish their basic knowledge and the institutions establish the organized framework for knowledge.	Tacit	(Nonaka I., A Dynamic Theory of Organizational Knowledge Creation, 1994, p. 21)
It could be related to the conative sciences		(Polanyi, 2009, p. X)
Descriptive term		(Organization For Economic Co-Operation, 1996, p. 13)
The tacit (uncodified) knowledge in the heads of employees, customer experience and past memories for vendors. Knowledge is broader that intellectual capital (IC) where some chose IC to include practice and process.	Informal/ uncodified and formal/codified	(O'dell & Grayson, 2012, pp. 3-5)
Knowledge is an information in action		
The knowledge is a tacit and implicit	Subjective matter	(Nonaka & Takeuchi, The knowledge-Creating Company, 1995, p. 61)
The contribution and collaboration of organization forms a knowledge		(Nonaka & Takeuchi, The knowledge-Creating Company, 1995, p. 25)
The right action to believe based on a justification for increase the capabilities of a specific and competent entity action	General	(Coulby & Jones, Postmodernity and European Education Systems: Cultural diversityand centralist knowledge, 1995, p. 25)
Knowing the target skills	Indented outcomes	(Sahdra & Thagard, 2003, p. 478)
The knowledge is the ability to retrieve relevant information		(DeVito, 2008, p. 34)
Spontaneous (causal) or implicit (rooted in the action) or explicit (clear and generalized) or rational (with knowledge) or realistic utilitarian pragmatism (for the organization) or police.	Based on condition and context	(Alavi & Leidner, Mar., 2001, p. 111)
Blog and stored were received in the form of booklets and documents and procedures in some media. Management tool; it will be utilized for the management of organizational knowledge	Tacit	(Hunt, 2003, p. 107)
Knowledge is useful include scientific information and data	General	(Mokyr, 2004, p. 5)
The knowledge is developed through the explicit information that could be tested and gets the outcomes to be used in solving a certain problem.	Implicit	(Audi, 2003, p. 265)
The person should be sure of the validity of knowledge or belief so that they use it to make decisions in order to solve problems and identify and implement actions.		(Hunt, 2003, p. 107)
	General	(Krauss, 2005, p. 759)
	Applicable, General and specific	(Farenhorst & Boer, 2009, p. 22)
Knowledge is the ability to develop a specific subject	Religious, moral, social phenomenology, and experimental technique done by individual and group	(Ryle, 2009, pp. 41, 46)
		(Sachs, 2010, pp. 221-225)
Knowledge is in form the data and information stored and retrieve in literature	tacit	(Bennet & Bennet, Knowledge, Theory and Practice in Knowledge Management: Between Associative Patterning and Context-Rich Action, 2014, pp. 14-15)
In some cases, knowledge has a deeper understanding of the meaning and making sensations	Explicit	
Knowledge contains concepts and objectives of intuition. It also gives insight, creativity, judgments and the ability to anticipate the results of our actions		

Boekhorst (Becoming Information Literate in the Netherlands, 2003) describe the illiteracy opposite to the general scientific literacy; technical, visual and cultural literacy which they are all the illiterate belongs to the umbrella literacy of information. The fundamental differences come between the information literacy and computer literacy. The literacy information are a European and American movement which has been prevailed in the eighties in the last century and then moved to all parts of the world; and continued till nowadays (Virkus, 2013, p. 251), (Klaus, 2000). At present, no longer focus on increasing literacy and numeracy rates is in the global interest rather than the necessity literacy information that is closely linked to digital with computers.

The most important issues are the knowledge that in connection with the term ability to do something successfully or efficiently. The information literacy is a collection of techniques requiring somebody to identify when data is needed and have the powers to locate, evaluate, and use the required information (American Association for Higher Education, 1989, pp. 2-3). This means that the focus has become a necessity on attempts to expand the intellectual ability of the individual through working in groups. Thereby, the literacy rate among adults is used as an indicator of human capital, comes the definition of literacy that the ability to read, write and understand (Woßmann, 2003, p. 243). It is not generally accepted in the Arabic language phrase, or that they have a common definition in dictionaries or language dictionaries. More than that, it is a term that does not use commonly than before in the field of architecture and urbanism at the educational and practical levels. In this work, the knowledge is sculpted as a term to mean the process of activating the knowledge and practical steps to follow to achieve a professional organization's intention. Definitely, the knowledge, data, information, skills and experience are acquired through the education, learning and training experience that is gained through the colleagues (Abusaada, 2015, pp. 57-66). The quality of a college is measured by the resources for learning on the campus and the extent to which students become independent, self-directed learners. And yet we found that today, about one out of every four undergraduates spend no time in the library during a normal week, and 65 percent use the library four hours or less each week. The gap between the classroom and the library reported on almost a half-century ago, still exists today.

The current work refers the development of this phrase; intellectual illiteracy, which is an unacceptable situation in professional practice. This case may reach to become a negative phenomenon in the field of architecture and urbanism. Moreover, it can be considered a new expression or a term in the field of urban design explains the intellectual illiteracy in the area of architecture and urbanism. But, if the literature describes the literacy in the condition of the ability to use the techniques of using and launching the information to produce the knowledge, the current work describes the scholarship that participant in the field of Architecture should have to use knowledge to produce and share ideas and intellectual production. The term can describe the persons who cannot produce and share ideas to solve a certain problem that the local community could have. This disability is a genetic problem rather than what these persons have gained through their educational and practical experience which should be resilient and robust to adequate the changes either in time and places. What they gain, help in producing the ideas with no reflection to the individual's mental ability. This is the reason to say no, arguing that all young people have creative abilities differently (Robinson, 1999, p. 37). Creativity can be defined as a fictional innovative activity for the production of original outputs of the value of any produce something original (Robinson, 1999, pp. 28,30). As long touted as confidential knowledge as implicit values and non-physical or intangible assets (Kaya, Sahin, & Gurson, 2010, p. 154), (Nonaka & Takeuchi, 1995, p. 8), this paper discusses how to make use of knowledge to improve professional practice in term of real results. And,

Figure 3. The importance of knowledge source: The authors based on (North & Kumta, 2014, p. 8)

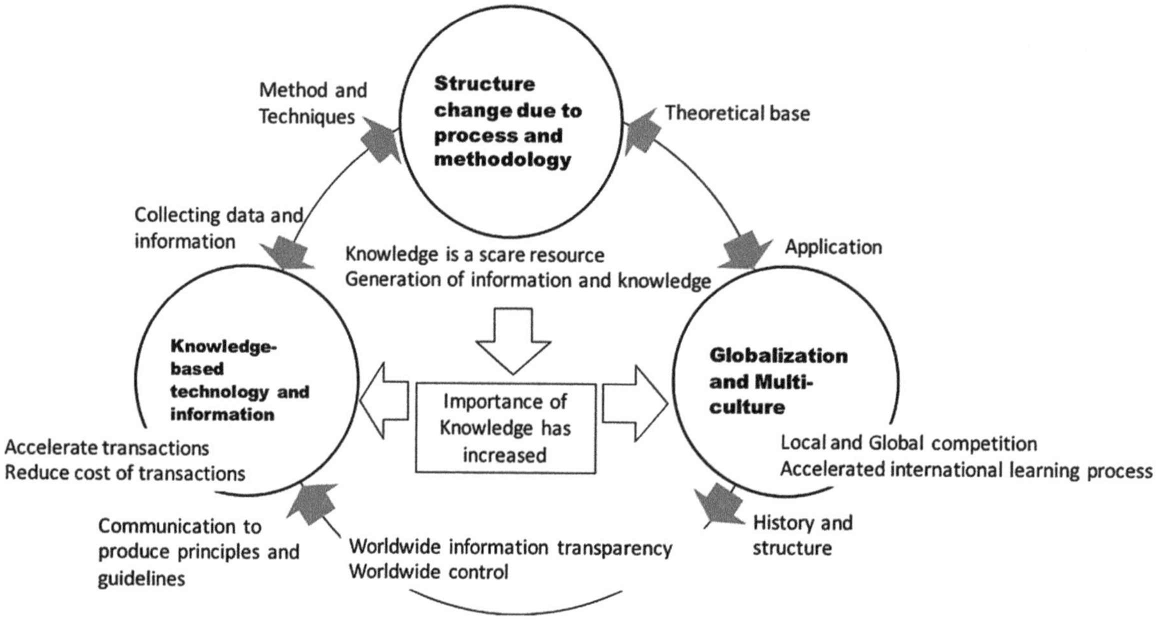

it searches for how to deal with the knowledge through an intellectual process structured methodology in addition to how to create knowledge as a synthesis process cause the growth of knowledge is the root of economic change for any society (Mokyr, 2004, p. 1). Crainer & Dearlove (2003, p. 102) also writes that knowledge has become the most important factor affecting knowledge in economic life. According to Kaya, et al (2010, p. 154), the knowledge is the first step in people's minds, if possible, sharing it can convert it from a hidden knowledge to explicit knowledge and the to become an asset. So it is necessary to have a huge impact on the architectural status quo.

In the nineties of the past millennium, a contemporary theory about the importance of knowledge in the community has been emerged to discuss the revenue returns of this the theory. It defines the members of a community who are working together to create and share knowledge. Once they finished work together to create a collective experience and based on them they start to engage in their business (North & Kumta, 2014, pp. 55-56). The concept is to recognize the organization as a place where personal knowledge and own intelligence unite to form a collective and productive intelligence that can be put to entrepreneurial use. From this viewpoint, companies exist because they are in the position to convert individual knowledge into the collective knowledge and employ it for an enterprise purpose (North & Kumta, 2014, pp. 55-56). Accordingly, the business is successful If people make their proper knowledge and experience available for an individual operation. Also, the process comes smoothly if the knowledge has been transferred from the individual to collective level and the activities are aligned with an entrepreneurial spirit to achieve the objectives. In a similar way, Albert Einstein said that the function of education is to open way of thinking, knowledge, moreover, that the role is the only way to meet this goal (Einstein, 1954, p. 40). Many experts pointed out concerning the philosophy of education that the aim of teaching is to help students to develop the intellectual tools and learning strategies which are needed to gain the knowledge that allows people to think and produce products (Bransford, L.Brown, & R.Cocking, 2000, p. 5).

Writings by Ausburn & Ausburn (1978, p. 464) and Kozhevnikov (2007, p. 465) have pointed the importance of the cognitive learning style and deal with it as a way to acquire and process information to gain oriented knowledge. In this way, the direction is towards measuring individual differences in cognition regarding the central character traits, as well as using the knowledge in the application of cognitive style of learning. Taking into account, the knowledge has nothing to do with human intelligence or personality as much as it can be understood as the individual's way and even the way the usual upper and plans strategies and disorderly behavior. They also describe him as bipolar, comprehensive and stands in the middle between the analytical and logical thinking. The cognitive learning style also organizes and shows the information and expertise and raise the intellectual capacity and addresses solves problems at all stages, as it cares to remember, learn, reflect and communicate with other individuals (Paul & Elder, 2008, pp. 8-9) (Kozhevnikov, 2007, p. 464) (Cassidy, 2004, pp. 420-421).

Furthermore, cognitive learning helps to develop the intellectual skills by referring to knowledge gained whether acquired, produced or applied, and focuses on the skills behind the knowledge, the logic, the critical thinking, creativity and the ability to analysis, as Robinson (1999, p. 106) describes the ability to think about their own thinking (beyond knowledge or metacognition), is necessary in a constantly changing world in term of the process rather than a product. Table 4 indicates the thinkers thought and Metacognition.

Table 4. Metacognition

Thinkers	Year	The Essence	Cited
Lloyd Humphreys	1968	- A manifestation of intellectual ability. - Include mental ability, cognitive abilities of humans, and the acquisition of general cognitive skills that are available to a person at a certain point in time.	(Humphreys, 1968)
John Flavell The term was coined in 1970	1976-1979	- Identify the cognitive processes at one and organize those processes (skills). - A kind of cognitive processes with human and non-human environment, - Continuity for a variety of information processing activities.	(Flavell J. H., 1976) (Flavell J. H., 1979, p. 906)
John H. Flavell	1979	- 'Thinking about Thinking. - The interaction between the person characteristics of the task properties - The available strategies in the learning situation.	
David R. Cross; Scott G. Paris	1988	- Knowing the children about their activities of thinking and learning, and how to control it.	(Cross & Paris, 1988, p. 131)
Arthur L. Costa	1991	- The ability to know what you know and what we do not know.	(Costa, 1991)
Marcel V.J. Veenman, Jan J. Elshout, and Martin G. M. Groen	1993	- Set of the determinants of education.	(Veenman, Elshout, & Groen, Thinking Aloud: Does it Affect Regulatory Processes in Learning?, 1993)
Marcel V.J. Veenman, Pascal Wilhelm, and Jos J. Beishuizen	2004	- Metacognitive skills have a surplus value. - On the top of the intellectual ability to learn through prediction.	(Veenman, Wilhelm, & Jos J. Beishuizen, The Relation Between Intellectual and Metacognitive Skills from a Developmental Perspective, 2004, pp. 91-92)
Frans J. Prins, Marcel V.J. Veenman, and Jan J. Elshout	2006	Of Knowledge through the cognitive processes of a particular person, and how to organize these processes.	(Prins, Veenman, & Elshout, 2006, p. 375)

THE INTELLECTUAL ILLITERACY (IL) IN URBAN DESIGN

Instructors may feel that graduates don't write well enough, and don't think clearly enough. Besides, some students don't have a good ethical sense as they don't understand the relationship of business to the larger social and public policy. In United States, graduates aren't globally aware (Rehm, 2006). From a side as Gerald Graff (2003, p. 3) and Schmoker (2007, p. 65) mention that 20% of the students are all who are willing to gain knowledge in the university. The illiteracy can be used as a justification for the act of learning. On the other side, the academic need to be aware of the efficient teaching and the learning process, as well as the need to necessary, flexible and stimulating procedure to identify the skills supporting the professional practice. Regarding supporting excellence in the current literary, the common ground between the students and instructors aims to comes over the intellectual illiteracy in the area of urban design process targeting the efficiency which concerns the ability to act in a particular context. Also, the knowledge needs the context to be found (Nonaka, Toyama, & Byosiere, 2001, p. 499) which makes thinking about how to deal with the knowledge in the context of the field of urban design as an imperative issue.

This work picks and identifies some of the IL in the field of Urban Design. Moreover, it tries to incorporate between the concepts of knowledge, intellectual capacity and cognitive capacity of the human being. The concept is what could be deduced from the theory of metacognition through the review intended cognitive learning style as governor of the framework for this study. To achieve this intent literary, the work focuses on some of the results of current studies in the scale of teaching and learning which have focused on the relation between the architect and its final product to discuss the process and how it produced based on a certain input of knowledge that the induvial had gained and provided.

Notably, the intellectual illiteracy can be categorized through two main tracks (Table 5). The first is the character of IL and the second is limited to the indicators for defining these characteristics qualifies. These indicators depend on measuring the degree of intellectual illiteracy in the area of jurisdiction of the urban designers' skills with respect to individual's abilities. These abilities are related to the experience and innovations through the gained knowledge as well as the process of producing a contemporary knowledge taking into consecration that the cognitive learning can enhance the quality of the indented product; the students (Robinson, 1999, p. 102). However, without going into details of the reasons for the decline of appropriate intellectual capacity required for the qualified professionals, the fourteen following points indicate some of the reasons that lead to intellectual illiteracy in the field of urban design (Etzkowitz & Leydesdorff, 2000, p. 114).

Hence turns out that, the second set of indicators which mean by the extent of knowledge of the diverse topics support the creation of new ideas. At the same time, both two concerns with how to pursue creative or innovative work through the accurate and systematic process, as the deficiencies in the ability to create and innovate ideas that must be interpreted as indented outcomes. Additionally, the theorists should have facilitated presenting theories and new ideas in the schools of Architecture.

A PROBLEM TOWARD A DEPTH IN THOUGHT

The current manuscript aims at fostering specific questions that related to the knowledge in the scientific research. How are the selected topics in these scientific research related to the current context? What about reviewing the produced thought done by specialists on the intellectual literacy in the Western

Table 5. Characteristics and measuring indices of the intellectual illiteracy in the field of urban design (Abussada, 2015)

<table>
<tr><th colspan="2">Group 1: The Characteristics of Intellectual Illiteracy</th><th>Group 2: The Measuring Criteria</th></tr>
<tr><td rowspan="6">Using & Sharing Knowledge</td><td>• There is a lack of basic knowledge of critical thinking.</td><td>• There is a lack of basic knowledge of critical thinking.</td></tr>
<tr><td>• The inability to retrieve appropriate information on promoting and contributing latest scientific knowledge.</td><td>• Increase the chaotic thoughts and confused thinking that neglects the fact, which is that each department is entirely linked with the entire system.</td></tr>
<tr><td>• The failure to extract fundamental data and information on supporting and adding latest, precise knowledge.</td><td>• Lose the desired ways to grow the creativity and to share ideas with others.</td></tr>
<tr><td>• A lack of the skills of disseminating knowledge.</td><td>• Lose interest in the growth of ideas and innovative thinking and refuse the exchange of ideas with others.</td></tr>
<tr><td>• Incompetence to adapt to the infrastructure of knowledge.</td><td>• The lack of potential to create a new vision for the future based on sound decisions has become a problem.</td></tr>
<tr><td>• The useless efforts to communicate or to share knowledge among other specialties.</td><td>• Several issues with limited conclusions, rather than those that are not closed and open-ended, have arisen.</td></tr>
<tr><td rowspan="3">Solving Problems</td><td>• Insufficiency of the principles that are linked with organized, underlying knowledge is a cause for missing the person's aptitude to solve any problem.</td><td>• There is a lack of intellectual ability to understand and perceive the design concepts.</td></tr>
<tr><td>• Lacking the skills that help to provide the sufficient input to solve the problems.</td><td>• There is an inability to apply knowledge so as to propose solutions responding to the demands of the urban context.</td></tr>
<tr><td>• Insists on using the old and traditional way to deal the knowledge to the solve the uncommon problems, whatever the results.</td><td>• Failure to implement the theories is, in fact, due to several reasons:
A) the inadequacy of the appropriate model;
(B) the absence of certainties and advanced views;
(C) the amount of attention is very low concerning the factors that affect urban development;
(D) each new development effort is independent of context.</td></tr>
<tr><td rowspan="6">The Quality of Knowledge</td><td>• The vulnerability of the diversity of the global culture and personal experiences effect on the quality of knowledge. The inability to focus on the details plus dealing with generalities instead of specifics.</td><td>• There is a difficulty as regards the possibility of analyzing and evaluating ideas entirely neutrally, as well as the point that there is an absence of the ability to think critically.</td></tr>
<tr><td>• Insufficiency of the principles that are linked with organized, underlying knowledge is a cause for missing the person's aptitude to solve any problem.</td><td>• There is a lack of availability of proper performance; the latter allows reading about and following up new ideas.</td></tr>
<tr><td>• Incompetence to adapt to the infrastructure of knowledge.</td><td rowspan="4">• There is a failure to provide unusual, imaginative, and innovative ideas. This is having the following effects:
- The product is losing its uniqueness.
- An inability to transform creative ideas into tangible products has emerged.
- There is a failure to assess critical thinking or anything correctly.
- There is an inability to use specific criteria to evaluate the thinking and decision-making processes.
- There is a failure to formulate or reformulate the problem as an integral part of the work.</td></tr>
<tr><td>• The obvious confusion in the area of discipline, not only on the level of words, phrases, and terminology but also regarding the expression by using drawing, writing, and oral expression.</td></tr>
<tr><td>• A lack of production of new knowledge even through continuous scientific research activities.</td></tr>
<tr><td>• The lack of ability to recognize unique capabilities, and the inability to achieve a variety of institutional knowledge.</td></tr>
</table>

thought that influence on the planning and design of the city? How do the professionals deal with the conflict in different disciplines that are related to urban design? Can knowledge contribute to decoding the controversy? Is there a possibility to establish an urban design which is based on the theory of knowledge that could cope the local context?

Predominantly, most forums which had been held by estimated institutions or universities select the most urgent problem in certain territories. In these, the theorizing process is continuous with refraction to the real ground. Examples are given to the subjects related to sustainability, quay of life, utopian urbanism, eco-friendly, green Architecture, Generic City, city branding, and son n so forth. These happen for many years which leads to the foundation of several organizations with no real impact on enhancing the scene in some devolving countries. Moreover, how in a developing world could afford the cost of establishing the system of green architecture in a city with more than 70% of its area is informal communities? The knowledge assets The idea of the current work depends on reviewing some theory of pedagogy and the history of knowledge theory. Additionally, the value judgments would be considered from the perspective of management of the comprehensive processes of a certain institution that it can use to raise the value of its students as the main product. The challenge for cities is to create dynamic environments where created and people with innovations feel happy and at ease: attractive areas, with good amenities, good jobs, good food, a great ambiance, and good connections.

The problematic issue is how to start from others' end with a different way of thinking to be in term of knowledge is gained and transferred to people and refracted well in the context. It can also be noted that some of these forums aimed at reducing the gap between education and practice, but it was mostly without any benefit on the ground. On the contrary, some Western and American scientific forums have a similar contribution to the development of the design of the city which conceded very clear. The first urban design conference held on 9-10 April 1956 to define the essence of urban design is a good example to get befits of the thought in the said forum and its recreation on the field of education, research, and professional practice. Besides, the conference discussed the participation of the architect and urban planner or urban design, as well as a series of acts of that, should be taken by other professionals (Marshall R., 2012, pp. 110-111). It is also in the year 1993, based on the new urbanism conference (CNU) in the Alexandria, Virginia, garden cities movement has founded to solve certain pressure in cities. In this conference, the charter of new urbanism was launched to be applicable in 2000 (Leccese & Mccormick, 1996-1996, p. 1).

More than that, most of these studies in the developing countries never refers to the actual real life, but it is the reality of a paper by default, it does not represent the real world. Whereby, there is no actual data on the extent of the deterioration of the real situation in these unknown cities to commonly known sites for the researchers. While some of these forums wanted to solve the current problems of chaos in traditional urban areas, the latest European and American issues were selected to abdicate on the local context. In this, Alatas, F. (2003, p. 604) refers to the dependency of developing countries on the production of knowledge gained from the western culture which has a diffract context in the application. The same researcher also pointed out that the real problem lies in the emergence of intuitive thinking arising from over-reliance on Western intellectual contribution in the various fields of knowledge (Alatas S. H., 2006, p. 8).

The problem is in some countries in the developing world through their forums focus on the latest intellectual models traded in the areas of knowledge in the competence of Architecture and Urbanism that established in developed courtiers. Applying the imported knowledge in a different context faces a lot of difficulties (Elshater, 2014), (Salama, Remali, & Rahimian, 2017).

According to the transformation of an approach to the urban conservation of highly valuable areas, instead of using the idea of urban renewal (UR), it should highlight the next review. In the period after World War II, in Europe in 1940, UR was started. It emerged by handling the sites that were damaged due to this war. The concept of UR was sustained for almost twenty years, from 1940 till 1960, and was proposing to activate the urban centers of the city. The Oxford Concise Dictionary identifies UR, in general, as a concept that "regenerates and makes it new again." It also means "restores and retrieves." The UN definitions diversified to explain what happens in the physical, urban, and building environment due to the impact of economic and social aspects (Couch, 1990, p. 1). Also, it is defined as a societal movement aimed at modernizing, regenerating, and reshaping the urban character of the city (Kemp, 2001, p. 10) (Komex, 2014, p. 363). Beside this, it was also aiming at reducing the extent of the deterioration of the living conditions in the urban community, such as high unemployment rates in cities that have a high population density. In the United States of America, between the period of 1954-1959, UR had been aroused due to the desire to redevelop the deteriorating residential areas in American cities. Also, in the United States, in 1954, UR emerged in the housing act as an urgent requirement. The primary objective of this law was to save the urban centers in the downtown areas of American cities on the one hand and to allow the city to compete with the new surroundings in the suburbs on the contrary. The first question of this act is how to meet the needs of the American people. Thus, the beginning of this act focuses on the social requirements of the people. In this era, "housing act" not only faced the idea of slum clearance but also it tries to stop the policies of rehabilitation and to change the housing code that does not belong to the people.

Implicitly, the historical review can be trail the beginning of the Alan Jacobs and Donald Appleyard in their manuscript entitled "Toward an Urban Design Manifesto" that had been published in 1987. From their point of view, Urban Design has become an urgent need for a new manifesto towards utopia which in some cases should be preferred by all. Otherwise, it is essential to be given a choice of the kind of community that people would like to live in the sort of choice (Jacobs & Appleyard, 1987, p. 120).

After fifty years of Le Corbusier's and the modernity thoughts (SIAM), a producer of a Charter of Athens. Moreover, after twenty years have been passed since the first urban design conference, which was held at Harvard University in the 1950s, and the case is still standing at the same level that SIAM started (Jacobs & Appleyard, 1987, p. 113). Despite the different problems of the past from what is happening today throughout the urban sprawl in European, American metropolitan cities in an opposite way to the situation in third world countries which are representing those similar problems in their living environments. These problems can be recognized in the uncontrolled urban sprawl, gigantism in the globalization process, the expansion of privatization and the loss of the manifestations of public life (Jacobs & Appleyard, 1987, pp. 113-115).

A chapter of the manuscript of Kuhn, Thomas S. (1970, p. 67) entitled "The Structure of Scientific Revolutions" mentions the essential need of awareness o be in line with paradigm change. This declaration should be taken into consideration in term of the what could be gain from the western knowledge to match the other contexts through different fields of specialization. Whereby the contribution of the universities in these western communities is widely recognized. For example, at the University of Liverpool in England in the year 1910, the civic design was produced as a tool to design a certain approach of the architectural side within the town planning process. The Civic Design is a European practice that focuses on the common good of our community by pulling upon all of all institution tools in the certain area behind our usual role focuses on governmental alone. The civic design is practiced with the knowing that without expectation, our societal challenges are not problems to be resolved, but rather a series of dilemmas to be better managed (Crouch, 2002, p. 69).

Arguably, the urban design discipline has paradigms of the art of the city. It is a scientific art and not a pseudoscience in the level of research, education, and practice. At the beginning of the 1950s, it had emerged as a concept note at Harvard University (Marshall R., 2012, p. 110). Throughout the last five decades, it had passed with two notable paradigm shifts in several places in the world to be ended at two scopes of interest: the urban rehabilitation and new development projects. In the region of the Middle East and Northern Africa (MENA), several cities may have an essential need for improving the interaction between the theory and practices in term of design aspects; this discipline, with new approaches, is matching with the urban context. Today, the urban designers in this region need to develop the outcomes of the American's and European's thoughts and praxis to be more robust toolkits with the ideologies in the field of urban design within the three mentioned levels.

In the developing countries, despite the thousands of published scientific papers presented in the recent past years which have included many of the suggestions and solutions but the current urban situation is getting worse. With reference to some of the issues that are still discussed on tables, the American and European literature do not contribute to raising the tacit and implicit knowledge. For being in the developing country that does not produce the knowledge, an essential need to adapt the import and develop the information or give structure change, knowledge base technology and open a track for globalization in thought, not in place and form. We can say that quite a lot of theoretical knowledge in the area of specialization of the urban design is still unknown for a large number of practitioners. For example, all of the terms of reference aimed at achieving an appropriated city in which we live, but some professionals are unaware of how to apply the principles of both the competence to achieve this goal. These professional aims to have a product as a quantity, not quality. The quantitate and qualified product of the product usually obtained when is knowledge base. The professional practice in the field of urban design that does not know how to distinguish between urban design and other fields such architecture, housing and urban planning and design, site planning and architecture, are very week to produce a good product. Moreover, a few of them do not even accept these differences, and even refuse to use the theories and methods of urban design independently of their areas of expertise. In this matter, Cuthbert (2006, p. 249) concludes that urban design is still for architects and planners a chance colonial another area of knowledge.

Ultimately, I would rather say that people have created cities, as cities remained to create people. This means that there is an interactive relationship between the people and the city. This relationship between them is fateful; both of them try to change the other. Hence, it is not necessary to make arguments about any point that starts this effect, whether from people or the city, because the key intent is focused on understanding the human-city relationship to provide a better living for both. In conclusion, two identical talks of Marks, 'Change the world,' and Rimbaud, 'Change life,' could inspire us to how urban design could change. To contrive a kind of change, vision may come for the task of urban design to have a modified, integrated, and transitioning role with different disciplines for any human settlement on the earth (Figure 4). Moreover, knowledge of urban design should be widening to host a holistic scope that involves the academic and non-academic discipline. The process of good alienation needs a common ground of knowledge.

A NEW THEORY OF KNOWLEDGE-BASED URBAN DESIGN

Generally speaking, the theory is a set of interrelated forms (variables) that describes a well-organized declaration of the rules, principles, or propositions that help to explain, interpret, predict, and present a

Figure 4. The transdisciplinary urban design
Source: Designed by the second author as a keynote speaker in Symposium "Designing Urban Design," in October 2016, Ankara (Elshater & Abusaada, 2016, p. 113)

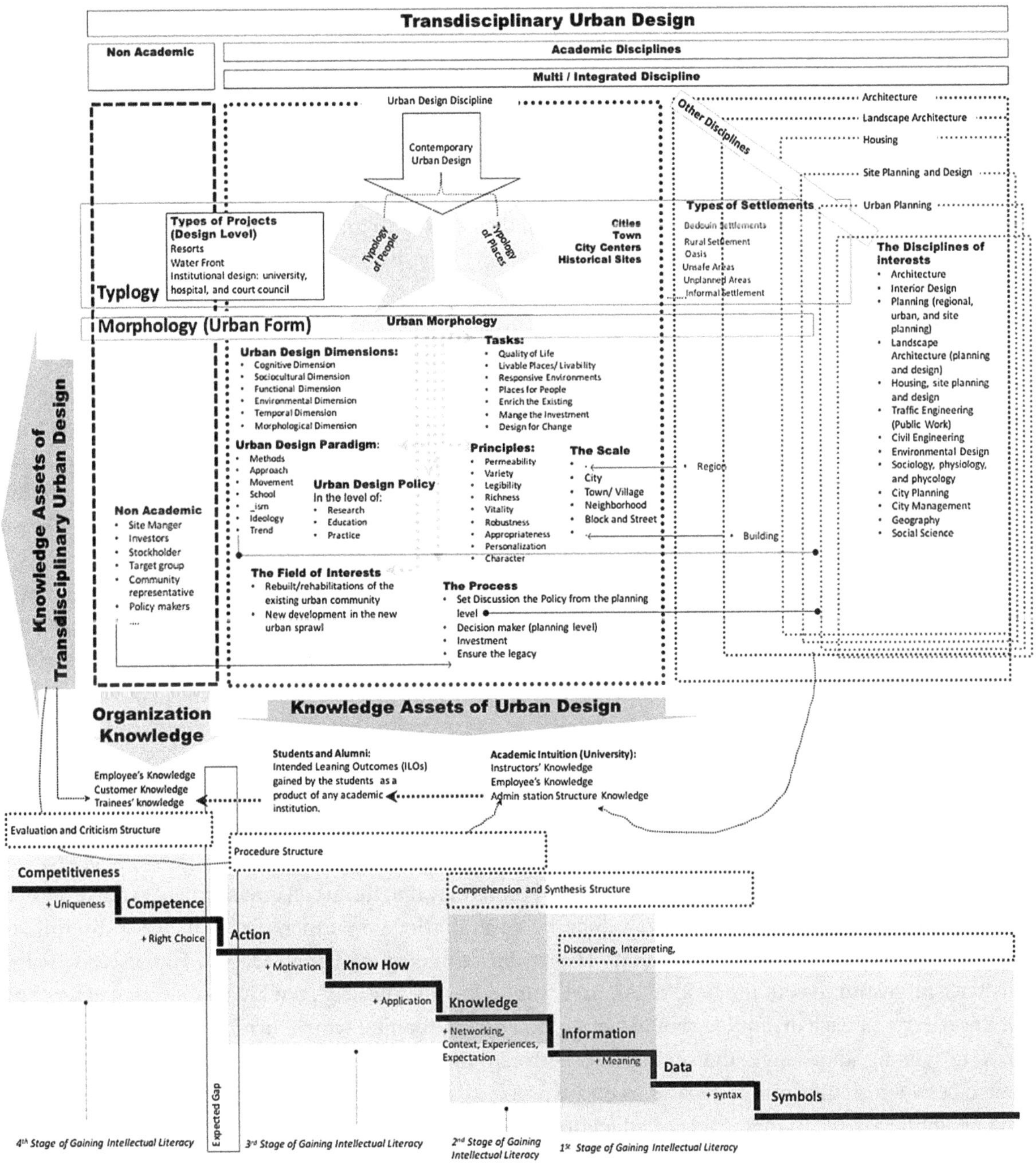

systematic view of scientific issues and societal phenomena. Establishing a theory in the field of urban design to get the benefit of knowledge-based contribution can select between two types of theory; substantive and normative. For social science, the substantive will be adapted concerning some inquiries:

- What knowledge and competence do we need in the field of urban design to stand in a clear position with other disciplines?
- How can we acquire and generate a common ground of knowledge conveniently to the changes happen by time?
- How do we change for the intellectual literacy in the field of urban design?

There are many approaches about how to make a change. The most commonly accepted model was introduced by Kotter; professor at Harvard University with eight-step change process in his book "*Leading the Change*" (Kotter, 2012). The eight principles are for the intuitional change to keep sustain position through the knowledge capital. Reflecting these eight steps were on the field of urban design institution as well the outcome product of the University. The following points could be adapted from Kotter's eight principles that shown in gray to add more concepts in black. The concept of the theory could be seen in term of nine principles. Before going in discussing each item, it critical to stand on the common ground of concepts. The organization or institution in the process of gaining knowledge is the university, research center or professional practice. They all are included in the process of producing the intellectual literacy with a different way of handling. The target groups are the students, the instructors, technical supporter, administrative structure, researchers, trainees and recipient society. The leader of knowledge starts at the level starts at the symbols and ends at the competitiveness. It passes through 4 stages of gaining intellectual literacy. After the third which comes synchronize with the graduation from the university, a gap could be found that should have a bridging process, Figure 4.

Generally speaking, the knowledge comes to solve a problem. In the case of urban design and after subsequent decades of unchecked sprawl, more people than ever are moving in to live in a better city. Dense urban living has been directed as a relief for the context and environmental crises of our time. However, is the internal displacement among cities better or worse for the well-being? Although it is hard to answer the question 'What knowledge makes a good city?', we have to put into consideration that sometimes, the goodness is affected from outside the city. The environmental crises caused by overcrowding, traffic pollution, noise, and industrial emissions are just a few of the issues that have to be continuously monitored and addressed to achieve a high quality of life without high environmental costs. However, doing this will also bring benefits beyond city borders.

It may come first at the knowledge capital. This is not to say that the urban environment is not designed in detail rather than in a detailed process done by several alliance partners from different disciplines with different knowledge and background. The proposed theory of Urban Design Based-Knowledge deals with all institutions in the field of Architecture as having knowledge with a significant asset. The tacit knowledge of each discipline should keen its knowledge capital which turns to be an asset. In other words, in gaining knowledge, the segregation between disciple is essential in the primary levels. The alliance between all disciplines to solve a certain problem, integration and transdisciplinary approaches could be applied at the higher levels of education and in professional practice.

The first principle for establishing a new theory of urban design based-knowledge concerns acceptance of the current schema with a well to change for the better. The second comes with the transparency which should refer in data/ information collecting and sharing. The third deals with the process of discovering the current scenarios of developing and sense of urgency. The fourth principle concerns the process of the election rather than selecting the tool, techniques used, the group of work and target audience which in our case of urban design discourse is representing in the field of professional practice. Appropriateness as a keyword is chosen as the fifth item to handle how the group of work could be satisfied with the selected and elected material. The sixth principle aims to form a powerful guiding coalition to empower others to act on the put vision. The seventh is for continuous improvement through the consolidation development and producing still more change. The eighth and ninth principles come for communicating and marketing the idea to keep it sustain and the institution in the track of spreading, circulation, pervasion then producing the knowledge (Figure 5).

Figure 5. The ten principles of transforming the organization toward knowledge capital

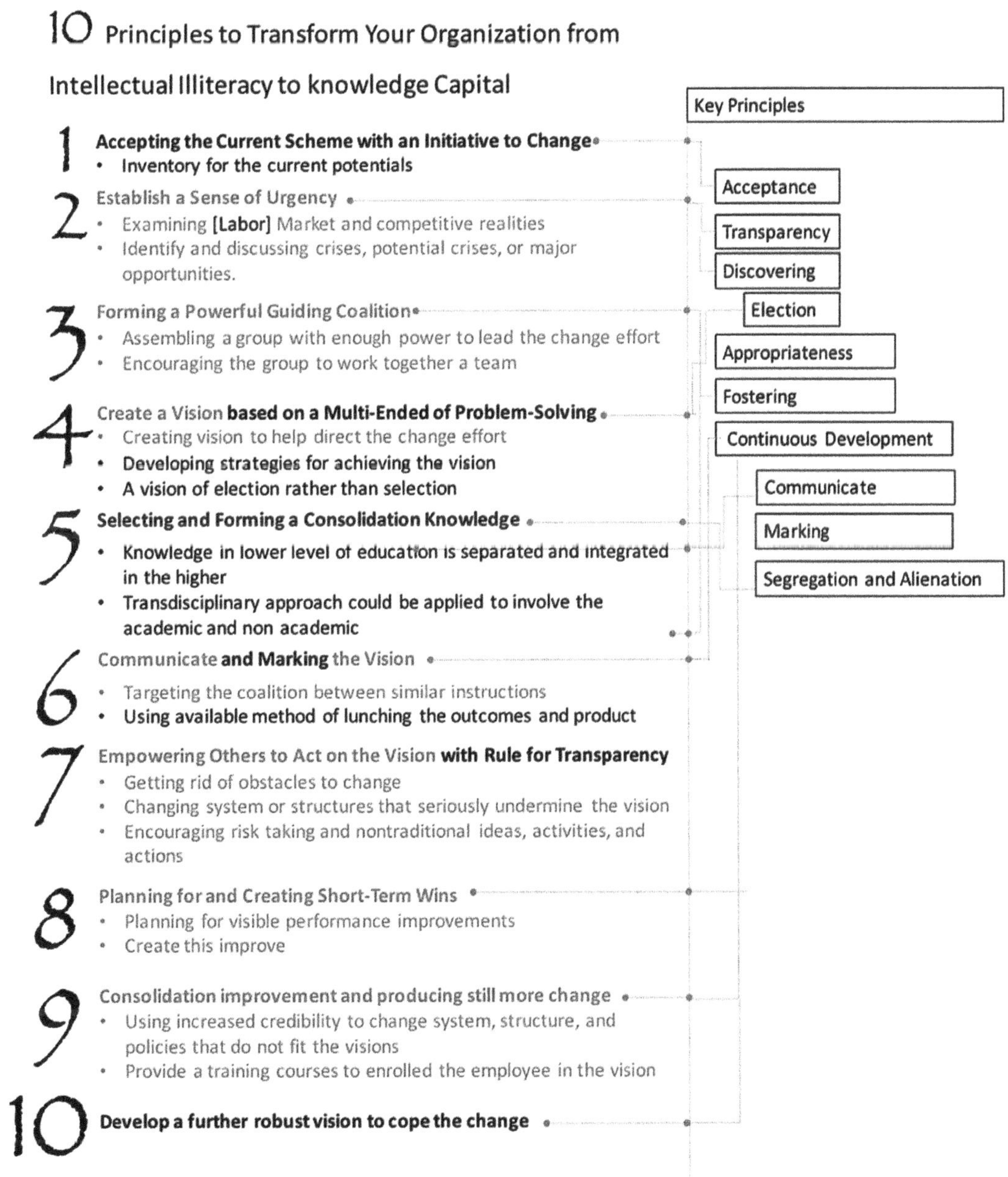

REFERENCES

Abusaada, H. G. (2015). *Architecture of the Repercussions of the Imagination: Renewal of Intellectual Discourse*. Cairo, Egypt: Association of Retrieving Planning and Architecture Heritage.

Abussada, G. H. (2015). *The Art of the City, Refutation of Intellectual Discourse as an Introductory to Knowledge Enlightenment.* PartridgeAfrica.

Alatas, S. F. (2003). Academic Dependency and the Global Division of Labour in the Social Sciences. *Current Sociology, 51*(6), 559–613. doi:10.1177/00113921030516003

Alatas, S. H. (2006). The Autonomous, the Universal & the Future of Sociology. *Current Sociology, 54*(7), 7–23. doi:10.1177/0011392106058831

Alavi, M., & Leidner, D. (2001, March). Review: Knowledge Management and Knowledge Management Systems: Conceptual Foundations and Research Issues. *Management Information Systems Quarterly, 25*(1), 107–136. doi:10.2307/3250961

American Association for Higher Education. (1989). *Presidential Committee on Information Literacy.* Chicago: American Library Association.

Audi, R. (2003). *Epistemology: A contemporary introduction to the theory of knowledge.* New York: Routledge.

Ausburn, L. J., & Ausburn, F. B. (1978). Cognitive Styles: Some information and implications for instructional design. *Educational Communication,* (26), 337–354.

Australia's National Dictionary. (1981). *The Macquarie Dictionary.* Sydney: Macquarie Library Pty.

Barret, B. (2010). Usine e-Portfolios to Evaluate Intellectual Capital of OnLine Learners. In S. C. Sirrano (Ed.), *Proceedings of the 2nd European Conference on Intellectual Capital: ISCTE* (pp. 67-76). Lisbon, Portugal: Academic Publishing Limited.

Becker, G. S. (1962). Investment in Human Capital: A Theoretical Analysis. *The Journal of Political Economy, part 2. Investment in Human Beings, 70*(5), 9–49.

Bennet, A., & Bennet, D. (2014). Knowledge, Theory and Practice in Knowledge Management: Between Associative Patterning and Context-Rich Action. Journal of Entrepreneurship, Management and Innovation, 10(1), 5-55.

Blakeley, N., Lewis, G., & Mills, D. (2005). *The Economics of Knowledge: What Makes Ideas Special for Economic Growth?* New Zealand Treasury, Policy Perspectives Paper 05/05.

Boekhorst, A. K. (2003). Becoming Information Literate in the Netherlands. *Library Review, 52*(7), 298–309. doi:10.1108/00242530310487399

Bontis, N. (1998). Intellectual capital: An exploratory study that develops measures and models. *Management Decision, 36*(2), 63–76. doi:10.1108/00251749810204142

Bontis, N., Keow, W. C., & Richardson, S. (2000). Intellectual Capital and Business Performance in Malaysian Industries. *Journal of Intellectual Capital, 1*(1), 85–100. doi:10.1108/14691930010324188

Bransford, J., Brown, L. A., & Cocking, R. (2000). How People Learn Brain, Mind, Experience, and School. Washington, DC: The National Academies Press.

Cassidy, S. (2004). Learning Style: An Overview of Theories, Models and Measures. *Educational Psychology*, *24*(4), 419–444. doi:10.1080/0144341042000228834

Clark, D. a. (2006). *The Elgar Companion to Development Studies*. Edward Elgar Publishing. doi:10.4337/9781847202864

Costa, A. L. (1991). The Search For Intelligent Life. In A. L. Costa (Ed.), *Developing Minds: A Resource Book for* (pp. 100–106). Alexandria, VA: Association for Supervision and Curriculum.

Couch, C. (1990). *Urban Renewal: Theory and Practice*. London: Macmillan Education Ltd. doi:10.1007/978-1-349-20912-5

Coulby, D., & Jones, C. (1995). *Postmodernity and European Education Systems: Cultural diversity and centralist knowledge*. London: Trentham Books.

Crainer, S., & Dearlove, D. (2003). *Business, The Universe and Everything: Conversations with the World's Greatest Management Thinkers*. Chichester, UK: Capeston.

Cross, D. R., & Paris, S. G. (1988). Developmental and Instructional Analyses of Children's Metacognition and Reading Comprehension. *Journal of Educational Psychology*, *2*(2), 131–142. doi:10.1037/0022-0663.80.2.131

Crouch, C. (2002). *Design Culture in Liverpool, 1880-1914: The Origins of the Liverpool School of Architecture*. Liverpool University Press.

Cuthbert, A. R. (2006). *The Form of Cities: Political Economy and Urban Design*. Oxford, UK: Blackwell. doi:10.1002/9780470774915

DeVito, T. R. (2008). *A Study of the Teaching Strategies of Paramedic Educators as they Relate to Models of Adult Education*. ProQuest.

Dictionary, T. O. (1989). The Oxford English Dictionary (2nd ed.; vol. 7). Oxford, UK: Oxford University Press.

Edvinsson, L., & Sullivan, P. (1996). Developing a Model for Managing Intellectual Capital. *European Management Journal*, *14*(4), 356–364. doi:10.1016/0263-2373(96)00022-9

Eggs, C. (2012). Trust Building in Communities of Practice. *Proceedings of the 4th European Conference on on Intellectual Capital*, 172-169.

Einstein, A. (1954). *Ideas and Opinions* (S. Bargmann Trans. & Ed.). New York: Crown Publishers, Inc.

Elshater, A. (2014). Prosperity of Thought Versus Retreat of Application: A Comprehensive Approach in Urban Design Teaching. International Journal of Architectural Research, 8.

Elshater, A., & Abusaada, H. G. (2016). *What is Urban Design? Teaching and Learning*. Partridge Africa.

Etzkowitz, H., & Leydesdorff, L. (2000). The Dynamics of Innovation: From National Systems and "Mode 2" to a Triple Helix of University–Industry–Government Relations. *Research Policy*, *29*(2), 109–123. doi:10.1016/S0048-7333(99)00055-4

Farenhorst, R., & Boer, R. C. (2009). *Architectural Knowledge Management: Supporting Architects and Auditors.* The Dutch Joint Academic and Commercial Quality Research & Development (Jacquard) Program on Software Engineering Research, The Dutch Research School for Information and Knowledge Systems. SIKS Dissertation series.

Feiwel, G. R. (1975). *The intellectual capital of Michal Kalecki: A Study in Economic Theory and Policy.* University of Tennessee Press.

Flavell, J. H. (1976). Metacognitive Aspects of Problem Solving. In L. B. Resnick (Ed.), The Nature of Intelligence (pp. 231-236). Academic Press.

Flavell, J. H. (1979). Metacognition and Cognitive Monitoring: A New Area of Cognitive–Developmental Inquiry. *The American Psychologist*, *34*(10), 906–911. doi:10.1037/0003-066X.34.10.906

Fowler, H. W., Fowler, F., & Sykes, J. B. (1976). *Concise Oxford Dictionary of Current English.* Oxford, UK: Oxford University Press.

Goldman, A. I. (1967). A Causal Theory of Knowing. *The Journal of Philosophy*, *64*(12), 357–372. doi:10.2307/2024268

Graff, G. (2003). *Clueless in Academe: How Schooling Obscures the Life of the Mind.* New Haven, CT: Yale University press.

Hayek, F. A. (1945). The Use of Knowledge in Society. *The American Economic Review*, *35*(4), 519–530.

Humphreys, L. G. (1968). The Fleeting Nature of the Prediction of College Academic Success. *Journal of Educational Psychology*, *59*(5), 375–380. doi:10.1037/h0026234 PMID:5722409

Hunt, D. P. (2003). The Concept Of Knowledge and How To Measure It. *Journal of Intellectual Capital*, *4*(1), 100–113. doi:10.1108/14691930310455414

Jacobs, A., & Appleyard, D. (1987). Toward an Urban Design Manifesto. *Journal of the American Planning Association*, *53*(1), 112–120. doi:10.1080/01944368708976642

Kaya, F. B., Sahin, G. G., & Gurson, P. (2010). Intellectual Capital in Organizations. *Problems and Perspectives in Management*, *8*(1), 153–160.

Kemp, R. L. (2001). *The inner city: A Handbook for Renewal.* McFarland & Company, Inc.

Klaus, C. B. (Ed.). (2000). *Information Literacy Around the World: Advances in Programs and Research. The University of Michigan.* Centre for Information Studies, Charles Sturt University.

Kok, A. (2007). Intellectual Capital Management as Part of Knowledge Management Initiatives at Institutions of Higher Learning. *Electronic Journal of Knowledge Management*, *5*(2), 181–192.

Komex, E. (2014). Architectural Contextualism and Emerging Hybrid Morphologies: the case of Olympic Sculpture Park for the Seatle Art Museum. In M. B. Kuijper (Ed.), *New Urban Configurations* (pp. 979–980). Amsterdam: IOS Press.

Kotter, J. (2012). *Leading Change*. Boston: Harvard Business Review Press.

Kozhevnikov, M. (2007). Cognitive Styles in the Context of Modern Psychology: Toward a Cognitive Styles in the Context of Modern Psychology: Toward an. *Psychological Bulletin*, *133*(3), 464–481. doi:10.1037/0033-2909.133.3.464 PMID:17469987

Krauss, S. E. (2005, December). Research Paradigms and Meaning Making: A Primer. *Qualitative Report*, *10*(4), 758–770.

Kuhn, T. S. (1970). *The Structure of Scientific Revolutions* (2nd ed.). International Encyclopedia of Unified Science.

Kuwayama, T., & Bremen, J. V. (1997). Native Anthropologists: With Special Reference to Japanese Studies Inside and Outside Japan. *Japan Anthropology Workshop*.

Le Dantec, C. A., & Do, E. Y.-L. (2009). The mechanisms of value transfer in design meetings. *Design Studies*, *30*(2), 119–137. doi:10.1016/j.destud.2008.12.002

Leach, A. (2006). The Conditional Autonomy of Tafuri's Historian / De Provisorische Autonomie van. *Oase Architecture Journal*, *69*, 14–29.

Leccese, M., & Mccormick, K. (1996). Charter of the New Urbanism. In *The fourth Congress for the New Urbanism (CNU IV)*. Charleston, SC: McGraw-Hill, Inc.

Lytras, M. D., Russ, M., Maier, R., & Naeve, A. (2000). *Knowledge Management Strategies: A Handbook of Applied Technologies*. New York: IGI Publishing.

Marshall, A. (1890). Principles of Economics (Originally published in 1890 ed., Vol. 1). Princeton, NJ: Macmillan and Company.

Marshall, R. (2012). Josep Louis Sert's Urban Design Legacy, From Josep Louis Sert: The Architect of Urban Design (2008). In M. Larice & E. Macdonald (Eds.), The Urban Design Reader (2nd ed.; pp. 106-117). Routledge.

Mojtahedi, P. (2013). The Impact of Intellectual Capital on Earning Quality: Evidence from Malaysian Firms. *Australian Journal of Basic and Applied Sciences*, *7*(2), 535–540.

Mokyr, J. (2004). *The Gifts of Athena: Historical Origins of the Knowledge Economy*. Oxford, UK: Princeton University Press.

Nickitas, D. M., Middaugh, D. J., & Aries, N. (2011). *Policy and Politics for Nurses and Other Health Professionals*. London, UK: Jones and Bartlete Publishers Internationa.

Nonaka, I. (1994). A Dynamic Theory of Organizational Knowledge Creation. *Organization Science*, *5*(1), 14–37. doi:10.1287/orsc.5.1.14

Nonaka, I., & Takeuchi, H. (1995a). *The knowledge-Creating Company*. Oxford, UK: Oxford University Press.

Nonaka, I., & Takeuchi, H. (1995b). The Knowledge-Creating Company. *Creativity Research Journal, 10*(4), 285–301.

Nonaka, I., Toyama, R., & Byosiere, P. (2001). A Theory of Organizational Knowledge Creation: Understanding the Dynamic Process of Creating Knowledge. In M. D. Nonaka (Ed.), *Handbook of organizational learning and knowledge* (pp. 487–491). Oxford, UK: Oxford University Press.

North, K., & Kumta, G. (2014). *Knowledge Management: Value Creation Through Organizational Learning*. Springer International Publishing Switzerland. doi:10.1007/978-3-319-03698-4

O'Dell, C. C., & Grayson, J. (2012). *If Only We Knew What We Know: The Transfer of Internal Knowledge and Best Practice*. New York: Free Press.

Organization For Economic Co-Operation. (1996). *The knowledge-based Economy*. Paris: Organization For Economic Co-Operation and Development OECD.

Paul, R., & Elder, L. (2008). *The Thinker's Guide to The Nature and Functions of Critical & Creative Thinking*. The Foundation for Critical Thinking. Retrieved 11 15, 2014, from http://www.criticalthinking.org/files/CCThink_6.12.08.pdf

Plato, . (1935). *Plato's Theory of Knowledge: The Theaetetus and the Sophist of Plato* (F. M. Cornford, Trans.). Routledge and Kegan Paul Ltd.

Polanyi, M. (2009). *The Tacit Dimension*. University Of Chicago Press.

Prins, F. J., Veenman, M. V., & Elshout, J. J. (2006). The Impact of Intellectual Ability and Metacognition on Learning: New Support for the Threshold of Problematicity Theory. *Learning and Instruction, 16*(4), 374–387. doi:10.1016/j.learninstruc.2006.07.008

Rehm, D. (2006, April 14). *The Diane Rehm Show. U.S. College Education*. Washington, DC: WAMU.

Robinson, K. (1999). *National Advisory Committee on Creative and Cultural Education, All Our Futures: Creativity, Culture and Education.* The Secretary of State for Education and Employment and the Secretary of State for Culture, Media and Sport. London: National Advisory Committee on Creative and Cultural Education (NACCCE). Retrieved from http://sirkenrobinson.com/pdf/allourfutures.pdf

Rokeach, M. (1973). *The Nature of Human Values*. New York: Free Press.

Ryle, G. (2009). The Concept of Mind. Chicago: Routledge.

Sachs, W. (2010). *The Development Dictionary, a guide to knowledge as power* (2nd ed.). London: Zed Books.

Sahdra, B., & Thagard, P. (2003). Procedural knowledge in molecular biology. *Philosophical Psychology, 16*(4), 477–498. doi:10.1080/0951508032000121788

Salama, A. M., Remali, A. M., & Rahimian, F. P. (2017). A decade of architectural and urban research. *International Journal of Architectural Research, 11*(1), 6-28.

Schmoker, M. (2007). Reading, Writing, and Thinking for All. *EL Educational Leadership, 64*(7), 63-66.

School of Management, Granfeild University. (n.d.). *Understanding Corporate Value: Managing and reporting intellectual capital.* London: Institute of Management Accountants (CIMA).

Souleh, S. (2014). The impact of Human Capital Management on the Innovativeness of research Center: The Case of Scientific Research Centers in Algeria. *International Journal of Business and Management, 2*(4), 80–96.

Starovic, D., & Marr, B. (2003). *Understanding Corporate Value: managing and reporting intellectual capital. The Chartered Institute of Management Accountants (CIMA), School of Management.* London, UK: CIMA.

Stewart, T. A. (1997). *Intellectual Capital: The New Wealth of Organizations.* New York: Doubleday/Currency.

Thomson, D. S., Austin, S. A., Devine-Wright, H., & Mills, G. R. (2003). Managing Value and Quality in Design. *Building Research and Information, 31*(5), 334–345. doi:10.1080/0961321032000087981

Ting, K.-S. (2012). How Accumulation of Intellectual Capital of IC Design Firms Listed in Taiwan Impacts Organization Performances: Organizational Learning Capability as the Mediator. *The Journal of Global Business Management, 8*(1), 60–73.

Veenman, M. V., Elshout, J. J., & Groen, M. G. (1993). Thinking Aloud: Does it Affect Regulatory Processes in Learning? *Tijdschrift voor Onderwijsresearch*, (18): 322–330.

Veenman, M. V., Wilhelm, P., & Jos, J. (2004). The Relation Between Intellectual and Metacognitive Skills from a Developmental Perspective. *Learning and Instruction, 14*(1), 89–109. doi:10.1016/j.learninstruc.2003.10.004

Virkus, S. (2013). Information Literacy in Europe: Ten Years Later. In S. Kurbanoglu, E. Grassian, D. Mizrachi, R. Catts, & S. Špiranec (Eds.), *Worldwide Commonalities and Challenges in Information Literacy Research and Practice. 397* (pp. 250–257). Istanbul: Springer Link. doi:10.1007/978-3-319-03919-0_32

Volker, L. (2010). *Deciding about Design Quality.* Leiden: Sidestone Press.

Volker, L., & Prins, M. (2006). Critical Reflections on Measuring the Effect of Steering Activities in Architectural Design. In D. Boyd (Ed.), *22nd Annual ARCOM Conference* (pp. 897-906). Birmingham, UK: Association of Researchers in Construction Management.

Winden, W. v. (2011). *Creating knowledge hotspots in the city: Practical guidelines for developing campuses, science quarters, creative districts and other knowledge hotspots.* Amsterdam: European Union.

Woßmann, L. (2003). Specifying Human Capital. *Journal of Economic Surveys, 17*(3), 239–270. doi:10.1111/1467-6419.00195

Chapter 12
A Holistic Assessment of Education City in Doha:
The Borderless Knowledge Hub

Ali A. Alraouf
Qatar Urban Planning, Qatar

ABSTRACT

Qatar, while developing its vision for the future, decided to adopt the knowledge economy as the new pillar for its economy and development. The chapter focuses on examining the impact of the one of the main and iconic national mega project in the capital Doha, the project named Education City (EC). The chapter scrutinizes EC's contribution to a more resilient future for Qatar. The chapter assesses the relative roles of such an influential project in preparing or hindering Qatar's moving towards the post-carbon paradigm. The project is examined using multilayered criteria, which include achieving urban diversity, relevance to knowledge-based urban development, supporting the diversification of the local economy, and accommodating multicultural society. The chapter concludes that education city is the most crucial urban projects in Qatar geared towards sustaining the knowledge economy as it creates ripples of change, knowledge dissemination, and a culture of innovation and creativity within the city.

INTRODUCTION

Since the 1970s, the small Arab states in the Gulf region have managed to transform from primitive Bedouin societies into giants of economic growth and urban development. The Gulf States while mostly young and small, they are the largest builders and developers in the world. Every single capital Gulf city is characterized with shopping malls, skyscrapers, artificial islands, gigantic airports, real-estate fantasies and landmark museums. Yet, they have also realized that another transformation is needed from oil-based to post-oil societies. With oil resources running out or prices are dropping sorely, a focus on the post-oil era is a priority. Assessing the pace of urban development in contemporary Gulf cities revealed a number of critical issues (Wippel, 2014). On one hand, the speed of development has social cost, negative relation with the past and the claim for identity loss. On the other hand, such rapid developments contributed

DOI: 10.4018/978-1-5225-3734-2.ch012

Copyright © 2018, IGI Global. Copying or distributing in print or electronic forms without written permission of IGI Global is prohibited.

to economic diversification, cultural tourism and city branding (Dinnie, 2011). The overarching issue is exploring critically the ways in which the Gulf States prepare for the post-oil era, by diversification of their assets, boosting real estate sector, and creating a knowledge economy. Hertog (2016) illustrates how the Gulf Cooperation Council (GCC) oil monarchies have been using their oil wealth to buy the accoutrements of 'good citizenship' and 'progressiveness' in the international arena through costly policy projects that involve urban interventions like the building of international museums, universities and 'zero-carbon cities' – urban enclaves with an audience that is almost exclusively international. This interpretation is valid for some Gulf States particularly the Emirate of Dubai. The mega projects reflect a desire to gain international recognition via exhibiting full adoption of Western norms and influential principals. The case of Masdar city in Abu Dhabi which was declared as 'the first zero-carbon city' in the world and ended up with a deserted real-estate project is a compelling evidence (Goldenberg, 2016). Yet, for a more holistic understanding one can't see all the cultural and educational projects in all Gulf cities as a catalyst for Western recognition. For that reason, the case of Doha is stimulating as such interventions are made to pave the way for a new development vison structured upon the value of knowledge economy and knowledge-based urbanity. In the coming section, the chapter illustrates Qatar's strategy towards investment in knowledge-based urban development. The case of Education City (EC), the unprecedented model within the whole world will be extensively analyzed a multi layered approach discussing the hierarchy of the project's development from a strategic level all the way to the quality of architecture and urbanism.

THE INEVITABILITY OF INVESTING IN EDUCATION AND KNOWLEDGE

Knowledge has become a crucial factor for production in the era of knowledge economics. Knowledge economy provides a more solid base for the future development particularly in the post globalized era (Foray, 2004). With the fall in oil prices underlining the risks of an over dependence on hydrocarbons revenues, Qatar has continued with its economic diversification drive. Human development is one of the four pillars of the country's economic plan, Qatar National Vision 2030 (QNV 2030). Along with

Figure 1. Doha concluded that moving from oil based urbanism to KBUD is a must strategy for a more sustainable future (©Alraouf)

fostering economic, social and environmental development, working to enable all of Qatar's people to sustain a prosperous society represents one of the state's major goals for the coming years. Before rising to the position of the Amir, Sheikh Tamim bin Hamad Al Thani led the Supreme Committee responsible for implementing QNV 2030. In its National Development Strategy (NDS) 2011-16, the committee highlighted the importance of education in driving the state's push toward a knowledge-based economy. Evidently, improving education forms part of the first pillar of Qatar National Vision 2030, the country's long-term development plan aimed at reducing dependency on hydrocarbons and creating a diversified economy driven by services. Improving education forms an essential part of Qatar National Vision (QNV) 2030's main pillars. The Qatar National Vision 2030 (QNV2030) is a master vision and roadmap towards Qatar becoming an advanced society capable of sustainable development with the goal of providing a high standard of living for all citizens by the year 2030. The National Vision foresees development in four interconnected pillars; Human development, Social development, Economic development and Environmental development. QNV 2030 is a development strategy launched in October 2008 and outlines how Qatar will use the vast revenues from its substantial hydrocarbon resources to transform itself into a modern knowledge-based economy (QNV, 2008). Qatar was clearly a forerunner within the Gulf context to pursue the post-oil globalization and diversification discourse in spite of being the third exporter of natural gas in the world:

Qatar is giving 2.8% of our GDP to research. This is something again that is a breakthrough, as nobody was even thinking of research as a tool or component for advancement in this part of the world. (Sheikha Moza bint Nasser, Chairperson of Qatar Foundation)

The capital city, Doha, now a metropolis with more than 2 million residents, had less than 500,000 residents in 1995. This is more than a four-fold increase in less than 25 years and most of that growth has occurred since 2005, when the population was about 821,000 (Alraouf, 2016). This rapid increase is not the result of natural population growth, but rather a highly planned effort to recruit workers from around the world. The constraints on Qatar's development choices pushed the leadership to adapt a mixed strategy of traditional and innovative approaches to educational development. Qatar invested substantially in reforms of the school system. It also invested profoundly in the national university, Qatar University, to expand access, improve its educational programs, adapt them to the needs of Qatar's society and workforce, and expand its capacity to conduct research. Qatar University (QU) is responsible for the vast majority of enrolments, with more than 17,000 students currently attending undergraduate and graduate courses and programs across its nine colleges. QU has also attempted to foster a research culture by setting up 14 research centers of excellence that correspond to national needs. An ambitious five-year research roadmap entitled "Advancing Research for Qatar's Future", launched by Qatar university in 2014, tackles four priority areas: energy, environment and resource sustainability; social change and identity; population, health and wellness; and ICT. As (Crist, 2015) explains, Qatar recruited global education professionals, most notably the RAND Corporation[1], to advise and assist with development and reform plans for the entire educational system. It also paid close attention to global educational benchmarks and standards set by UNESCO, OECD, and the World Bank. In 2009, Qatar Foundation established the Qatar Science and Technology Park to promote innovative partnerships between the research and development wings of global corporation and the Qatar government. QF's research is led through its R&D arm, which serves as the "custodian" of the national research strategy and directs funding for research through the Qatar National Research Fund. Since 2012, QF established a collection of independent research institutes within Education City that will house researchers and research facilities addressing many of the country's national priorities comprised of the Qatar Biomedical Research Institute (QBRI), Qatar Environment and Energy Research Institute (QEERI), and Qatar Computing Research Institute (QCRI). Qatar R&D also oversees the Qatar Science and Technology Park (QSTP), which serves to bring industry and academics together in an innovative environment at Education City, incubating knowledge with the eventual goal of commercializing results (Crist, 2015; OBG, The Report, 2015). Finally, QF's flagship $7.9bn Sidra Medical and Research Centre is destined to be a major center for research in the health sector. It will function as a teaching hospital affiliated with the Weill Cornell Medical College in Qatar and as a medical research center[2].

ESTABLISHING QATAR AS A HUB FOR KNOWLEDGE AND RESEARCH

By any measure, Qatar's growth is phenomenal; in the past decade the population has trebled, and the size of metropolitan Doha's built environment has increased fourfold (Alraouf, 2017). From its humble origins as a fishing and pearling village, Doha has emerged as a growing world city, where ambition and means are fueling exciting experiments in education, health, sports and culture (Fromherz, 2012; Kamrava,2013; Alraouf, 2008; 2016; 2017). The need to diversify the state's economy and shift from a hydrocarbon-based economy to a knowledge-based one is a key stipulation of the (QNV) 2030 and the Qatar National Development Strategy (QNDS) 2011–2016. Central to the Amir's vision is the recognition that, as plentiful as Qatar's natural resources may be, their value will one day be significantly diminished by the emergence of sustainable forms of energy production (Woodman, 2008). More significantly, the country's long-term development plan aimed at reducing dependency on hydrocarbons and creating a diversified economy driven by principles of knowledge economy:

Education can also be used as a soft power and as a soft force to transform societies. When I say transform societies it means we can tackle issues in political, social, cultural, economic areas. These are the most important things. (Sheikha Moza bint Nasser, Chairperson of Qatar Foundation)

The combination of a massive labor deficit and the abundance of discretionary wealth cemented the necessity for a new alternative of development and investment. Qatar's national vision of transitioning towards a knowledge-based economy is rooted in developing the state as a regional and increasingly global leader in research and development (R&D). The government has gradually strengthened the human and capital resources required to achieve this goal through the transformation of its education systems and with major investments in developing an advanced academic and research environment. The Qatar National Research Strategy, which was launched in 2012, outlines an extensive framework of goals and objectives under five priority themes that reflect local needs. The government has signalled the importance of these initiatives with commitments to allocate 2.8% of total government revenue to finance the development of facilities and research. Qatar Foundation (QF), in particular, has played a critical role in funding research and by developing leading centers for research in medicine, science and technology.

One of the most concrete evidences that Qatar is determined to shift its development plan into a new horizon is Education City (EC). Education City, Qatar Foundation's massive flagship educational project, is perhaps the largest single educational project undertaken anywhere in the world. EC was and still envisioned as a foremost manifestation of the country's future vison. EC is a cluster of Western universities that have established campuses in Doha over the past two decades. These have mostly congregated in Education City, a multibillion-dollar complex on Doha's western outskirts, designed as a center for knowledge and innovation and spearheaded by Qatar Foundation (QF), a non-profit organization focused on education, science and community development. EC is a completely unprecedented development in the field of international branch campuses (IBCs) and global higher education (Crist, 2015). Willoughby (2008, p.8) notes that the early founding and eventual success of the American University of Beirut (1866) and the American University of Cairo (1919) increased the familiarity of Arab families with American "curricular principles" and contributed to a regional reputation of American universities for high quality education alternatives for their children. Over the past twenty years, EC grew from a single school to a multi university campus with students from over 50 countries and an enormous research fund, offering endless opportunities for the advancement of knowledge and research across all disciplines (Jodido, 2014b). EC is located on the outskirts of Doha (Al-Rayyan area); it covers 14 square kilometers and houses educational facilities from school age to research level and branch campuses of some of the world's leading universities. Education City has evolved substantially since the establishment of QF in 1995. The essence of the development, and of the whole QF, was to create a niche for Qatar as an emerging education and research hub. EC is an initiative of Qatar Foundation for Education, Science and Community Development which was founded in 1995. EC is basically a cluster of Western universities that have established campuses there over the past two decades. It is planned and designed as a center for knowledge and innovation and spearheaded by Qatar Foundation (QF), a non-profit organization focused on education, science and community development.

Education City provides a nearly complete range of educational opportunities (except doctoral programs) from pre-school children through to university students. Its elementary and secondary school offerings include a highly regarded K-12 school (Qatar Academy), an international school on the International Baccalaureate model (Al Jazeera Academy), a school for children with special needs (Awsaj Academy), an Academic Bridge Program (ABP) which prepares high school graduates for college admission. Qatar Foundation's first agreement with an American university to provide education in Doha was made in 1998 with Virginia Commonwealth University's School of the Arts (VCUQ). However, this was not initially a branch campus arrangement. VCUQ ran educational programs but it was not authorized to grant a degree. Some in QF leadership believe that the decision to create an IBC cluster model was taken well after the arrangement with VCU. In 2001, Qatar Foundation announced its agreement with Weil Cornell Medical School to open a branch campus and offer a complete medical degree. From that date, in rapid succession, Qatar Foundation announced deals with several elite American universities to open IBCs in Doha: Texas A & M in 2003, Carnegie Mellon in 2004, Georgetown University School of Foreign Service in 2005, and Northwestern in 2008, followed by deals with two European universities, HEC Paris in 2010 and University College London in 2012 (Crist, 2015; Jodidio, 2014). Education City houses nine universities in all: eight foreign and one Qatari, Hamad bin Khalifa University, founded in 2011.

THE URBAN EVOLUTION OF EDUCATION CITY

The narrative of Education City's urban development was originated in 1999 after the appointment of the internationally claimed Japanese architect Arata Isozaki to develop the masterplan for EC. The decision resulted from the Qatar Foundation's commitment to ensuring design quality but more significantly form the country's leadership's vison for the future of Qatar[3]. The Amir, Sheikh Hamad Al Thani (*AlAmir*

Figure 2. Weil Cornell Medical School designed by world-renowned architect Arata Isozaki, Contemporary in concept, the design nonetheless features many references to traditional Islamic and Gulf architecture from geometric patterns on exterior and interior walls to wind towers in the courtyard (©Alraouf)

Al Waled, father of Sheikh Tamim, the current Amir) invited Isozaki for a visit to the site allocated for the project and stated the main objective; to put Qatar on the cultural, knowledge and educational map regionally and globally. Significantly, Sh. Mooza bint Al Misnid, the first lady, attended every cycle and milestone of the masterplan development as the consultant revealed[4]. While Isozaki was already engaged in the Gulf and the Middle East but a new interest was developed regarding the design and planning opportunities in Qatar. The early involvement with Qatar Foundation in the development of the blue print for what is to become one of the major undertakings in education and culture in the Middle East, the Qatar Education City established a different era for the firm's involvement in the Middle East. The process through which the masterplan was developed was based on creating independent yet integrated knowledge centers connected via main green spine and oasis like connections with various quality of open spaces.

Figure 3. The boundaries of Education city were changing on a swiftly manner due to the Qatar's commitment to transform the project into a holistic evidence that the KBUD is the future (Source: Courtesy of QF.org)

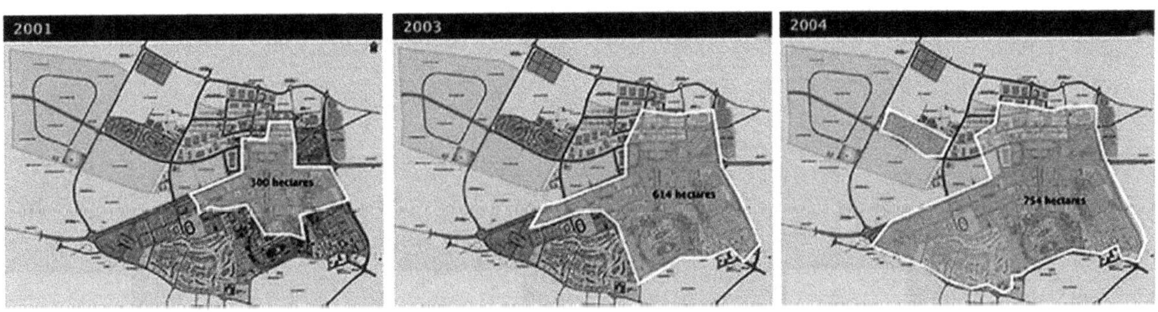

Figure 4. The master plan of education city as finally crystalized after cycles of development (Source: Courtesy of QF.org)

The masterplan was also based on the concept an organic system for growth and therefore the plan was not an end product. The Green Spine acts as a central landscaped area around which QF's early university buildings were grouped. It was designed to present a grand open vista with Qatar National Convention Centre acting as an indoor gathering place as the north anchor and, at the spine's southern end, the Ceremonial Court provides a focus for outdoor gatherings. The first cycle of Education City masterplan was produced in 2001 and was later subjected to more than twenty cycles of change, improvements and developments (Ahmadi, 2015; Jodio, 2014). The area designated for the project started with nearly 200 hectares and is exceeding 700 hectares in 2017. In addition to the major responsibility of the masterplan, Isozaki also was assigned for some key architectural entities designed and completed in the Education City, such as the ceremonial court[5] which was inspired by the mosque typology particularly influential elements like the minaret, courtyard, water fountains and geometrical patterns. and the Qatar National Convention Center (QNCC). As a symbol of physical and spiritual nourishment, the Sidra tree, Qatari local tree, has shaded scholars and students from the harsh desert sun for centuries. It is a powerful symbol for the Qatar Foundation — stressing the value of knowledge and community and was integrated symbolically in the design of QNCC.

Figure 5. Qatar National Convention Center designed by Arata Isozaki and Akoi Associates where the local Sidra tree was used to emphasize the Qatari Identity and contextual relevance (©Alraouf)

EC provides various facilities to support its main function of efficient education, research and knowledge dissemination. The holistic nature of EC clearly seen in the multi layered facilities added gradually to the project and transform it from a purely contained educational facility into a community magnet. Therefore, facilities established within the education city can be broadly categorized into three distinctive areas. First, the principal education facilities which include: Qatar academy, Virginia Commonwealth University, Weill Cornell Medical College, Texas A&M University, Carnegie Mellon University, Georgetown University School of Foreign Service, Hamad Bin Khalifa University and Northwestern University. Educational institutions at Education City offer programs that focus on their particular strengths. Georgetown, for instance, delivers programs in international politics, while Texas A&M awards degrees in engineering, VCU delivers programs in interior, fashion and graphic design, University College London offers opportunities to gain degrees in museum, cultural and heritage studies and HEC Paris focuses on business and executive education. While International Branch Campuses (IBCs) have been in operation since 1955 (Crist, 2015), not until Education City had multiple IBCs been assembled into a combined campus, "a university of universities" (Witte, 2010, p.18).

THE ARCHITECTURE AND URBANISM OF EDUCATION CITY

With renowned architects contributing to the design of the campus's various buildings, EC became a national landmark signifying the role Qatar Foundation plays as a catalyst for the nation's transition from a hydrocarbon-based economy to a knowledge-based economy. The architectural manifestation of EC starts from Qatar Academy (1996) to Qatar Faculty of Islamic Studies (2014) to Northwestern University new campus completion (2016). Within these two decades of development, EC projects illustrate a permanent commitment towards excellence that ensures people are offered an environment which not only provide world-class educational experience but also social integration, inspiration, and knowledge dissemination. Almost every single building is used as a knowledge-based physical representation of how architecture can be used as a catalyst for learning, inspiration and unique spatial experiences (Alraouf, 2016; 2017). As (Alami, 2015) argues visitors from all over the world frequently express that walking through Education City makes them feel like being in a museum of architecture where masterpieces are made public, not only to raise city fabric quality but primarily to educate community to a more responsible architecture. The interesting aspect here is that all of these buildings remain human in volume, size and scale to maintain the human experience as the significant objective of the project as a whole. The main idea was allowing the presence of world architects to participate in a dialogue challenging the notions of architecture, locality, education, identity and community. So while, it was expected that individual buildings should be able to express their own identity through their architectural theme, while acting in synergy with each other:

To look at Education City is to see the proof that QF is fulfilling its mission of contributing to the building of a sustainable and prosperous society, and of supporting the transition of Qatar to a knowledge-based economy. The campus is an organic realm of knowledge and cultural exchange, where a new generation is being nourished within a unique learning environment. (Telefat, 2015)[6]

Education City began with Qatar Academy, a single school offering primary, middle and international baccalaureate diploma programs along with an early-childhood center, in 1995. The construction of the academy was followed by buildings for the Qatar Foundation (QF) Headquarters and a facility for VCU, all of which were designed by local architectural consultancies to resemble the traditional architecture of Qatar and the region (Ahmadi, 2015).

The whole project started with a school for girls to provide education and teach Etiquette. As was described by the designer of the first educational facility on the project, Ibrahim Jaidah, the prominent Qatari architect, boundaries and the QF's original headquarters; the school was the seed that created this magnificent place called Education City, where we celebrate contemporary Arabic architecture and challenge the best architects in the world not just to create buildings, but to create buildings that celebrate a culture (Jaidah, 2015). At that time, according to Jaidah, it was impossible to envisage what Education City would become. In its current status, Education city houses educational facilities from school age to research level and branch campuses of some of the world's leading universities.

The commitment to ensuring design quality was further demonstrated through selecting internationally renowned architects to design the various buildings for the EC campus, including Ricardo and Victor Legorreta, Rem Koolhaas, Antoine Predock and Cesar Pelli. Victor Legorreta, the founder of Legorreta + Legorreta designed a number of key buildings in Education City including Carnegie Mellon University in Qatar, Texas A&M University in Qatar, Georgetown University School of Foreign Service in Qatar, and the Student Center. Legorreta's approach to design EC buildings was based on learning from the architecture of Islamic communities around the world including Mexico. He concluded that the common thread is that human architecture is articulated around feelings and therefore it is the kind of architecture which provokes feelings[7]. It has romantic content and in some situations encourages mysterious spatial experiences. Specifically, He stated that his team was able to develop a language for the four projects in EC assembled from an integration of formal patterns (Victor Legorreta, 2015). These patterns include extensive use of geometry, contrast of natural light and shade, use of roofs and terraces, variety of water elements, walls and solid planes, repetition of arches and domes, and architecture around courtyards. In Carnegie Mellon University in Qatar, College of Business and Computer Science designed in 2008, the concept was to create a street inside the building to emphasize the publicness. While, the Student Center Building which was designed in 2011 was seen as the *Souq* or the market of the university and therefore the mass is penetrated from different entrances and experienced through number of street like passages. Such conceptual basis in EC significant buildings, designed by Legorreta, supports the identity of the project as a knowledge-based urban development. Information is becoming so available in our digital era but knowledge can emerge from interactions and confrontations that EC buildings provided.

Another significant educational building is Northwestern University (NWQ) designed by the winner of the American Institute of Architects 2006 Gold Medal, architect Antoine Predock. Predock is the lead designer of all of the projects produced by Antoine Predock Architect PC. As a specialized architect in designing educational facilities and cultural buildings, Predock acknowledges that he is a true believer in the importance of seeing the architect as a traveler. He admits that his travels to Italy, Morocco, Egypt and finally Qatar deeply affected his thoughts about the nature and the built environment. In Doha, he was interested in creating freehand studies of the sand dunes dynamics and forms (Predock, 2015). Additionally, he experimented with the geometry of the crescent and the generative patterns that can be produced. Located in the southeast quadrant of Education City and set as a joint between two campus axes, the Northwestern College of Media and Communications' design philosophy translates and mediates the surrounding environment and site adjacencies into an interwoven movement of interior and exterior space. Consisting of textured outer stone walls, the building tells a story of place while inwardly transforming to a realm of digital era. The skyline or the outline of the NWQ becomes

Figure 6. Northwestern University (NWQ) architect Antoine Predock (©Alraouf) (Part 1)

Figure 7. Northwestern University (NWQ) architect Antoine Predock (©Alraouf) (Part 2)

a rugged Qatari landscape in abstraction, while expressing a diagram of journalistic ideals (Predock, 2015). Knowing that the design task in hand is Northwestern University Media and Communication School, Predock originated the idea that the building should attain pedagogical objectives and allowing for formal, informal and fun ceremonies and events to take place. Hence, a matrix of open informal gathering spaces juxtaposes against soft arcing paths tracing through the building. The NWQ is divided into three sections: The crescent on the west, the curved arc on the east, and the bar on the north. The building creates a narrative interweaving of the courtyards and open patios in addition to allowing a spatial progression out through the courtyard and to the Gardens. The building embodies architectural elements from Qatar's desert landscape and local culture and acts as a forum for technological innovation, education and cultural exchange.

Second main component of EC, is the science and technology facilities which include Qatar Science and Technology Park (QSTP), Sidra Medical and Research Centre, and Qatar Research institute among other facilities. Finally, the third component of EC is community facilities which include EC community housing, Mathaf; Arab Museum of Modern Art, National Library, Al-Shaqab Equestrian Center, Qatar

Figure 8. The architecture of Carnegie Mellon University blending with the external landscape particularly the backyard fountain (© Alraouf)

National Convention Centre, Qatar Foundation Headquarters, Al Shaqab Hotel, Solis Hotel, Oxygen Park and Health and wellness facilities (www.qf.org.qa). The idea is to support the EC with all kinds of mixed use developments that guarantee the vibrancy of the project. Such activities would also enhance connecting EC's different components and improving its urban experience for users and visitors alike. As clearly seen in the second and third components of EC, the presence of inviting activities that would attract city dwellers from different gender and age groups is an ultimate objective. A great deal of this project' success would rely on its ability to provide an experience of place that engages people from different cultural backgrounds in a vibrant mix of activities within acceptable catchment boundaries. When it comes to creativity in suggesting land uses and functions within the project, diversified suggestions were selected without out having a direct relation with education, research. Rather, it would speak to the nature of EC as a hub for exploring, creativity and knowledge.

An excellent evidence is the EC library which is not perceived as a typical campus faculty and students library but rather a national knowledge forum for the whole of Qatar.

The new National Library (QNL) is one of the projects which will help substantially to bring the community to Education City and help in avoiding transforming the territory into a kind of gated community. The project will offer residents of Qatar state-of-the-art public facilities and technologies alongside a variety of learning spaces, performance venues and cafés. The library's form consists of two square plates (138m wide), pulled apart and folded diagonally at the corners to create a shell-like container. The sloped interior surfaces of the plates create three large terraces that are stacked with 300 bookshelves, visible from a central communal space called the urban plaza. The Urban Plaza is directly connected with the main entrance which is a kind of continuation of the external road. Hence, people will be moving smoothly from the public space to the semipublic to the urban plaza to intensify the notion that QNL is a public space for all. For architect Rem Koolhaas, who designed the building, the design is intended to inspire in the same way that an open book inspires and promote the importance of reading through accessibility and visibility of content. The QF's new headquarters in EC is also designed by Rem Koolhaas. The concept of the building design emerged from the requirements and qualities of an innovation hub, and how creativity and ingenuity can only flourish in an environment that allows it to do so. Consequently, in the design of QF Headquarters, Koolhaas acknowledges the need for a more simple, pure and neutral form to contrast the dynamic architectural languages used in the rest of EC' buildings. He selected the mass of the cube to resemble such needed simplicity. Meanwhile, the building was inspired by Islamic aesthetics and poetics of spaces where the serenity and tranquility of the external composition contrast the vibrancy and the vitality of the internal spaces.

Figure 9. The new National Library (QNL) designed by Rem Koolhaas who stressed the openness and publicness of the library and created strong connectivity with the urban setting, community and the city (©Alraouf)

Figure 10. The architectural dialogue between buildings stimulate visitors and users' minds and help using architecture as a tool for learning and knowledge dissemination. In this case the dialogue is between NWQ and CIS (Source: Courtesy of QF.org)

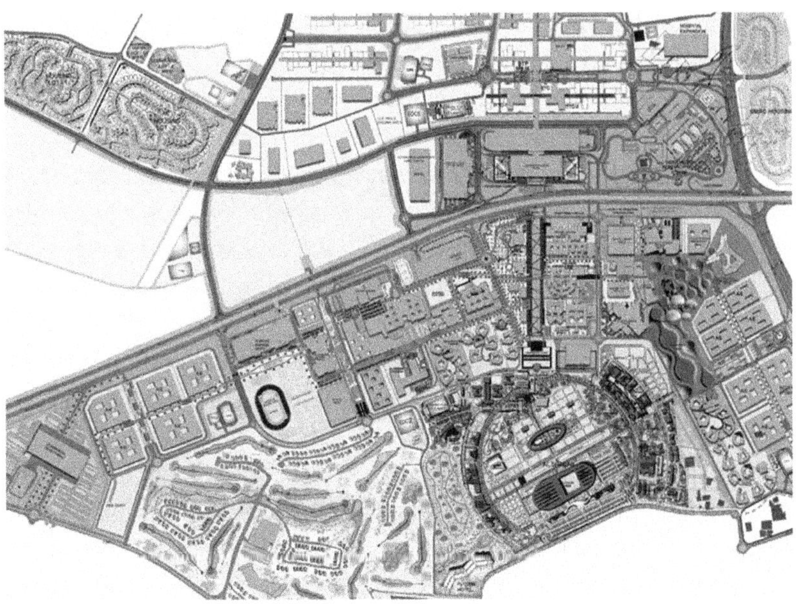

Other leading architects, whose imprint can be seen at QF, emphasized the concept of creating buildings with a purpose that extends far beyond their function. Ali Mangera, Director of Mangera Yvars Architects, the architects for the World Architecture Festival Award-winning building that comprises the Education City Mosque and Qatar College of Islamic Studies (QCIS), which can be best described as a "visible, dynamic, and inclusive" building that respects and contemporizes the tenets of Islam[8]. The QCIS building occupies the north-east corner of Education City, which opens in towards the rest of the campus. QCIS perfectly illustrates the underlying philosophy and conceptual base of EC. Every single building was seen as an opportunity to confront static cultural concepts or stagnated architectural doctrines (Alraouf, 2016). Whereas people expect a rational and typical Islamic style building to host such curriculum, the preferred design was the one with the strongest narrative: two ribbons start from the building entrance and harmoniously tweak in the building until they reach the minaret, pointing toward the sky (Alami, 2015):

Indeed, a true innovator in terms of acknowledgement of context, program configuration and architectural design, the QFIS's impact is even greater as an ideological statement. In times of heated theological discourse and divisiveness in the discourse of Islamic teachings, it offers a platform for social re-construct and re-calibration, based on a shared appreciation of the processes of learning, of progress and of capacity for reinvention, of sharing knowledge and most importantly, of self-growth and critical thought. (Mirincheva, 2017)

The building, opened in 2015, could easily be regarded as one of the most socially eloquent, culturally erudite and design innovative structures in Qatar (Mirincheva, 2017). The project also provided a new paradigm in educational and religious building which resonates with the historical precedents of traditional university in traditional cities within the Muslim communities. Because of the role of the mosque as a community space in Islam, the QCIS becomes a collective communal agency, a 'beacon of knowledge and light', as described by its tenants, that simultaneously gathers and disperses in a series of spaces that seem indispensable to one another and in a complete synergy. In historical cases of traditional educational centers like Al Azhar in Cairo, Al Qirawan in Tunisia and Al Mustansiriya in Baghdad, there was no clear distinction between the college, the mosque and the community facilities (Hakim, 1986; Mortada, 2003). Consequently, such places were the real heart for their cities playing multi roles including educational, spiritual, economical, social and even recreational:

The scriptural relevance of knowledge and faith underpinned the many advances of Islamic civilization where faith supported scholarly endeavors in areas such as mathematics, philosophy, astronomy and the arts. The brief led to developing the scheme where faith and knowledge are wrapped around one another, physically, formally and programmatically. (Mangera Yvars Architects, 2017)

The designers stated that the main functions of QCIS are learning and praying; two notions which deeply related to the concepts of knowledge and light. Based on such understanding, the design team focused on five main principles; geometry, light, color, water and garden. More importantly, the design for the QFIS is not without profound historical reference. It is based on the Islamic '*Kulliyya*' – a place of education and prayer, built on the belief that all knowledge comes from faith. A concept which was originated in Middle Eastern and Islamic communities cities as a place for learning and worship. The external and internal walls were used as exhibition of Islamic art particularly calligraphy and geometrical ornaments. The designers considered the building to be a contemporary message about Islam which can confront the current image associated with Islam. So the project was an opportunity not only to change the perception about typical architectural elements like the minaret and the prayers space but also about the essence of Islam. Even the mosque space itself, as the courtyard space, is not formalized, rather it becomes part of the experience of discovery, which explains its lack of processional entrance, its multiple entry points and levels. Its volume is lifted off the ground and supported by five formidable size pillars, representing the five pillars of Islam, *Shahada* (knowledge), *Salat* (prayer), *Zakat*(charity), *Siyam* (fasting)and *Hajj* (pilgrimage); also wrapped in calligraphy. QCIS is paving the way for constructing a new paradigm in education, sacred architecture and knowledge-based urbanism. The QCIS conveys an unmistakably urban quality, manifested in the synergetic alternation of massing and landscape, solids and voids, sun and shade, and in the clear acknowledgement and close relationship with the adjacent Northwestern University building and Oxygen Park (Mirincheva, 2017).

The role of the signature architects also known as "Starchitects"[9] practicing in the Middle East and the Gulf was revisited within the boundaries of Education City. They are here not just to put yet one more replica of their slandered formal signature but rather to experiment, produce new languages, challenged by cultural context and help in stimulating minds. Their role was also challenged in finding answers on the role architecture can play in inspiring social change. By creating public space you are able to create chances for social change. The goal of establishing Education City was to create an environment that inspires knowledge and facilitates the exchange of knowledge. Hence, there was a need for spaces to incorporate four key elements: diversity, inclusivity, stability, and the enablement of new and imaginative thinking. EC provided spaces that allow people to be inspired, to collaborate, to think, and to be stimulated, you are laying the foundations for innovation.

What has been achieved thus far in EC has been recognized as a unique national, regional and global destination that is currently designated as one of four metropolitan centers for the greater city of Doha (QNDF, 2016; Ahmadi, 2015, p.53). Connecting EC to various destinations across the city of Doha is

Figure 11. The College of Islamic Studies and Education city mosque allocated on the border of EC and attracting city dwellers to perform prayers and enjoy the adjacent parks (Source: Courtesy of QF.org)

also underway as part of the planned Qatar metro scheme, where four major stations will be located at the parameter of the campus. The presence of local architects and engineers like Amina Alahmadi, Jassim Telefat and Mohammed Ouassim Alami achieved a positive confrontation to the meticulously selected eminent architects. The ability to embrace QF's vision and mission, and to translate and integrate the richness of Islamic, Gulf and Qatari heritage into contemporary and forward-thinking design, was the main condition to engage them in the designing of Education City's defining buildings. Therefore, architects selected to participate in achieving such a state-of-the-art campus, such as Arata Isozaki and Legorreta+Legorreta – amongst many others – were selected to enrich EC environment with innovative approaches and ideas strong enough to induce a behavior change towards the best, and a community engagement for sustainable practices.

EDUCATION CITY AS A VIBRANT KNOWLEDGE HUB FOR ALL

With all the previously analyzed qualities of EC, another crucial aspect to be assessed is integration of the EC with the community and the city. There are different aspects related to the presence of American universities in the Gulf and Qatar. As Vora (2015) suggests branch campuses have a particularly important relationship with emerging forms of racial consciousness, identity, and politicization among students, both citizen and foreign resident. While such educational and research entities are providing excellent learning opportunities for students from Qatar and the region yet their cultural impact should be considered and assessed on a regular basis. Vora (2015) claims that it might be perceived as an entity of a broader project of postcolonial and transnational engagement with the newly emerging knowledge economy. Looser (2012) provides an earlier parallel interpretation suggesting that the shift from studying abroad to studying in high-profile North American universities. Such shift creates a new geography of "area," that includes shifting conceptions of citizenship, sovereignty, and cultural difference. Hence, these universities are defining new kinds of global social space resulted from "neoliberal" global economics. Based on such concerns, the case of Education city in Qatar should consider the varied implications resulted from being inward entity intensifying a separation from the rest of the community and the city.

EC transcends the typical notion of education cluster to pave the way for a vibrant knowledge center which integrates with the city and the community. The challenge of transforming EC into a gated community was faced with the insertion of number of facilities and activities geared towards inviting community members with different cultural and social groups to use its spaces and places. In the field work within EC, the author documented influx of community members particularly form adjacent neighborhood and also from the rest of Doha coming to use the community-based facilities particularly the unique mosque at CIS and the Oxygen park. The relationship of the mosque with the adjacent Oxygen Park and Qur'anic Botanic Garden is another important factor in exploring different ways to relate community to knowledge, environment and experience. The idea of Oxygen Park is to introduce a green lung in the campus, inviting students and visitors alike to refresh their mind, body, and spirit through active exercise, relaxation, and exploration. Oxygen Park is an open invitation to community to enjoy outdoor landscaped areas, while the Qur'anic Botanic Garden hosts botanical species mentioned in the Holy Qur'an and Hadith. Both express a didactic and innovative way to push for positive change and contribute to social development.

Education City is currently at a critical juncture: planned growth is increasing the campus population and development footprint; planned transit investments are creating greater opportunities for collegial connectivity. An Ascending fear that EC would transform into a kind of gated community divorced for the city and its community, has required a new project which was initiated by the local team and titled: EC Masterplan Integration. The project focuses on revisiting Education City's planning, assess its current performance and propose schemes that will provide improved connectivity and integration of systems, public realm and overall development. The intent of the Master Plan Integrator, currently being developed by Moriyama & Teshima, is to guide Education City - creating a flexible, sustainable framework for development and holistic decision-making. It builds on past planning initiatives, beginning with the 2001 Arata Isozaki master plan. The Master Plan Integrator is envisaged as a living document — providing a dynamic framework for both Institution and City to thrive in an integrated manner. A campus master plan must be many things — functional, sustainable, and technically sound but never losing sight of its main objective of providing a setting that symbolizes and inspires human excellence. Whether walking through Oxygen Park, relaxing at Al Shaqab Hotel, or enjoying the atmosphere of the Qatar International Golf Club, another common thread through Education City's new projects is their very inter-connectedness. All of these projects are intended to complement each other and be easily accessible, from within and outside Education City and to maximize the benefits of EC to the wider community. As well as being home to prestigious universities and schools, cutting-edge research centers and laboratories, a string of new developments are under way to further increase public accessibility to the flagship community of Qatar Foundation (QF). The plans are ambitious and multi-faceted, including world-class hotels, thoughtfully designed public open space, high level sports, and recreation facilities to achieve a better connected educational hub, city and community. To help transforming EC into a model not only for Doha and Qatar but for the rest of Gulf and Middle Eastern Cities, the place is planned as a car-less environment with the aim to transform it in the future into car-free environment. Therefore, there is a huge emphasis on the enhancement of the pedestrian experience in the campus. Different methods were implemented including pedestrian friendly walkways, the 'people mover' system, the e bikes network will contribute and the imminent opening of adjacent Metro station which were incorporated in the final master plan of the city. All of which to build a car-less environment, where people decide to abandon their vehicle for a more convenient and healthy lifestyle.

CONCLUSION

The strategic objectives of megaprojects in Qatar are achieved via branding the State as a new destination for knowledge, education, research, cultural events, and sports international competitions. It is also achieved via establishing Qatar's new identity as a context for knowledge and creativity attracting knowledge workers from all over the globe. A project like Education City is constructing a new identity for Qatar and help in going beyond the traditional comprehension of State's identity as a historical reference rather than future contribution. Such a project reflects Qatar as a benchmark for globalization, seamlessly bringing together different influences and perceptions of modernity. The analyzed projects within the Education City development, demonstrate the aspiration to become centers of urban life for all citizens. They also provided evidences to a solid trend towards promoting the sustainable urbanism by being inclusive and achieving the principles of the just city open for all. Qatar's new identity is articulated around the notion of knowledge and education. Therefore, investing in building universities, research centers, museums and vibrant public spaces, is actually investment in the intellectual, cultural and knowledge capabilities of the society as a whole. The analysis, provided in the context of the chapter, illustrates that architecture and urban design of mega urban projects like Education City in Qatar, are crucial factors in the success of establishing knowledge based urban development. Provocative and exciting architecture invites people to explore the spaces and to be engaged in new experiences. Education city is geared towards economic diversification, urban diversity, knowledge-based urban development and social urban justice.

Creating knowledge and innovation hubs is not restricted to building of enclaves but should be seen as a strategy for the whole city and a manifestation of a holistic approach adopted by the whole State. History and modern times are full of examples to support such conclusion as we have seen in the analysis of Education city in Qatar. The whole notion of knowledge in Greek civilization was based on the presence of Agoura where people debate, discuss and interact. The city of Baghdad in Iraq was famous for the cultural context and the presence of *Dar Al Hikama* with all its books and manuscripts accessible to everyone in the city. The artistic movement in Florence affected the whole city and transforms it into the European center of enlightenment. Another crucial contemporary example is Google headquarters with its distinctive colorful, informal, diversified spatial experiences and living room quality setting added substantially to the identity of the place as an entity for innovation and creativity. Education city's model proved that the whole environment leads to innovation, inspiration and knowledge transfer. Inspiration and stimulation resulted from bringing nature to external and internal spaces. EC acknowledges that establishing a relation with the city and the community is important as in the age of digital media, educational buildings should provide a different experience than what can be gained digitally. Open and public spaces are equally important in the success of Education City as they invite different people from the city to interact and have such back yard closeness in different green spaces and courtyards. Education city is a mosaic of nationalities, cultures, disciplines and spatial experiences and these are the conditions for an inspiring and stimulating knowledge-based urban development.

The fact that Education City's master plan went through twenty four cycles of development is an evidence of a different understanding of planning. In the context of EC, the masterplan was never perceived as a static reference but rather dynamic always unfinished guidelines which allow the organic and dynamic development of the project. Such process also allows the incorporation of any fundamental changes in the vison of EC, QF, Qatar or the whole region. Such flexibility was evident when Qatar faced four main and unprecedented challenges in the last decade; the financial global crisis in 2008, winning the bid for hosting the FIFA 2022 cup in 2010, the drop of oil prices in 2014 and the blockade in June 5th, 2017[10]. Much has been achieved since the first buildings were erected almost two decades ago, but Education City is not yet complete. What exists so far forms part of an ongoing masterplan that has evolved, and continues to evolve, in a way that brings complementary elements that, when combined, create the optimum environment for a thriving and expanding hub of knowledge serving all the community of Qataris, expats and beyond.

REFERENCES

Ahmadi, A. (2015). A City for Education. *Architectural Design*, *85*(1), 46–53. doi:10.1002/ad.1854

Alami, M. O. (2015, March 15). Realizing a Masterplan with Architectural Works of Art. *QF Telegraph*.

Alraouf, A. A. (2008). Emerging Middle Eastern knowledge cities: the unfolding story. In T. Yigitcaular & V. Koray (Eds.), *Knowledge Based Urban Development: Planning and Application in the Information Era*. IGI Global Publishing. doi:10.4018/978-1-59904-720-1.ch014

Alraouf, A. A. (2016). "Dohaization": An Emerging Interface between Knowledge, Creativity, and Gulf Urbanity. In Gulf Cities as Interfaces. Cambridge, UK: Gulf Research Centre Cambridge.

Alraouf, A. A. (2017). Interrogating Qatar's Urbanity as a Catalyst for Building Knowledge-Based Societies and Economies. In R. G. Bertelsen, N. Noori, & J.-M. Rickli (Eds.), *Strategies of Knowledge Transfer For Economic Diversification In The Arab States Of The Gulf* (pp. 53–66). London: Gerlach Press.

Crist, J. T. (2015). Innovation in a Small State: Qatar and the IBC Cluster Model of Higher Education. *The Muslim World Journal.*, *105*(1), 93–115. doi:10.1111/muwo.12082

Dinnie, K. (2011). *City Branding: Theory and Cases*. Palgrave Macmillan. doi:10.1057/9780230294790

Foray, D. (2004). *The Economics of Knowledge*. Cambridge, MA: MIT Press.

Fromherz, A. (2012). *Qatar: a Modern History*. Washington, DC: Georgetown University Press.

Goldenberg, S. (2016). Masdar's zero-carbon dream could become world's first green ghost town. *The Guardian*. Retrieved from https://www.theguardian.com/environment/2016/feb/16/

Gray, M. (2013). *Qatar: Politics and the Challenges of Development*. Boulder, CO: Lynne Rienner Publishers.

Hakim, B. (1986). Arabic-Islamic Cities: Building and Planning Principles. Academic Press.

Hertog, S. (2016). A Quest for Significance: Gulf Oil Monarchies' International 'Soft Power' Strategies And Their Local Urban Dimensions. The London School of Economics and Political Science, LSE Kuwait Program, Paper Series, 42.

Jaidah, I., & Bourennane, M. (2010). *The History of Qatari Architecture 1800-1950*. Skira.

Jodidio, P. (2014). (ed): Education City; Qatar Foundation, Doha "About Qatar Foundation". Qatar Foundation.

Jodido, P. (2014). *The New Architecture of Qatar* (1st ed.). New York: Skira Rizzoli Publications.

Kamrava, M. (2013). *Qatar: Small State, Big Politics*. New York: Cornell University Press.

Kihato, C. (2010). *Urban Diversity: Space, Culture, and Inclusive Pluralism in Cities Worldwide*. Johns Hopkins University Press.

Learning from Education City International Conference. (2015). Organized by QF and AIA Middle East Chapter in Doha, Qatar. Retrieved from http://www.qf.org.qa/learningfromec/speakers

Looser, T. (2012). The Global University, Area Studies, And The World Citizen: Neoliberal Geography's Redistribution Of The "World". *Cultural Anthropology*, *27*(1), 97–117. doi:10.1111/j.1548-1360.2012.01128.x

Mirincheva. V. (2017, March 7). The Qatar Faculty of Islamic Studies by Mangera Yvars is a process of continuous learning and enlightenment. *The Architectural Review*.

Mortada, H. (2003). *Traditional Islamic Principles of Built Environment*. London: Routledge Curzon.

Oxford Business Group (OBG). (2016). *The Report. Qatar*. Author.

Qatar General Secretariat of Development Planning (QSDP). (2009). *Qatar National Vision 2030. Advancing Sustainable Development, Qatar's Second Human Development Report*. Gulf Publishing and Printing Company.

Qatar General Secretariat of Development Planning (QSDP). (2011). *National Development Strategy 2011-2016*. Doha: Gulf Publishing and Printing Company.

Qatar National Development Framework (QNDF). (2016). *The Ministry of Municipality and Environment*. Author.

Qatar Statistics Authority. (2015). *QSA Population*. Retrieved February 22, 2015, from http://www.qsa.gov.qa/eng/populationstructure.htm

QSDP. (2011). *National Development Strategy 2011–2016*. Doha, Qatar: Gulf Publishing and Printing Company.

Roberts, D. B. (2015). *Qatar: Securing the Global Ambitions of a City-state*. London: C Hurst & Co Publishers Ltd.

The Foundation. (2016, January 19). *Learning from Education City*. Author.

Thierstein, A., & Schein, E. (2008). Emerging Cities on the Arabian Peninsula: Urban Space in the Knowledge Economy Context. *Archnet-IJAR: International Journal of Architectural Research*, *2*(2), 178–195.

United Nations Development Programme (UNDP). (2003). *Arab human development*. Author.

Vora, N. (2015). Is the University Universal? Mobile (Re)Constitutions of American Academia in the Gulf Arab States. *Anthropology & Education Quarterly*, *46*(1), 19–36. doi:10.1111/aeq.12085

Willoughby, J. (2008). *Let a Thousand Models Bloom: Forging Alliances with Western Universities and the Making of the New Higher Educational System in the Gulf*. Washington, DC: American University. Retrieved from http://www.american.edu/academic.depts/cas/econ/workingpapers/workpap.htm

Wippel, S. (Ed.). (2014). *Under Construction: Logics of Urbanism in the Gulf Region*. London: Ashgate.

Witte, S. (2010). *Inside Education City: The Persistent Demographic and Gender Imbalance in Qatar*. United Nations Publications.

ENDNOTES

1. The RAND Corporation is a nonprofit institution that helps improve policy and decision-making through research and analysis. RAND has conducted research on Qatari issues since 2003. From 2003 to 2013, much of this work was performed in partnership with the Qatar Foundation in the RAND-Qatar Policy Institute. Most RAND analyses have focused on Qatar's education system, but the research agenda also includes health, infrastructure, labor markets, and science and technology. https://www.rand.org/topics/qatar.html

2 Last year international media reported that QF's annual bill to cover operating expenses for the six US universities in Qatar surpassed $400m. The investment seems to be paying dividends: in the World Economic Forum's "Global Competitiveness Report 2016/17, Qatar placed 30th out of 138 countries, topping the GCC rankings for higher education.

3 The evolution of EC was critically discussed in 'Learning from Education City', a conference organized by QF in partnership with Columbia University's Graduate School of Architecture, Planning, and Preservation, and in collaboration with the American Institute of Architects Middle East Chapter, and was held at Hamad bin Khalifa University (HBKU) from 27-28 November 2015.

4 An interview with architect A. Akoi, partner in Arata Isozaki and Akoi Associates conducted on 28th November, 2015 during the conference "Learning from Education City".

5 The Ceremonial Court provides a multi-functional open-air setting for the celebration of special events such as graduation ceremonies, lectures and music concerts. Two settings are provided: a formal stage area to the south with a seating capacity of 3,000, and an informal amphitheater style seating arrangement for up to 3,000 people to the north of the venue. The facility, which has a gross floor area of 1,880 square meters, is located in the central zone of the campus, adjacent to Al Shaqab Academy and at the end of the central green spine.

6 In an interview conducted by the author dated 27th November, 2015, with Engineer Jassim Telefat, Group Executive Director, Capital Projects and Facilities Management, QF.

7 An interview was conducted with Victor Legorreta in 2015 as he was attending Learning from Education City Conference in Doha, Qatar.

8 The building was Shortlisted for the 2017 Moira Gemmill Prize and was described as A university in Doha fluidly wraps around the campus mosque minarets – a beacon of knowledge and prayer.

9 For a holistic understanding of the term and the phenomena, refer to Edwin Heathcote, Age of the 'starchitect' published in the Financial Times. January 26, 2017. Heathcote argues that Modern architecture is the story of the starchitect, the architect as lone genius, the brilliant flair of the sketch on the napkin, the celebrity, the worldwide renown. He illustrates across the world starchitecture has given branding to blockbuster buildings. In Gehry's Bilbao Guggenheim and his sparkling Spruce Street tower, in Herzog & de Meuron's cavernous Tate Modern and in Zaha Hadid's Olympic aquatics center, in Rem Koolhaas's Seattle Public Library and in Norman Foster's Gherkin, each of these buildings has stimulated both the cities they are in and the (still sparse) public debate about contemporary architecture.

10 In the early hours of Monday June 5th 2017, three countries from the Gulf Cooperation Council (GCC) including Saudi Arabia, United Arab of Emirates and Bahrain joined by Egypt decided to have a total blockade and imposing trade and travel bans over Qatar due to major political disputes.

Chapter 13
Cities of GCC in Post-Hydrocarbon Era:
Challenges and Opportunities

Ahmed O. El-Kholei
Arabian Gulf University, Bahrain

Odeh Al-Jayyousi
Arabian Gulf University, Bahrain

ABSTRACT

Gulf Cooperation Council (GCC) countries are highly urbanized. The states of GCC countries are considered rentier states and suffer from the Dutch disease. Acknowledging this fact, many GCC States endeavored to diversify their economic base by attempting to transfer their economies from hydrocarbon-based to knowledge-based economy. Many reports and studies claim these attempts still in need to be integrated within their urban settings, not just a development at the hinterlands of existing cities. The chapter outlines key challenges and opportunities for cities of GCC to transfer their urban development into a knowledge base. The chapter calls for an enabling environment for knowledge transfer, a transition towards a green economy, and institutional development by building and fostering global partnerships for knowledge, innovation, and energy.

1. INTRODUCTION

1.1. The State of Cities in GCC Countries

Today, the GCC is highly urbanized. In 2012, at least 70 percent of the total population lived in cities. For example, almost 100 percent of the population of Kuwait and Qatar lives in urban settlements (see Figure 1). However, late rates of urban growth have been relatively reasonable (UN-Habitat, 2012). The average annual change between 2010 and 2015 was 0.1, 0.0, 0.6, 0.1, 0.3, and 0.4 percent in Bahrain, Kuwait, Oman, Qatar, Saudi Arabia and the United Arab Emirates, respectively (United Nations, 2014).

DOI: 10.4018/978-1-5225-3734-2.ch013

Copyright © 2018, IGI Global. Copying or distributing in print or electronic forms without written permission of IGI Global is prohibited.

There are various reasons for this situation. Atop of these reasons is oil and natural gas. The economies of GCC generated employment opportunities that attracted internal migrants and expatriate labor. Another major reason is maintaining high rates of natural population growth, where death rates declined because of improved health services while birth rates continued to be high. "Despite these slowing urban growth rates, the urban populations in all countries will continue to grow more rapidly than the total populations" (UN-Habitat, 2012, p. 128). The added population will be in existing cities. Between 2010-2015, the growth rate of Riyadh was about four percent (UNDESA, 2014).

Factors of geopolitical elements affected all countries located on the eastern side of the Arabian Peninsula. Gulf States are at the crux of global politics and trade. They were subject to external influences from Africa, India, Iran, the Levant and transformations from within the Arabian Peninsula (Riad, 1983). In 1981, the six countries founded the Gulf Cooperation Council (GCC) a regional intergovernmental political and economic bloc.

The residents of the Arabian Gulf states based their livelihoods on the strategic location of their port cities, Figure 2, where they mastered the arts of navigation and building ships and boats. They made use of the morphology of the coast and the use of a compass. In addition to transportation and trade, the residents of GCC states depended on extracting natural resources demanded in global markets, namely, pearls and petroleum (UN-Habitat, 2012). The fact that the Gulf states depended on producing goods and providing services, such as trade and transportation, that global markets demand explains why this region is at the center of world politics that global powers control (Riad, 1983). During the 19th century, local Arab powers, the Ottomans and British Empire competed to dominate the Gulf region thus affecting trade, particularly with India. Before 1930s, the Gulf region experienced an economic boom as a res ult of flourishing pearl trade and domination of the British influence that brought stability to the region. Between 1930-1940 due, in part, to the Japanese cultured pearls, together with the global economic

Figure 1. Proportion urban population as percent of total population, 1990-2050
Source: United Nations, Department of Economic and Social Affairs, Population Division (2014). World Urbanization Prospects: The 2014 Revision, Highlights (ST/ESA/SER.A/352).

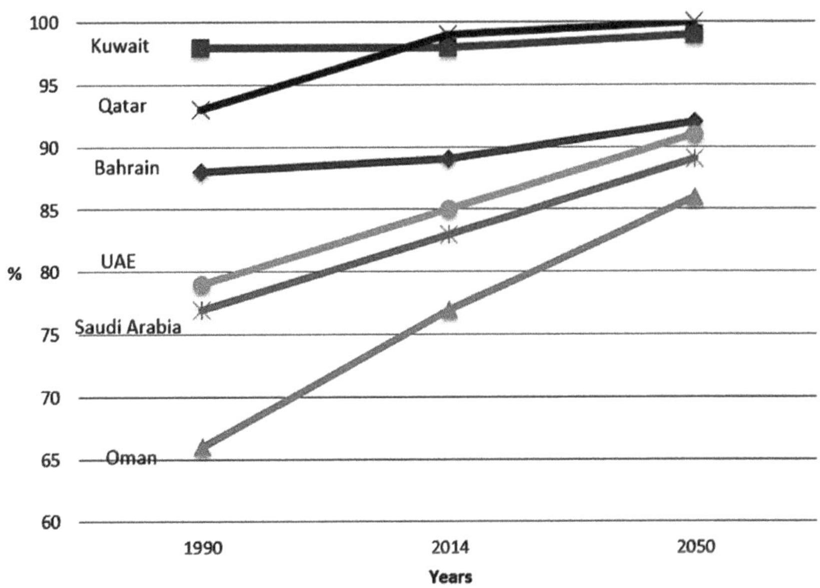

Figure 2. Major cities of GCC countries
Source: UN-Habitat. (2012). The State of Arab Cities 2012 Challenges of Urban Transition. Retrieved from http://www.citiesalliance.org/sites/citiesalliance.org/files/SOAC-2012.pdf

recession and World War II (WWII), the economy of the Gulf started to lose momentum. Starting the 1950s, the economy of the Gulf region started to flourish following the production of petroleum and natural gas (Riad, 1983).

The oil boom, particularly following 1973, contributed significantly to the economic expansion of the economy of the Gulf region. At that time:

City growth rates [were] among the highest in the world ...The high growth rates [were] essentially due to massive foreign migration into the region and to extremely high natural increase rate — an abnormal condition in an urban process approaching saturation point. (El-Arifi, 1986, p. 223)

The development of Gulf cities was fast and exponential both in spatial and demographic terms (Kamrava, 2015; Kamrava et al., 2015).

The urban system of GCC countries consists of 24 cities (those of population 300 thousand and over); 14 of them are in Saudi Arabia alone. One-third of the cities of the GCC countries have a population of one million and over. They are Riyadh, Jeddah, Mecca, Dammam and Medina, Saudi Arabia; Kuwait City, Kuwait; and Abu Dhabi and Dubai, UAE. Sharjah is expected to join them in the near future (UNDESA, 2014).

This fact means that the national urban systems and the Gulf urban system as well suffer from urban primacy. It is the status where the urban population is not evenly distributed among the cities within nationally defined boundaries. Most of the newcomers (both newly born and migrants) will live in existing cities.

In 1961, Berry proposed that urban primacy exists in developing countries that gained their political and economic independence. The primate city is often the capital and the chief port. He argued that urban primacy does not associate with the level of development. El-Shakhs (1972) found a noteworthy relationship between city-size distribution and level of economic development. At the stage of an economic take-off, the national urban system will suffer from primacy because of migration to the primate city. As the economy enters the stage of economic maturity, the urban system experiences a process of polarization reversal, where urban population starts to move to other cities. Smith (1985a, 1985b) proposed that urban primacy partners with class relations and offshoots with the reliance of the economy on exporting raw materials. Urban primacy associates with many urban ills, such as environmental degradation, the quest for job opportunities, lack of social justice and the need for shelter. It means imbalances and implies certain levels of bias (Abu-Lughod & Hay Jr., 1977; Berry, 1961; El-Kholei & Wahbi, 2010; El-Shakhs, 1972; Jayne & Bell, 2009; Smith, 1985a, 1985b).

Freshwater resources are extremely limited in the region. The availability of freshwater resources is the prime reason for the development of human settlements in GCC states in their particular locations (Bamakhrama, 2015; Bonine, 1983; El-Arifi, 1986; Ramadan, 2015; Riad, 1983). The State dedicated major mega-infrastructures to capital cities and chief ports – a direct outcome of urban primacy. The role of these cities in the national development and the economy of the region is unquestionable. Moreover, all indicators suggest that future urbanization will take place in these settlements as it is, probably less costly in economic and political terms (Bamakhrama, 2015; Bonine, 1983; El-Arifi, 1986; Ramadan, 2015; Riad, 1985; UN-Habitat, 2012).

Considering the global discourse on climate change and the imperatives to make a transition to low carbon economy, GCC countries are taking steps to diversify the economy and mainstream eco-solutions and practices in economy and society. Such a transition to sustainability implies the embodiment of new knowledge and worldview to cope with change and risks due to changes in the energy mix, subsidies, governance, and business model.

A knowledge society is a community that is capable to acquiring and harnessing knowledge for development (Fergany, Bennani, Elsadda, Jadaane, & Kubursi, 2003; United Nations Department of Economic and Social Affairs, 2005; United Nations Development Programme, 2006). According to Nonaka (1994, 1997, 2007), knowledge comes with two complementary facets: explicit and implicit. Explicit knowledge consists of formal and standardized information like codes and manuals; while tacit knowledge is implicit and verbal. Combining and internalizing explicit and tacit knowledge is a condition for generating and manufacturing of knowledge (Nonaka, 1994, 1997, 2007). Knowledge workers and communities of practice enable the process of knowledge development (Drucker, 2003a, 2003b).

The Arab world had limited capacity to create knowledge which in turn affected the trajectory of progress and prosperity. Unlike the industrialized countries, the Arab region had undergone different socio-technological transformation to catch up or leapfrog to a knowledge-based economy (Fergany et al., 2003).

This chapter investigates the sufficient and necessary conditions for the urban knowledge-based development of GCC cities. The chapter investigates cities whose urban development is knowledge-based, then attempts to identify the challenges and opportunities for Knowledge-Based Urban Development (KBUD) in GCC given that globalization and emerging web-based technologies in the era of Internet offer new opportunities for the evolution of a new model of urban development that is innovative and sustainable. Recommendations for actions conclude the paper.

1.2. Attempts to Switch to KBUD

Recognizing their well-integration in the world economy, and need to limit their reliance on exporting oil and natural gas, GCC countries adopted various strategies to achieve their aim. According to macroeconomic indicators, all GCC countries have experienced relatively strong growth in the the non-oil economic sector. Expanding sectors included tourism; trade; infrastructures and construction; finance, insurance and real estate; and services (El-Ali, 2016). "To reduce its dependence on oil, the UAE has launched a diversification and liberalization program to transform the conventional labor-intensive economy to one based on knowledge, technology, and skilled labor … The impact of diversification is apparent: the contribution of the non-oil sector rose from 46 per cent of GDP in 1975 to 90 percent in 2000 and 95 per cent in 2005. The largest share gains were in the trade, construction and real estate sectors which, between 2000 and 2005, grew by 6.7, 4.1 and 2.3 per cent respectively" (UN-Habitat, 2012, p. 133).

There are various attempts in the region to develop a knowledge-based economy. Dubai Internet City is the location of 1,200 companies with more than 10 thousand employees providing business and community infrastructures for ICT (UN-Habitat, 2012). In 2008, Masdar City was developed on the hinterlands of Abu Dhabi to advance the clean energy industry in Abu Dhabi and around the world (Masdar City, n.d., 2008; The Guardian, n.d.). In Qatar, Education City, a 10 thousand sq. meters, was developed at the outskirts of Doha to be the hub of knowledge and research facilities by hosting the world's most prestigious universities and institutes (UN-Habitat, 2012).

The attempts of UAE to shift from hydrocarbon-based economy to a knowledge-based economy rests on three pillars: human capital, financial capital, and technological capital (Al-Jayyousi, 2015). Only at the juncture of these three pillars innovation can be possible (Byat & Sultan, 2014). UAE invested in telecommunications infrastructure and services, and education as well. The UAE has spent substantially on education and developing capabilities. The UAE allocates more than 20 percent of the total government budget for education, which is higher than the benchmark average, i.e., 13 percent. Also, UAE is attracting foreign talents. In 2013, immigrants represented 96 percent of the UAE workforce, and 99.5 percent of the four million that the private sector employed that year (Byat & Sultan, 2014).

Knowledge cities and their primary cities in GCC and other Arab countries seem to suffer a condition of "ectopic pregnancy." Developed Middle Eastern knowledge-based cities, such as Dubai's Internet City and Knowledge Village, and Qatar's Educational City and Science and Technology Oasis, are technologically isolated entities (Alraouf, 2014).

The force that results and shapes modern Gulf cities is the conceptual and/or physical interaction between sub-cities (mega-projects) and their primate cities (Bamakhrama, 2015). He noticed that it is common in cities of GCC, such as Dubai, Riyadh and Abu Dhabi, to find mega-projects given the name 'city' within their title. He first, examined the naming problem of the sub-city, as it demonstrates the tension between competing identities, thus generating a set of effects that could either emphasize or blur the overall urban image. Next, Bamakhrama (2015) tried to reveal how Dubai utilizes two seemingly conflicting growth strategies (sprawl and infill) to grow as a primate city and to integrate its sub-cities, i.e., mega projects mentioned earlier. Finally, he argued that Dubai's internal structure for urban management promotes good governance and decentralized decision-making.

2. CONDITIONS FOR KBUD

The Global and World Cities Research Network (GaWC) is research group that inquires about into the external relations of world urban settlements. According to GaWC, the World is a city-centered space of flows. Using a system of interlocked network model, the specialists at GaCW measure urban areas regarding their advanced producer services. Indirect assessments of flows are deducted to calculate a settlement's connectivity. It measures a city's integration into the global urban system. The connectivity measures are used to classify urban areas into levels of world city integration (Ago, 2015; Hu, 2015b; Ley & Newton, 2010; O'Connor, Derudder, & Witlox, 2015; Paganoni, 2015; Söderström, 2014). By building service values matrix for 175 leading advanced producer services firms across 526 urban areas, GaWC scientists could group these 526 urban areas into the accompanying classes:

1. Alpha++ cities, such as London and New York. They emerge clearly more engaged in global economy than other urban areas and establish their than all different urban areas and establish their own particular advanced level of reconciliation (Ago, 2015; Du & Ren, 2011; Hu, 2015a, 2015b; Ley & Newton, 2010; O'Connor et al., 2015; Söderström, 2014);
2. Alpha+ cities are those urban areas that are highly integrated and connected to the world economy. They complement the role of both London and New York, by filling-in advanced service needs of the global economy, particularly those of the Pacific Asia (Ago, 2015; Du & Ren, 2011; Hu, 2015a, 2015b; O'Connor et al., 2015; Söderström, 2014);
3. Alpha & alpha- cities are those cities that link major economic regions into the global economy (Ago, 2015; Du & Ren, 2011; Hu, 2015a, 2015b; O'Connor et al., 2015; Söderström, 2014);
4. All beta level cities are important world urban areas. They are influential in connecting their countries into the global economy (Ago, 2015; Du & Ren, 2011; Hu, 2015a, 2015b; O'Connor et al., 2015; Söderström, 2014);
5. All gamma level cities are cities that can be world urban communities. They can connect smaller locales of their nations into the world economy, or essential world urban communities whose major worldwide capacity is not in advanced producer service (Ago, 2015; Du & Ren, 2011; Hu, 2015a, 2015b; O'Connor et al., 2015; Söderström, 2014); and lastly;
6. Cities with the sufficiency of services are those urban settlements that are not world urban regions as GaWC portrayed. Instead, they have adequate administrations so as not to be unmistakably subject to world urban groups. Two particular characterizations of the city are fundamental at this level of consolidation smaller capital urban areas, and traditional manufacturing settlements (Ago, 2015; Du & Ren, 2011; Hu, 2015a; O'Connor et al., 2015; Söderström, 2014).

To conceptually identify the pillars of KBUD, it is essential to review experiences of cities of knowledge-based economy. Case study is a useful tool for examining development. Unlike extensive studies that look for commonalities and use sophisticated statistical methods, case study is an intensive inquiry of a specific status (Shuttleworth 2015). The following case studies are meant to induce the major attributes for knowledge-based urban development.

2.1. Case Studies

2.1.1. Boston, USA

Boston developed as port on the eastern coast of the USA. Boston and its metropolitan area is the location of world research institutes that is central to innovation. In 2012, Boston was among the alpha minus group of cities according to GaWC list. Boston is an important global city as it connects the northeastern states of the US into the world economy. According to the 2008 Location Quotient,[1] Boston's basic industries include hospitals, health care and social assistance, educational services, legal services, securities, insurance, and banking (Lima, Melnik, Avault, Blake, & Borella, 2011). All these industries depend on both knowledge and innovation.

2.1.2. Brisbane, Australia

Brisbane is a major Australian city and port, with rich architectural heritage, and the hub of major businesses, such as information technology, and biotechnology. The city is well connected to other settlements through various routes and modes of transportations. Brisbane is home to Australia's highest rated universities, namely University of Queensland (UQ), Queensland University of Technology (QUT) and Griffith University. Brisbane is the venue of several annual events, such as the Ekka (the Royal Queensland Exhibition), and world sports occasions, such as the 1987 Rugby World Cup, 1992 Cricket World Cup and 2024 Olympic Games. As part of its "Smart State" initiative, the Queensland State Government encouraged the expansion of technology and science industries in Brisbane and Queensland at large. The Government funded numerous biotechnology and research units at several universities in Brisbane (Brisbane City Council, n.d.; Mostafa & Mohamed, 2016; Queensland Government, n.d.; Yigitcanlar & Velibeyoglu, 2008).

2.1.3. Dortmund, Germany

Dortmund is an administrative, commercial and cultural hub located north of the Rhine. It used to be the home of German steel, coal and beer industries. Dortmund is the home of renowned educational institutions, such as the Technical University of Dortmund and Dortmund University of Applied Sciences and Arts, International School of Management. The economy of the city declined as a result of deindustrialization. In the early 1980s, the city moved to be the site of high innovative businesses. The city established a mono functional innovation hub at the outskirts of the city. Dortmund is building up another "new era" information hotspot on the Phoenix site, which used to be an industrial site close to the downtown area. Unlike to the first technology estate, this one is redeveloped blending various uses including housing, recreation, and other functions. To give it personality, the development is unequivocally connected to the industrial history of the region. Parts of the industrial heritage are saved and reconverted. This endeavor to safeguard or make "personality" is common for post-modern knowledge cities (City of Dortmund, 2015; van Winden, n.d., 2010).

2.1.4. Manchester

Manchester evolved as a port and major industrial center. During the 19th century, Manchester was known for cotton mills, textiles, and trade. The Cotton Exchange was developed in Manchester because of booming businesses. Following WWII, Manchester started to experience serious economic losses because of decline in cotton business. The Exchange closed in 1968. Today, the basic exporting economic sectors of Manchester, both its metropolitan area and region, include professional services, ICT, digital and biomedical knowledge. In 2009, Manchester and its region produced goods and services worth £30,890 million (URBACT, 2015).

2.1.5. Singapore

Singapore has a diverse population and rich culture. Singapore is a city-state, which was among the first generation of Asian tigers. Singapore is a financial and transportation hub. In 2016, Singapore ranked as number one country among 139 countries best prepared for the new digital economy (Breene, 2016). In 2014, Singapore scored 0.912 on the Human Development Index (HDI) with a per capita Gross Domestic Product (GDP) of $56,319 (UNDP, 2015).

"The multi-cultural Singaporean workforce is highly educated, highly motivated and highly productive. It is also proficient in English. An open immigration policy has served to enhance Singapore's talent pool. In the last decade, Singapore has successfully grown its R&D base, drawn top scientific and creative talent and nurtured R&D collaborations between the public sector and private enterprise. Today, Singapore holds global leadership positions in areas of manufacturing such as electronics and petrochemicals" (Singapore Economic Development Board, 2016).

In 2012, Singapore was on GaCW list ranked among the alpha plus category. It means that Singapore is one of the cities that are highly integrated into the global economy as it avails advanced service needs for the Pacific Asia region (Global and World Cities, 2016).

The Singaporean experience is relevant to GCC cities. Singapore is an island city-state that emerged as a port. In the 1960s, Singapore encouraged the development of manufacturing sector. Later, Singapore attracted oil companies, such as Shell and Esso, to establish oil refineries. The country capitalized on its location to expand tertiary sector, such as wholesale, transport, etc. Since the 1980s, the Government of Singapore experienced significant transformations that allowed opposition leaders to serve as members of the parliament.

Boston, Brisbane, Manchester, Singapore and other knowledge-based cities have several common characteristics and attributes. They have administrations of high agility to transform from industrial-based economy to knowledge-based economy, where the basic economic sector is no more manufacturing but services in the form of education and health, as in the case of Boston. The secret of such agility is in the administration and management of these cities to attract talents and human capital and to harness science and technological innovation for both prosperity and sustainability.

3. TRANSITION FROM INDUSTRIAL TO POST-INDUSTRIAL CITY

3.1. Modernism: The Garden City and City Beautiful Movements

In the wake of the industrial revolution, the city was the site of both innovation and industrial production. The environmental degradation and social injustice were clear symptoms of urban ills. The call for reforming the built environment came in the early 1990s. In Europe, Ebenezer Howard suggested the Garden City. In the USA Burnham and Frank Law Olmsted among others called for the City Beautiful movement. Both movements aimed to introduce beautification and monumental grandeur[2] in cities to develop moral and civic virtue among urban populations (Catanese, 1988; Foglesong, 2016). Cities, according to these theories, are planned in their entirety, nothing is left to chance. They are planned for mass production based on the concepts of economies of scale and agglomeration of economies, then flourish according to their comparative advantage.

In 1925, Burgess examined the internal structure of Chicago. He concluded that the internal structure of the city is based on a monocentric model where the city has Central Business District (CBD) from which prices of land, heights of buildings and densities (both population and buildings) decline with distance away from the CBD. The city consists of homogeneous functional zones, such as industry, commercial, services, and residence. Later, number of studies affirmed the monocentric model, such as that of Wingo (1961), Kain (1962), Alonso (1965), Mills (1967) and Muth (1969) developed several proofs of the model (Heilbrun, 1981; Hoover & Giarratani, 1984; Mills & Hamilton, 1989; Mohan, 1979). Both the sector model (1939) and multi-nuclei model (1945) were developed to complement and further enhance the monocentric model for an enhanced comprehension of the internal structure of the city (Harris & Ullman, 1945; Hoyt, 1939).

Notice these attempts associated with the rise of modernity and modernism where Western societies moved from the medieval era into another form of capitalism characterized by the rise of nation-state of democratic political institutions with strong industrial economic base. Urbanization is another facet of the modern age. The transition towards modernism entailed some cultural transformations, such as secular outlook, and demographic shifts, such as a sharp decline in population growth because of decline in birth and death rates, and entry of women all levels of employment and business. Probably the most important imperatives for the transition towards the modern age are innovation and scientific discoveries that associate with the use of technology thus requiring advanced, standardized education. This is not the case of Arab cities, particularly those of the GCC region, as the UNDP Human Development Report noted earlier in 2003.

3.2. The End of Modernism

In the mid-1970s, Pruitt-Igoe project, a public housing developed in the 1950s, was demolished. It marks the end of modernism in advanced industrial countries. The project was developed based on the concept of "form follows function." It reflected the anomalies of high-rise buildings and modern architecture and city planning at large.

In the 1960s, the civil rights movement gained momentum. In 1968, the civil unrest in France brought the economy to a break. Protests swept US cities demanding an end of the Vietnam war, which was never declared war. Labor unions turned to be powerful organizations. After 1973, the prices of petroleum increased dramatically. The environmental movement accelerated after publishing Carson's book, *Silent Spring*. The economies of Western countries started to face serious difficulties. It was time for a change.

3.3. Globalization: Another Phase of Capitalism

The response was a swing towards the right conservative side giving rise to Reagan and Thatcher in the USA and the UK leading to a new phase of capitalism known as globalization that availed the freedom of the flows of capital and labor beyond nationally defined boundaries. Production plants moved from cities of developed countries to those of developing countries. It was the dawn of the post-industrial city where the service sector generates more revenue and growth compared to manufacturing sectors.

The monocentric model explaining the internal structure of the city is no longer applicable for a post-industrial city, marking the emergence of a new paradigm. It was the time for the Los Angles School to replace the Chicago School, which is discussed later.

3.4. The Rise of Postmodernity: Neoliberalism Another Phase of Capitalism?

In the 1960s, postmodernism appeared as a cultural facet of post-industrial societies that affected numerous aspects including, but not limited to, architecture, media, education and the built-environment. After comparing modernism to post-modernism. Harvey (1989) argued that cultural, political and social changes were taking place since 1972 that associated with ways people experienced space and time. The time-space compression associated with the emergence of flexible modes of capital accumulation, which meant a change in the organization of capitalism. Once these changes are juxtaposed against the basic rules of capital accumulation, postmodernism is not an indication of a post-capitalist society (Harvey, 1989).

The Los Angeles School emerged in the 1980s to displace the Chicago School of Urbanism. The movement is grounded in the postmodernist movement. The writings of a diverse variety of neo-Marxist scholars, such as Soja, Davis, Dear, Scott and Flusty, dealt exclusively with Los Angeles. They attempted to explain both the form and culture of Los Angeles spreading into the desert and up- and down the coast. The economic base of Los Angeles changed. The services sector expanded while manufacturing plants migrated to cities of developing countries. The transformation of the economic base led to a growing city that encapsulated both contrasts and tensions. The scholars of the Los Angeles School argue that their city is a model of the twentieth and twenty-first centuries. Their writings depend on the work of theorists, such as Foucault, Baudrillard and Derrida, who associate with postmodernism.

The transformation of industrial societies into post-industrial societies means it is time for services, as an economic sector, to spearhead urban and regional economies. It is the era of cognitive–cultural capitalism. At the center of it is creativity and innovation is the processes of learning, and manifest in particular location patterns and social relations (Mahmoudi & Levenda, 2016; Scott, 2011, 2014). Cognitive–cultural capitalism is a strong conceptual framework to examine current processes of urbanization observed in cities today (Scott, 2014).

In sum, capitalism and its transformations were among the chief reasons for transformations in the epistemological foundations of the western city. However, oil-economy, consumerism and dependency models shaped cities in GCC; and limited their capacity to co-create and adapt locally rooted models of knowledge formation and urban development.

4. WHAT IS KNOWLEDGE-BASED URBAN DEVELOPMENT?

In 1996, the OECD defined the knowledge-based economy as those "directly based on the production, distribution, and use of knowledge and information" (Organisation for Economic Co-operation and Development, 1996, p. 7). High-technology investments, high-technology industries, more highly-skilled labor and associated productivity gains are among the attributes of knowledge-based economies that lead to enhanced productivity and economic growth (Roberts, 2009). Besides investing in knowledge, knowledge distribution through formal and informal networks is a necessary condition for economic performance that will increase demand for more highly-skilled workers. Last but not least is the science system that consists of public research laboratories and institutes of higher education responsible for vital functions in the knowledge-based economy, including knowledge production, transmission, and transfer (Organisation for Economic Co-operation and Development, 1996).

Based on the definition above, industrial economies can transform to become a knowledge-based economy only when manufacturing processes are founded on producing, utilizing and distributing information and knowledge (Rittgasszer, 2013). Yigitcanlar and Lönnqvist (2013) argued that in addition to low-priced labor and natural resources, knowledge, as a special resource, is turning to spearhead a city's competitive advantage. Only when the city is capable of advancing and using its knowledge resource to develop new and innovative products, then the city can easily respond to challenges resulting from the knowledge-based economy (Yigitcanlar & Lönnqvist, 2013).

To assess and compare the comparative advantage of a knowledge-based city, it is of utmost importance to first examine its institutional framework as it determines its future vision. Studying the institutional framework of the city is crucial for other three dimensions, i.e., economic, social-cultural, and territorial (both natural and built environments) dimensions. The institutional framework of a city, i.e., a structure for urban governance and management, supports interventions to improve the other three areas. Second, is to investigate its economic base to assess its knowledge capital. In this case, knowledge is not treated as an exogenous element of development, but a key endogenous resource necessary for economic growth (Yigitcanlar & Lönnqvist, 2013). The third dimension is a social-cultural dimension. It is the residents' competencies central for community development. Human and social capital is important for a knowledge-based economy of specific characteristics including, but not limited to accepting diversity and social justice (Yigitcanlar & Lönnqvist, 2013). The fourth dimension is territorial (Yigitcanlar & Lönnqvist, 2013). The environmental-urban dimension aims to balance amongst preserving and improving the built and natural environment, which develops a robust, knowledge-cluster based development path towards sustainable urban development thus improving the quality of life (Yigitcanlar & Lönnqvist, 2013). Using this four-dimensional criterion, Yigitcanlar and Lönnqvist (2013) were able to compare Helsinki, Finland, to a set of post-industrial cities, mainly Boston, San Francisco, Birmingham, Manchester, Melbourne, Sydney, Toronto, and Vancouver:

The results of the study not only reveal a clearer understanding of Helsinki's benchmarked performance and competitive edge considering the regional policy context along with strategic directions in strengthening its international standing and competitiveness but also provide useful insights for other urban regions that aspire to such development. (Yigitcanlar & Lönnqvist, 2013, p. 357)

Urban development associates with the ability to bind various kinds of energy for human prosperity and progress. Energy has a critical role in defining and shaping the urban development, the governance of cities and even the extent of innovation in the urban space and built environment. The emergence of fossil oil in the early 20th century resulted in urban sprawl, the gap between rural and urban development models and imbalance in urban development. However, with the innovations of ICT and concerns of environment and climate change, a transition to green energy informed new urban development models including e-city, eco-city, and smart city. There is a strong historical connection between human security, energy use, and the urban development and knowledge economy. However, in an era of globalization, information technology, and sustainability, the question becomes: can renewable energy provide a new paradigm in KBUD in the Middle East?

GCC countries, such as the United Arab Emirates (UAE), Qatar and Saudi Arabia, have planned and are implementing strategies to shift to renewable energy and a knowledge-based economy. This move is likely to introduce a new paradigm in urban development that is strengthened by knowledge, decentralized modes of energy delivery like Feed-in-Tariff (FIT) and new roles for the private sector and the support for SMEs in green technologies (Al-Jayyousi, 2015). The model of Masdar City in the UAE is a testimony of adopting and diffusing clean technology. This model needs, however, to be tested to draw lessons learned and best practices for replication.

Knowledge-based urban development (KBUD) implies organizational and social learning processes and harnessing of both common knowledge and ICT technology conducive for informed decisions regarding energy efficiency, technology transfer, investment policy in renewable energy, land use, zoning and urban development. Besides, a shift from a model of Rentier States to KBUD associates with policies related to green building, green technology, and green economy and green growth.

The resilience and sustainability of cities depend on the ability to balance between economic, social and ecological components. At the heart of this balance is the institutional framework that governs relationships between these three spheres. As presented earlier, producing, utilizing and distributing information and knowledge are central to manufacturing processes that is a *sine qua non* for economic growth and development. If knowledge is important for manufacturing development, and economic advancement at large, then proper administration and management are essential for the city to be able to re-discover its potentials and change its economic base.

5. CHALLENGES AND OPPORTUNITIES

Historically, GCC countries were subjected to the Dutch disease, "a phenomenon reflecting changes in the structure of production in the wake of a favorable shock (such as a large natural resource discovery, a rise in the international price of an exportable commodity, or the presence of sustained aid or capital inflows)" (Brahmbhatt, Canuto, & Vostroknutova, 2010, p. 1). In the past, as mentioned earlier, they depended on trade and transportation, then the pearl industry, and now the production and exporting oil. However, they have learnt the lesson. They are determined to diversify their economic base and transform their economies from oil-dependency to knowledge-based economy.

GCC countries, as other countries of the Arab world, need to move away from the rentier state, as it has serious implications for the economy and society at large. "Rentier state theory (RST) is a political economy theory that seeks to explain state-society relations in states that generate a large proportion of their income from rents, or externally-derived, unproductively-earned payments" (Gray, 2011, p. 1). The economy of a rentier state depends on exporting raw material, such as oil, where this exporting economic sector employs few native population. In 1990, Beblawi noticed that the oil boom since the 1970s had had a significant impact on Arab countries, both oil and non-oil producing countries. Arab countries transformed into rentier states, yet at various levels, where "income is no longer a reward of serious and hard work, it is very often related to special circumstances, chances, location, etc. In a word, we are living in a rentier universe which has affected both the state and the citizen" (Beblawi, 1990, p. 98).

The key challenges and opportunities for GCC to make a transition to the knowledge-based economy may be summarized as follows.

5.1. Dependency on Oil Exports and Regional Instabilities

Political and economic instability due, in part, to fluctuations of oil prices and armed conflicts in the Middle East is a challenge for GCC countries that hinders their ability for long term planning. In the 21st century, as GCC countries endeavor to compete in a global economy, they confront various challenges. Atop of these difficulties are fluctuating oil and gas prices, the rise of cleaner sources of energy, the need to diversify the economic base, and a growing population that will require natural resources, such as freshwater; social services, such as education and health care; and physical infrastructures, such as roads and sewerage, to continue developing human capital and generate jobs for GCC residents. To tackle these difficulties, the Arab Gulf states are shifting gear towards knowledge-based economic development. To enhance human capital, GCC countries continue to invest in education, ICT, and Science, Technology, and Innovation (STI). However, there is an opportunity to capitalize on benefits from these investments, and there are numerous open doors for GCC states to make use of knowledge-based economic development (Tadros, 2015).

Furthermore, the scene in the Arab world is changing and presenting GCC countries with opportunities. Since the 1980s, a delicate but continual shift has been taking place in the centers of the Middle East of economic, commercial, diplomatic, and political importance swinging gradually away from the Levant and North Africa and toward the Arabian Gulf region (Kamrava, 2015; Kamrava et al., 2015). There are several reasons for such transformation. Atop of these reasons is the political instability. Egypt, Syria, and Iraq have been unstable for the past decade. Iraq and Syria were subject to economic sanctions since the 1990s. Egypt started experiencing political instabilities since the mid-2000s. These countries, together with Lebanon, which is not politically stable either, used to be the centers of innovation and creativity in the Arab region. They used to publish more books, and produce more art than other countries in the region. The second reason is the economic and financial conditions in these countries push educated professionals outside their countries to Western countries, and the GCC region seeking better pay, and improved working conditions regarding laboratories, equipment, assistants, funds and so forth.

5.2. Human Capital and Education Infrastructure

Inadequate human capital and education infrastructure and systems that enhance critical thinking, research, and innovation capacity are among the serious challenges to transform the economy of GCC cities to be based on knowledge. One central aspect of launching and sustaining an innovative environment is attracting foreign talents. In 2013, Immigrants constituted 96 percent of the total workforce of UAE. They represented 99.5 percent of the UAE's four million employees working for private-sector companies (Byat & Sultan, 2014).

Despite the above challenges, several opportunities exist if a purposeful and systematic reform is carried out to address the root causes of these challenges. These include a reform in the STI governance, investment in education and STI, supporting an enabling environment for knowledge creation, sustainability, and citizenship.

Some positive developments toward a knowledge economy are already taking place. For example, GCC countries invested in educating younger generations. The UAE allocated more than 20 percent of total government budget for education, which is more than the target average of 13 percent (Byat & Sultan, 2014).

These measures depict the quantitative aspects that result from reforms in education. On the qualitative side, there have been attempts to enhance the quality of education and research in the GCC countries. In debates concerned with modern knowledge economies concepts, such as education and universities, besides biotechnology, intellectual property, and ICT development, are usually examined with little intensive critical analysis. Facing fierce competition in international markets and the flow of intellectual capital, the concept of the role of primary, secondary and tertiary education will necessarily be transformed in developing countries (Weber, 2011). Liberal studies and the possibility of instruction as the planning for good citizenship, self-revelation, and self-satisfaction are being reexamined within national training needs. For this reason, Qatar Foundation's Education City is committed to meet part of the present and future training inside the setting of the learning economies of MENA and the Arabian Gulf (Weber, 2011).

The result is developed human resources, Table 1. The HDI rank and scores reflect improved per capita GDP and the investments that States of GCC countries have allocated for education and health services. The States of GCC countries invested in infrastructures, particularly drinking water, wastewater management facilities, and electricity. Further, the States of GCC invested in ICT infrastructures, and have taken steps to avail many governmental services electronically that depend on the high quality of human resources. If GCC countries lack key natural resources, such as freshwater, they have human resources that can represent an opportunity for development plans in the future.

The report of GaWC released in 2012, and mentioned earlier, included nine cities from the GCC countries, Table 2. Dubai was listed as an alpha + city as it is highly integrated into the world economy. It complements the role of both London and New York and serves the needs of Pacific Asia. Another

Table 1. GCC countries on the HDI, 2014

Country	Score 2014	HDI Rank 2014	Rank 2014
Bahrain	0.824	VH	45
Kuwait	0.816	VH	48
Oman	0.793	H	52
Qatar	0.850	VH	32
Saudi Arabia	0.837	VH	39
United Arab Emirates	0.835	VH	41

Source: UNDP (2015)

Table 2. GCC cities according to their level of connectivity, 2012

	City	Group	Description
1	Dubai, UAE	Alpha +	Highly integrated city that complements London and New York, largely filling in advanced service needs for the Pacific Asia.
2	Riyadh, Saudi Arabia	Beta	Important world cities. They are instrumental in linking their region or state into the world economy.
3	Doha, Qatar	Beta	
4	Abu Dhabi, UAE	Beta -	
5	Manama, Bahrain	Beta -	
6	Kuwait City, Kuwait	Beta -	
7	Jeddah, Saudi Arabia	Gamma +	Cities are those who can be world cities linking smaller regions or states into the world economy, or important world cities whose major global capacity is not in advanced producer services.
8	Muscat, Oman	Gamma	
9	Dammam, Saudi Arabia	Sufficiency	Cities that are not world cities as defined here but they have sufficient services so as not to be overtly dependent on world cities. Two specialized categories of the city are common at this level of integration: smaller capital cities, and traditional centers of manufacturing regions.

Source: The World According to GaWC 2012

five cities are listed as beta cities as indicated in Table 2. This situation is another outcome of the efforts and funds the States of GCC countries invested in both the people and the place.

The results of the 2014 GII[3] indicate that GCC countries are atop their neighbors, except Israel. The UAE, Saudi Arabia, and Qatar lead Arab countries. They came atop the list of Arab countries. Countries that used to be leading the Arab world, such as Egypt, came in a lower rank or did not make it to the list, Table 3. These results indicate that the GCC countries are ample to be the centers of creativity and innovation.

In 2015, Tadros highlighted and reviewed knowledge-based economy, the information society, innovation ecosystem, and key Science and Technology Indicators (STI) for selected countries, including the GCC states, and compared them with the BRICS group of countries (Tadros, 2015).[4] Additionally, he then compared the performance of GCC and BRICS countries regarding The Networked Readiness Index 2015, The Global Innovation Index 2014, Key STI Indicators, and the Doing Business 2015: Going Beyond Efficiency (Tadros, 2015).

5.3. Enabling Environment

Establishing an enabling environment for the manufacturing of knowledge in urban development stems from adopting the principles of good urban governance for social equity, diversified economy, renewable energy, and public participation. GCC countries have to build a business-friendly environment characterized by the rule of law, transparency and accountability, funding mechanisms and venture capital to generate job opportunities for GCC residents, and attract creative and talented businesspersons and visionaries market has proven research output and groundbreaking concepts (Tadros, 2015).

Table 3. Rank and score of GCC countries and their neighbors on GII, 2014

Country	Score (0–100)	Rank	Income	Efficiency Ratio
Israel	55.46	15	HI	0.79
Cyprus	45.82	30	HI	0.77
United Arab Emirates	43.25	36	HI	0.54
Saudi Arabia	41.61	38	HI	0.74
Qatar	40.31	47	HI	0.60
Turkey	38.20	54	UM	0.93
Bahrain	36.26	62	HI	0.60
Jordan	36.21	64	UM	0.80
Kuwait	35.19	69	HI	0.78
Oman	33.87	75	HI	0.58
Lebanon	33.60	77	UM	0.59
Egypt	30.03	99	LM	0.76
Iran, Islamic Republic of	26.14	120	UM	0.57

Note: (HI) High Income; (UM) Upper-middle Income; (LM) Lower Middle Income
Source: Dutta, S., Lanvin, B., & Wunsch-Vincent, S. (2014)

Realizing and revitalizing the notion of culture as a creative asset is stressed in the work of Landry (2008) when he asserts the importance of culture as a creative resource. Florida (2002) stressed the idea that "place is the key economic and social organizing unit of our time" since it creates a sense of meaning and purpose for people, environment, and economy. Establishing an enabling ecosystem for culture-based urban development is essential for KBUD. This requires a process of combination and internalization of tacit and explicit knowledge that determine the capacity of an organization to learn as depicted in Figure 3 (Nonaka, 1994, 1997, 2007; Takeuchi & Nonaka, 1995). Having a shared vision for the identity of urban development in GCC, absorbing lessons learned from best practices worldwide, instilling a culture of R&D on regional priorities to develop a "an innovative region", and localizing a model of urban development that resonate with culture and ecology is key for an enlightened model for KBUD in GCC.

6. CONCLUSION, RECOMMENDATIONS AND PLANNING IMPLICATIONS

The necessary conditions to transform the GCC countries to KBUD include a transformation of city governance, aligning education to regional vision, building a knowledge base for best practices, and strategic alliances in STI and green energy. However, knowledge creation in an urban context is framed by institutional context, history, and culture. It is evident that in GCC there is a disconnect between the four pillars of innovation; i.e., Individual, Community, Organization and National (ICON)) at one level and there is also another disconnect at the core as manifested in dislocation of culture and ecology from urban development as manifested in technical and economic innovation. These two systemic and structural barriers limit the propensity to develop a KBUD.

Figure 3. Model for knowledge co-creation in support of KBUD
Source: Al-Jayyousi (2015)

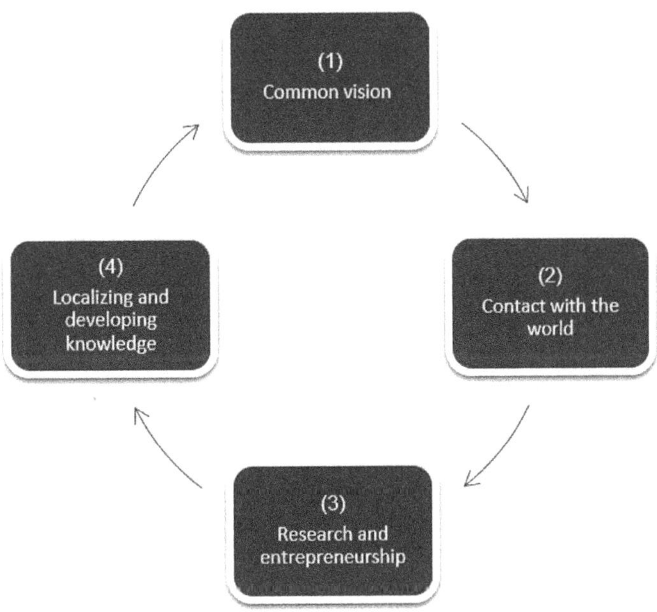

The enablers for KBUD in the cities of GCC lie on enhancing quality education in urban planning, supporting civic intelligence and nurturing reflective practitioners. Identifying and unlocking the potential for the individual lies at the heart of KBUD. The innovative individual (or knowledge worker) is the catalyst and lever for re-connecting the city and community with organizational and societal learning processes. Learning organizations are the cornerstone for establishing a KBUD since they ensure connectivity between individuals, cities, organizations, and the national system of innovation. A key characteristic of a learning organization includes having a shared vision, team learning, system thinking, and capacity for knowledge-creation. Realizing and operationalizing a regional model for learning and creative cities requires the formation of research alliances and research teams in GCC to capitalize on resources and to focus R&D on relevant and regional priorities.

The transition to a green economy in GCC is part of an ecological modernization which is a key reform to be embodied in GCC at all levels to overcome the "Dutch disease syndrome". This in turn will result in a transformation of city governance and mental models for KBUD. Moreover, it is noteworthy that the post-hydrocarbon era is likely to witness a shift in governance structures and the center of gravity in alliances between GCC and emerging economic block like BRICS. The creation of international organizations and knowledge-based models and green energy such as IRENA and MASDAR city and Qatar Foundation in Qatar and KACST in KSA provide a hub for "sustainability-innovation" nexus which will inform a KBUD model for GCC including eco-cities, green building, green SMEs, green technology, and green industry and infrastructure.

On the other hand, it is imperative to reform the urban planning education and praxis to respond to the rational imperatives of KBUD; i.e., sustainability, equity, and innovation. Planners need to acquire the following three competencies:

1. Analytical knowledge, such as environmental science, for technical actions;
2. Hermeneutic knowledge, such as economics, political sciences, and sociology, for communicative actions central to arbitration, negotiation and mediation needed to reach a solution that is viable and acceptable;
3. Critical knowledge, such as ethics and philosophy, needed for planners to emancipate from their biases, and to work with the people not for them, by showing them the way through enabling and empowerment.

The following are a set of recommendations.

6.1. An Enabling Environment for the Knowledge Transfer

It is recommended to develop and instill a culture of STI in GCC through forming research groups and alliances to contribute to KBUD. These STI alliances are likely to enhance the scale and velocity of knowledge co-creation and cross-fertilization, which in turn will inform sustainable innovation and education models that will transform the urban development practice in GCC. It is critical to benefit from models of KBUD worldwide (like models in Boston, Singapore, etc.) which harness technology, knowledge, and innovation for sustainability.

Besides, the paradigm of KBUD emerges from a mental model for a livable and creative city. Hence, the interplay between the five capitals; i.e., human, social, natural, manufactured, business, and intellectual is key for GCC regional model of urban development. Also, a community of practice is a basic lever and enabler for knowledge creation in urban development. There are several necessary conditions to ensure a proper embodiment of KBUD models which include reform of education and practice of urban development, good urban governance systems, and a culture of innovation and inquiry. This enabling environment provides fertile opportunities for knowledge creation from the interaction of reflective practitioners with policy makers and civil society.

6.2. Transition to a Knowledge-Based and Green Economy in GCC

The climate change commitments and the global argument for peak oil is leading the policy debate in GCC to make a transition to renewable energy. This shift in policy is reflected in practice and civil society debate in green growth and green economy. The ecological footprints and velocity and scale of pollution, desertification, species extinction, and waste production are compounded to shape a new discourse for KBUD within "sustainability-innovation" nexus. The implications for such a transition are compelling regarding the developmental models in the GCC, consumption patterns, green SMEs, green technology, and cleaner production. A macro- shift in the economy, society and ecology is emerging at many fronts in GCC as illustrated knowledge-based hubs and green technology in MASDAR city and Qatar Foundation and KACST.

Besides, a transition to a low carbon economy in GCC associates with knowledge creation and new governance of natural resources. This shift is likely to have deep implications regarding innovation policy, green construction, and the paradigm of teaching engineering and urban planning at the university level. It is recommended to enhance the organizational capacity in GCC to cope with global changes regarding climate change and technological innovations in green building and renewable energy.

6.3. New Global Partnerships for Knowledge, Innovation, and Energy

The globalization forces and the impact of the culture of the post-industrial era along with the shift in global energy markets, compel the formation of new alliances in the GCC. New entrants to the green construction and energy markets will define a new era of urban development and open innovation. These deep and radical transformations in market and policy in hydrogen, solar and wind energy will inform new practice for KBUD. KBUD is underpinned having a culture of innovation and knowledge creation that help to complete the triangle of knowledge, science, and research. However, to instill a culture of learning, reflection, and a KBUD, it is necessary to develop information assets and knowledge base for ensuring sustainable development and innovation.

REFERENCES

Abu-Lughod, J., & Hay, R. Jr. (1977). *Third World Urbanization*. London, UK: Methuen and Co. Ltd.

Ago, A. (2015). Global Cities vs Other Cities in Europe. In G. Mattarocci & D. Pekdemir (Eds.), *European Real Estate: Asset Class Performance and Optimal Portfolio Construction Asset Class Performance and Optimal Portfolio Construction* (pp. 43–66). London: Palgrave Macmillan UK; doi:10.1057/9781137436122_3

Al Beblawi, H. (1990). The Rentier State in the Arab World. In G. Luciani (Ed.), *The Arab State* (pp. 85–98). London, UK: Routledge.

Al-Jayyousi, O. (2015). *Renewable Energy in the Arab World - Transfer of Knowledge and Prospects for Arab Cooperation*. Amman, Jordan: Friedrich Ebert Stiftung; doi:10.1007/s13398-014-0173-7.2

Bamakhrama, S. S. (2015). *Cities within Cities: An Urbanization Approach in the Gulf Countries*. Los Angeles, CA: University of California.

Berry, B. J. L. (1961). City Size Distributions and Economic Development. *Economic Development and Cultural Change*, *9*(4), 573–588. doi:10.1086/449923

Bonine, M. E. (1983). Cities of the Middle East and North Africa. In S. D. Brunn & J. F. Williams (Eds.), *Cities of the World, World Regional Urban Development*. New York, NY: Harper & Row, Publishers.

Brahmbhatt, M., Canuto, O., & Vostroknutova, E. (2010). *Dealing with Dutch Disease A Model of Dutch Disease* (Poverty Reduction and Economic Management (PREM) No. 16). Retrieved from www.worldbank.org/economicpremise

Breene, K. (2016). *The countries best prepared for the new digital economy*. Retrieved October 28, 2016, from https://www.weforum.org/agenda/2016/07/countries-best-prepared-for-the-new-digital-economy/

Brisbane City Council. (n.d.). *Welcome to Brisbane City*. Retrieved from https://www.brisbane.qld.gov.au/

Byat, A. B., & Sultan, O. (2014). The United Arab Emirates: Fostering a Unique 101 Innovation Ecosystem for a Knowledge-Based Economy. In S. Dutta, B. Lanvin, & S. Wunsch-Vincent (Eds.), *The Global Innovation Index 2014: The Human Factor in Innovation*. (pp. 101–112). Cornell University, INSEAD, and the World Intellectual Property Organization (WIPO).

Catanese, A. J. (1988). Evolution and Trends. In A. J. Catanese & J. Snyder (Eds.), *Urban Planning* (pp. 3–64). New York: McGraw Hill Company.

City of Dortmund. (2015). *PHOENIX Dortmund - enter a location into the future*. Retrieved from http://www.phoenixdortmund.de/de/home/index.html

Drucker, P. F. (2003a). *Peter Drucker on the profession of management*. Harvard Business School Press.

Drucker, P. F. (2003b). *The Essential Drucker*. New York: Harper Business. Retrieved from http://books.google.com/books?id=bpy7KvlKOv4C&pgis=1

Du, J., & Ren, J. (2011). An economic view on Beijing's construction of a world city. In *2011 International Conference on E-Business and E-Government (ICEE)* (pp. 1–4). Shanghai, China: IEEE.doi:10.1109/ICEBEG.2011.5876668

El-Ali, H. (2016, August 14). Economic diversification and job creation in the Gulf States. *Al-Yaum*. Retrieved from http://www.alyaum.com/article/4151670

El-Arifi, S. A. (1986). The Nature of Urbanization in the Gulf Countries on JSTOR. *GeoJournal*, *13*(3), 223–235. doi:10.1007/BF00704813

El-Kholei, A. O., & Wahbi, S. (2010). Human Settlements. In A. F. Abdel Kadr & M. S. Abido (Eds.), *Environmental Outlook for Arab Region* (pp. 131–165). Nairobi, Kenya: United Nations Environment Programme, CEDARE and League of Arab States. Retrieved from http://eoar.cedare.int/report/EOAR_Full Report (EN).pdf

El-Shakhs, S. (1972). Development, primacy and systems of cities. *Journal of Developing Areas*, (7): 11–36. PMID:12312642

Fergany, N., Bennani, F., Elsadda, H., Jadaane, F., & Kubursi, A. (2003). *The Arab Human Development Report 2003*. Retrieved from http://hdr.undp.org/sites/default/files/rbas_ahdr2003_en.pdf

Foglesong, R. E. (2016). *Planning the Capitalist City: The Colonial Era to the 1920s*. Princeton, NJ: Princeton University Press. doi:10.1002/9781119084679.ch5

Gray, M. (2011). *A Theory of "Late Rentierism" in the Arab States of the Gulf* (Occasional Paper No. 7). Retrieved from https://repository.library.georgetown.edu/bitstream/handle/10822/558291/CIRSOccasionalPaper7MatthewGray2011.pdf?sequence=5

Harris, C. D., & Ullman, E. L. (1945). The Nature of Cities. *The Annals of the American Academy of Political and Social Science: Building the Future City*, *242*(1), 7–17. doi:10.1177/000271624524200103

Harvey, D. (1989). *The Condition of Postmodernity*. Oxford, UK: Basil Blackwell.

Heilbrun, J. (1981). *Urban Economics and Public Policy (2nd ed.)*. New York, NY: St. Martin's Press.

Hoover, F., & Giarratani, E. (1984). *An Introduction to Regional Economics* (3rd ed.). New York, NY: Alfred A. Knopf.

Hoyt, H. (1939). *The Structure and Growth of Residential Neighbourhoods in American Cities*. Washington, DC: Academic Press.

Hu, R. (2015a). Competitiveness, Migration, and Mobility in the Global City: Insights from Sydney, Australia. *Economies*, *3*(1), 37–54. doi:10.3390/economies3010037

Hu, R. (2015b). Sustainable Development Strategy for the Global City: A Case Study of Sydney. *Sustainability*, *7*(4), 4549–4563. doi:10.3390/su7044549

Jayne, M., & Bell, D. (2009). Urban Order. *International Encyclopedia of Human Geography*, 70–76.

Kamrava, M. (2015). Contemporary Port Cities in the Persian Gulf: Local Gateways and Global Networks. In M. Kamrava, A. Keshavarzian, S. Ramos, A. Kanna, A. M. Salama, F. Wiedmann, & M. Bontenbal (Eds.), *Gateways to the World: Port Cities in the Gulf*. Doha, Qatar: Center for International and Regional Studies.

Kamrava, M., Keshavarzian, A., Ramos, S., Kanna, A., Salama, A. M., Wiedmann, F., … Bontenbal, M. (2015). *Gateways to the World: Port Cities in the Gulf*. Doha, Qatar: Academic Press.

Ley, A., & Newton, P. (2010). Creating and Sustaining Liveable Cities. In K. Seetharam & B. Yuen (Eds.), *Developing Living Cities: From Analysis to Action* (pp. 191–229). Singapore: World Scientific Publishing and Imperial College Press. doi:10.1142/9789814304504_0008

Lima, A., Melnik, M., Avault, J., Blake, N. D., & Borella, N. (2011). *Boston by Numbers*. Boston, MA: Boston Redevelopment Authority. Retrieved from http://www.bostonredevelopmentauthority.org/getattachment/946803b2-6f1c-40b2-8b6b-c01c8c4bced1/

Mahmoudi, D., & Levenda, N. (2016). *Beyond the screen: Uneven geographies, Digital Labour, and the city of Cognitive-Cultural Capitalism*. Academic Press.

Masdar City. (2008). *Masdar City at a glance: Key buildings*. Academic Press.

Masdar City. (n.d.). *Pioneering Innovation at Masdar City. Academic Press.*

Mills, E. S., & Hamilton, B. W. (1989). *Urban Economics (4th ed.)*. Boston: Scott, Foreman and Company.

Mohan, R. (1979). *Urban Economic and Planning Models*. Baltimore, MD: Johns Hopkins University Press.

Mostafa, A. M., & Mohamed, K. Y. (2016). An Approach for Promoting Urban and Architectural Potentials for Supporting Knowledge Economy, Case Study: Brisbane. *Procedia - Social and Behavioral Sciences, 216*, 20–29. doi:10.1016/j.sbspro.2015.12.003

Nonaka, I. (1994). *A Dynamic Theory of Organizational Knowledge Creation*. Retrieved from http://www.jstor.org/stable/2635068

Nonaka, I. (1997). Nonaka's Four Modes of Knowledge Conversion. In *Knowledge Advantage Conference*. Retrieved from http://www.uky.edu/~gmswan3/575/nonaka.pdf

Nonaka, I. (2007). The Knowledge-Creating Company. *Harvard Business Review*. Retrieved from https://hbr.org/2007/07/the-knowledge-creating-company

O'Connor, K., Derudder, B., & Witlox, F. (2015). Logistics Services: Global Functions and Global Cities. *Growth and Change, 47*(4), 481–496. doi:10.1111/grow.12136

Organisation for Economic Co-operation and Development. (1996). *The Knowledge-based Economy*R-etrieved from https://www.oecd.org/sti/sci-tech/1913021.pdf

Paganoni, M. C. (2015). Introduction — City Branding and New Media: Linguistic, Discursive and Semiotic Aspects. In *City Branding and New Media* (pp. 1–12). London: Palgrave Macmillan UK. doi:10.1057/9781137387967_1

Queensland Government. (n.d.). *Brisbane, Queensland, Australia*. Retrieved October 22, 2016, from http://www.queensland.com/en-us/explore-queensland/brisbane

Ramadan, E. (2015). Sustainable Urbanization in the Arabian Gulf Region: Problems and Challenges. *Citation: Ramadan E Arts Social Sci J, 64172*(10910), 2151–6200. doi:10.4172/2151

Riad, M. (1983). The Arabian Gulf and Its People Prior to 1930. *The Gulf and Arabian Peninsula Studies, 9*(26), 215–398.

Riad, M. (1985). Some Aspects of Petro-Urbanism in the Gulf States. *Arabia Gulf Studies, 37*, 63–84.

Rittgasszer, I. (2013). Knowledge-based Urban Development, as a New Development Paradigm. *University of Szeged, Doctoral School in Economics*, 36–46.

Roberts, J. (2009). The global knowledge economy in question. *Critical Perspectives on International Business*, *5*(4), 285–303. doi:10.1108/17422040911003033

Scott, A. J. (2011). Emerging cities of the third wave. *City*, *15*(3–4), 289–321. doi:10.1080/13604813.2011.595569

Scott, A. J. (2014). Beyond the Creative City: Cognitive–Cultural Capitalism and the New Urbanism. *Regional Studies*, *48*(4), 565–578. doi:10.1080/00343404.2014.891010

Singapore Economic Development Board. (2016). *Knowledge-Based Economy*. Retrieved October 29, 2016, from https://www.edb.gov.sg/content/edb/en/why-singapore/about-singapore/values/knowledge.html

Smith, C. (1985a). Class relations and urbanization in Guatemala: Toward an Alternative Theory of Urban Primacy. In M. Timberlake (Ed.), *Urbanization in the World-Economy* (pp. 121–167). New York, NY: Academic Press.

Smith, C. (1985b). Theories and Measures of Urban Primacy: A Critque. In M. Timberlake (Ed.), *Urbanization in the World-Economy* (pp. 87–117). New York, NY: Academic Press.

Söderström, O. (2014). Trajectories of Urban Change in Two Ordinary Cities. In *Cities in Relations* (pp. 31–59). Oxford, UK: John Wiley & Sons, Ltd.; doi:10.1002/9781118632758.ch2

Tadros, M. E. (2015). *The Arab Gulf States and the Knowledge Economy: Challenges and Opportunities*. Washington, DC: Academic Press.

Takeuchi, H., & Nonaka, I. (1995). *The Knowledge Creating Company*. Oxford, UK: Oxford University Press.

The Guardian. (n.d.). *World's first zero-carbon city: Masdar in pictures*. Retrieved from https://www.theguardian.com/environment/gallery/2011/apr/26/masdar-eco-city-abu-dhabi

UN-Habitat. (2012). *The State of Arab Cities 2012 Challenges of Urban Transition*. Retrieved from http://www.citiesalliance.org/sites/citiesalliance.org/files/SOAC-2012.pdf

UNDESA. (2014). *World Urbanization Prospects: The 2014 Revision, Highlights. New York, United*. New York, NY: United Nations, Department of Economic and Social Affairs, Population Division. Retrieved from https://esa.un.org/unpd/wup/Publications/Files/WUP2014-Highlights.pdf

UNDP. (2015). *Human Development Report 2015*. New York, NY: Work for Human Development.

United Nations Department of Economic and Social Affairs. (2005). *Understanding Knowledge Societies*. Retrieved from https://publicadministration.un.org/publications/content/PDFs/E-Library Archives/2005 Understanding Knowledge Societies.pdf

United Nations Development Programme. (2006). *Knowledge Services and Learning*. New York, NY: United Nations. Retrieved from http://content-ext.undp.org/aplaws_publications/1463060/Knowledge-Services-Learning.pdf

URBACT. (2015). *Manchester*. Retrieved October 28, 2016, from http://urbact.eu/manchester

van Winden, W. (2010). Knowledge and the European City. *Tijdschrift voor Economische en Sociale Geografie*, *101*(1), 100–106. doi:10.1111/j.1467-9663.2009.00591.x

van Winden, W. (n.d.). *Urban knowledge economies affected by the crisis?* Retrieved from http://urbact.eu/sites/default/files/import/general_library/article-WINDEN_01.pdf

Weber, A. S. (2011). The role of education in knowledge economies in developing countries. In *3rd World Conference on Educational Sciences* (Vol. 15, pp. 2589–2594). Elsevier Science, B. V. doi:10.1016/j.sbspro.2011.04.151

Yigitcanlar, T., & Lönnqvist, A. (2013). Benchmarking knowledge-based urban development performance: Results from the international comparison of Helsinki. *Cities*, *31*, 357–369. doi:10.1016/j.cities.2012.11.005

Yigitcanlar, T., & Velibeyoglu, K. (2008). Knowledge-Based Urban Development: The Local Economic Development Path of Brisbane, Australia. *Local Economy*, *23*(3), 195–207. doi:10.1080/02690940802197358

ENDNOTES

1 Location Quotient is a ratio of the products per economic sector (i) in a city to the total goods and services the city produced divided by the products per economic sector (i) at the national level to the total goods and services the nation produced. If the ratio is greater than one, then that economic sector is basic, if less than the economic sector is service. Basic economic sectors are economic sectors that export their products and services. They are the economic sectors that spearhead the economy of the city and its region.

2 Upon embarking on preparing the plan for Chicago, Illinois following a destructive fire in 1906, Burnham's planning principle was "make no small plans."

3 The Global Innovation Index (GII) 2014 examines 143 economies around the world using 81 indicators covering an array of issues. It is useful in analyzing global innovation trends (Soumitra Dutta, Lanvin, & Wunsch-Vincent, 2014).

4 Brazil, Russia (Russian Federation), India, China, and South Africa.

Compilation of References

Abdel Raouf, A. (2014). Social inclusion between identity dilemmas and the trap of globalization: The challenges and transformations of the modern Gulf city of Amran. In *The Dialectic of social inclusion, state and nation-building in the Arab nation*. Arab Centre for Research and Policy Study.

Abdelhalim, K. (2010). Participatory upgrading of informal areas: a decision-maker's guide of action. Cairo: Participatory Development Program in Urban Areas (PDP) in Egypt.

Abdullah, M., & Atar, M. (2006). *Souq Waqif.* Doha: Al Diwan Al Amiri.

Abu-Anzeh, N., & Ledraa, T. (2007). Planning the Knowledge City: Can it be an option for Riyadh? In *Knowledge Cities, Future of Cities in The Knowledge Economy* (pp. 116–141). Scholar Press.

Abu-Lughod, J., & Hay, R. Jr. (1977). *Third World Urbanization*. London, UK: Methuen and Co. Ltd.

Abusaada, H. G. (2015). *Architecture of the Repercussions of the Imagination: Renewal of Intellectual Discourse*. Cairo, Egypt: Association of Retrieving Planning and Architecture Heritage.

Abussada, G. H. (2015). *The Art of the City, Refutation of Intellectual Discourse as an Introductory to Knowledge Enlightenment.* PartridgeAfrica.

Ago, A. (2015). Global Cities vs Other Cities in Europe. In G. Mattarocci & D. Pekdemir (Eds.), *European Real Estate: Asset Class Performance and Optimal Portfolio Construction Asset Class Performance and Optimal Portfolio Construction* (pp. 43–66). London: Palgrave Macmillan UK; doi:10.1057/9781137436122_3

Ahmadi, A. (2015). A City for Education. *Architectural Design*, *85*(1), 46–53. doi:10.1002/ad.1854

AKDN. (2013). *AKDN – Aga Khan Development Network*. Retrieved from http://www.akdn.org/architecture/project.asp?id=3564 〉

Al Beblawi, H. (1990). The Rentier State in the Arab World. In G. Luciani (Ed.), *The Arab State* (pp. 85–98). London, UK: Routledge.

Al Buainain, F. (1999). *Urbanisation in Qatar: A Study of the Residential and Commercial Land Development in Doha City, 1970 -1997* (Ph.D. Thesis). University of Salford, Salford, UK.

Al Hathloul, S. (2004). Planning in the Middle East, moving Toward the Future. *Habitat International*, *18*(5), 641–643. doi:10.1016/j.habitatint.2004.04.004

Al Qassemi, S. S. (2013). Thriving Gulf Cities Emerge as New Centers of Arab World. *Al-Monitor: The Pulse of the Middle East*. Retrieved from http://www.al-monitor.com/pulse/originals/2013/10/abu-dhabi-dubai-doha-arab-centers.html#ixzz4sLNSlI3A

Alami, M. O. (2015, March 15). Realizing a Masterplan with Architectural Works of Art. *QF Telegraph.*

Alatas, S. F. (2003). Academic Dependency and the Global Division of Labour in the Social Sciences. *Current Sociology, 51*(6), 559–613. doi:10.1177/00113921030516003

Alatas, S. H. (2006). The Autonomous, the Universal & the Future of Sociology. *Current Sociology, 54*(7), 7–23. doi:10.1177/0011392106058831

Alavi, M., & Leidner, D. (2001, March). Review: Knowledge Management and Knowledge Management Systems: Conceptual Foundations and Research Issues. *Management Information Systems Quarterly, 25*(1), 107–136. doi:10.2307/3250961

Al-Bader, J. (2012). *Visual Ethnography in Three Preschools in Kuwait (Middle East). Arizona State University.* ProQuest.

Al-Bader, J. (2017). Spaces for reviving traditions: Vol. 282. *Legitimating Tradition, Kuwait, 2016.* Berkley, CA: The International Association for the Study of Traditional.

Alexandra, J., Laura, W., Neil, L., David, C., & Marc, C. (2006). *Ideopolis: Knowledge City-Regions.* London: The Work Foundation.

Alexandria University, Faculty of Arts. (n.d.). *TAFL Center (Teaching Arabic as Foreign Language).* Retrieved from http://arts.alexu.edu.eg/tafl/

Alexandrina, B. (n.d.a). *BA African Networks.* Retrieved from http://afn.bibalex.org/GeneralPortal.aspx

Alexandrina, B. (n.d.b). *Overview, Mission, Objectives.* Retrieved from https://www.bibalex.org/en/page/about

Alexandrina, B. (n.d.c). *The BA Embassies of Knowledge.* Retrieved from https://www.bibalex.org/en/project/details?documentid=1300&keywords=

Algohary, S., & El-faramawy, A. (2010). *Egyptian Approach to Informal Settlements Development.* Informal Settlements Development Facilities. Available at: http://www.slideshare.net/GRFDavos/egypt-for-idrc-2-june-2010-finalpptx

Al-Jayyousi, O. (2015). *Renewable Energy in the Arab World - Transfer of Knowledge and Prospects for Arab Cooperation.* Amman, Jordan: Friedrich Ebert Stiftung; doi:10.1007/s13398-014-0173-7.2

Al-Kholaifi, M. J. (2003). *The Traditional Architecture in Qatar.* Doha: National Council for Culture, Arts and Heritage. (In Arabic)

Al-Nakib, F. (2016). *Kuwait Transformed: A History of Oil and Urban Life.* Stanford University Press.

Al-Nakib, F. (2016). *Kuwait transformed: a history of oil and urban life.* Stanford, CA: Stanford University Press.

Alomaim, A. (2016). *Nation Building in Kuwait 1961–1991. University of California Los Angeles.* ProQuest.

Alraouf, A. (2005). Knowledge Cities: Examining the Discourse: Smart Villages, Internet Cities or Creativity engines. *Proceedings of the International Symposium on Knowledge Cities.* The World Bank and Arab Urban Development Institute.

Alraouf, A. (2006). *Dubaization vs. Glocalization: Territorial Outlook of Arab/Gulf Cities Transformed.* The 9th Sharjah Urban Planning Symposium (SUPS), Sharjah, UAE.

Alraouf, A. A. (2008). Emerging Middle Eastern knowledge cities: the unfolding story. In *Knowledge-Based Urban Development: Planning and Applications in the Information Era.* Retrieved from http://www.igi-global.com/chapter/emerging-middle-eastern-knowledge- cities/25495

Alraouf, A. A. (2012). *Knowledge Cities: Examining the Discourse Smart Villages, Internet Cities or Creativity Engines.* Retrieved from http://qu.academia.edu/AliAlraouf/Papers/126203/Knowledge_Cities_Examining_The_Discourse_Smart_Villages

Alraouf, A. A. (2016). "Dohaization": An Emerging Interface between Knowledge, Creativity, and Gulf Urbanity. In Gulf Cities as Interfaces. Cambridge, UK: Gulf Research Centre Cambridge.

Alraouf, A. A. (2017). Interrogating Qatar's Urbanity as a Catalyst for Building Knowledge-Based Societies and Economies. In Strategies of Knowledge Transfer for Economic Diversification in the Arab States of the Gulf. London: Gerlach Press.

Alraouf, A. A. 2011. Assembling Identity for an Emerging Urbanity. Doha, Qatar, as a Creative City. *The City: 2nd International Conference The City: Culture, Society, and Technology.*

Alraouf, A. (2016a). "Dohaization": An Emerging Interface between Knowledge, Creativity, and Gulf Urbanity. In *Gulf Cities as Interfaces* (pp. 47–68). Cambridge, UK: Gulf Research Centre Cambridge.

Alraouf, A. (2016b). *One Nation, One Myth and Two Museums Heritage, Architecture and Culture as Tools for Assembling Identity in Qatar.* In P. Erskine-Loftus (Ed.), *Representing the Nation: Heritage, Museums, National Narratives, and Identity in the Arab Gulf States* (pp. 79–94). Routledge.

Alraouf, A. (2017). Interrogating Qatar's Urbanity as a Catalyst for Building Knowledge-Based Societies and Economies. In R. G. Bertelsen, N. Noori, & J.-M. Rickli (Eds.), *Strategies of Knowledge Transfer for Economic Diversification in the Arab States of the Gulf* (pp. 53–66). London: Gerlach Press.

Alraouf, A. (2017). Interrogating Qatar's Urbanity as a Catalyst for Building Knowledge-Based Societies and Economies. In R. G. Bertelsen, N. Noori, & J.-M. Rickli (Eds.), *Strategies Of Knowledge Transfer For Economic Diversification In The Arab States Of The Gulf* (pp. 53–66). London: Gerlach Press.

Alraouf, A. A. (2008). Emerging Middle Eastern Knowledge Cities: the Unfolding Story. In T. Yigitcaular & V. Koray (Eds.), *Knowledge Based Urban Development: Planning and Application in the Information Era* (pp. 240–259). IGI Global. doi:10.4018/978-1-59904-720-1.ch014

Alraouf, A. A. (2010). *From Knowledge to Creativity Economy, Qatar Urbanity Transformed. In Third Knowledge Cities Summit (KCS) 2010* (pp. r16–r19). Melbourne, Australia: Academic Press.

Alraouf, A. A. (2013). Manama, Bahrain. In M. Fraser & N. Golzari (Eds.), *Architecture and Globalization in The Persian Gulf Region.* London: Ashgate.

Alraouf, A. A. (2017). Interrogating Qatar's Urbanity as a Catalyst for Building Knowledge-Based Societies and Economies. In R. G. Bertelsen, N. Noori, & J.-M. Rickli (Eds.), *Strategies of Knowledge Transfer For Economic Diversification In The Arab States Of The Gulf* (pp. 53–66). London: Gerlach Press.

Alraouf, A. A. 2012. An Emerging Urbanity in Knowledge Economy Paradigm: The Case of Doha, *Qatar. International Conference on Realigning Power Geometries in the Arab World.* Leipzig University.

Al-Thani, A. (2011). *The Paradox of Development: A Comparison between.* Dubai, UAE: Intellectual Magazine of SFS-Q.

Al-Yousef. (2013). *Yusuf Kalifa, United Arab Emirates at a Crossroads, Arab future, 12th and 400.* Beirut: Centre for Arab Unity Studies.

American Association for Higher Education. (1989). *Presidential Committee on Information Literacy.* Chicago: American Library Association.

Ampujo, M., & Koivisto, J. (2014). From 'Post-Industrial' to 'Network Society' and Beyond: The Political Conjunctures and Current Crises of Information Society Theory. *TripleC*, *12*(2), 447–463.

Anderson, G. (2004). *Reinventing the Museum, Historical and Contemporary Perspectives on the Paradigm Shift*. AltaMira Press.

Anderson, R., & Al-Bader, J. (2006). Recent Kuwaiti architecture: Regionalism vs. globalization. *Journal of Architectural and Planning Research*, *23*(2), 134–146.

Android Technology Fair, R. T. E. X. (2014). *Exhibitors Handbook*. Retrieved from http://www.rt-exhiption.com

Anholt, S. (2009). *Places: Identity, Image and Reputation*. Palgrave Macmillan. doi:10.1057/9780230251281

Antonelli, C. (1997). New Information Technology and the Knowledge-Based Economy. The Italian Evidence. *Review of Industrial Organization*, *12*(4), 593–607. doi:10.1023/A:1007798532691

Arab Republic of Egypt, Ministry of Communications and Information Technology (MCIT). (n.d.a). *Building Digital Bridges: Egypt's Vision of the Information Society 2003*. Retrieved from http://www.mcit.gov.eg/Upcont/Documents/BuildingBridges_all.pdf

Arab Republic of Egypt, Ministry of Communications and Information Technology (MCIT). (n.d.b). *Egypt's Information Society 2005*. Retrieved from http://www.mcit.gov.eg/Upcont/Documents/EgyInfo_Society.pdf

Arab Republic of Egypt. (2012). *Egypt's ICT strategy 2012-2017: The Egyptian Digital Society in Knowledge Economy*. Ministry of Communications and Information Technology. Retrieved from http://www.mcit.gov.eg/Upcont/Documents/ICT%20Strategy%202012-2017.pdf

Arnstein, S. (1969). A Ladder of Citizen Participation. *JAIP*, *35*(4), 216–224.

Arrighi, G. (1996). *The Long Twentieth Century: Money, Power, and the Origins of Our Times*. London: Verso.

Associates, A. B. T. ADames and Moore, & GOHBPR. (1982). Informal Housing in Egypt. Cairo: U.S. Agency for International Development.

Aubert, E. J. (2005). Knowledge Economies: A Global Perspective. In A. Bounfour & L. Edvinsson (Eds.), *Intellectual Capital for Communities: Nations, Regions, and Cities* (pp. 61–69). Burlington, MA: Elsevier Butterworth-Heinemann. doi:10.1016/B978-0-7506-7773-8.50007-8

Aubert, J., & Reiffers, J. (2004). *Knowledge Economies in the Middle East and North Africa: Toward New Development Strategies. WBI Learning Resources*. Washington, DC: World Bank. doi:10.1596/0-8213-5701-8

Audi, R. (2003). *Epistemology: A contemporary introduction to the theory of knowledge*. New York: Routledge.

Ausburn, L. J., & Ausburn, F. B. (1978). Cognitive Styles: Some information and implications for instructional design. *Educational Communication,* (26), 337–354.

Australia's National Dictionary. (1981). *The Macquarie Dictionary*. Sydney: Macquarie Library Pty.

Azua, J. (2006). Bilbao: From the Guggenheim to the Knowledge City. In F. J. Carrillo (Ed.), *Knowledge Cities: Approaches, Experiences and Perspectives* (pp. 97–112). Burlington, MA: Elsevier Butterworth-Heinemann. doi:10.1016/B978-0-7506-7941-1.50011-7

Baker, C. (2005). *Cultural Studies: Theory and Practice*. London: Sage.

Bamakhrama, S. S. (2015). *Cities within Cities: An Urbanization Approach in the Gulf Countries*. Los Angeles, CA: University of California.

Baqir, M. N., & Kathawala, Y. (2004). Ba for knowledge cities: A futuristic technology model. *Journal of Knowledge Management*, *8*(5), 83–95. doi:10.1108/13673270410558828

Barcelona City Government. (2003). *Culture, The Motor of the Knowledge City: Strategic Plan of the Cultural Sector of Barcelona*. Barcelona: Steering Council of the Strategic Plan of the Cultural sector of Barcelona.

Barret, B. (2010). Usine e-Portfolios to Evaluate Intellectual Capital of OnLine Learners. In S. C. Sirrano (Ed.), *Proceedings of the 2nd European Conference on Intellectual Capital: ISCTE* (pp. 67-76). Lisbon, Portugal: Academic Publishing Limited.

Başaran, F. (2014). *İletişim ve Emperyalizm: Türkiye'de Telekomünikasyonun Ekonomi Politiği*. Ankara: Ütopya.

Batty, M. (2007). *Cities and Complexity: Understanding Cities with Cellular Automata, Agent-based Models, and Fractals*. Boston: MIT Press.

Baum, S., O'Connor, K., & Yigitcanlar, T. (2009). The implications of creative industries for regional outcomes. *International Journal of Foresight and Innovation Policy, 5*(1/2/3), 44-64.

Baum, S., Yigitcanlar, T., Horton, S., Velibeyoglu, K., & Gleeson, B. (2007). *The role of community and lifestyle in the making of a knowledge city*. Brisbane: Griffith University.

Baum, S., Yigitcanlar, T., Horton, S., Velibeyoglu, K., & Gleeson, B. (2007). *The Role of Community and Lifestyle in the Making of a Knowledge City. Report*. Brisbane: Griffith University.

Bayat, A. (2009). *Life as Politics: How Ordinary People Change the Middle East*. Cairo: AUC Press.

Bayat, A., & Denis, E. (2000). Who is Afraid of Ashwaiyyat?: Urban Change and Politics in Egypt. *Environment and Urbanization*, *12*(2), 185–199.

Becker, R., Caceres, H., Hanson, K., Loh, J. M., Urbanek, S., Varshavsky, A., & Volinsky, C. (2011). A Tale of One City: Using Cellular Network Data for Urban Planning. IEEE Pervasive Computing.

Becker, G. S. (1962). Investment in Human Capital: A Theoretical Analysis. *The Journal of Political Economy, part 2. Investment in Human Beings*, *70*(5), 9–49.

Bell, D. (1973). *The Coming of Post Industrial Society*. New York: Basic Books.

Beniger, J. (1986). *The Control Revolution: Technological and Economic Origins of the Information Society*. Cambridge, MA: Harvard University Press.

Bennet, A., & Bennet, D. (2014). Knowledge, Theory and Practice in Knowledge Management: Between Associative Patterning and Context-Rich Action. Journal of Entrepreneurship, Management and Innovation, 10(1), 5-55.

Berg, B. L. (2000). *Qualitative Research Methods for the Social Sciences (4th ed.)*. Allyn & Bacon.

Berry, B. J. L. (1961). City Size Distributions and Economic Development. *Economic Development and Cultural Change*, *9*(4), 573–588. doi:10.1086/449923

Bharadwaj, V. (2012). *Museums, Cultural Jewels in the Gulf*. NYTimes.com

Bibliotheca Alexandrina. (n.d.). Retrieved from http://www.bibalex.org/ar/Page/About

Bibliotheca, A. H. P. (n.d.). *About the BA*. Retrieved from https://www.bibalex.org/en/default

Black, G. (2005). *The Engaging Museum: Developing Museums For Visitor Involvement*. London: Routledge.

Blakeley, N., Lewis, G., & Mills, D. (2005). *The Economics of Knowledge: What Makes Ideas Special for Economic Growth?* New Zealand Treasury, Policy Perspectives Paper 05/05.

Boekhorst, A. K. (2003). Becoming Information Literate in the Netherlands. *Library Review*, *52*(7), 298–309. doi:10.1108/00242530310487399

Bonine, M. E. (1983). Cities of the Middle East and North Africa. In S. D. Brunn & J. F. Williams (Eds.), *Cities of the World, World Regional Urban Development*. New York, NY: Harper & Row, Publishers.

Bontis, N. (1998). Intellectual capital: An exploratory study that develops measures and models. *Management Decision*, *36*(2), 63–76. doi:10.1108/00251749810204142

Bontis, N., Keow, W. C., & Richardson, S. (2000). Intellectual Capital and Business Performance in Malaysian Industries. *Journal of Intellectual Capital*, *1*(1), 85–100. doi:10.1108/14691930010324188

Bounfour, A., & Edvinsson, L. (2005). *Intellectual Capital for Communities: Nations, Regions, and Cities*. London: Routledge.

Bourdieu, P. (1984). *Distinction: A social critiques of the judgement if taste*. Harvard University Press.

Brahmbhatt, M., Canuto, O., & Vostroknutova, E. (2010). *Dealing with Dutch Disease A Model of Dutch Disease* (Poverty Reduction and Economic Management (PREM) No. 16). Retrieved from www.worldbank.org/economicpremise

Bransford, J., Brown, L. A., & Cocking, R. (2000). How People Learn Brain, Mind, Experience, and School. Washington, DC: The National Academies Press.

Breene, K. (2016). *The countries best prepared for the new digital economy*. Retrieved October 28, 2016, from https://www.weforum.org/agenda/2016/07/countries-best-prepared-for-the-new-digital-economy/

Brisbane City Council. (2012). *Brisbane Long Term Infrastructure Plan 2012 – 2031*. Brisbane City Council.

Brisbane City Council. (n.d.). *Welcome to Brisbane City*. Retrieved from https://www.brisbane.qld.gov.au/

Byat, A. B., & Sultan, O. (2014). The United Arab Emirates: Fostering a Unique 101 Innovation Ecosystem for a Knowledge-Based Economy. In S. Dutta, B. Lanvin, & S. Wunsch-Vincent (Eds.), *The Global Innovation Index 2014: The Human Factor in Innovation*. (pp. 101–112). Cornell University, INSEAD, and the World Intellectual Property Organization (WIPO).

CAPMS. (2016). Census. *Central Agency for Public Mobilization and Statistics*. Available at: http://www.capmas.gov.eg/

Carrillo, F. (2006). The century of knowledge cities. In Knowledge cities: Approaches, experiences, and perspectives. New York: Butterworth–Heinemann.

Carrillo, F. (2011). *knowledge cities, entrances, experiences and visions* [Arabic translation]. Khalid Ali Yusuf.

Carrillo, F. (2002). Capital systems: Implications for a global knowledge agenda. *Journal of Knowledge Management*, *6*(4), 379–399. doi:10.1108/13673270210440884

Carrillo, F. (2004). Capital cities: A taxonomy of capital accounts for knowledge cities. *Journal of Knowledge Management*, *8*(5), 28–46. doi:10.1108/1367327041058738

Carrillo, F. J. (2006). Introduction: the century of knowledge cities. In J. Carrillo (Ed.), *Knowledge Cities: Approaches, Experiences and Perspectives* (pp. xi–xv). Oxford, UK: Butterworth-Heinemann/Elsevier. doi:10.1016/B978-0-7506-7941-1.50003-8

Carrillo, F. J. (2006). *Knowledge Cities Approaches, Experiences, and Perspectives*. Elsevier's Science & Technology Rights.

Carrillo, F. J. (2009). Demarcation and levels of analysis in knowledge-based development. *Journal of Knowledge-Based Development*, *13*(5), 208–213.

Carrillo, F. J. (Ed.). (2005). *Knowledge Cities: Approaches, Experiences, and Perspectives*. London: Routledge.

Carrillo, F. J., Yigitcanlar, T., García, B., & Lönnqvist, A. (2014). *Knowledge and the City: Concepts, Applications and Trends of Knowledge-Based Urban Development*. London: Routledge.

Carrillo, J., Yigitcanlar, T., Garcia, B., & Lonnqvist, A. (2014). *Knowledge and the city: concepts, applications and trends of knowledge-based urban development*. New York, NY: Routledge.

Cassidy, S. (2004). Learning Style: An Overview of Theories, Models and Measures. *Educational Psychology*, *24*(4), 419–444. doi:10.1080/0144341042000228834

Castells, M. (1997). The Rise of the Network Society (Vols. 1-3). Blackwell.

Castells, M. (1989). *The Informational City: Information Technology, Economic Restructuring, and the Urban-Regional Process*. Oxford, UK: Blackwell.

Castells, M. (1989). *The Informational City: Informational Technology, Economic Restructuring and the Urban-Regional Process*. Oxford, UK: Basil Blackwell.

Castells, M. (1997). *The Information City: Economy, Culture and Society*. Oxford, UK: Blackwell.

Castells, M. (2001). *The Rise of the Network Society*. Oxford, UK: Blackwell.

Castells, M., & Hall, P. (1994). *Technopoles of the World: The Making of 21st-Century Industrial Complexes*. London: Routledge.

Castells, M., & Ince, M. (2003). *Conversations with Manuel Castells*. Cambridge, UK: Polity.

Catanese, A. J. (1988). Evolution and Trends. In A. J. Catanese & J. Snyder (Eds.), *Urban Planning* (pp. 3–64). New York: McGraw Hill Company.

Center for Knowledge Systems. (2003). *Forum on Knowledge-based Development, 2003*. Retrieved from http://www.knowledgesystems.org/

Charles, D. R., & Wray, F. (2008). *Science cities in the UK*. Available at www. D1074616.domain.com/worldcapitalinstitute/sites/default/files/

Chatzkel, J. (2004). Greater Phoenix as a knowledge capital. *Journal of Knowledge Management*, *8*(5), 61–72. doi:10.1108/13673270410558783

Cheng, P., & Choi, C. (2004). Knowledge repositories in knowledge cities. *Journal of Knowledge Management*, *8*(5), 96–106. doi:10.1108/13673270410558800

Chen, S., & Choi, C. J. (2004). Creating a knowledge-based city: The example of Hsinchu Science Park. *Journal of Knowledge Management*, *8*(5), 73–82. doi:10.1108/13673270410558792

City of Dortmund. (2015). *PHOENIX Dortmund - enter a location into the future*. Retrieved from http://www.phoenix-dortmund.de/de/home/index.html

Clark, D. a. (2006). *The Elgar Companion to Development Studies*. Edward Elgar Publishing. doi:10.4337/9781847202864

Collier, P. (2013). *Exodus: How Migration is Changing Our World.* New York: Oxford University Press.

Cooke, P. (2006). *Regional Development in the Knowledge Economy (Regions and Cities).* London: Routledge.

Corey, K., & Wilson, M. (2006). *Urban and regional technology planning: planning practice in the global knowledge economy.* New York: Routledge.

Corrado, C., Haskel, J., & Jona-Lasinio, C. (2017). Knowledge Spillovers, ICT and Productivity Growth. *Oxford Bulletin of Economics and Statistics*, *79*(4), 592–618. doi:10.1111/obes.12171

Costa, A. L. (1991). The Search For Intelligent Life. In A. L. Costa (Ed.), *Developing Minds: A Resource Book for* (pp. 100–106). Alexandria, VA: Association for Supervision and Curriculum.

Couch, C. (1990). *Urban Renewal: Theory and Practice.* London: Macmillan Education Ltd. doi:10.1007/978-1-349-20912-5

Coulby, D., & Jones, C. (1995). *Postmodernity and European Education Systems: Cultural diversity and centralist knowledge.* London: Trentham Books.

Crainer, S., & Dearlove, D. (2003). *Business, The Universe and Everything: Conversations with the World's Greatest Management Thinkers.* Chichester, UK: Capeston.

Crist, J. T. (2015). Innovation in a Small State: Qatar and the IBC Cluster Model of Higher Education. *The Muslim World Journal.*, *105*(1), 93–115. doi:10.1111/muwo.12082

Cross, D. R., & Paris, S. G. (1988). Developmental and Instructional Analyses of Children's Metacognition and Reading Comprehension. *Journal of Educational Psychology*, *2*(2), 131–142. doi:10.1037/0022-0663.80.2.131

Crouch, C. (2002). *Design Culture in Liverpool, 1880-1914: The Origins of the Liverpool School of Architecture.* Liverpool University Press.

Cuthbert, A. R. (2006). *The Form of Cities: Political Economy and Urban Design.* Oxford, UK: Blackwell. doi:10.1002/9780470774915

D. Evers H. (2002) *Knowledge Society and the Knowledge Gap.* Paper read at an International Conference, Globalisation, Culture and Inequalities, Kebansaan, Malaysia.

Danahar, P. (2015). *The New Middle East: The World After the Arab Spring.* London: Bloomsbury.

Davidson, C. M. (2008). *Dubai: The Vulnerability of Success.* Colombia University Press.

Denis, E., & Séjourné, M. (2002). *ISIS: Information System for Informal Settlements.* Cairo: Ministry of Planning, GTZ, CEDEJ.

Department of Science. (2014). *Information Technology, Innovation and the Arts:" Queensland Cultural Precinct.* Queensland Government.

Department of Transport and Main Roads. (2011). *Connecting SEQ 2031 – An Integrated Regional Transport Plan for South East Queensland.* The State of Queensland.

DeVito, T. R. (2008). *A Study of the Teaching Strategies of Paramedic Educators as they Relate to Models of Adult Education.* ProQuest.

Dictionary, T. O. (1989). The Oxford English Dictionary (2nd ed.; vol. 7). Oxford, UK: Oxford University Press.

Dinnie, K. (2011). *City Branding: Theory and Cases.* Palgrave Macmillan. doi:10.1057/9780230294790

Doğan Şirketler Grubu Holding, A. Ş. (2015). *Moving Forward... Moving Beyond...*Retrieved October 21, 2016 from http://www.doganholding.com.tr/_files/en/annual-report/DOHOL_2015_Annual_Report.pdf

Dovey, K. (2005). *Fluid City: Transforming Melbourne's Urban Waterfront*. London: Routledge.

Drucker, P. F. (2003a). *Peter Drucker on the profession of management*. Harvard Business School Press.

Drucker, P. F. (2003b). *The Essential Drucker*. New York: Harper Business. Retrieved from http://books.google.com/books?id=bpy7KvlKOv4C&pgis=1

Dubai from Sand to Silicon, Growth of Creative Industries, The Dubai Experience. (n.d.). Retrieved from http://www definitely dubai.com

Dubai Statistics Centre. (2012). Dubai, UAE: Dubai in Figures.

Dubai Strategic Plan. (2007). Emirate of Dubai. UAE: Academic Press.

Du, J., & Ren, J. (2011). An economic view on Beijing's construction of a world city. In *2011 International Conference on E-Business and E-Government (ICEE)* (pp. 1–4). Shanghai, China: IEEE.doi:10.1109/ICEBEG.2011.5876668

Durmaz, B., Yigitcanlar, T., & Velibeyoglu, K. (2008). Creative cities and the film industry. *The Open Urban Studies Journal*, *1*(1), 1–10. doi:10.2174/1874942900801010001

Dvir, R. (2003). *Innovation Engines for Knowledge Cities*. In ENTOVATION 100 roundtable and the Latin American Knowledge Development forum, Monterrey, Mexico.

Dvir, R., & Pasher, E. (2004). *Innovation Engines for Knowledge Cities: An Innovation Ecology Perspective*. Academic Press.

Dvir, R. (2006). Knowledge City, Seen as a Collage of Human Knowledge Moments. In F. J. Carrillo (Ed.), *Knowledge Cities: Approaches, Experiences, and Perspectives* (pp. 245 272). Amsterdam: Elsevier. doi:10.1016/B978 0 7506 7941-1.50022-1

Dvir, R., & Pasher, E. (2004). Innovative Engines for Knowledge Cities: An Innovation Ecology Perspective. *Journal of Knowledge Management*, *8*(5), 16–27. doi:10.1108/13673270410558756

Dyker, D., & Radosevic, S. (2000). Building the Knowledge-Based Economy in Countries in Transition – from Concepts to Policies. *Journal of Interdisciplinary Economics*, *12*(1), 41–70. doi:10.1177/02601079X00001200103

Economics, S. G. S. (2002). *Towards a knowledge city strategy, Technical Report*. Melbourne, Australia: Melbourne City Council.

Edvardsson, I., Yigitcanlar, T., & Pancholi, S. (2016). Knowledge cities research and practice under the microscope: A review of the literature. *Knowledge Management Research and Practice*, *14*(4), 537–564. doi:10.1057/s41275-016-0003-0

Edvinsson, L. (2003). *Introduction to issues in Knowledge Management*. Henley Knowledge Management Forum.

Edvinsson, L. (2003). *Introduction to Issues in Knowledge Management*. Oxfordshire, UK: Henley Knowledge Management Forum.

Edvinsson, L. (2006). Aspects on the City as a Knowledge Tool. *Journal of Knowledge Management*, *10*(5), 6–13. doi:10.1108/13673270610691134

Edvinsson, L., & Sullivan, P. (1996). Developing a Model for Managing Intellectual Capital. *European Management Journal*, *14*(4), 356–364. doi:10.1016/0263-2373(96)00022-9

Eggs, C. (2012). Trust Building in Communities of Practice. *Proceedings of the 4th European Conference on on Intellectual Capital*, 172-169.

Einstein, A. (1954). *Ideas and Opinions* (S. Bargmann Trans. & Ed.). New York: Crown Publishers, Inc.

El Mallakh, R. (1979). *Qatar, Development of an Oil Economy*. London: Croom Helm.

El Mouelhi, H. (2014). Culture and informal urban development - The case of Cairo's 'Ashwa'eyat (informal settlements). Berlin: German Academic Exchange Service (DAAD).

El-Ali, H. (2016, August 14). Economic diversification and job creation in the Gulf States. *Al-Yaum*. Retrieved from http://www.alyaum.com/article/4151670

El-Arifi, S. A. (1986). The Nature of Urbanization in the Gulf Countries on JSTOR. *GeoJournal*, *13*(3), 223–235. doi:10.1007/BF00704813

Eldefrawi, S. (2015). Community and Neighbourhood in Egyptian Context, case Formal and Informal Settlements - Cairo. *International Journal of Social Science and Humanity*, *5*(3), 281–286. doi:10.7763/IJSSH.2015.V5.467

El-Kholei, A. O., & Wahbi, S. (2010). Human Settlements. In A. F. Abdel Kadr & M. S. Abido (Eds.), *Environmental Outlook for Arab Region* (pp. 131–165). Nairobi, Kenya: United Nations Environment Programme, CEDARE and League of Arab States. Retrieved from http://eoar.cedare.int/report/EOAR_Full Report (EN).pdf

El-Shakhs, S. (1972). Development, primacy and systems of cities. *Journal of Developing Areas*, (7): 11–36. PMID:12312642

Elshater, A. (2014). Prosperity of Thought Versus Retreat of Application: A Comprehensive Approach in Urban Design Teaching. International Journal of Architectural Research, 8.

Elshater, A., & Abusaada, H. G. (2016). *What is Urban Design? Teaching and Learning*. Partridge Africa.

Emirate of Dubai. (n.d.). In *Wikipedia, the free encyclopedia*. Retrieved from http://www.wikipedia, org/wiki

Engelke, P. (2015). Brainstorming the Gulf: Innovation and the Knowledge Economy in the GCC. Washington, DC: The Atlantic Council's Brent Scowcroft Center on International Security.

ENTOVATION 100. (2003). *The Latin American knowledge development forum*, Monterrey, Mexico.

ENTOVATION 100. (2004). *Roundtable*. Barcelona, Spain.

Ergazakis, Metaxiotis, & Psarras. (2004). Towards knowledge cities: conceptual analysis and success. *Journal of Knowledge Management, 8*(5).

Ergazakis, E., Ergazakis, K., Metaxiotis, K., & Charalabidis, Y. (2009). Rethinking the development of successful knowledge cities: An advanced framework. *Journal of Knowledge Management*, *13*(5), 214–227. doi:10.1108/13673270910988060

Ergazakis, K., Metaxiotis, K., & Psarras, J. (2004). Towards Knowledge Cities: Conceptual Analysis and Success Stories. *Journal of Knowledge Management*, *8*(5), 5–15. doi:10.1108/13673270410558747

Ergazakis, K., Metaxiotis, K., & Psarras, J. (2006). Knowledge cities: The answer to the needs of knowledge-based development. *Journal of Information and Knowledge Management Systems*, *36*(1), 67–81.

Ergazakis, K., Metaxiotis, K., & Psarras, J. (2006a). An emerging pattern of successful knowledge cities' main features. In F. J. Carrillo (Ed.), *Knowledge Cities: Approaches, Experiences and Perspectives* (pp. 3–15). Oxford, UK: Butterworth-Heinemann/Elsevier. doi:10.1016/B978-0-7506-7941-1.50004-X

Ergazakis, K., Metaxiotis, K., & Psarras, J. (2006b). Knowledge cities: The answer to the needs of the knowledge-based development. *VINE. The Journal of Information and Knowledge Management Systems*, *36*(1), 67–81.

Ergazakis, K., Metaxiotis, K., Psarras, J., & Askounis, D. (2006). A unified methodological approach for the development of knowledge cities. *Journal of Knowledge Management*, *10*(5), 65–78. doi:10.1108/13673270610691189

Erskine-Loftus, P. (2013). *Reimagining Museums: Practice in the Arabian Peninsula*. Cambridge, MA: MuseumsEtc.

Esmaeilpoorarabi, N., Yigitcanlar, T., & Guaralda, M. (2016a). Towards an urban quality framework: Determining critical measures for different geographical scales to attract and retain talent in cities. *International Journal of Knowledge-Based Development*, *7*(3), 290–312. doi:10.1504/IJKBD.2016.078556

Esmaeilpoorarabi, N., Yigitcanlar, T., & Guaralda, M. (2016b). Place quality and urban competitiveness symbiosis? A position paper. *International Journal of Knowledge-Based Development*, *7*(1), 4–21. doi:10.1504/IJKBD.2016.075444

Etzkowitz, H., & Leydesdorff, L. (2000). The Dynamics of Innovation: From National Systems and "Mode 2" to a Triple Helix of University–Industry–Government Relations. *Research Policy*, *29*(2), 109–123. doi:10.1016/S0048-7333(99)00055-4

European Commission. (2000). *Innovation Policy in a Knowledge-Based Economy*. Brussels: Office for Official Publications of the European Communities.

Evans, G. (2009). Creative Cities, Creative Spaces and Urban Policy. *Urban Studies (Edinburgh, Scotland)*, *46*(5-6), 1003–1040. doi:10.1177/0042098009103853

Farenhorst, R., & Boer, R. C. (2009). *Architectural Knowledge Management: Supporting Architects and Auditors*. The Dutch Joint Academic and Commercial Quality Research & Development (Jacquard) Program on Software Engineering Research, The Dutch Research School for Information and Knowledge Systems. SIKS Dissertation series.

Features Dubai Strategic Plan. (2015). *Dubai where the future begins: The official website of the secretariat of the Executive Council of the Emirate of Dubai*. Retrieved from http://WWW.TEC.GOVE.AE/TEC/IMAGES/PDF/DSP

Feiwel, G. R. (1975). *The intellectual capital of Michal Kalecki: A Study in Economic Theory and Policy*. University of Tennessee Press.

Fergany, N., Bennani, F., Elsadda, H., Jadaane, F., & Kubursi, A. (2003). *The Arab Human Development Report 2003*. Retrieved from http://hdr.undp.org/sites/default/files/rbas_ahdr2003_en.pdf

Fernandez-Maldonado, A. M. (2012). Designing: combining design and high-tech in Eindhoven knowledge city. In T. Yigitcanlar, K. Metaxiotis & F. Carrillo (Eds.), Building prosperous knowledge cities: Policies, plans and metrics. Edward Elgar. doi:10.4337/9780857936042.00019

Fernandez-Maldonado, A. M., & Romein, A. (2008). A Knowledge-Base Urban Paradox:The Case of Delft. In T. Yigitcanlar, K. Velibeyoglu, & S. Baum (Eds.), *Knowledge-Based Urban Development Planning and Applications in the Information Era*. Hershey, PA: Information Science Reference. doi:10.4018/978-1-59904-720-1.ch013

Flavell, J. H. (1976). Metacognitive Aspects of Problem Solving. In L. B. Resnick (Ed.), The Nature of Intelligence (pp. 231-236). Academic Press.

Flavell, J. H. (1979). Metacognition and Cognitive Monitoring: A New Area of Cognitive–Developmental Inquiry. *The American Psychologist*, *34*(10), 906–911. doi:10.1037/0003-066X.34.10.906

Florida, R. (1995). Toward the Learning Region. *Futures*, *27*(5), 527–536. doi:10.1016/0016-3287(95)00021-N

Florida, R. (2000). *The Economic Geography of Talent*. Pittsburgh, PA: Carnegie Mellon University.

Florida, R. (2002). *The rise of the creative class and how it is transforming work, leisure, community and every-day life*. New York: Basic Books.

Florida, R. (2002). *The Rise of the Creative Class and How it's Transforming Work,L eisure, Community and Everyday Life*. New York: Basic Books.

Florida, R. (2002). *The Rise of the Creative Class*. New York: Basic Books.

Florida, R. (2005). *Cities and the Creative Class*. New York: Routledge.

Florida, R. (2008). *Who's your city?* New York: Basic Books.

Florida, R. (2008). *Who's Your City?* New York: Basic Books.

Foglesong, R. E. (2016). *Planning the Capitalist City: The Colonial Era to the 1920s*. Princeton, NJ: Princeton University Press. doi:10.1002/9781119084679.ch5

Foray, D. (2004). *The Economics of Knowledge*. Cambridge, MA: MIT Press.

Fowler, H. W., Fowler, F., & Sykes, J. B. (1976). *Concise Oxford Dictionary of Current English*. Oxford, UK: Oxford University Press.

Fram, S., & Margolis, E. (2001). Architectural and build environment discourses in an educational context: The Gottscho and Schleisner collection. *Visual Studies*, *26*(3), 229–243. doi:10.1080/1472586X.2011.610946

Frane, A., Tomsic, M., Ronecevic, B., & Makarovic, M. (2005). *The challenges of sustained development: the role of socio-cultural factors in east-central Europe*. Budapest: Central European University Press.

Franz, P. (2012). *Competing: important stimuli for knowledge cities to become prosperous. In Building Prosperous Knowledge Cities, Policies, Plans and Metrics*. Edward Elgar Publishing.

Fraser, M., & Golzari, N. (Eds.). (2013). *Architecture and Globalization in The Persian Gulf Region*. London: Ashgate.

Friedmann, J. (2010). Place and place-making in cities: A global perspective. *Planning Theory & Practice*, *11*(2), 149–165. doi:10.1080/14649351003759573

Fromherz, A. (2012). *Qatar: a Modern History*. Washington, DC: Georgetown University Press.

Galaby & Abdrabo. (2013). Knowledge-based development, an Alternative Development Policy: Analysis of the Discourse of knowledge precincts in Egypt. *Egyptian Journal for Development and Planning, 21*(1).

García, S. I. (2009). *Valencia, awarded as one of the Most Admired Knowledge Cities 2009*. Retrieved from http://www.globalcitiesdialogue.com/index.php/home/88-news-from-our-members/122-valencia-awarded-as-one-of-the-most-admired-knowledge-cities-2009.html

Garcia, B. (2004). Developing futures: A knowledge-based capital for Manchester. *Journal of Knowledge Management*, *8*(5), 47–60. doi:10.1108/13673270410558774

Garrett-Jones, S. (2007). Knowledge and cooperation for regional development. *Prometheus*, *25*(1), 31–50. doi:10.1080/08109020601172886

Gehi, J. (2010). *Cities for People*. Island Press.

General Directorate of State Hydraulic Works. (2015). *Devlet Su İşleri Genel Müdürlüğü 2015 Yılı Faaliyet Raporu*. Ankara: DSİ.

George Sun, L. T. A. Academy. (2010). *Land Transport in Singapore*. Retrieved from http://www.gist.edu.sg/cmsresource/Travel%20conference/Land%20Transport%20in%20Singapore.pdf

Georgiou, M. (2013). *Media and the City: Cosmopolitanism and Difference*. Cambridge, UK: Polity Press.

Geray, H. (2003). *İletişim ve Teknoloji: Uluslararası Birikim Düzeninde Yeni Medya Politikaları*. Ankara: Ütopya.

Gertler, M. (2004). *Creative Cities, What are they for? How do they work? And what do Build them?* Back ground Paper (f 48), Canadian Policy Research Network. Retrieved from http://www. cprn. Org

Gibbons, F., & Moore, L. (2011). Turkey's Great Leap Forward risks cultural and environmental bankruptcy. *The Guardian*. Retrieved October 21, 2016 from https://www.theguardian.com/world/2011/may/29/turkey-nuclear-hydro-power-development

Gilder, G. (1995, February 27). *Forbes ASAP*.

Goldenberg, S. (2016). Masdar's zero-carbon dream could become world's first green ghost town. *The Guardian*. Retrieved from https://www.theguardian.com/environment/2016/feb/16/

Goldman, A. I. (1967). A Causal Theory of Knowing. *The Journal of Philosophy*, *64*(12), 357–372. doi:10.2307/2024268

Gonzalez, M., Alvarado, J., & Martinez, S. (2005). A compilation of resources on knowledge cities and knowledge-based development. *Journal of Knowledge Management*, *8*(5), 107–127.

Gorz, A. (2009). *The Immaterial: Knowledge, Value and Capital*. London: Seagull Books.

Gottmann, J. (1977). Megapolis and Antipolis: The Telephone and the Structure of the City. In P. de Sola (Ed.), *The Social Impact of the Telephone*. Cambridge, MA: MIT Press.

Gower, P. (1997). *Banking Development in the Czech Republic: an Analysis of Credit Allocation* (Ph.D. Thesis). University of Sussex.

Graff, G. (2003). *Clueless in Academe: How Schooling Obscures the Life of the Mind*. New Haven, CT: Yale University press.

Gray, M. (2011). *A Theory of 'Late Rentierism' in the Arab States of the Gulf.* Occasional Paper No. 7, Center for International and Regional Studies, Georgetown University School of Foreign Service in Qatar.

Gray, M. (2011). *A Theory of "Late Rentierism" in the Arab States of the Gulf* (Occasional Paper No. 7). Retrieved from https://repository.library.georgetown.edu/bitstream/handle/10822/558291/CIRSOccasionalPaper7MatthewGray2011.pdf?sequence=5

Gray, M. (2013). *Qatar: Politics and the Challenges of Development*. Boulder, CO: Lynne Rienner Publishers.

GSDP. (2011). *(General Secretariat of Development Planning) National Development Strategy 2011–2016*. Doha, Qatar: Gulf Publishing and Printing Company.

Hakim, B. (1986). Arabic-Islamic Cities: Building and Planning Principles. Academic Press.

Hall, P. (1998). *Cities in Civilization*. London: Weidenfeld and Nicolson.

Hall, P. (2000). Creative cities and economic development. *Urban Studies (Edinburgh, Scotland)*, *37*(4), 639–649. doi:10.1080/00420980050003946

Hall, P. (2002). *Cities of Tomorrow: An Intellectual History of Urban Planning and Design in the Twentieth Century*. Blackwell Publishing.

Hall, P. (2004). Knowledge Creativity, Culture, and the City. *Built Environment*, *30*(3), 256–258. doi:10.2148/benv.30.3.256.54306

Harris, C. D., & Ullman, E. L. (1945). The Nature of Cities. *The Annals of the American Academy of Political and Social Science: Building the Future City*, *242*(1), 7–17. doi:10.1177/000271624524200103

Harvey, D. (1989). *The Condition of Postmodernity*. Oxford, UK: Basil Blackwell.

Harvey, D. (1992). *The Condition of Postmodernity: An Enquiry into the Origins of Cultural Change*. Oxford, UK: Blackwell.

Harvey, D. (2009). *Social Justice and the City (Geographies of Justice and Social Transformation)* (Revised edition). University of Georgia Press.

Harwit, E. (2008). *China's Telecommunications Revolution*. Oxford, UK: Oxford University Press. doi:10.1093/acprof:oso/9780199233748.001.0001

Hassan, A. (1994). *City planning in the state of Qatar. Doha*. Doha: Qatar University Publications. (In Arabic)

Hassanein, N., & Mohamed, M. (2007). Sudan Electronic City, an Integrated Technology Park. In *Knowledge Cities, Future of Cities in The Knowledge Economy* (pp. 160–183). Scholar Press.

Hawkins, R. (1997). Prospect for a Global Communication Infrastructure in the 21st Century: Institutional Restructuring and Network Development. In A. Sreberny-Mohammadi, D. Winseck, J. McKenna, & O. Boyd-Barrett (Eds.), *Media in Global Context: A Reader* (pp. 177–193). London: Arnold.

Hayek, F. A. (1945). The Use of Knowledge in Society. *The American Economic Review*, *35*(4), 519–530.

Heilbrun, J. (1981). *Urban Economics and Public Policy (2nd ed.)*. New York, NY: St. Martin's Press.

Henten, A., Skouby, K. E., & Falch, M. (1996). European Planning for an Information Society. *Telematics and Informatics*, *13*(2-3), 177–190. doi:10.1016/S0736-5853(96)00010-X

Hertog, S. (2016). A Quest for Significance: Gulf Oil Monarchies' International 'Soft Power' Strategies And Their Local Urban Dimensions. The London School of Economics and Political Science, LSE Kuwait Program, Paper Series, 42.

Hillenbrand, R. (1998). *Islamic Art and Architecture*. London: Thames & Hudson.

Hoover, F., & Giarratani, E. (1984). An Introduction to Regional Economics (3rd ed.). New York, NY: Alfred A. Knopf.

Hospers, G-J. (2014). *Creative Cities: Breeding Places in Knowledge Economy*. Back Ground Paper (f/48, Auges dt 20904). Retrieved from http://www.cpth.org

Hoyt, H. (1939). The Structure and Growth of Residential Neighbourhoods in American Cities. Washington, DC: Academic Press.

Humphreys, L. G. (1968). The Fleeting Nature of the Prediction of College Academic Success. *Journal of Educational Psychology*, *59*(5), 375–380. doi:10.1037/h0026234 PMID:5722409

Hunt, D. P. (2003). The Concept Of Knowledge and How To Measure It. *Journal of Intellectual Capital*, *4*(1), 100–113. doi:10.1108/14691930310455414

Hu, R. (2015a). Competitiveness, Migration, and Mobility in the Global City: Insights from Sydney, Australia. *Economies*, *3*(1), 37–54. doi:10.3390/economies3010037

Hu, R. (2015b). Sustainable Development Strategy for the Global City: A Case Study of Sydney. *Sustainability*, *7*(4), 4549–4563. doi:10.3390/su7044549

Information Society Commission. (2002). *Building the Knowledge Society*. Report to Government.

ITI. (n.d.). *Vision and Mission*. Retrieved from http://www.iti.gov.eg/overview.aspx?page=1

Jacobs, A., & Appleyard, D. (1987). Toward an Urban Design Manifesto. *Journal of the American Planning Association*, *53*(1), 112–120. doi:10.1080/01944368708976642

Jaidah, I., & Bourennane, M. (2010). *The History of Qatari Architecture 1800-1950*. Skira.

Jameson, F. (2003). *Postmodern, or cultural logic of late capitalism*. Durham, NC: Duke University Press.

Jayne, M., & Bell, D. (2009). Urban Order. *International Encyclopedia of Human Geography*, 70–76.

Jayne, M. (2006). *Cities and consumption*. London: Routledge. doi:10.4324/9780203358733

Jodidio, P. (2014). (ed): Education City; Qatar Foundation, Doha "About Qatar Foundation". Qatar Foundation.

Jodidio, P. (2009). *Museum of Islamic Art, Doha, Qatar*. New York: Prestel.

Jodido, P. (2014). *The New Architecture of Qatar* (1st ed.). New York: Skira Rizzoli Publications.

Kaaki, L. (2008). *The stunning renovation of Souq Waqif*. Arab News. Retrieved from http://archive.arabnews.com

Kamberelis, G. (2010). Focus Groups: Contingent Articulations of Pedagogy, Politics, and Inquiry. *Collecting and Interpreting Qualitative Materials*, *3*, 1–17.

Kamrava, M., Keshavarzian, A., Ramos, S., Kanna, A., Salama, A. M., Wiedmann, F., … Bontenbal, M. (2015). Gateways to the World: Port Cities in the Gulf. Doha, Qatar: Academic Press.

Kamrava, M. (2013). *Qatar: Small State, Big Politics*. New York: Cornell University Press.

Kamrava, M. (2015). Contemporary Port Cities in the Persian Gulf: Local Gateways and Global Networks. In M. Kamrava, A. Keshavarzian, S. Ramos, A. Kanna, A. M. Salama, F. Wiedmann, & M. Bontenbal (Eds.), *Gateways to the World: Port Cities in the Gulf*. Doha, Qatar: Center for International and Regional Studies.

Kaplan, S., Grünwald, L., & Hirte, G. (2016). The effect of social networks and norms on the inter-regional migration intentions of knowledge-workers: The case of Saxony, Germany. *Cities (London, England)*, *55*, 61–69. doi:10.1016/j.cities.2016.03.017

Kaya, F. B., Sahin, G. G., & Gurson, P. (2010). Intellectual Capital in Organizations. *Problems and Perspectives in Management*, *8*(1), 153–160.

Kazgan, G. (2002). *Tanzimat'tan 21. Yüzyıla Türkiye Ekonomisi: Birinci Küreselleşmeden İkinci Küreselleşmeye*. İstanbul: İstanbul Bilgi Üniversitesi Yayınları.

Kefela, G. T. (2010). Knowledge-based economy and society has become a vital commodity to countries. *International NGO Journal*, *5*(7), 160–166.

Kemp, R. L. (2001). *The inner city: A Handbook for Renewal*. McFarland & Company, Inc.

Khalifa University of Science, Technology and Research (KUSTAR). (2008). *Our mission*. Retrieved from http://www.kustar.ac.ae/main/index.php?page=themission

Khalifa, M. (2015). Evolution of informal settlements upgrading strategies in Egypt: From negligence to participatory development. *Ain Shams Engineering Journal*, *6*(4), 1151–1159. doi:10.1016/j.asej.2015.04.008

Kihato, C. (2010). *Urban Diversity: Space, Culture, and Inclusive Pluralism in Cities Worldwide*. Johns Hopkins University Press.

King, A. D. (2004). *Spaces of Global Cultures, Architecture, Urbanism, Identity*. London: Routledge.

Kipper, R. (2009). Cairo: a broader view. In R. Kipper & M. Fischer (Eds.), *Cairo's informal areas between urban challenges and hidden potentials* (pp. 12–15). Cairo: GTZ Egypt.

Kıyan, Z., & Yüksel, H. (2011). The GATS and the Globalizing Public Services: The Case of Turkey and Türk Telekom. *AİD TODAİE's Review of Public Administration*, *5*(1), 35–68.

Klaus, C. B. (Ed.). (2000). *Information Literacy Around the World: Advances in Programs and Research. The University of Michigan*. Centre for Information Studies, Charles Sturt University.

Knight, R. (2008). Knowledge based development. In Knowledge-based urban development. IGI Global.

Knight, V. R. (1995). Knowledge-based development: Policy and planning implications for cities. Urban Studies, 32(2), 225-260.

Knight, R. (1995). Knowledge-based development: Policy and planning implications for cities. *Urban Studies (Edinburgh, Scotland)*, *32*(2), 225–260. doi:10.1080/00420989550013068

Knight, R. (2008). Knowledge based development. In T. Yigitcanlar, K. Velibeyoglu, & S. Baum (Eds.), *Knowledge-based urban development* (pp. xiii–xviii). Hersey, PA: IGI Global.

Knowledge Village in Dubai. (n.d.). In *Wikipedia, the free encyclopedia*. Retrieved from http: www.wikipedia, org/wiki

Kok, A. (2007). Intellectual Capital Management as Part of Knowledge Management Initiatives at Institutions of Higher Learning. *Electronic Journal of Knowledge Management*, *5*(2), 181–192.

Komex, E. (2014). Architectural Contextualism and Emerging Hybrid Morphologies: the case of Olympic Sculpture Park for the Seatle Art Museum. In M. B. Kuijper (Ed.), *New Urban Configurations* (pp. 979–980). Amsterdam: IOS Press.

Komninos, N. (2002). *Intelligent Cities: Innovation, Knowledge Systems and Digital Spaces*. London: Routledge.

Kothin, J., & Devol, R. (2001). *Knowledge-Value Cities in the Digital Age*. Santa Monica, CA: Milken Institute.

Kotler, P. (1993). *Marketing Places*. Free Press.

Kotter, J. (2012). *Leading Change*. Boston: Harvard Business Review Press.

Kozhevnikov, M. (2007). Cognitive Styles in the Context of Modern Psychology: Toward a Cognitive Styles in the Context of Modern Psychology: Toward an. *Psychological Bulletin*, *133*(3), 464–481. doi:10.1037/0033-2909.133.3.464 PMID:17469987

Krauss, S. E. (2005, December). Research Paradigms and Meaning Making: A Primer. *Qualitative Report*, *10*(4), 758–770.

Kristofer, D. (2012). *Dubai model; Diversification and slowdown in the political economy of the Gulf region. Centre for Regional and International Studies*. Qatar: Faculty of International Affairs, Georgetown University.

Kuhn, T. S. (1970). *The Structure of Scientific Revolutions* (2nd ed.). International Encyclopedia of Unified Science.

Kumara. (2008). Speed implementation for provision of urban infrastructure: A case of Mysore city. *ITPI Journal*, *5*(4).

Kunzmann, K. (2008). Spatial dimensions of knowledge production. In Knowledge-based urban development. IGI Global.

Kunzmann, K. (2004). Culture, Creativity and Spatial Planning. *TPR*, *75*(4), 383–404.

Kunzmann, K. (2008). Spatial dimensions of knowledge production. In T. Yigitcanlar, K. Velibeyoglu, & S. Baum (Eds.), *Knowledge-based urban development:Planning and application in the information era* (pp. 296–300). Hersey, PA: IGI Global.

Kuwayama, T., & Bremen, J. V. (1997). Native Anthropologists: With Special Reference to Japanese Studies Inside and Outside Japan. *Japan Anthropology Workshop*.

Laguerre, M. S. (2006). *The Digital City: The American Metropolis and Information Technology*. Palgrave Macmillan.

Landry, C., & Wood, P. (Eds.). 2007. The Intercultural City: Planning for Diversity Advantage. London: Earthscan Publications Ltd.

Landry, C. (2000). *The creative city: a tool kit for urban innovators*. London: Earhscan.

Landry, C. (2000). *The Creative City: A Toolkit for Urban Innovators*. London: Earthscan Publications.

Landry, C. (2006). *The Art of City Making*. London: Earthscan Publications Ltd.

Laszlo, K. C., & Laszlo, A. (2007). Fostering a Sustainable Learning Society Through Knowledge-based Development. *Journal of Systems Research and Behavioral Science, 24*(5). Retrieved from http://onlinelibrary.wiley.com/doi/10.1002/sres.850/pdf

Laszlo, K. C., & Laszlo, A. (2007). Fostering a Sustainable Learning Society through Knowledge-Based Development. *Systems Research and Behavioral Science*, *24*(5), 493–503. doi:10.1002/sres.850

Laszlo, K., & Laszlo, A. (2002). Evolving knowledge for development: The role of knowledge management in a changing world. *Journal of Knowledge Management*, *6*(4), 400–412. doi:10.1108/13673270210440893

Lazlo & Lazlo. (2009). Fostering Sustainable Learning Society Through Knowledge Based Development. *System Research & Behavioral Science*, (24).

Le Dantec, C. A., & Do, E. Y.-L. (2009). The mechanisms of value transfer in design meetings. *Design Studies*, *30*(2), 119–137. doi:10.1016/j.destud.2008.12.002

Leach, A. (2006). The Conditional Autonomy of Tafuri's Historian / De Provisorische Autonomie van. *Oase Architecture Journal*, *69*, 14–29.

Learning from Education City International Conference. (2015). Organized by QF and AIA Middle East Chapter in Doha, Qatar. Retrieved from http://www.qf.org.qa/learningfromec/speakers

Leccese, M., & Mccormick, K. (1996). Charter of the New Urbanism. In *The fourth Congress for the New Urbanism (CNU IV)*. Charleston, SC: McGraw-Hill, Inc.

Lever, W. (2002). Correlating the knowledge-base of cities with economic growth. Urban Studies, 39(5-6), 859–870.

Lever, W. (2002). Correlating the Knowledge-base of Cities with Economic Growth. *Urban Studies (Edinburgh, Scotland)*, *39*(5–6), 859–870. doi:10.1080/00420980220128345

Ley, A., & Newton, P. (2010). Creating and Sustaining Liveable Cities. In K. Seetharam & B. Yuen (Eds.), *Developing Living Cities: From Analysis to Action* (pp. 191–229). Singapore: World Scientific Publishing and Imperial College Press. doi:10.1142/9789814304504_0008

Lima, A., Melnik, M., Avault, J., Blake, N. D., & Borella, N. (2011). *Boston by Numbers*. Boston, MA: Boston Redevelopment Authority. Retrieved from http://www.bostonredevelopmentauthority.org/getattachment/946803b2-6f1c-40b2-8b6b-c01c8c4bced1/

Lonnqvist, A., Kapyla, J., Salonius, H., & Yigitcanlar, T. (2014). Knowledge that matters: Identifying regional knowledge assets of Tampere Region. *European Planning Studies*, *22*(10), 2011–2029. doi:10.1080/09654313.2013.814621

Looser, T. (2012). The Global University, Area Studies, And The World Citizen: Neoliberal Geography's Redistribution Of The "World". *Cultural Anthropology*, *27*(1), 97–117. doi:10.1111/j.1548-1360.2012.01128.x

Lorimer, J. (1970). *Gazetteer of the Persian Gulf.* Dohah.

Luhmann, N. (2012). *Theory of Society*. Stanford, CA: Stanford University Press.

Lynch, K. (1960). *The Image of the City*. Boston: The MIT Press.

Lytras, M. D., Russ, M., Maier, R., & Naeve, A. (2000). *Knowledge Management Strategies: A Handbook of Applied Technologies*. New York: IGI Publishing.

MacDonald, F., & Fattah, Z. (2017). 100 Days of the Big Gulf Feud. *Bloomberg Business Week*.

Madanipour, A. (2011). *Knowledge Economy and the City: Spaces of Knowledge*. New York: Routledge.

Mahmoudi, D., & Levenda, N. (2016). *Beyond the screen: Uneven geographies, Digital Labour, and the city of Cognitive-Cultural Capitalism*. Academic Press.

Maldonado, A., & Romein, A. (2010). The role of organisational capacity and knowledge-based development. *Int. J. Knowledge-Based Development*, *1*(1), 79–96. doi:10.1504/IJKBD.2010.032587

Malone, T., & Yohe, G. (2002). Knowledge partnerships for a sustainable, equitable and stable society. *Journal of Knowledge Management*, *6*(4), 368–378. doi:10.1108/13673270210440875

Manchester City Council. (2015). *2015 – UK-GBC City Conference Summary Report*. Manchester, UK: Green Building Council.

Manuel, C. (1989). *The Informational City*. Williston, VT: Blackwell.

Marcus, G. (1995). Ethnography in/of the world system: The emergence of multisite ethnography. *Annual Review of Anthropology*, *24*(1), 95–117. doi:10.1146/annurev.an.24.100195.000523

Marshall, A. (1890). Principles of Economics (Originally published in 1890 ed., Vol. 1). Princeton, NJ: Macmillan and Company.

Marshall, R. (2012). Josep Louis Sert's Urban Design Legacy, From Josep Louis Sert: The Architect of Urban Design (2008). In M. Larice & E. Macdonald (Eds.), The Urban Design Reader (2nd ed.; pp. 106-117). Routledge.

Martínez, D. S. (2006). A Comparative Framework for Knowledge Cities. In F. J. Carrillo (Ed.), *Knowledge Cities: Approaches, Experiences and Perspectives* (pp. 17–30). Burlington, MA: Elsevier Butterworth-Heinemann. doi:10.1016/B978-0-7506-7941-1.50005-1

Masdar City. (2008). *Masdar City at a glance: Key buildings*. Academic Press.

Masdar City. (n.d.). *Pioneering Innovation at Masdar City. Academic Press.*

Masdar Institute of Science and Technology (MIST). (2010). *Vision & mission*. Retrieved from http://www.masdar.ac.ae/aboutus/VisionMission.php

McAfee & Brynjolfsson. (2007). Investing in the IT That Makes a Competitive Difference. *Harvard Business Review.*

Mehrem, H. (2014). *What to do with Egypt's Informal Economy?* Available at: http://www.egypt-business.com/Paper/details/1448-What-to-do-with-Egypts-Informal-Economy/11368

Mehta, V. (2015). *Public Space*. London: Routledge.

Méndez, R., & Moral, S. S. (2010). Spanish Cities in the Knowledge Economy: Theoretical Debates and Empirical Evidence. *European Urban and Regional Studies*, *18*(2), 136–155. doi:10.1177/0969776410381039

Metaxiotis, K., Carrillo, J., & Yigitcanlar, T. (Eds.). (2010). *Knowledge-based development for cities and societies: an integrated multi-level approach.* Hersey, PA: Information Science Reference. doi:10.4018/978-1-61520-721-3

Metaxiotis, K., & Psarras, J. (2004). Applying knowledge management in higher education: The creation of a learning organization. *Journal of Information and Knowledge Management*, *6*(4), 1–7.

Michaud, P., & Tcheremenska, A. (2003). *Montreal, Knowledge city.* Retrieved from http://ville.montreal.qc.ca/pls/portal/docs/page/contenus_partages_en/vie_montreal/media/documents/mtl-knowledge.pdf

Mieg. (2012). Sustainability and innovation in urban development: concept and case. *Journal of Sustainable Development, 20*(4), 251-263.

Miles, M., & Hall, T. (Eds.). (2003). *Urban Futures*. London: Routledge.

Mills, E. S., & Hamilton, B. W. (1989). *Urban Economics (4th ed.)*. Boston: Scott, Foreman and Company.

Ministry of Communications and Information Technology. (2007). *Egypt's National Vision for Information Society (2000- 2005); Egypt's ICT National Strategy 2007- 2010*. Author.

Ministry of Development. (2014). *2015-2018 Bilgi Toplumu Stratejisi ve Eylem Planı*. Ankara: MoD. Retrieved October 21, 2016 from http://www.telkoder.org.tr/docDownload.php?docID=2287

Ministry of Development. (2015). *2015-2018 Information Society Strategy and Action Plan.* Ankara: MoD. Retrieved October 21, 2016 from http://www.bilgitoplumu.gov.tr/en/wp-content/uploads/2016/03/Information_Society_Strategy_and_Action_Plan_2015-2018.pdf

Ministry of Education. (2012). *Education in Singapore*. Retrieved from www.moe.gov.sg

Ministry of Information, Communications and the Arts. (2012). *Singapore culture statistics 2012*. Retrieved from www.mica.gov.sg

Mirincheva. V. (2017, March 7). The Qatar Faculty of Islamic Studies by Mangera Yvars is a process of continuous learning and enlightenment. *The Architectural Review.*

Mitchell, T. (2002). *Rule of Experts, Egypt, Techno-Politics, Modernity*. Berkeley, CA: University of California press.

Mitchell, W. (1995). *City of Bits: Space, Place, and the Infobahn*. Cambridge, MA: MIT Press.

Mohan, R. (1979). *Urban Economic and Planning Models*. Baltimore, MD: Johns Hopkins University Press.

Mojtahedi, P. (2013). The Impact of Intellectual Capital on Earning Quality: Evidence from Malaysian Firms. *Australian Journal of Basic and Applied Sciences*, *7*(2), 535–540.

Mokyr, J. (2004). *The Gifts of Athena: Historical Origins of the Knowledge Economy*. Oxford, UK: Princeton University Press.

Monnavarian, A., Mosakhani, M., & Akbari, M. (2012). Is Tehran a knowledge city? *Journal of Place Management and Development, 5*(2), 158–173. doi:10.1108/17538331211250053

Monreal, C. O. (2016). Intelligent Technologies for Mobility in Smart Cities. *Hradstechnika, 71*, 29–36.

Monzon, A. (2015). Smart Cities Concept and Challenges: Bases for the Assessment of Smart City Projects. *Proceedings of the Smartgreens 2015, Smart cities, Green technologies, and Intelligent Transport Systems*, 17–31.

Moore, R. C., & Cosco, N. G. (2010). Using behavior mapping to investigate healthy outdoor environments for children and families. In C. W. Thompson, P. Aspinall, & S. Bell (Eds.), Innovative Approaches to Researching Landscape and Health: Open Space: People Space 2 (pp. 33–72). Taylor & Francis.

Morse, S. (2004). *Smart Communities*. Jossey-Bass.

Mortada, H. (2003). *Traditional Islamic Principles of Built Environment*. London: Routledge Curzon.

Moser, S., Swain, M., & Alkhabbaz, M. H. (2015). King Abdullah Economic City: Engineering Saudi Arabia's post-oil future. Cities, 45, 71–80.

Moss, W. (1998). Technology and Cities. *Cityscape: A Journal of Policy Development and Research, 3*(3), 107-127.

Mostafa, A. M., & Mohamed, K. Y. (2016). An Approach for Promoting Urban and Architectural Potentials for Supporting Knowledge Economy, Case Study: Brisbane. *Procedia - Social and Behavioral Sciences, 216*, 20–29. doi:10.1016/j.sbspro.2015.12.003

Mostafa, M. (2013). Closing the loop: teaching what we have learned from learning from Cairo-an academic perspective. In B. Stryker, O. Nagati, & M. Mostafa (Eds.), *Learning from Cairo: global perspectives and future visions* (pp. 134–136). Cairo: Cluster.

Murphy, B. (2011, February 15). *Bahrain Square Becomes New Center for Arab Anger*. Associated Press.

Musterd, S. and Gritsai. (2012). The creative knowledge city in Europe: Structural conditions and urban policy strategies for competitive cities. *European Urban and Regional Studies*, (April): 1–17.

Nafi, S. I., Alattar, D. A., & Furlan, R. (2015). Built Form of the Souq Waqifin Doha and User's Social Engagement. *American Journal of Sociological Research, 5*(3), 73–88.

Nagy, S. (2000). Dressing Up Downtown: Urban development and government public image in Qatar. *City & Society, 12*(1), 125–147. doi:10.1525/city.2000.12.1.125

Nam, T., & Pardo, T. (2011). Smart City as Urban Innovation: Focusing on Management, Policy, and Context. *Proceedings of the 5th International Conference on Theory and Practice of Electronic Governance*, 185–194. doi:10.1145/2072069.2072100

Narula, R. (2003). *Globlization & Technology; Interdependence, Innovation systems and Industrial policy*. MPC Book LTD.

Negroponte, N. (1995). *Being Digital*. New York: Alfred A. Knopf.

Netto, V. M. (2017). *The Social Fabric of Cites (Design and the Built Environment)*. New York: Routledge.

Nguyen, T. (2010). *Knowledge economy and sustainable economic development: A critical review*. Munich: de Gruyter Saur.

Nguyen, T. (2010). Knowledge Economy and Sustainable Economic Development. De Gruyter Saur, Munich. *International Journal of Knowledge-Based Development, 5*(3), 2014.

Nickerson, N. P. (1993). Understanding your consumers through behavioral mapping. *Parks & Recreation*.

Nickitas, D. M., Middaugh, D. J., & Aries, N. (2011). *Policy and Politics for Nurses and Other Health Professionals*. London, UK: Jones and Bartlete Publishers Internationa.

Nonaka, I. (1994). *A Dynamic Theory of Organizational Knowledge Creation*. Retrieved from http://www.jstor.org/stable/2635068

Nonaka, I. (1997). Nonaka's Four Modes of Knowledge Conversion. In *Knowledge Advantage Conference*. Retrieved from http://www.uky.edu/~gmswan3/575/nonaka.pdf

Nonaka, I. (2007). The Knowledge-Creating Company. *Harvard Business Review*. Retrieved from https://hbr.org/2007/07/the-knowledge-creating-company

Nonaka, I. (1994). A Dynamic Theory of Organizational Knowledge Creation. *Organization Science*, *5*(1), 14–37. doi:10.1287/orsc.5.1.14

Nonaka, I., & Takeuchi, H. (1995a). *The knowledge-Creating Company*. Oxford, UK: Oxford University Press.

Nonaka, I., & Takeuchi, H. (1995b). The Knowledge-Creating Company. *Creativity Research Journal*, *10*(4), 285–301.

Nonaka, I., Toyama, R., & Byosiere, P. (2001). A Theory of Organizational Knowledge Creation: Understanding the Dynamic Process of Creating Knowledge. In M. D. Nonaka (Ed.), *Handbook of organizational learning and knowledge* (pp. 487–491). Oxford, UK: Oxford University Press.

North, K., & Kumta, G. (2014). *Knowledge Management: Value Creation Through Organizational Learning*. Springer International Publishing Switzerland. doi:10.1007/978-3-319-03698-4

Northwestern University Qatar. (2014). *Social media ubiquiitous, more used than email*. Retrieved September 2017, from http://www.mideastmedia.org/survey/2015/chapter/social-media.html#subchapter4

O'Connor, K., Derudder, B., & Witlox, F. (2015). Logistics Services: Global Functions and Global Cities. *Growth and Change*, *47*(4), 481–496. doi:10.1111/grow.12136

O'Dell, C. C., & Grayson, J. (2012). *If Only We Knew What We Know: The Transfer of Internal Knowledge and Best Practice*. New York: Free Press.

OECD. (1996). *The knowledge-based economy*. Paris: OECD. Retrieved October 22, 2016 from https://www.oecd.org/sti/sci-tech/1913021.pdf

OECD. (1996). *The Knowledge-Based Economy. Science, Technology and Industry Outlook 1996*. Paris: Organisation for Economic Co-operation and Development.

Organisation for Economic Co-operation and Development. (1996). *The Knowledge-based Economy*Retrieved from https://www.oecd.org/sti/sci-tech/1913021.pdf

Organization For Economic Co-Operation. (1996). *The knowledge-based Economy*. Paris: Organization For Economic Co-Operation and Development OECD.

Orzan, S. (2014.) *An Interview with Damiano Cerrone, Co-Founder of SPIN Unit*. Retrieved September 2017, from http://www.startuberlin.com/spin-unit-damiano-cerrone-interview/

Othman, N. (1984). *With Their Bare Hands: The Story of the Oil Industry in Qatar*. London: Longman.

Ovalle, M., Marquez, J., & Salomon, S. (2004). A compilation of resources on knowledge cities and knowledge-based development. *Journal of Knowledge Management*, *8*(5), 107–127.

Ovalle, M., Marquez, J., & Salomon, S. (2004). A compilation of resources on knowledge cities and knowledge-based development. *Journal of Knowledge Management*, *8*(5), 107–127. doi:10.1108/13673270410558819

Overall Intelligent Change Coming. (n.d.). *Tech Magazine for All C4 No. 121*. Retrieved from http://www.dsg.gov.ae

Oxford Business Group (OBG). (2016). *The Report. Qatar*. Author.

Paganoni, M. C. (2015). Introduction — City Branding and New Media: Linguistic, Discursive and Semiotic Aspects. In City Branding and New Media (pp. 1–12). London: Palgrave Macmillan UK. doi:10.1057/9781137387967_1

Pancholi, S., Yigitcanlar, T., & Guaralda, M. (2014). Urban knowledge and innovation spaces: Concepts, conditions and contexts. *Asia Pacific Journal of Innovation and Entrepreneurship*, *8*(1), 15–38.

Pancholi, S., Yigitcanlar, T., & Guaralda, M. (2015). Place making facilitators of knowledge and innovation spaces: Insights from the European best practices. *International Journal of Knowledge-Based Development*, *6*(3), 215–240. doi:10.1504/IJKBD.2015.072823

Pancholi, S., Yigitcanlar, T., & Guaralda, M. (2017a). Place making in knowledge and innovation spaces: The Australia experience. *Technological Forecasting and Social Change*. doi:10.1016/j.techfore.2017.09.014

Pancholi, S., Yigitcanlar, T., & Guaralda, M. (2017b). Governance that matters: Identifying place-making challenges of Melbourne's Monash Employment Cluster. *Journal of Place Management and Development*, *10*(1), 73–87. doi:10.1108/JPMD-08-2016-0053

Paul, R., & Elder, L. (2008). *The Thinker's Guide to The Nature and Functions of Critical & Creative Thinking*. The Foundation for Critical Thinking. Retrieved 11 15, 2014, from http://www.criticalthinking.org/files/CCThink_6.12.08.pdf

Perry, B. (2008). Academic Knowledge and Urban Development: Theory, Policy, and Practice. In T. Yigitcanlar, K. Velibeyoglu, & S. Baum (Eds.), *Knowledge Based Urban Development: Planning and Applications in the Information Era*. Hershey, New York: IGI Global. doi:10.4018/978-1-59904-720-1.ch002

Perry, B., & May, T. (2010). Urban knowledge exchange: Devilish dichotomies and active intermediation. *International Journal of Knowledge-Based Development*, *1*(1/2), 6–24. doi:10.1504/IJKBD.2010.032583

Peyroux, E., Grossetti, M., & Eckert, D. (2009). Becoming a Knowledge City: The Example of Toulouse. *Built Environment*, *35*(2), 196–203. doi:10.2148/benv.35.2.196

Pfeifer, L. (2013) *The Planner's Guide to Tactical Urbanism*. Montreal: McGill. Pogue, D. *David Pogue tested 47 pill-reminder apps to find the best*. Retrieved September 2017, from https://finance.yahoo.com/news/david-pogue-tested-47-pill-reminder-apps-to-find-the-best-154017023.html

Piffero, E. (2009). Beyond rules and regulations: the growth of informal Cairo. In R. Kipper & M. Fischer (Eds.), *Cairo's informal areas between urban challenges and hidden potentials* (pp. 20–27). Cairo: GTZ Egypt.

Plato, . (1935). *Plato's Theory of Knowledge: The Theaetetus and the Sophist of Plato* (F. M. Cornford, Trans.). Routledge and Kegan Paul Ltd.

Pol, P., Winden, W., Woets, P., & Berg, L. (Eds.). (2005). European Cities in the Knowledge Economy: The Cases of Amsterdam, Dortmund, Eindhoven, Helsinki, Manchester, Munich, Munster, Rotterdam and Zaragoza (EURICUR. Institute for Comparative Urban Research). Ashgate Publishing.

Polanyi, M. (2009). *The Tacit Dimension*. University Of Chicago Press.

Ponzini, D., & Nastasi, M. (2011). *Starchitecture: Scenes, actors and spectacles in contemporary cities*. Turin: Allemandi.

Porter, M. E. (2000). Location, Competition, and Economic Development: Local Clusters in a Global Economy. *Economic Development Quarterly*, *14*(1), 15–34. doi:10.1177/089124240001400105

President Erdoğan Inaugurates Osmangazi Bridge. (2016, June 30). Retrieved October 21, 2016 from http://www.tccb.gov.tr/en/news/542/45570/president-erdogan-inaugurates-osmangazi-bridge.html

Prins, F. J., Veenman, M. V., & Elshout, J. J. (2006). The Impact of Intellectual Ability and Metacognition on Learning: New Support for the Threshold of Problematicity Theory. *Learning and Instruction*, *16*(4), 374–387. doi:10.1016/j.learninstruc.2006.07.008

Qatar General Secretariat of Development Planning (QSDP). (2009). *Qatar National Vision 2030. Advancing Sustainable Development, Qatar's Second Human Development Report*. Gulf Publishing and Printing Company.

Qatar General Secretariat of Development Planning (QSDP). (2011). *National Development Strategy 2011- 2016*. Doha: Gulf Publishing and Printing Company.

Qatar General Secretariat of Development Planning (QSDP). (2011). *National Development Strategy 2011-2016*. Doha: Gulf Publishing and Printing Company.

Qatar National Development Framework (QNDF). (2016). *The Ministry of Municipality and Environment*. Author.

Qatar Statistics Authority. (2015). *QSA Population*. Retrieved February 22, 2015, from http://www.qsa.gov.qa/eng/populationstructure.htm

QSDP. (2011). *National Development Strategy 2011–2016*. Doha, Qatar: Gulf Publishing and Printing Company.

QSDP. (2011). *Qatar General Secretariat of Development Planning National Development Strategy 2011–2016*. Doha, Qatar: Gulf Publishing and Printing Company.

Queensland Government. (2011). *Western Brisbane Transport Network strategy*. Minister for Transport.

Queensland Government. (n.d.). *Brisbane, Queensland, Australia*. Retrieved October 22, 2016, from http://www.queensland.com/en-us/explore-queensland/brisbane

Rahman, H. (2005). *The emergence of Qatar: the turbulent years, 1627-1916*. London: Kegan Paul.

Ramadan, E. (2015). Sustainable Urbanization in the Arabian Gulf Region: Problems and Challenges. *Citation: Ramadan E Arts Social Sci J*, *64172*(10910), 2151–6200. doi:10.4172/2151

Reades, J., Calabrese, F., Sevtsuk, A., & Ratti, C. (2007). Cellular Census: Explorations in Urban Data Collection. IEEE Pervasive Computing.

Rehm, D. (2006, April 14). *The Diane Rehm Show. U.S. College Education*. Washington, DC: WAMU.

Riad, M. (1983). The Arabian Gulf and Its People Prior to 1930. *The Gulf and Arabian Peninsula Studies*, *9*(26), 215–398.

Riad, M. (1985). Some Aspects of Petro-Urbanism in the Gulf States. *Arabia Gulf Studies*, *37*, 63–84.

Richer, R. (2009). *Conservation in Qatar: Impacts of Increasing Industrialization. Center for International and Regional Studies (CIRS)*. Qatar: Georgetown University.

Rico, T., & Exell, K. (Eds.). (2014). *Cultural Heritage in the Arabian Peninsula - Debates, Discourses and Practices*. London: Ashgate.

Rittgasszer, I. (2013). Knowledge-based Urban Development, as a New Development Paradigm. *University of Szeged, Doctoral School in Economics*, 36–46.

Rittgasszer, I. (2013). Knowledge-based Urban Development, as a New Development Paradigm. In *Regional Growth, Development and Competitiveness*. Szeged: Doctoral School in Economics.

Roberts, D. B. (2015). *Qatar: Securing the Global Ambitions of a City-state*. London: C Hurst & Co Publishers Ltd.

Roberts, J. (2009). The global knowledge economy in question. *Critical Perspectives on International Business*, *5*(4), 285–303. doi:10.1108/17422040911003033

Robinson, K. (1999). *National Advisory Committee on Creative and Cultural Education, All Our Futures: Creativity, Culture and Education*. The Secretary of State for Education and Employment and the Secretary of State for Culture, Media and Sport. London: National Advisory Committee on Creative and Cultural Education (NACCCE). Retrieved from http://sirkenrobinson.com/pdf/allourfutures.pdf

Rokeach, M. (1973). *The Nature of Human Values*. New York: Free Press.

Romein, A., Fernandez-Maldonado, A., & Trip, J. (2011). Delft blues, *Int. J. Knowledge-Based Development*, *2*(2), 148–165. doi:10.1504/IJKBD.2011.041245

Rosenberg, B. C. (2016). Shhh! Noisy Cities, Anti-Noise Groups and Neoliberal Citizenship. *Journal of Sociology (Melbourne, Vic.)*, *52*(2), 190–203. doi:10.1177/1440783313507493

Ryle, G. (2009). The Concept of Mind. Chicago: Routledge.

Sachs, W. (2010). *The Development Dictionary, a guide to knowledge as power* (2nd ed.). London: Zed Books.

Safouane, Y. (2015). Inventing New Cities: Case Studies from Morocco. In *(Re)inventing Cities: Successful Cases seminar*. Retrieved from http://www.ocppc.ma/events/seminars-series/reinventing-cities-successful-cases#.WbjEoFEjFnI

Sahdra, B., & Thagard, P. (2003). Procedural knowledge in molecular biology. *Philosophical Psychology*, *16*(4), 477–498. doi:10.1080/0951508032000121788

Sakr, T. (1993). *Early Twentieth-Century Islamic Architecture in Cairo*. Cairo: American University in Cairo Press.

Salama, A. M., Remali, A. M., & Rahimian, F. P. (2017). A decade of architectural and urban research. *International Journal of Architectural Research, 11*(1), 6-28.

Sanders, T. I. (2008). Complex system thinking and new urbanism. In *New Urbanism and Beyond designing cities for the future* (pp. 275–279). New York, NY: Rizzoli.

Sanyal, B. (2000). Planning's three challenges. In L. Rodwin & B. Sanyal (Eds.), *The profession of city planning: changes, images, and challenges 1950-2000* (pp. 312–333). Rutgers: The State of New Jersey.

Sarimin, M., & Yigitcanlar, T. (2011). Knowledge-based urban development of Multimedia Super Corridor, Malaysia: An overview. *International Journal of Knowledge Based Development*, *2*(1), 34–48. doi:10.1504/IJKBD.2011.040623

Sarimin, M., & Yigitcanlar, T. (2012). Towards a comprehensive and integrated knowledge-based urban development model. *International Journal of Knowledge Based Development*, *3*(2), 175–192. doi:10.1504/IJKBD.2012.047035

Sassen, S. (2001). The Global City: New York, London, Tokyo (2nd ed.). Academic Press. doi:10.1515/9781400847488

Sassen, S. (1991). *The Global City*. Princeton University Press.

Sassen, S. (2002). *Global Networks, Linked Cities: Urban connections In a Globalizing World*. New York: Routledge.

Saudi Arabian Consortium win Turk Telecom privatization tender. (2005, July 2). Retrieved October 21, 2016 from http://www.hurriyet.com.tr/saudi-arabian-consortium-win-turk-telecom-privatization-tender-331772

Saygı, N. (2002). Telekomünikasyon ve Bilgi Teknolojileri Pazarı: Mevcut Durum ve 10 Yıllık Perspektif. *Telekomünikasyon Ekseni, 4*, 17–34.

Schmoker, M. (2007). Reading, Writing, and Thinking for All. *EL Educational Leadership, 64*(7), 63-66.

School of Management, Granfeild University. (n.d.). *Understanding Corporate Value: Managing and reporting intellectual capital.* London: Institute of Management Accountants (CIMA).

Scott, A. J. (2006). Creative Cities; Conceptual Issues and Policy Questions. *Journal of Urban Affairs, 28*(1).

Scott, A. J. (2011). Emerging cities of the third wave. *City, 15*(3–4), 289–321. doi:10.1080/13604813.2011.595569

Scott, A. J. (2014). Beyond the Creative City: Cognitive–Cultural Capitalism and the New Urbanism. *Regional Studies, 48*(4), 565–578. doi:10.1080/00343404.2014.891010

Scott, J. C. (1999). *Seeing like a State: How Certain Schemes to Improve the Human Condition Have Failed.* Yale University Press.

Séjourné, M. (2009). The history of informal settlements. In R. Kipper & M. Fischer (Eds.), *Cairo's informal areas between urban challenges and hidden potentials* (pp. 16–19). Cairo: GTZ Egypt.

Sen, A. (1999). *Development as Freedom.* Oxford University Press.

Şenerdem, E. (2015, November 3). Bir Candy Crush nelere bedel? *BBC Türkçe.* Retrieved October 21, 2016 from http://www.bbc.com/turkce/ekonomi/2015/11/151103_candy_crush_nelere_bedel

Shaqrah, A. (2014). The Role of Greater Amman Municipality in the Making of a Knowledge City. *European Scientific Journal, 10*(28), 448–456. Retrieved from http://www.eujournal.org/index.php/esj/article/view/4410

Shehabi, A., & Jones, M. O. (Eds.). (2015). *Bahrain's Uprising.* London: Zed Books.

Shehayeb, D. (2009). Advantages of Living in Informal Areas. In R. Kipper & M. Fischer (Eds.), *Cairo's informal areas between urban challenges and hidden potentials* (pp. 34–43). Cairo: GTZ Egypt.

Shehayeb, D., & Eid, Y. (2007). Neighbourhood Design and Community Building: A model of social interaction. In *The appropriate home: Can we design"appropriate" residential environments?* (pp. 129–144). Cairo: HBNRC.

Sims, D. (2003). *Cairo, Egypt - understanding slums: case studies for the global report 2003.* UN Habitat. Available from: http://www.ucl.ac.uk/dpu-projects/Global_Report/pdfs/ Cairo.pdf

Sims, D. (n.d.). *Library - analytical materials.* The Habitat International Coalition's specialized Member group: Housing and Land Rights Network (HIC-HLRN). Available at: http://www.landpedia.org/landdoc/Analytical_materials/Sims_Residential_Informality_in_Greater_Cairo. pdf

Singapore Economic Development Board. (2016). *Knowledge-Based Economy.* Retrieved October 29, 2016, from https://www.edb.gov.sg/content/edb/en/why-singapore/about-singapore/values/knowledge.html

Smart Living City Dubai. (2014). Retrieved from http: //www.smart Living city. Com

Smart Village Egypt. (n.d.). *About Us.* Retrieved from https://www.smart-villages.com/en/page/page/147

Smith, C. (1985a). Class relations and urbanization in Guatemala: Toward an Alternative Theory of Urban Primacy. In M. Timberlake (Ed.), Urbanization in the World-Economy (pp. 121–167). New York, NY: Academic Press.

Smith, C. (1985b). Theories and Measures of Urban Primacy: A Critque. In M. Timberlake (Ed.), *Urbanization in the World-Economy* (pp. 87–117). New York, NY: Academic Press.

Söderström, O. (2014). Trajectories of Urban Change in Two Ordinary Cities. In *Cities in Relations* (pp. 31–59). Oxford, UK: John Wiley & Sons, Ltd.; doi:10.1002/9781118632758.ch2

Solvell, O. (2009). *Along-term Strategy for Dubai Bulding On Innovation and Clusters.* Dubia Economic Councial.

Soto, R. (2013). Education in Dubai From Quantity to Quality. Dubai Economic Council.

Souleh, S. (2014). The impact of Human Capital Management on the Innovativeness of research Center: The Case of Scientific Research Centers in Algeria. *International Journal of Business and Management, 2*(4), 80–96.

SRTA-City. (n.d.). *Vision & Mission.* Retrieved from http://mucsat.org/index.php?option=com_content&view=article&id=46&Itemid=63

Starovic, D., & Marr, B. (2003). *Understanding Corporate Value: managing and reporting intellectual capital. The Chartered Institute of Management Accountants (CIMA), School of Management.* London, UK: CIMA.

State Planning Organization. (2006). *Information Society Strategy (2006-2010).* Ankara: SPO. Retrieved from http://www.bilgitoplumu.gov.tr/Documents/5/Documents/Information_Society_Strategy.pdf

Stewart, T. A. (1997). *Intellectual Capital: The New Wealth of Organizations.* New York: Doubleday/Currency.

Stock, G. W. (2011). Informational Cities: Analysis and Construction of Cities in the Knowledge Society. *Journal of the American Society for Information Science and Technology, 62*(5), 963–986. doi:10.1002/asi.21506

Sullivan, P. (2012). *Qualitative Data Analysis: Using a dialogic approach.* Los Angeles: SAGE Publications Ltd. doi:10.4135/9781446268391

Tadamun. (2014). *Coming up short: Egyptian government approaches to informal areas.* The Tadamun Initiative. Available from: http://www.tadamun.info/

Tadros, M. E. (2015). The Arab Gulf States and the Knowledge Economy: Challenges and Opportunities. Washington, DC: Academic Press.

Takeuchi, H., & Nonaka, I. (1995). *The Knowledge Creating Company.* Oxford, UK: Oxford University Press.

Tan, Y. (2007). The Making of Urban Spaces for the Knowledge Economy: Global Practices. *Proceedings The 2nd International Symposium on knowledge cities: future of cities in the Knowledge Economy.*

Tan, Y. (2011). Knowledge-based urban development redefined: from theory to practice knowledge-based development of cities. *Proceedings of the 4th Knowledge Cities World Summit.*

Tan, Y., & Muna, S. (2010). Orchestrating knowledge-based urban development: lessons from multimedia super corridor, Malaysia. In Knowledge-Based Development for Cities and Societies – Integrated Multi-Level Approaches. IGI Global.

Taylor, P., Derudder, B., Saey, P., & Witlox, F. (2006). *Cities in Globalization: Practices, policies and theories.* London: Routledge.

Tharoor, I. (2017). The Persian Gulf crisis over Qatar, explained. *The Washington Post.* Retrieved from https://www.washingtonpost.com/news/worldviews/wp/2017/06/06/the-persian-gulf-crisis-over-qatar-explained/?utm_term=.507e62718366

The Commission for Architecture and the Built Environment and the Greater London Authority. (2009). *Open space strategies Best practice guidance.* Blackmore Ltd.

The Foundation. (2016, January 19). *Learning from Education City.* Author.

The Guardian. (n.d.). *World's first zero-carbon city: Masdar in pictures.* Retrieved from https://www.theguardian.com/environment/gallery/2011/apr/26/masdar-eco-city-abu-dhabi

The World Capital Institute & Teleos. (2009). *The Most Admired Knowledge Cities (MAKCi) Report.* Retrieved from http://www.worldcapitalinstitute.org/

The World Capital Institute & Teleos. (2012). *The Most Admired Knowledge Cities (MAKCi) Report.* Retrieved from http://www.worldcapitalinstitute.org/

Thierstein, A. (2017). Residence, workplace and commute: Interrelated spatial choices of knowledge workers in the metropolitan region of Munich. *Journal of Transport Geography, 62*, 197-212.

Thierstein, A., & Schein, E. (2008). Emerging Cities on the Arabian Peninsula: Urban Space in the Knowledge Economy Context. *Archnet-IJAR: International Journal of Architectural Research, 2*(2), 178–195.

Thomson, D. S., Austin, S. A., Devine-Wright, H., & Mills, G. R. (2003). Managing Value and Quality in Design. *Building Research and Information, 31*(5), 334–345. doi:10.1080/0961321032000087981

Ting, K.-S. (2012). How Accumulation of Intellectual Capital of IC Design Firms Listed in Taiwan Impacts Organization Performances: Organizational Learning Capability as the Mediator. *The Journal of Global Business Management, 8*(1), 60–73.

Toffler, A. (1971). *Future Shock.* New York: Bantam Books.

Toffler, A. (1981). *The Third Wave.* New York: Bantam Books.

Törenli, N. (2005). Türkiye'de Telefon Haberleşmesi Alanında Yaşanan Dönüşüm: Neo-liberal Politikalar Eşliğinde Ulus Devletin Elinden Alınan Politika Araçları. *Kültür ve İletişim, 8*(1), 11–40.

Turkish Statistical Institute. (2016). *Konut Satış İstatistikleri, Ağustos 2016.* Retrieved October 21, 2016 from http://www.tuik.gov.tr/PreHaberBultenleri.do?id=21716

Turner, P. (2010). *On IT strategies.* Enterprise Architecture Summer Camp.

Ulrichsen, K. C. (2011). *Insecure Gulf: The End of Certainty and the Transition to the Post-oil Era.* London: C Hurst & Co.

UNDESA. (2014). *World Urbanization Prospects: The 2014 Revision, Highlights. New York, United.* New York, NY: United Nations, Department of Economic and Social Affairs, Population Division. Retrieved from https://esa.un.org/unpd/wup/Publications/Files/WUP2014-Highlights.pdf

UNDP. (2015). *Human Development Report 2015.* New York, NY: Work for Human Development.

UNESCO. (2005). *Towards Knowledge Societies.* Paris: UNESCO Publications.

UNESCO. (2005). *Towards knowledge societies.* Paris: UNESCO Publishing.

UNESCO. (2005). *Towards Knowledge Society.* Paris: The United Nations Educational, Scientific, and Cultural Organisation.

UN-Habitat. (2012). *The State of Arab Cities 2012 Challenges of Urban Transition.* Retrieved from http://www.citiesalliance.org/sites/citiesalliance.org/files/SOAC-2012.pdf

United Nations Department of Economic and Social Affairs. (2005). *Understanding Knowledge Societies.* Retrieved from https://publicadministration.un.org/publications/content/PDFs/E-Library Archives/2005 Understanding Knowledge Societies.pdf

United Nations Development Program (UNDP). (2003). *Arab human development report 2003: Building a knowledge society*. New York: United Nations Publications.

United Nations Development Programme (UNDP). (2003). *Arab human development.* Author.

United Nations Development Programme. (2006). *Knowledge Services and Learning*. New York, NY: United Nations. Retrieved from http://content-ext.undp.org/aplaws_publications/1463060/Knowledge-Services-Learning.pdf

United Nations Organization. (2001). *Making new technologies work for human development, The Human Development Report 2001*. New York, NY: UNO.

University of Salford. (2011). *The campus plan: Urban initiatives*. Author.

Upbin, B. (2012). Facebook Buys Instagram for $1 Billion. Smart Arbitrage. *Forbes*. Retrieved October 21, 2016 from http://www.forbes.com/sites/bruceupbin/2012/04/09/facebook-buys-instagram-for-1-billion-wheres-the-revenue/#553c1ebe447f

URBACT. (2015). *Manchester*. Retrieved October 28, 2016, from http://urbact.eu/manchester

Uzunçarşılı Baysal, C. (2016, February 7). *Probing the 3rd Airport Project vis-a-vis Life, Nature, Environment and People*. Retrieved October 21, 2016 from http://www.kuzeyormanlari.org/2016/02/07/probing-the-3rd-airport-project-vis-a-vis-life-nature-environment-and-people/

Valverde, M. (2012). *Everyday Law on the Street: City Governance in an Age of Diversity (Chicago Series in Law and Society)*. The University of Chicago Press. doi:10.7208/chicago/9780226921914.001.0001

van den Berg, L., Pol, P. M., Winden, W., & Woets, P. (2005). European Cities in the Knowledge Economy: The Case of Amsterdam, Dortmund, Eindhoven, Helsinki, Manchester, Munich, Munster, Rutterdam and Zaragoza. Hants, UK: Ashgate.

van Winden, W. (n.d.). *Urban knowledge economies affected by the crisis?* Retrieved from http://urbact.eu/sites/default/files/import/general_library/article-WINDEN_01.pdf

Van Winden, W. (2008). Urban governance in the knowledge-based economy: Challenges for different city types. *Innovation, Management. Policy & Practice*, *10*(2-3), 197–210. doi:10.5172/impp.453.10.2-3.197

van Winden, W. (2010). Knowledge and the European City. *Tijdschrift voor Economische en Sociale Geografie*, *101*(1), 100–106. doi:10.1111/j.1467-9663.2009.00591.x

Van Winden, W., Berg, W., van Den, L., & Peter, P. (2007). European cities in the knowledge economy. *Urban Studies (Edinburgh, Scotland)*, *44*(3), 525–549. doi:10.1080/00420980601131886

Van Winden, W., Carvalho, L. D., Van Tujil, E., Van Haaren, J., & Van Den Berg, L. (2010). *Creating Knowledge Locations in Cities: Innovation and Integration Challenges*. Rotterdam: Euricur.

van Winden, W., & van den Berg, L. (2004). *Cities in the knowledge economy: new governance challenges*. European Institute for Comparative Urban Research.

van Winden, W., van den Berg, L., Carvalho, L., & van Tuijl, E. (2011). *Manufacturing in the New Urban Economy*. Routledge.

Veenman, M. V., Elshout, J. J., & Groen, M. G. (1993). Thinking Aloud: Does it Affect Regulatory Processes in Learning? *Tijdschrift voor Onderwijsresearch*, (18): 322–330.

Veenman, M. V., Wilhelm, P., & Jos, J. (2004). The Relation Between Intellectual and Metacognitive Skills from a Developmental Perspective. *Learning and Instruction*, *14*(1), 89–109. doi:10.1016/j.learninstruc.2003.10.004

Velibeyoglu, K., & Yigitcanlar, T. (2008). Understanding the supply side: ICT experience of Marmara region, Turkey. In T. Yigitcanlar, K. Velibeyoglu, & S. Baum (Eds.), *Creative Urban Regions*. Hershey, PA: Information Science Reference. doi:10.4018/978-1-59904-838-3.ch015

Velibeyoglu, K., & Yigitcanlar, T. (2010). An evaluation methodology for tangible and intangible assets of city-regions: The 6K1C framework. *International Journal of Services Technology and Management*, *14*(4), 343–359. doi:10.1504/IJSTM.2010.035783

Village, S. (n.d.). *Vision & Mission*. Retrieved from http://www.smart-villages.com/en/page/page/147

Virkus, S. (2013). Information Literacy in Europe: Ten Years Later. In S. Kurbanoglu, E. Grassian, D. Mizrachi, R. Catts, & S. Špiranec (Eds.), *Worldwide Commonalities and Challenges in Information Literacy Research and Practice. 397* (pp. 250–257). Istanbul: Springer Link. doi:10.1007/978-3-319-03919-0_32

Volker, L. (2010). *Deciding about Design Quality*. Leiden: Sidestone Press.

Volker, L., & Prins, M. (2006). Critical Reflections on Measuring the Effect of Steering Activities in Architectural Design. In D. Boyd (Ed.), *22nd Annual ARCOM Conference* (pp. 897-906). Birmingham, UK: Association of Researchers in Construction Management.

Vora, N. (2015). Is the University Universal? Mobile (Re)Constitutions of American Academia in the Gulf Arab States. *Anthropology & Education Quarterly*, *46*(1), 19–36. doi:10.1111/aeq.12085

Wagner, C. (2001). Megacities of the future. *The Futurist*, *35*(6), 8–9.

Wakefield, S. (2015). Museum Development in the Gulf: Narrative and Architecture. In K. Mitchell & G. Katodrytis (Eds.), *UAE and the Gulf: Architecture and Urbanism Now. Architectural Design* (pp. 20–27). London: Wiley. doi:10.1002/ad.1851

Wang. (2009). *Knowledge-based urban development in China* (PhD dissertation). The Newcastle University.

Weber, A. S. (2011). The role of education in knowledge economies in developing countries. In *3rd World Conference on Educational Sciences* (Vol. 15, pp. 2589–2594). Elsevier Science, B. V. doi:10.1016/j.sbspro.2011.04.151

Webster, F. (2006). *Theories of Information Society*. London: Routledge.

Weill, P., & Ross, J. (2009). *IT Savvy: What Top Executives Must Know to Go from Pain to Gain*. Harvard Business School Press.

Weil, S. (2007). *Making Museums Matter*. Smithsonian Institution Press.

White, A. (2010). How Doha's Dollars are changing the World. Arabian Business, 11(28), 26-34.

Whyte, W. H. (1980). *The Social Life of Small Urban Spaces*. Ann Arbor, MI: Edwards Brothers, Inc.

Wiedmann, F. (2012). Post-oil Urbanism in the Gulf: New Evolutions in Governance and the Impact on Urban Morphologies. Academic Press.

Wiedmann, F. (2010). *Post-oil Urbanism in the Gulf*. Stuttgart, Germany: University of Stuttgart.

Willoughby, J. (2008). *Let a Thousand Models Bloom: Forging Alliances with Western Universities and the Making of the New Higher Educational System in the Gulf*. Washington, DC: American University. Retrieved from http://www.american.edu/academic.depts/cas/econ/workingpapers/workpap.htm

Winden, W.V., Denberg, L.V., & Pol, P. (2007). European Cities In the knowledge Economy: Toward A Typology. *Urban Studies*, *44*(3), 525-549.

Winden, W. v. (2011). *Creating knowledge hotspots in the city: Practical guidelines for developing campuses, science quarters, creative districts and other knowledge hotspots*. Amsterdam: European Union.

Wippel, S. (Ed.). (2014). *Under Construction: Logics of Urbanism in the Gulf Region*. London: Ashgate.

Witte, S. (2010). *Inside Education City: The Persistent Demographic and Gender Imbalance in Qatar*. United Nations Publications.

Wong, C. Y. L., Choi, C. J., & Millar, C. C. J. M. (2006). The Case of Singapore as a Knowledge-Based City. In F. J. Carrillo (Ed.), *Knowledge Cities: Approaches, Experiences and Perspectives* (pp. 87–96). Burlington, MA: Elsevier Butterworth-Heinemann. doi:10.1016/B978-0-7506-7941-1.50010-5

Wood, P., & Landry, C. (2008). *The Intercultural City: Planning for Diversity Advantage*. London: Earthscan.

Woodman, E. (2008). *I.M. Pei's MIA opens in Doha*. Retrieved from http://www.bdonline.co.uk/story.asp?storycode=3129204

World Bank. (2008). *The Road Not Traveled: Education Reform in the Middle East and North Africa*. Washington, DC: World Bank.

World Capital Institute & Teleos. (n.d.). *The Most Admired Knowledge Cities (MAKCi) Report*. Retrieved from http://www.worldcapitalinstitute.org/

Woßmann, L. (2003). Specifying Human Capital. *Journal of Economic Surveys*, *17*(3), 239–270. doi:10.1111/1467-6419.00195

Yigitcanlar & Sarimin. (n.d.). Orchestrating knowledge-based urban development: lessons from multimedia super corridor, Malaysia. *International Journal of Knowledge-Based Development, 2*(1).

Yigitcanlar, T. (2005). The Making of Knowledge Cities: Lessons Learned from Melbourne. In *Proceedings of the International Symposium on Knowledge Cities*. The World Bank and Arab Urban Development Institute.

Yigitcanlar, T. (2005). *The Making of Knowledge Cities: Lessons Learned from Melbourne*. International Symposium on Knowledge Cities, Medina, Saudi Arabia.

Yigitcanlar, T. (2007). The Making of Urban Spaces for the Knowledge Economy: Global Practices. *Proceedings The 2nd International Symposium on Knowledge Cities: Future of Cities in the Knowledge Economy.*

Yigitcanlar, T. (2011). Knowledge-based urban development redefined: from theory to practice knowledge-based development of cities. In T. Yigitcanlar & C. Fachinelli (Eds.), *Summit Proceedings of the 4th Knowledge Cities World Summit.* The World Capital Institute and Ibero-American Community for Knowledge Systems, Bento Goncalves.

Yigitcanlar, T. (2011c). Knowledge-based development processes of an emerging knowledge city: Brisbane, Australia. *A|Z Journal,* 8(1), 53-67.

Yigitcanlar, T., & Lee, S. (2009). *Moving towards a knowledge city: Brisbane's experience in knowledge-based urban development*. The State of Australian Cities National Conference, University of Western Australia, Perth, Western Australia.

Yigitcanlar, T., & Velibeyoglu, K. (2008). Knowledge-based strategic planning. *3rd International Forum on Knowledge Asset Dynamics*, 296-306.

Yigitcanlar, T., Inkinen, T., & Makkonen, T., (2015). Does size matter? Knowledge-based development of second-order city-regions in Finland. *disP-The Planning Review, 51*(3), 62-77.

Yigitcanlar, T., Lonnqvist, A., Kapyla, J., & Salonius, H. (2012). Tampere region under the microscope: a critical analysis from the knowledge perspective. In *7th International Forum on Knowledge Asset Dynamics (IFKAD)*. University of Basilicata.

Yigitcanlar, T. (2003). *Bridging the Gap between Citizens and Local Authorities via e-government*. In *Symposium on E-government*, Muscat, Oman.

Yigitcanlar, T. (2007). The making of urban spaces for the knowledge economy: global practices. In I. Al-Furaih, A. Sahab, A. Hayajneh, A. Abdullah, M. Thalha, & M. Ibrahim (Eds.), *Knowledge Cities: Future of Cities in the Knowledge Economy* (pp. 73–97). Selangor, Malaysia: Scholar Press.

Yigitcanlar, T. (2009). Planning for knowledge-based urban development: Global perspectives. *Journal of Knowledge Management, 13*(5), 228–242. doi:10.1108/13673270910988079

Yigitcanlar, T. (2010). Knowledge-based devlopemnt of cities: a myth or reality? *Proceedings of REvive MTY forum 2010*, 3–4.

Yigitcanlar, T. (2010). Making space and place for the knowledge economy. *European Planning Studies, 18*(11), 1769–1786. doi:10.1080/09654313.2010.512163

Yigitcanlar, T. (2011). Redefining knowledge-based urban development. *International Journal of Knowledge Based Development, 2*(4), 340–356. doi:10.1504/IJKBD.2011.044343

Yigitcanlar, T. (2011b). Moving towards a knowledge city? Brisbane's experience in knowledge-based urban development. *International Journal of Knowledge-Based Organizations, 1*(3), 22–38. doi:10.4018/ijkbo.2011070102

Yigitcanlar, T. (2013). Building contemporary urban spaces of knowledge and innovation: Lessons from Australian practice. In *Proceedings of ICEIRD 2013*. Sehir University.

Yigitcanlar, T. (2014). Innovating urban policymaking and planning mechanisms to deliver knowledge-based agendas: A methodological approach. *International Journal of Knowledge-Based Development, 5*(3), 257. doi:10.1504/IJKBD.2014.065300

Yigitcanlar, T. (2014b). Position paper: Benchmarking the performance of global and emerging knowledge cities. *Expert Systems with Applications, 41*(12), 5549–5559. doi:10.1016/j.eswa.2014.03.032

Yigitcanlar, T. (Ed.). (2010a). *Sustainable urban and regional infrastructure development: technologies, applications and management*. Hersey, PA: Information Science Reference. doi:10.4018/978-1-61520-775-6

Yigitcanlar, T. (Ed.). (2010b). *Rethinking sustainable development: urban management, engineering and design*. Hersey, PA: Engineering Science Reference. doi:10.4018/978-1-61692-022-7

Yigitcanlar, T., Baum, S., & Horton, S. (2007). Attracting and retaining knowledge workers in knowledge cities. *Journal of Knowledge Management, 11*(5), 6–17. doi:10.1108/13673270710819762

Yigitcanlar, T., & Bulu, M. (2015). Dubaization of Istanbul: Insights from the knowledge-based urban development journey of an emerging local economy. *Environment & Planning A, 47*(1), 89–107. doi:10.1068/a130209p

Yigitcanlar, T., & Dur, F. (2013). Making space and place for knowledge communities: Lessons for Australian practice. *Australasian Journal of Regional Studies, 19*(1), 5–32.

Yigitcanlar, T., Edvardsson, I., Johannesson, H., Kamruzzaman, M., Ioppolo, G., & Pancholi, S. (2017a). Knowledge-based development dynamics in less favoured regions: Insights from Australian and Icelandic university towns. *European Planning Studies, 25*(12), 2272–2292. doi:10.1080/09654313.2017.1358699

Yigitcanlar, T., Guaralda, M., Taboada, M., & Pancholi, S. (2016). Place making for knowledge generation and innovation: Planning and branding Brisbane's knowledge community precincts. *Journal of Urban Technology, 23*(1), 115–146. doi:10.1080/10630732.2015.1090198

Yigitcanlar, T., & Lonnqvist, A. (2013). Benchmarking knowledge-based urban development performance. *Cities (London, England), 31*(1), 357–369. doi:10.1016/j.cities.2012.11.005

Yigitcanlar, T., Lonnqvist, A., & Salonius, H. (2014). Analysis of a city-region from the knowledge perspective: Tampere, Finland. *VINE: The Journal of Information and Knowledge Management Systems, 44*(3), 445–466. doi:10.1108/VINE-09-2013-0056

Yigitcanlar, T., Metaxiotis, K., & Carrillo, J. (Eds.). (2012). *Building prosperous knowledge cities: policies, plans and metrics*. London: Edward Elgar Publishing. doi:10.4337/9780857936042

Yigitcanlar, T., O'Connor, K., & Westerman, C. (2008). The making of knowledge cities: Melbourne's knowledge-based urban development experience. *Cities (London, England), 25*(2), 63–72. doi:10.1016/j.cities.2008.01.001

Yigitcanlar, T., Sabatini-Marques, J., Da Costa, E., Kamruzzaman, M., & Ioppolo, G. (2017b). Stimulating technological innovation through incentives: Perceptions of Australian and Brazilian firms. *Technological Forecasting and Social Change*. doi:10.1016/j.techfore.2017.05.039

Yigitcanlar, T., & Sarimin, M. (2011). The role of universities in building prosperous knowledge cities: The Malaysian experience. *Built Environment, 37*(3), 260–280. doi:10.2148/benv.37.3.260

Yigitcanlar, T., & Sarimin, M. (2015). Multimedia Super Corridor, Malaysia: Knowledge-based urban development lessons from an emerging economy. *VINE: The Journal of Information and Knowledge Management, 45*(1), 126–147. doi:10.1108/VINE-06-2014-0041

Yigitcanlar, T., & Velibeyoglu, K. (2008). Knowledge-Based Urban Development: The Local Economic Development Path of Brisbane, Australia. *Local Economy, 23*(3), 195–207. doi:10.1080/02690940802197358

Yigitcanlar, T., Velibeyoglu, K., & Baum, S. (Eds.). (2008a). *Knowledge-based Urban Development: Planning and Applications in the Information Era*. Hershey, PA: IGI Global. doi:10.4018/978-1-59904-720-1

Yigitcanlar, T., Velibeyoglu, K., & Baum, S. (Eds.). (2008b). *Creative Urban Regions: Harnessing Urban Technologies to Support Knowledge City Initiatives*. Hershey, PA: IGI Global. doi:10.4018/978-1-59904-838-3

Yigitcanlar, T., Velibeyoglu, K., & Martinez-Fernandez, C. (2008). Rising knowledge cities: The role of urban knowledge precincts. *Journal of Knowledge Management, 12*(5), 8–20. doi:10.1108/13673270810902902

Yigitcanta, T. (2010, November). Making Spaces and Places for the knowledge Based Development-Australian Cities. *European Planning Studies, 18*(11), 1770–1786.

Yin, R. K. (1994). *Case Study Research: Design and Methods*. Thousand Oaks, CA: Sage Publications.

Youssef, K., Ahmed, J., & Mohammed, A. (2013). The comparative importance of the architectural and urban potentials of knowledge cities (KCs). The 6th knowledge cities world summit, Istanbul, Turkey.

Zahlan, R. S. (1979). *The Creation of Qatar*. London: Harper and Row Publishers Inc.

Zahlan, R. S. (1998). *The Making of the Modern Gulf States: Kuwait, Bahrain, Qatar, the United Arab Emirates, and Oman*. Reading, UK: Ithaca Press.

About the Contributors

Ali A. Alraouf is a professor of architecture and urbanism. He is an architect and urban planner interested in research and practice related to architectural, urban, sustainable design and holistic planning. He was a Visiting Scholar at University of California at Berkeley-USA. Alraouf has held permanent and visiting teaching and research positions at regional and international universities. His research interests are: Doha's urban Model, Knowledge cities, Smart Urbanism and contemporary Gulf cities. He published more than 100 journal refereed papers, critical reviews, essays, in addition to books and book chapters. He delivered lectures and presentations in over 30 countries. He is the recipient of number of awards including Modern Science and Arts University (MSA) Teaching Excellence Award 2004, Best Research Paper in Sharjah International Conference for Urban Planning 2008 and Research Publication Achievement Award from University of Bahrain 2009. Alraouf was selected as member of 2012 Excel campaign at Qatar University. He is currently acts as head of Capacity Building, Research and Development unit in Urban Planning Dept. at Ministry of Municipality and Environment (MME). He is also the Chairman of Green Urbanism and Planning Group at Qatar Green Building Council.

* * *

Ahmed Hassan Abayazeed is an Egyptian architect. He received his Bachelor degree in Architecture in 2004 from The Faculty of Fine Arts at Alexandria University. In 2013, Abayazeed won a scholarship to study at a joint academic program (IUSD) hosted at the University of Stuttgart, Germany and Ain Shams University, Cairo where he earned his MSc double degree. His thesis topic concerns with residential urban spaces in Cairo's informal settlements. Abayazeed is working now as a senior urban designer at The National Organization for Urban Harmony (NOUH) where he participates in various projects covering a wide range of scope and complexity with special emphasis on urban design projects. Abayazeed's work and academic interests concern with public urban spaces, informal settlements, and urban design-related issues. He attended various workshops and summer schools. Also, he participated in international, local competitions and exhibitions and won several awards and certificates of merit.

Amal Abdrabo works as a sociology lecturer (PhD) at Alexandria University- Egypt. She graduated from the Faculty of Education at the same university majoring in philosophy and sociology in 2005. Her first MA degree was about "Social Movements and Human Rights: A Critical Discourse Analysis of Anti-globalization Discourse in the Egyptian Society between 2001 to 2010". Recently, she earned her PhD degree in sociology from the Faculty of Arts- Alexandria University. Her doctorate thesis entitled "Social Dimensions of Knowledge-based Development in Egypt: an Evaluation Study of a Sample of

Knowledge Precincts". She was also granted Building The Next Generation Fellowship at the American University in Cairo (2014-2015) where she finished her second MA degree in anthropology with a thesis entitled "We Live Like KHAYALAT (Scarecrows): An Ethnography of A Palestinian Village in Egypt". Her research interests cover development studies; refugees' studies; urbanization; migration; anthropology of development. The researcher published and co-authored a lot of academic papers covering the previously mentioned fields of research.

Hisham G. Abusaada obtained the MSc in 1987, and the PhD in 1992, both was from the Department of Architecture, Cairo University, Egypt. He is currently a Professor of Architecture and Urban Design in Housing and Building National Research Center-HBRC, Giza, Egypt. Absaada enrolled in the Urban Design program as courses coordinator in the Department of Landscape Architecture at King Faisal University, Saudi Arabia, from 1995 to 2004 and in several Egyptian Universities. He is an architect and urban designer, and author of numerous books and articles on urban design. He has more than thirty-five scientific papers and sixties essays in Arabic. He concerns with the socio-cultural aspects and problems of the urban community and development projects. He has several published books, including Architecture Evermore (2017), Partridge Africa; Back to the Order (2017), Lambert, Germany; What is Urban Design (2016) Partridge Africa, South Africa; The Unknown Cities (2016), Partridge Africa, A Penguin Random House Company, South Africa, The Art of the City (2015), Partridge Publishing Africa, A Penguin Random House Company, South Africa; Topics in Landscape Architecture profession (2007), Academic Book, Cairo, Egypt; Post Occupancy Evaluation (2004), Translated book, Faculty of Architecture and Planning, King Faisal University, Kingdom of Saudi Arabia; Efficiency and Urban Form Generation (1992), Academic Book, Cairo, Egypt.

Jawaher Al-Bader, Ph.D., is an assistant professor in the Department of Design Sciences at the College of Architecture at Kuwait University. She received her Ph.D. in Curriculum Instructions in Art Education from Arizona State University. Al-Bader also holds an MFA in Painting from Pratt Institute. Her MFA thesis installation 'Suspended Enclosures' explored the multidimensionality of space. Her undergraduate degrees include a BArch and BFA from the Rhode Island School of Design. Her PhD was under the mentorship of Visual Sociologist Dr. Eric Margolis, and Anthropologist Dr. Joseph Tobin which shaped her interest in Visual Ethnographic research. Prior to obtaining her PhD, Dr. Al-Bader worked in Boston for Jung Brannen Architects and in Kuwait for SSH. Her architectural works include the two campuses in Kuwait, Fawzia Al Sultan International School and Bayan Bilingual School.

Odeh Al-Jayyousi is the head of Technology and Innovation Management at the Arabian Gulf University in Bahrain. He was the vice president for science and research at the Royal Scientific Society (RSS) in Jordan during 2011- 2013. He was the regional director for IUCN – West Asia regional office during 2004-2011. Previously, he was a university professor in water resources and environment during 1994-2004. He was an academic director for M.Sc. Program in transformational management in the UK (1999-2004). In 2014, he worked as a consultant with UN ESWCA on Technology for Sustainable Development. His research interests include Technology for Sustainable Development, appropriate technologies, science policy, technology assessment, technology oversight, water and environmental policy, and innovation policy. He was a consultant with EU, ESCWA, World Bank, GIZ and USAID. He published several articles in international peer-reviewed journals including several books including two recent books; i.e., Islam and sustainable development (2012), UK and Renewable Energy and

Knowledge Management, 2015. He was the Dean of Scientific Research at Applied Science University, Jordan. He is a founding board member of Jordan Green Building Council and Fair Trade Jordan. He is a member of the Advisory Board for MSc program in IWRM between Cologne and Jordan University; Board member of several think tanks WANA Forum, and Social Forum and Economic Forum. He was a keynote speaker at many global events including Global Thinkers Forum and Sustainability Forum. He is a recipient of the award for scientists and social innovations, 2014.

Anas Alomaim is a professor of architecture at Kuwait University. After finishing his Bachelor of Science in Architecture at Kuwait University he moved to New York City to do his Masters of Architecture and Urban Design at Columbia University. Alomaim received his PhD in Architecture from the University of California Los Angeles and had the opportunity to practice architecture and teach in several companies and institutions in London, New York City, Los Angeles, and Kuwait. Alomaim co-founded Mirzam Manifesto, an initiative that aims to bring people of various backgrounds and disciplines under one roof to examine the current trends of local cultures and to critically analyze the products of the contemporary generation.

Jamal Ahmad Abd el-Hameed is a professor of Architecture, Faculty of Fine Arts, Minia University. Graduated from Department of Architecture, Faculty of Engineering, Cairo University. 1991, Master in 1998 and PhD 2003 in Architecture Acoustics field from Cairo University, Lectured in many Egyptian and K.S.A universities and institutes for undergraduate and postgraduate, Participated in preparation of many architectural designs and urban planning Projects. Also prepared environmental and Acoustic studies in architecture.

Ahmed El-Kholei is Professor of Urban Planning, Department of Natural Resources and Environment, AGU. He holds a Ph.D. degree in Regional Planning from the University of Illinois at Urbana-Champaign, USA; MSc degree in Urban Planning and Policy Development from Rutgers; in addition to MA and BA degrees in Architecture from Faculty of Fine Arts, Cairo, Egypt. He taught at the University of Illinois at Urbana-Champaign and Michigan State University, USA, and Arab Academy for Science and Technology, Menofia University, and Ain Shams University, Egypt. He provided technical assistance in participatory strategic and action planning for urban and regional planning, and national environmental management programmes. He participated in designing and evaluating several national and regional development projects. He worked with several agencies including, but not limited to, UNDP, UN Environment, FAO, IFAD, WFP, GEF, ECA, AfDB, League of Arab States and GIZ. In 2006, the UN Secretary-General appointed him as a member of the Advisory Group for Central Emergency Relief Fund (CERF) of OCHA for two years for his outstanding expertise in the fields of environment management and urban planning. He coordinated the activities to elaborate Egypt's National Environmental Action Plan. His research interests include urban and regional planning theories, methods and models, environmental management, disaster risk reduction and sustainable development.

Abeer Elshater is an associate professor at Ain Shams University. She obtained her BSc in urban design and spatial planning in 1999 from Ain Shams University, Cairo, Egypt. In 2009, she received her Ph.D. in urban design from the same university. Since then, she has acted as an assistant professor then an associate professor, teaching and supervising multidisciplinary topics in the ideology of urban design. She has worked on some international research projects with international universities. In 2011, she joined the program Integrated Urbanism & Sustainable Design—IUSD as a teaching staff and academic adviser of post-graduate students. She has published two books entitled "Urban Design Paradigm" (2015), and "The Unknown Cities" (2016) as well as twenty –one scientific manuscripts in international journals and periodicals. She is a vice-director of Contagious Improvement of Quality Assurance Unit—CIQAU at Faculty of Engineering, Ain Shams University — ASU.

Ali Abdel Razek Galaby was born on 14/8/1941 in Egypt and works as Professor of Sociology Faculty of Arts Alexandria University and he got a Master's degree 1970 and Ph.D. 1973 from Alexandria University and he had worked as an expert at the National Centre for Social Research and Crime Cairo 1973 and head the Department of Sociology Alexandria 1990, Faculty of Social Sciences Qatar 1997 and advisor to the National Centre for Research 2008 and decision of the Standing Committee promotions Supreme Council for Universities 2013 and 2016 and traveled on a scientific mission to the United States and Austria 1974 and seconded to work in a number of universities Arabic Beirut King Abdulaziz Qatar al-Jazair United Arab Emirates and he got the scientific promotion 1982 and Excellence 2004 membership of the Association Egyptian and Arab for sociology he participated in conferences and seminars for children's work UNESCO and the National Research Centre, 1992 and organized crime in the Arab nation Riyadh 1998 and social capital in Egypt Bibliotheca Alexandrina 2003 Social Responsibility and Citizenship 2009 National Centre for Research on the dialectic of social integration and nation-building in the Arab nation Qatar 2013 information systems in our life Alexandria 2016. His research has been presented at conferences on social inclusion and active citizenship Qatar 2013 Quality Assurance at universities Arabic Sharjah 2014 Egyptian knowledge Circles Alexandria 2016 and research published in scientific journals based on Knowledge Development Institute National Planning 2013 Globalization and the Identity Crisis Journal of the Arabic sociology 2017 and contributed to the authoring and translation of several books and number of research projects, the evaluation of scientific production and the validity of articles submitted for publication in a number of scientific journals.

Robert Gurney graduated from Rhode Island School of Design in 1997 with a Bachelors of Fine Arts, BArch in Architecture, and a History of Art concentration. He practiced as an architect, urban planner and as construction manager until receiving his Master in Urban and Environmental Planning from Arizona State University in 2012. His built work ranges from interiors for health clubs and restaurants, the design of educational campuses, design of several 80+ story residential high rise's in Abu Dhabi and Dubai, to a large scale urban planning project in Amman Jordan. Currently he is practicing as an architect Kuwait.

Zafer Kıyan is a research assistant at the Department of Journalism of the University of Ankara, since May of 2009. He obtained his Ph.D. degree from Ankara University in 2015. He is currently conducting his research at the Center for Internet Studies and Digital Life at the University of Navarra as visiting scholar. His research interests are the political economy of media and communication, information society studies, technology and culture, Internet and society, commodification of culture, social media, and protest movements studies. Kıyan is the author of "GATS and the restructuring of telecommunication in Turkey" (2011), "Mobile democracy discourse in a Turkish experiment" (2012), and "Traces of digital capitalism in communication field: Processes of production, circulation, labor and consumption" (2015) amongst others.

Khaled Youssef Mohamed is a Lecturer of Architecture at the Faculty of Fine Arts, Minia University. Khaled obtained his PhD from the department of Architecture in 2017. His dissertation was about introducing a methodology for upgrading the urban and architectural potentials supporting formation of Knowledge Cities. Dr. Khaled has many papers published in this discipline.

Ayman Mohammad Mostafa graduated from the department of Architecture, Ain Shams University, 1991. He is an associate professor of urban planning, with many published papers about indices and their relationship with urban development. He is an expert in architecture, urbanism, urban observatory, indices building and connecting the same to policies and urban planning.

Rabee Reffat is the Professor of Architecture and Digital Technologies at the Architecture Department, Faculty of Engineering, Assiut University, Assiut, Egypt. He earned his PhD in Architecture and Design Computing from the University of Sydney, Australia. He worked as an Assistant and Associate Professor at the University of Sydney, Australia and KFUPM, Saudi Arabia. His areas of research excellence include: utilization of advanced and intelligent technologies in architecture, heritage, construction, maintenance and energy saving; and using the applications of artificial intelligence and machine learning in planning, designing, constructing and managing the built environment; Intelligent, green and sustainable buildings; Virtual design studios & e-learning; Virtual heritage; Energy efficiency and renewable energy; Creative and knowledge-based environments, Architectural creativity; and Digital architecture. Prof. Reffat has published over 90 research papers in international refereed journals and conferences. He delivered over 60 presentations in more than 25 countries in the five continents. He successfully managed and completed over 15 research projects funded by Australian Research Council, University of Sydney and the CRC Construction Innovation in Australia, KFUPM and KACST in Saudi Arabia, and STDF in Egypt. Prof. Reffat has a substantial architectural design experience in the building and construction industry and contributed in designing distinctive and major buildings in Australia and the Middle East, and he is currently the director of QASP (Quality Architecture and Strategic Planning) consultation office in Egypt.

Hakan Yüksel received his MA in Information and Communication Sciences from University of Paris 13 in 2003. In 2007 he got his second MA in Journalism from Ankara University in Turkey. He was hired as Research Assistant by Ankara University in 2009. He received his PhD in Journalism from Ankara University in 2013. He worked as Junior Lecturer between 2013 and 2017 in the Faculty of Communication of Ankara University. He has various scientific publications on information society policies, new communication technologies, social media, political economy of communication, and communication history. He is also a member of the Alternative Media Association of Turkey.

Index

U

W

Purchase Print, E-Book, or Print + E-Book

IGI Global books can now be purchased from three unique pricing formats: Print Only, E-Book Only, or Print + E-Book. Shipping fees apply.

www.igi-global.com

Recommended Reference Books

ISBN: 978-1-5225-0717-8
© 2017; 296 pp.
List Price: $190

ISBN: 978-1-5225-0320-0
© 2016; 502 pp.
List Price: $205

ISBN: 978-1-4666-8358-7
© 2015; 2,307 pp.
List Price: $2,150

ISBN: 978-1-5225-1674-3
© 2017; 1,536 pp.
List Price: $2,200

ISBN: 978-1-5225-0053-7
© 2016; 618 pp.
List Price: $300

ISBN: 978-1-5225-0731-4
© 2017; 609 pp.
List Price: $300

Looking for free content, product updates, news, and special offers?
Join IGI Global's mailing list today and start enjoying exclusive perks sent only to IGI Global members.
Add your name to the list at **www.igi-global.com/newsletters.**

Publishing Information Science and Technology Research Since 1988

IGI Global
DISSEMINATOR OF KNOWLEDGE

www.igi-global.com | Sign up at www.igi-global.com/newsletters | facebook.com/igiglobal | twitter.com/igiglobal

Stay Current on the Latest Emerging Research Developments

Become an IGI Global Reviewer for Authored Book Projects

The overall success of an authored book project is dependent on quality and timely reviews.

In this competitive age of scholarly publishing, constructive and timely feedback significantly decreases the turnaround time of manuscripts from submission to acceptance, allowing the publication and discovery of progressive research at a much more expeditious rate. Several IGI Global authored book projects are currently seeking highly qualified experts in the field to fill vacancies on their respective editorial review boards:

Applications may be sent to:
development@igi-global.com

Applicants must have a doctorate (or an equivalent degree) as well as publishing and reviewing experience. Reviewers are asked to write reviews in a timely, collegial, and constructive manner. All reviewers will begin their role on an ad-hoc basis for a period of one year, and upon successful completion of this term can be considered for full editorial review board status, with the potential for a subsequent promotion to Associate Editor.

If you have a colleague that may be interested in this opportunity, we encourage you to share this information with them.

www.igi-global.com

InfoSci®-Books

A Database for Information Science and Technology Research

Maximize Your Library's Book Collection!

Invest in IGI Global's InfoSci®-Books database and gain access to hundreds of reference books at a fraction of their individual list price.

The InfoSci®-Books database offers unlimited simultaneous users the ability to precisely return search results through more than 80,000 full-text chapters from nearly 3,900 reference books in the following academic research areas:

Business & Management Information Science & Technology • Computer Science & Information Technology
Educational Science & Technology • Engineering Science & Technology • Environmental Science & Technology
Government Science & Technology • Library Information Science & Technology • Media & Communication Science & Technology
Medical, Healthcare & Life Science & Technology • Security & Forensic Science & Technology • Social Sciences & Online Behavior

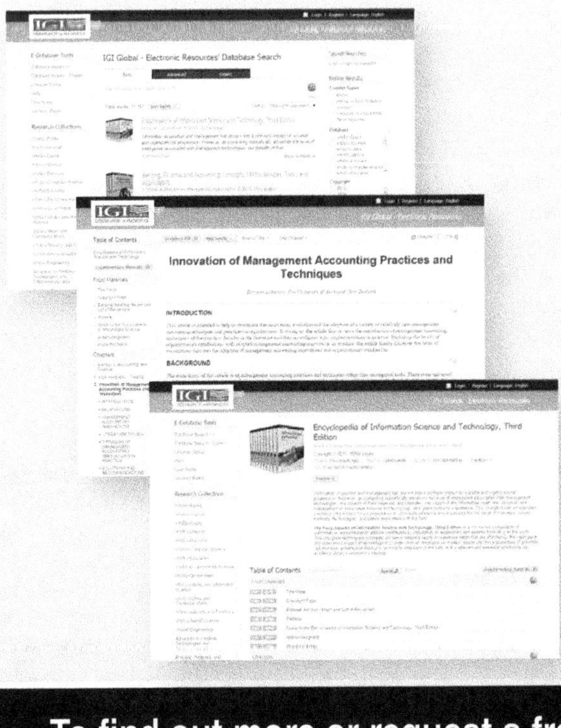

Peer-Reviewed Content:

- Cutting-edge research
- No embargoes
- Scholarly and professional
- Interdisciplinary

Award-Winning Platform:

- Unlimited simultaneous users
- Full-text in XML and PDF
- Advanced search engine
- No DRM

Librarian-Friendly:

- Free MARC records
- Discovery services
- COUNTER4/SUSHI compliant
- Training available

To find out more or request a free trial, visit:
www.igi-global.com/eresources

IGI Global
DISSEMINATOR OF KNOWLEDGE
www.igi-global.com

IGI Global
DISSEMINATOR OF KNOWLEDGE
www.igi-global.com

IGI Global Proudly Partners with

eContent Pro International

Expert Copy Editing

eContent Pro International copy editors, with over 70 years of combined experience, will provide complete and comprehensive care for your document by resolving all issues with spelling, punctuation, grammar, terminology, jargon, semantics, syntax, consistency, flow, and more. In addition, they will format your document to the style you specify (APA, Chicago, etc.). All edits will be performed using Microsoft Word's Track Changes feature, which allows for fast and simple review and management of edits.

Additional Services

eContent Pro International also offers fast and affordable proofreading to enhance the readability of your document, professional translation in over 100 languages, and market localization services to help businesses and organizations localize their content and grow into new markets around the globe.

IGI Global Authors Save 25% on eContent Pro International's Services!

Scan the QR Code to Receive Your 25% Discount

The 25% discount is applied directly to your eContent Pro International shopping cart when placing an order through IGI Global's referral link. Use the QR code to access this referral link. eContent Pro International has the right to end or modify any promotion at any time.

Email: customerservice@econtentpro.com

econtentpro.com

Information Resources Management Association

Advancing the Concepts & Practices of Information Resources Management in Modern Organizations

Become an IRMA Member

Members of the **Information Resources Management Association (IRMA)** understand the importance of community within their field of study. The Information Resources Management Association is an ideal venue through which professionals, students, and academicians can convene and share the latest industry innovations and scholarly research that is changing the field of information science and technology. Become a member today and enjoy the benefits of membership as well as the opportunity to collaborate and network with fellow experts in the field.

IRMA Membership Benefits:

- **One FREE Journal Subscription**
- **30% Off Additional Journal Subscriptions**
- **20% Off Book Purchases**
- Updates on the latest events and research on Information Resources Management through the IRMA-L listserv.
- Updates on new open access and downloadable content added to Research IRM.
- A copy of the Information Technology Management Newsletter twice a year.
- A certificate of membership.

IRMA Membership $195

Scan code or visit **irma-international.org** and begin by selecting your free journal subscription.

Membership is good for one full year.

www.irma-international.org

IGI Global
DISSEMINATOR OF KNOWLEDGE
www.igi-global.com

Available to Order Now

Order through www.igi-global.com with **Free Standard Shipping**.

The Premier Reference for Information Science & Information Technology

100% Original Content
Contains 705 new, peer-reviewed articles with color figures covering over 80 categories in 11 subject areas

Diverse Contributions
More than 1,100 experts from 74 unique countries contributed their specialized knowledge

Easy Navigation
Includes two tables of content and a comprehensive index in each volume for the user's convenience

Highly-Cited
Embraces a complete list of references and additional reading sections to allow for further research

Included in:
InfoSci®-Books

Encyclopedia of Information Science and Technology Fourth Edition

A Comprehensive 10-Volume Set

Mehdi Khosrow-Pour, D.B.A. (Information Resources Management Association, USA)
ISBN: 978-1-5225-2255-3; © 2018; Pg: 8,104; Release Date: July 2017

The **Encyclopedia of Information Science and Technology, Fourth Edition** is a 10-volume set which includes 705 original and previously unpublished research articles covering a full range of perspectives, applications, and techniques contributed by thousands of experts and researchers from around the globe. This authoritative encyclopedia is an all-encompassing, well-established reference source that is ideally designed to disseminate the most forward-thinking and diverse research findings. With critical perspectives on the impact of information science management and new technologies in modern settings, including but not limited to computer science, education, healthcare, government, engineering, business, and natural and physical sciences, it is a pivotal and relevant source of knowledge that will benefit every professional within the field of information science and technology and is an invaluable addition to every academic and corporate library.

Scan for Online Bookstore

Pricing Information

Hardcover: **$5,695** E-Book: **$5,695** Hardcover + E-Book: **$6,895**

Recommend this Title to Your Institution's Library: www.igi-global.com/books

www.igi-global.com/infosci-ondemand

InfoSci®-OnDemand

Continuously updated with new material on a weekly basis, InfoSci®-OnDemand offers the ability to search through thousands of quality full-text research papers. Users can narrow each search by identifying key topic areas of interest, then display a complete listing of relevant papers, and purchase materials specific to their research needs.

Comprehensive Service

- Over 81,600+ journal articles, book chapters, and case studies.
- All content is downloadable in PDF format and can be stored locally for future use.

No Subscription Fees

- One time fee of $37.50 per PDF download.

Instant Access

- Receive a download link immediately after order completion!

"It really provides an excellent entry into the research literature of the field. It presents a manageable number of highly relevant sources on topics of interest to a wide range of researchers. The sources are scholarly, but also accessible to 'practitioners'."

- Lisa Stimatz, MLS, University of North Carolina at Chapel Hill, USA

"It is an excellent and well designed database which will facilitate research, publication and teaching. It is a very very useful tool to have."

- George Ditsa, PhD, University of Wollongong, Australia

"I have accessed the database and find it to be a valuable tool to the IT/IS community. I found valuable articles meeting my search criteria 95% of the time."

- Lynda Louis, Xavier University of Louisiana, USA

Database Platform Features:

- Comprehensive Pay-Per-View Service
- Written by Prominent International Experts/Scholars
- Precise Search and Retrieval
- Updated With New Material on a Weekly Basis
- Immediate Access to Full-Text PDFs
- No Subscription Needed
- Purchased Research Can Be Stored Locally for Future Use

Recommended for use by researchers who wish to immediately download PDFs of individual chapters or articles.

www.igi-global.com/e-resources/infosci-ondemand

IGI Global
DISSEMINATOR OF KNOWLEDGE
www.igi-global.com

www.ingramcontent.com/pod-product-compliance
Lightning Source LLC
LaVergne TN
LVHW062140300926
849161LV00010B/2587
* 9 7 8 1 5 2 2 5 3 7 3 4 2 *